THE
Locavore's Kitchen

THE
Locavore's
Kitchen

MARILOU K. SUSZKO

*A Cook's Guide
to Seasonal Eating
and Preserving*

Ohio University Press   Athens

Ohio University Press / Swallow Press, Athens, Ohio 45701
ohioswallow.com

Printed in the United States of America
Ohio University Press / Swallow Press books are printed on acid-free paper ⊗ ™

20 19 18 17 16 15 14 13 12 11   5 4 3 2 1

Library of Congress Cataloging-in-Publication Data
Suszko, Marilou K.
 The locavore's kitchen : a cook's guide to seasonal eating and preserving / Marilou
K. Suszko.
    p. cm.
 Summary: "The Locavore's Kitchen invites readers to savor homegrown foods
that come from the garden, the farm stand, or local farmers markets through
cooking and preserving the freshest ingredients. In more than 200 recipes that
highlight seasonal flavors, Marilou K. Suszko inspires cooks to keep local flavors
in the kitchen year round. She helps readers learn what to look for when buying
seasonal homegrown or locally grown foods as well as how to store fresh foods and
which cooking methods bring out fresh flavors and colors. Suszko shares tips and
techniques for extending seasonal flavors with detailed instructions on canning,
freezing, and dehydrating and which methods work best for preserving texture and
flavor"— Provided by publisher.
 Includes bibliographical references and index.
 ISBN 978-0-8214-1938-0 (pbk.) — ISBN 978-0-8214-4355-2 (electronic)
 1. Cooking, American. 2. Local foods. 3. Food supply—Seasonal variations. 4.
Locavores. 5. Cooking (Natural foods) 6. Cookbooks. I. Title.
 TX715.S9536 2011
 641.3'02—dc22
                                2011010202

To farmers, artisans, and producers
everywhere. Your work
is a locavore's
passionate pursuit.

To family and friends who respect
my quest for the best
in the food we share.

Contents

Fall 127

Winter 201

Preserving the Harvest 215
in the Locavore's Kitchen

Acknowledgments

How do I begin to thank those who nurtured me with healthy doses of encouragement, support, information, patience, and great seasonal and local foods? I suppose at the beginning.

To my editor, Gillian Berchowitz, and the staff at Ohio University Press for their guidance and patience.

To my many farmer friends and chefs, too many to mention and too humble to take credit, yet always generous with advice and information, especially the following, for their expert guidance:

Janet O'Donnell, Master Herbalist

Doug Raubenolt, Tea Hills Farm

Dr. Dave Smith, Freshwater Farms

The members of Lorain County Beekeepers Association

To the following food preservation experts for their opinions, advice, and guidance:

Janet Cassidy, Ohio Farm Bureau Federation

Linnette Goard, Extension Educator, Family and Consumer Sciences, Ohio State University Extension

Susan S. Shockey, Ph.D., CFCS OSU Extension Educator, Family and Consumer Sciences

To Marcia DePalma and the staff at Laurel Run Cooking School for assistance, support, and allowing me to teach others about great local flavors.

To Christina Matijasic, Edgewater Graphics, Vermilion, for her guidance and advice.

To my recipe testers, accomplished cooks all who were my biggest fans and gentlest critics:

Laura Allegretto, Lois Allegretto, Lynn Louise Allegretto, Venessa Allegretto, Marianne Bodine, Kate Bogart, Campbell, Maggie Daly, James Daly, Shelia Greene, Mary Jane Grob, Sara Hasley, Molly Kavanaugh, Jim Keske, Shirley Koachway, Patricia Kishman, Trish Kosik, Cara Lawson, Cindy LeBlanc, Jean Liljegren, Tammy Martin, Tom Maurer, Christina Matijasic, Jean Niedzwicki, Sharon Steinhoff, Daria Sulpizio, Tina Swinehart, Therese Ward, Janice Zweigart

THE
Locavore's Kitchen

local
*pertaining to
a city, town, or
small district*

+ vore
*a combining
form meaning
"one that eats"*

= locavore

In 2007, the *Oxford American Dictionary* became longer by one curious yet satisfying word: locavore.

Tucked among the more than a quarter million other words we use in daily conversation appeared this fresh term coined by Jessica Prentice, a chef and local foods advocate from the San Francisco Bay area. She created it in a pressure moment to kick off an "Eat Local Challenge" designed to inspire others in her community to think, act, and live as locavores—people passionate about buying, cooking, and eating food grown, raised, or produced close to home, usually within 100 miles of their kitchens. The call to "eat local" quickly evolved into a national movement encouraging people to buy from farmers markets and local farms, join community-supported agriculture programs (CSAs), and grow their own food.

"Locavore" is the perfect label for a new generation of cooks and consumers. It comes with more honor than "foodie" and less pretense than "food snob." Locavores rally around wonderful food finds and want them served up closer to home with sides of social, economic, and environmental consciousness. Locavores want to know if the food they are buying and eating is good for all: their families, the farmers, the land, and the environment. The word arrives with perfect timing, as cooks and consumers alike have turned some serious attention to what is on their dinner plates.

While the word "locavore" has made our vocabularies one word richer, and the principle behind it has made our culinary lives all the better, the truth is that there is nothing new or revolutionary about this way of living or eating. It's simply a new spin on the way that generations ate and enjoyed food— fresh food—before the market on the corner turned into a supermarket and improved transportation and distribution systems changed the way we ate for good. For *good*?

While it does allow us to stock our pantries with cinnamon, chocolate, bananas, and other ingredients that can't be grown locally—things we consider essentials or staples—the same system also fills the produce section of grocery stores with fruits and vegetables, meats and poultry, cheeses, and even honey from other parts of the country, the same ones we grow or produce in our own communities. We have to remind ourselves not to let the convenience factor overshadow what we could logically and easily get from our own regions. It doesn't make sense to watch local apple orchards go out of business while supermarkets stock apples that come from thousands of miles away. Do we really want to be knee deep is tasteless strawberries in December; stringy, tough asparagus in August; and rock-hard peaches in April? It's all there in the produce department—but it doesn't come with the flavor, quality, and nutritional value to make it worth the convenience.

These days, we're concerned with food safety, the cost of food, and the ways our food distribution systems tax the environment. We're looking to put flavor and quality back into what nourishes us. Our own gardens, roadside stands, farmers markets, and CSAs represent a victory over tasteless, nutrition-poor, and tired-looking produce as well as over cost and are a step in the right direction for conserving energy, protecting the environment, and encouraging self-reliance.

Even if this is the first time you've heard this word "locavore," you can't miss the fact that more than 4,800 farmers markets set up all across the nation on a weekly basis throughout the growing season, some even through the winter months. Have you noticed that more and more of your neighbors and friends are planting tomatoes, growing their own salad greens, and sharing their overabundance of zucchini with you and others in the neighborhood?

And instead of just watching someone cook a meal on television, one that we can neither taste nor smell, we're returning to the kitchen to learn, relearn, or hone our cooking skills—and we're finding that it's fun, rewarding, economical, easy, and most of all delicious—simply delicious. When we eat locally and with the seasons, the kitchen is a constantly evolving place that keeps pace with the harvest—one week it's fresh peas, the next it's chard. A few weeks down the road, it will be green beans and cucumbers. Eating with the seasons keeps our kitchen fresh in so many ways. We're also finding out that it's not always about the recipe, but about the ingredients. Simple fresh ingredients don't need much help to make simply wonderful dishes.

This book presents an opportunity for you think and act like a locavore in your own kitchen with information about what you choose to eat—from fruits and vegetables to meat and poultry, dairy products, and much more—plus delicious recipes that make the best of what is already a good thing.

Do you have what it takes to become a locavore? Of course. Everyone who craves fresh food with flavor and better nutrition and who in any measure aims to keep food dollars close to home by supporting local farmers markets and small family farms or by growing food at home is a locavore.

Where Locavores Shop

Locavores embrace shopping for their food. For them, it's not a chore, it's a pleasure, an adventure, and often a welcome challenge with delicious rewards. What's not to love about shopping at a farmers market, strolling the aisles in search of the next great flavor of the season and shaking hands with the farmer who grows your food? The adventure comes when you stumble across a great find when you least expect it, like exotic wild mushrooms or whole milk with a plug of cream at the top. The challenge presents itself when you're determined to find a local source for an ingredient you keep as a staple in your cupboard, like locally grown and milled wheat or spelt. So where do you go to find this kind of fun?

First, make it a point to talk with other people you know who seek out locally grown foods. They are valuable resources to lead you to the great ingredients and foods they gather from local sources. There are no secrets between locavores. Sharing information is good for all, especially the farmers who appreciate opportunities to expand their market.

Here are a few likely places where locavores shop to find fresh, seasonal, and local food. Looking for places like these close to where you live? Go to the Resources section on page 241, which will point you in the right direction.

Farmers Markets

No doubt if you're living the life of a locavore already, you know what a farmers market is. These public, mostly outdoor venues pop up on a weekly basis when the local harvest season begins. Typically amidst a lively, energetic atmosphere, you'll find multiple farmers from a specific region selling their products directly to consumers. The selection at farmers markets is characterized by a wide array of fresh and diverse local food—freshly harvested, in-season produce, pasture-raised meats, poultry and eggs, artisan cheeses, maple syrups, hand-harvested honey, and more. This is where the consumer can get the freshest local and seasonal products and where farmers can get the best price for their good work. It brings the two together in a setting where they can exchange information about the products and develop a friendship over food.

Farm Market or On-Farm Market

For the most direct route from the field to the customer, some farms create a farm market, also called an on-farm market, where they sell what is produced on that farm. Like a farmers market, the selection changes as the season moves from one fruit or vegetable to the next. To round out their selection and broaden the shopping experience for their customers, many will feature other local and regional products, such as honey, syrup, and produce or products from neighboring farms.

Roadside Stands

There's usually nothing fancy about roadside stands, humble little structures found along country roads that open with the first pickings of asparagus and close with the last pumpkin out of the field. They are simple but most effective in their marketing approach—local, fresh, seasonal produce catches the eye of the passerby, making it hard to resist. As the term implies, the stands are located along the road where it's convenient for customers to purchase produce on their way home. And fresh? It's not likely to get better than this.

Community-Supported Agriculture (CSAs)

CSAs are becoming a popular way for anyone to buy local, seasonal food directly from a farmer. If you don't have a garden or like to work in the first, CSAs are the perfect solution for staying connected to locally grown, seasonal foods. Here's how one works. Farmers sell seasonal shares or subscriptions to their CSAs to the public. For that investment, you will get a regular delivery to feed your family, usually once a week while the harvest is on. The farmers benefit from this arrangement by creating a demand for their harvest before work in the field begins and by developing relationships with those for whom they grow. The buyers get the freshest, most nutritious food possible and are often introduced to a variety of new vegetables and ways to prepare them. Knowing the farmer adds a level of confidence for the consumer. Produce is the main attraction, yet some CSAs broaden the selection by offering eggs, meats, poultry, cheese, fruits and flowers, honey and maple syrup. When you join a CSA, you assume some risk. If it's a bad year in the field for greens, you lack an abundance of salad, but if it's a banner year for tomatoes, think salsa, pasta sauce, juice, chutney, ketchup, and more!

Community Gardens

In neighborhoods and cities all over the country, community gardens are springing up. While there's no one model of what makes a community garden, it's basically a joint effort of a group of neighbors to turn an open space, which could be a field, empty parking lot, even rooftop, into a productive garden to feed people in the community. The harvest can be shared among those who work the garden, or participants can have their own dedicated plots. A community garden can produce foods that are as diverse as its community of gardeners and can provide wonderful social benefits like getting to know your neighbors.

Grocery Stores

Over the past ten years, the focus on local foods has encouraged people to get out of the aisles of traditional grocery stores where the "fresh" produce selection was neither seasonal nor locally grown and sometimes not very fresh. Today's independent grocers and supermarket chains have stepped up to the demands and desires of local food enthusiasts and often stock their bins with fresh, seasonal produce from local producers, clearly identifying the local source with special signage. If you're curious about the sources of certain produce, ask the produce manager. Sometimes you'll be surprised that the green beans or potatoes are from close by.

Food Cooperatives

These are grocery stores that are community supported, community owned, and typically filled with foods that are local, organic, vegan, or grass-fed and with other foods that appeal to locavores and ecologically conscious eaters. To shop there, you usually have to be a member. That means you pay a fee or buy a share, much like buying stock in the stock market. Membership not only gets you through the door with convenient access to local foods but gives you a vote on matters that affect the operation of the coop.

Pick Your Own

Some orchards and berry farms invite the customers into the fields to pick their own apples, pears, stone fruits, strawberries, raspberries, blueberries, and more, typically at a discount over the price at the market stand since you're doing some of the work. Not only is it a delightful way to spend a few hours, but it doesn't get any fresher than when you pick your own.

Home Gardens

Whether it's your own or your neighbor's, home vegetable gardening has enjoyed a revival as we prime our taste buds for great local flavors. The garden can be any size, from a half acre to a raised bed to maybe a few pots on the patio. How enthusiastic you are about growing your own foods depends on space, time, and desire. Today's gardeners are getting more creative about incorporating edibles into their landscaping, making the most productive use of the space that surrounds them. Horseradish sends up big, beautiful foliage; chard makes for an interesting border plant; herbs fill plenty of blank spots; and pots can be used to plant tomatoes, lettuces, herbs, and more.

Creating the Locavore's Kitchen,
or How to Use This Book

Buying, growing, cooking, and preserving locally grown food is not a fad or a trend. It's a lifestyle that can be lived in any measure. Whether you call yourself a locavore or just someone who prefers to eat fresh seasonal food, you'll find inspiration in this book to make the most of locally grown and raised foods and seasonal flavors. The goal is to fill your plate and kitchen with foods you can easily find at farmers markets, at local farms, and out of your own garden. But beware: one great flavor of the season will lead to the next, and before you know it, you'll find yourself passionately pursuing the goal of putting seasonal flavors on the table year round. This book will make it an attainable goal by arming you with knowledge, encouraging you to think ahead, and creating the desire to seize the moment in the harvest.

That's how you can begin to use this book: in the moment. If it's spring and asparagus season is upon us, start at the beginning of this book with recipes that make the most of the flavor that launches the growing season. Perhaps it's the end of summer heading into fall, and the local apple harvest is in full swing; the middle of the book will put you in the middle of orchard fruits—pears and apples. Make an apple pie or pear sauce, slice the fruit and use in a salad, or simply eat them out of hand. If it's the middle of winter and the seasonal harvest is long over, there are still ways to begin putting local ingredients on the table with locally raised meats and poultry, dairy products, grains, and more that you can find locally and at late-season farmers markets. It's never too late in the year or too early in the season to think about how you can create a locavore's kitchen.

In Season

Throughout this book, you'll find plenty of foods in the sections called "In Season." These sections follow the natural rhythm of the season by reminding you what popular and commonly found fruits and vegetables are coming out of the garden, farmers markets, or local farms during the growing seasons—spring, summer, and fall. For each "In Season" selection, you'll learn in "Choosing the Best" how to recognize signs of peak ripeness and quality, while "How to Store Fresh" introduces ways to extend the useful life of fresh food as well as the best flavor and texture. "To Prepare for Cooking" includes information important for preparing a recipe or for enjoying produce out of hand; and "Pick or Buy Now, Enjoy Later" introduces ways to preserve the same flavors and textures you enjoy now for later.

Once you know this, dive into the recipes that feature these seasonal foods. More than 275 recipes throughout the book focus on seasonal, local foods—simple recipes that put flavors at the center of attention. It's natural that "things that grow together, go together," and you'll often find this to be true with the other ingredients featured in a recipe. You'll find that when you use fresh, local, seasonal foods at their peak flavor, the simplest recipes can have the most complex flavors.

Local Flavor

As you follow this book from one delicious season to the next, you'll find sections called "Local Flavor" where the spotlight is on easy-to-find local foods like meats and poultry, dairy products, maple syrup and honey, wines, and more—foods that you can reasonably rely on finding throughout your region year round, whether directly at the farm or at farmers markets. While produce has seasons that come and go, many of these foods can add that local component to the table any time of year.

Making Your Own

One of the most fun and rewarding aspects of a locavore's kitchen is the opportunity to say, "I did it myself!" This book has more than a dozen "Making Your Own" projects that turn one fabulous local ingredient into another. If you've found wholesome dairy products, turn them into thick, refreshing yogurt, sweet butter, or tangy crème fraîche, even ricotta cheese. Turn the cabbage harvest into sauerkraut and freshly milled grain into a loaf of wholesome wheat bread that can be your family's everyday loaf. Learn to make a basic piecrust that will follow you from pie to pie throughout the local growing season. Each project is simple, requiring little or no special equipment or unusual ingredients.

The time to think about preserving the flavors of the season is while you're enjoying them. Canning and preserving foods is becoming more popular as an inexpensive and effective way to capture seasonal flavors and introduce them to your menus off season, when the taste of local blackberries or green beans could brighten up a winter meal. "Preserving the Harvest in the Locavore's Kitchen" will show you the simplest and most inexpensive ways to stock up on the flavors you love now but will appreciate in the winter as well. Asparagus in season? Freeze a stash for winter soups. More tomatoes than you bargained for from your garden? Think canned tomatoes, salsa, and sauce, or oven-dried tomatoes, a respectable cousin of sun-dried. Herbs galore? It's easy and efficient to air-dry this harvest of flavor to keep the spice cabinet stocked until next growing season.

Preserving the Harvest

You'll also find more than 25 recipes that preserve seasonal ingredients by turning them into delicious sauces, salsa, chutneys, jams, jellies, and preserves as well as by canning whole fruits, classic pickles, and pickled vegetables. Sure, it takes some work. But it's *delicious* work with great fringe benefits, namely seasonal flavors remembered from last spring, summer, and fall. Think about it. Start small with one recipe and you'll see. There's a feeling of great accomplishment and satisfaction when you open your cupboard or freezer in February and know that locally grown food will be featured on your menu that day.

Whether you're completely new to canning, thinking about reviving your skills, or a seasoned canning enthusiast, the time to think about preserving the harvest is before it happens. Gather your recipes and sharpen your skills before the harvest comes on. Be sure to capture foods you intend to preserve at their peak flavor and texture. For information about preserving seasonal foods through canning and freezing, read "Preserving the Harvest in the Locavore's Kitchen" on page 215.

HOW TO USE THIS BOOK

Dedicating your household to eating locally grown, homegrown foods during the harvest season should be a joy, not a chore, and the journey to create a locavore's kitchen does not happen overnight. Pick and choose the ways you want to start incorporating locally grown and seasonal food into your life or adding even more local components to your kitchen. Do what you can in any measure to bring local flavors back into your kitchen. Your efforts will pay off in many ways: taste, fresh and nutritious food, and goodwill in supporting small family farms and local agriculture.

Let the harvest begin!

Spring

Spring is nature's wake-up call to tell us that another growing season is upon us. Some call it a rebirth, others a renewal, and then there are those who consider it a reward for waiting patiently for the return of great seasonal flavors. The harvest begins gradually with thick, succulent stalks of asparagus, spicy radishes, bouquets of salad greens, bright-stemmed chards, rosy rhubarb, and aromatic herbs. Spring foods are the "appetizers" to the abundance that awaits in the summer and fall.

Even though cold weather is just behind us, spring is the time to think about ways to translate some of what we enjoy now by preserving through canning and freezing so that the taste of spring is no further than our own kitchen when that's all we need to get us through the winter.

in season...
asparagus

Ah, asparagus! The green soldiers of spring. When sturdy shoots begin to pop up in the fields, it's Mother Nature's signal that another harvest season is under way and better eating is ahead. Get your fill of the juicy, toothsome, homegrown spears while you can because an early blast of summer heat can cut the season short, leaving you wanting more.

While asparagus makes an appearance year round in grocery stores, it can't compare with the flavor and texture of fresh picked. Asparagus has a naturally high sugar content and once picked begins to turn to starch and a tough, stringy chew. After a few days, the tender spears lose their snap, tenderness, and sweet flavor.

Choosing the Best. Spears should be straight, a bright grassy green color, and firm to the touch. The tips should be tightly closed with a dark green or purplish tinge, a sign of good quality. Yellowed or dried tips mean the asparagus is too old, and if the tips look like they are opening up, the asparagus is past its prime.

How to Store Fresh. It's best to use fresh asparagus the same day you buy it, but you can store it for up to four days and still anticipate good taste. Trim the stalks by snapping or cutting off the tough bottoms. Wrap a wet paper towel around the bottoms and place the bundle in a plastic bag. Store in the coldest part of the refrigerator, preferably the crisper.

To Prepare for Cooking. Asparagus tips trap sand as they grow. To clean, hold the bunch upside down and swish gently in cold water. Snap off the tough, woody bottoms by bending each stalk at the natural breaking point, where the color changes from white to green, about an inch from the base. Some prefer to trim the tiny scales along the shaft of the asparagus, but when the asparagus is truly fresh, that's a step you can skip.

Pick or Buy Now, Enjoy Later. Blanching and freezing asparagus or pickling in vinegar brine are the best ways to help the spears retain their bright green color and delicate flavor. Some of the toothy texture will be sacrificed in freezing, so don't expect the same bite or firmness as fresh asparagus. Frozen asparagus in best used in baked casseroles and in egg dishes, or pureed into soups like Asparagus Soup with Blue Cheese on page 205.

Freeze this season's asparagus! To learn how, go to page 218. Or preserve the seasonal flavor of asparagus with Pickled Asparagus Spears on page 6.

Asparagus Frittata with Spring Mint

Makes 6 to 8 servings

Mint is a vibrant yet subtle companion to the first pickings of asparagus. And because mint and asparagus are among the first vegetables and herbs to be harvested in the spring, they give credence to the saying "What grows together, goes together."

4 large fresh eggs

⅓ cup ricotta cheese or softened goat cheese

1½ tablespoons chopped fresh mint

¼ teaspoon salt

¼ teaspoon freshly ground black pepper

3 tablespoons grated Parmesan cheese, divided use

2 tablespoons unsalted butter

1 pound slender asparagus spears, trimmed, cut into ½-inch pieces

3 scallions, green part only, thinly sliced

Preheat the broiler.

Whisk the first 5 ingredients and 2 tablespoons of the Parmesan in a medium bowl to blend. Set aside.

Heat the butter in a medium nonstick broiler-proof skillet over medium heat. Add the asparagus and toss to coat. Cover the skillet; cook until the asparagus is crisp-tender, about 4 minutes. Add the scallions; stir 30 seconds. Stir in the egg mixture. Cover, reduce the heat to low, and cook until almost set on top, about 4 to 5 minutes.

Sprinkle the frittata with the remaining 1 tablespoon Parmesan. Place under the broiler until the top is set and starts to brown, about 2 minutes. Use a spatula around the edges of the frittata to loosen. Slide out onto a serving plate and serve.

● ●

all that's asparagus is not green

Green is the most common color of asparagus you'll find at farmers markets, but once in a while a creative farmer will slip in some purple or white asparagus just to keep you on your toes and pique your interest. What's the difference?

Purple varieties of asparagus are sweeter and more tender than their green counterparts. A showpiece for salads, purple asparagus is best in recipes where it's used raw or lightly steamed. It will lose its purple color when overcooked.

White asparagus is grown in the dark, under mounds of soil, so it lacks the chlorophyll that would make it green. It doesn't see the light until it is harvested. It is milder in flavor and more tender than green asparagus and often costs more.

a mint of mints

With more than two hundred varieties of garden mint found in home gardens, deciding which to use is a matter of taste, but consider this rule of thumb. Use spearmint for warm dishes and peppermint for cool or uncooked dishes. By and large, these basic varieties of mint are interchangeable in recipes if you don't have the choice. Reserve specialty mints like chocolate, orange, or pineapple mint for recipes where the leaf is used whole or as an edible garnish where unique taste can be fully appreciated.

Spring Soup

Makes 4 to 6 servings

A freezer stocked with asparagus and peas is your ticket to this luscious Spring Soup any time of year, but try it fresh first! The simplicity of the ingredients is intentional. Trust them to shine without competing with other seasonings.

5 cups rich chicken stock or vegetable broth

3 small shallots, minced

1 clove garlic, minced

2 pounds peas in the pod, shelled, about 2 cups, divided use

1 pound fresh asparagus, trimmed, cut into 1-inch pieces, tips reserved for garnish

1/3 cup long-grain white rice, cooked, divided use

1/2 tablespoon kosher salt

Freshly ground black pepper, to taste

Bring the chicken broth to a boil in a medium-sized saucepan. Add the shallots, garlic, and half of the peas. Simmer for 5 minutes. Puree the mixture along with 3 tablespoons of the cooked rice in a blender. Return to the saucepan, taste, and season with salt and pepper.

Return the soup to a boil over medium heat. Stir in the remaining peas and cook until tender, about 3 minutes. Add the asparagus and remaining rice and cook for an additional 2 minutes. Ladle into warm soup bowls and garnish with the reserved asparagus tips.

Beer-Battered Asparagus Spears

Makes 10 to 12 appetizer servings

This is one of those recipes that disappear almost as fast as they come out of the pan. Use thicker spears of fresh homegrown asparagus, tender to begin with. A quick bath in the hot oil makes them almost melt in your mouth ... and using beer from a local microbrewery keeps it all in the local family.

....

How do you know if the oil is hot enough? Place a drop of batter in the oil. If it sizzles immediately, it's ready! Too hot? The oil smokes.

2 pounds fresh asparagus, washed, dried, tough ends trimmed

1 1/2 cups all-purpose flour

1 1/2 teaspoons garlic powder

1 teaspoon kosher salt

1 teaspoon freshly ground black pepper

1 1/2 cups beer (or 1 12-ounce bottle)

Canola or vegetable oil, for frying

In a shallow baking dish, combine the flour and the seasonings. Slowly stir in the beer until the batter is smooth and thick enough to cling to the asparagus (using all of the beer may not be necessary).

Heat about 1 inch of oil in a large frying pan over medium-high heat. Dredge the asparagus through the batter, coating each stalk completely. Fry in the hot oil until golden and puffy, about 4 minutes, turning once. If the spears are browning too quickly, reduce the heat a little.

Drain the spears on a paper towel–lined tray before serving.

Asparagus Pesto Pizza

Yields enough for two 12-inch pizzas

While thicker asparagus is more toothsome than thin, sometimes you end up with slender spears, often pencil thin, that find a great home in this recipe. Use this pesto for a fresh, seasonal twist on the classic pizza, or tossed with hot pasta, or stirred into scrambled eggs.

To save some of the asparagus pesto for later, simply freeze small portions in freezer-proof containers for up to 6 months. Come winter, you'll be glad you made the effort.

Asparagus Pesto:

1 pound asparagus, tough ends trimmed

½ cup plus 2 tablespoons extra virgin olive oil

2 cloves garlic

½ cup packed fresh basil leaves, plus extra for garnish

2 tablespoons nuts (walnuts, pine nuts, or pecans)

¾ cup grated Romano cheese, divided use

Salt and freshly ground black pepper

2 prepared 12-inch pizza shells

2 cups crumbled goat or feta cheese

To make the pesto, preheat the oven to 425°F. Drizzle the 2 tablespoons of oil over the asparagus and toss to coat evenly. Spread in a single layer on a baking sheet and roast for 10 minutes, or until the spears are just tender and lightly browned. Remove from the oven and let cool slightly.

Place the garlic, basil leaves, and nuts in the bowl of a food processor. Pulse until ground to a fine texture. Add the cooled asparagus and ½ cup of the Romano cheese and pulse until coarsely chopped. With the motor running, slowly add the ½ cup of olive oil until smooth and emulsified. Season to taste with salt and pepper. (Pesto can be divided into smaller portions and frozen at this point if it is not to be used immediately.)

To assemble the pizzas, put the pizza shells on baking trays. Divide the asparagus pesto between the two shells, spreading evenly to an inch from the edge. Sprinkle the remaining Romano cheese followed by the goat cheese evenly over both pizzas.

Bake for 10 to 12 minutes or until the cheese is softened and very lightly browned. Let cool for a few minutes and serve.

Chilled Asparagus and Red Onion Salad

Makes 6 to 8 servings

While thicker spears are certainly meatier and better for recipes that call for high temperatures, here is a special place for thinner, more delicate spears. The vinegar does the work to "cook" or tenderize the asparagus in the hour it sits before serving.

1 pound fresh asparagus, trimmed

1 small red onion, finely diced

1 cup coarsely grated Parmesan or Romano cheese

½ cup red wine vinegar

2 tablespoons extra virgin olive oil

Coarse sea salt

Cracked black pepper, to taste

Slice the asparagus spears crosswise on the diagonal into very thin slices, about ⅛ inch thick. Place in a medium bowl and add the red onion and cheese, tossing to combine. Add the red wine vinegar and oil and toss again. Set aside for one hour, tossing once or twice, to allow the flavors to meld. When ready to serve, sprinkle with sea salt and cracked black pepper, to taste.

Crunchy Asparagus Spears

Makes 6 servings

¼ cup mayonnaise

2 tablespoons Dijon mustard

1 teaspoon fresh lemon juice

½ teaspoon coarse salt

¼ teaspoon freshly ground black pepper

1 cup panko crumbs

2 tablespoons extra virgin olive oil, divided use

1 pound thick asparagus, tough ends trimmed

Preheat the oven to 450°F.

Whisk together the mayonnaise, mustard, lemon juice, salt, and pepper in a shallow baking dish, wide enough to dip the spears in the mixture.

Spread the breadcrumbs on a rimmed baking sheet. Oil another rimmed baking sheet with 1 tablespoon of the oil.

Roll each stalk of asparagus in the mayonnaise mixture. Roll in the breadcrumbs until coated.

Transfer to the oiled baking sheet. Repeat with the remaining spears. Sprinkle the remaining tablespoon of oil over the top.

Roast the asparagus 13 to 15 minutes, until the crumbs are golden and the asparagus is crisp-tender. Serve immediately.

Contrary to what you may have heard in the past, thick spears are better than thin . . . and freshly picked trump them both! Rolled in panko, a very crunchy Japanese breadcrumb, these spears make a nice side dish or can be served as an appetizer with a mustard dipping sauce. Simply mix the mustard of your choice with some crème fraîche or sour cream thinned with a little milk. Learn to make your own crème fraîche on page 50.

A suitable substitute for the panko would be fresh breadcrumbs, lightly toasted. To make the crunchiest possible breadcrumbs, remove the crusts from slices of bread and process into coarse crumbs in a food processor fitted with the steel blade. Spread on a baking sheet and place in a 400°F oven until dry and lightly toasted. Make extra and store in a sealed container.

Pickled Asparagus Spears

Makes 6 pint jars

5 pounds fresh asparagus, washed and tough bottoms trimmed

1 large red onion, thinly sliced

6 cloves garlic, peeled and crushed

4 cups distilled white vinegar

4 cups water

6 tablespoons pickling salt or kosher salt

3 teaspoons dill seed or 6 sprigs of fresh dill

Cut the asparagus spears to 4-inch lengths to fit in 6 wide-mouthed pint jars. (Reserve the trimmed portions for another use.) Pack jars with asparagus (tips pointing up), onion, and a clove of garlic in each.

Combine the vinegar, water, pickling salt, and dill seed in a medium saucepan and bring to a boil. Pour the hot liquid into the jars to within ½ inch of the rim (leaving headspace), making sure that the spears are covered. Seal and process for 20 minutes.

Pickled asparagus is a delicious way to bring spring into your kitchen any time of the year. While it might be tempting to dive into these slender green gems right away, give them at least five days to bathe in their vinegary brine to develop the best flavor. Then use them in salads or as a snack.

New to pickling? For a step-by-step guide to the basics, see "Pickled Vegetables, Relishes, and Salsas" on page 239.

in season ...
rhubarb

It's a sure sign of spring when rhubarb emerges from its long winter's nap. Rhubarb is the "tart" of the garden, teasing us into thinking it's a fruit by headlining in pies, cobblers, and jams, in the company of a hefty measure of sugar to tame its sour disposition. In reality, rhubarb is an uncommon vegetable that doesn't often find its way into savory dishes but should! Some flavors are flattered by the sourness of rhubarb, so you'll often find it teamed with sugary ripe strawberries or spiced with ginger.

Rhubarb is largely water, breaking down easily and quickly in sauces and jams, but perhaps too quickly when a chunky texture is desired—so some recipes benefit from a watchful eye. Highly acidic, rhubarb turns a murky brown when cooked in copper, aluminum, or cast iron, so choose nonreactive cookware.

Choosing the Best. Whether you're preparing to pick rhubarb straight from the garden or buying a bundle at a farmers market, choose firm, straight stalks (also called *petioles*) with smooth, shiny patinas. For all rhubarb, only the stalks are used, as the leaves are highly toxic. Between varieties, the color of the stalks varies from an intense ruby red to a soft speckled pink to a light green with a hint of blush. The redder stalks offer the best flavor and are more likely to maintain their rosy hue when cooked.

How to Store Fresh. When properly stored, fresh rhubarb can be kept for up to three weeks in the refrigerator. Cut off the leaves and discard them. Brush off any soil that clings to the stalks, but save washing for later. Store in a plastic bag in the coolest part of the refrigerator, preferably the crisper.

To Prepare for Cooking. Rinse stalks stored in the refrigerator and refresh them by trimming ¼ inch from each end. Let stand in cold water for an hour before using. Peeling the rhubarb is often unnecessary, but larger stalks often have a stringy covering running down the back that can be stripped off. A pound of rhubarb yields about 3 cups chopped or ¾ cup cooked.

Pick or Buy Now, Enjoy Later. Rhubarb freezes beautifully with little fuss. Come fall and winter, frozen rhubarb can be baked into pies, breads, and desserts or stirred into stews and soups like the Savory Lentil and Rhubarb Soup on page 206.

Freeze this season's rhubarb! To learn how, go to page 218.
Or preserve the seasonal flavor of rhubarb in Grilled Rhubarb and Lemon Preserves on page 10.

Ginger Rhubarb Crisp

Makes 8 servings

Aside from pies, rhubarb is traditionally found in crisps and cobblers. The ingredients in this recipe are what you expect in a cobbler, but add just a couple of tablespoons of candied ginger and wow! Let's just say this isn't your grandmother's rhubarb crisp! It's a perfect union of tart and sweet . . . with a delightful, spicy kick!

1 cup old-fashioned rolled oats

¾ cup packed dark brown sugar

½ cup all-purpose flour

½ teaspoon salt

½ cup unsalted butter, cut into small pieces and chilled

4 cups chopped rhubarb, 1-inch pieces

2 tablespoons finely chopped candied ginger

½ cup sugar

Vanilla ice cream, to accompany

If candied ginger is not available, add 1 ½ teaspoons of ground ginger to the dry ingredients.

Preheat the oven to 350°F. Grease an 8-inch square baking dish.

Combine the oats, brown sugar, flour, and salt in a medium bowl. Cut the butter into the dry ingredients using a pastry blender until the mixture is crumbly. Place half of the mixture into the baking dish, pressing gently to form a bottom crust. Top with the rhubarb and sprinkle with the chopped ginger and sugar. Top with the remaining oatmeal mixture.

Bake for about 45 minutes or until the rhubarb is tender and the crust is brown. Serve with a scoop of vanilla ice cream.

Rhubarb Coffee Cake

Makes two 8-inch square cakes

The combination of cherry-red stalks of rhubarb and the brown sugar batter makes this coffee cake wonderfully moist. It's a special treat warm from the oven, slathered with real butter, and enjoyed with a cup of hot coffee in the morning. Serve it as a cake after dinner with a dollop of lightly sweetened whipped cream or a scoop of vanilla ice cream.

1 ½ cups packed dark brown sugar

⅔ cup vegetable oil

1 large egg

1 cup buttermilk

2 ½ cups all-purpose flour

1 teaspoon baking soda

1 teaspoon salt

1 teaspoon pure vanilla extract

2 cups diced rhubarb, about ½-inch pieces

½ cup coarsely chopped walnuts

1 tablespoon unsalted butter, at room temperature

¼ cup granulated sugar

This coffee cake feeds a crowd, but if you're lacking a crowd at the moment, wrap the cooled cake tightly in foil and freeze for up to 3 months.

Preheat the oven to 350°F. Grease or butter two 8-inch square baking pans.

Mix the brown sugar and vegetable oil together in a large bowl until smooth. Add the egg, buttermilk, flour, baking soda, salt, and vanilla. Blend until moist. Fold in the rhubarb and walnuts. Divide the batter evenly between the pans.

In a food processor, combine the butter and sugar until the mixture resembles wet sand. Scatter evenly over the surface of the batter.

Bake for 40 to 45 minutes, or until a toothpick inserted in the center comes out clean. Let cool in pan for 5 minutes before turning out onto a baking rack.

Serve warm or let cool completely before serving.

Rhubarb and Strawberry Compote over Rustic Cornmeal Shortcakes

Rhubarb's most constant companion is the strawberry. Not only do they come in season at the same time, but their bright flavors— one tart, the other sweet—are the perfect springtime complement to each other. Spoon this combination over these rustic shortcakes.

Makes 8 servings

Compote

1 pound strawberries, washed and hulled
1 pound rhubarb stalks, cut into ¾-inch pieces
1 teaspoon grated lemon zest
1 tablespoon freshly squeezed lemon juice
¾ cup sugar

Cornmeal Shortcakes

1½ cups all-purpose flour
½ cup coarsely ground cornmeal
3 tablespoons poppy seeds
1 tablespoon plus 1 teaspoon baking powder
¼ teaspoon kosher salt
4 tablespoons sugar, divided use
4 tablespoons cold unsalted butter, cut into small cubes
1 cup heavy cream, plus extra for brushing
Lightly sweetened whipped cream, to accompany

To prepare the compote, cut the strawberries into quarters. Set aside 1 cup. Place the remaining berries in a medium saucepan. Add the rhubarb pieces. Add the lemon zest and lemon juice to the pan. Add the sugar and stir to coat.

Cook over medium-high heat, stirring occasionally to dissolve the sugar. The fruit will release a lot of liquid. Boil for 5 to 7 minutes until the rhubarb is softened. Remove from the heat and stir in the reserved strawberries. Cool to room temperature and then refrigerate in a covered container until chilled.

Preheat the oven to 425°F.

To prepare the shortcakes, place the flour, cornmeal, poppy seeds, baking powder, salt, and 3 tablespoons of sugar in a food processor. Pulse to combine. Add the butter and pulse until the mixture resembles coarse meal. With the machine running, quickly pour in the cup of cream. When the dough begins to come together, stop the machine.

Turn the dough out onto a lightly floured surface. With floured hands, shape it into a rough 6-inch circle, about ¾ inch thick. Cut the round into 6 wedges. Place the wedges on a baking sheet, brush each with cream, and sprinkle the remaining tablespoon of sugar over the tops. Bake for 15 to 20 minutes, until the shortcakes are set and lightly golden. Cool to room temperature.

To serve, spoon the compote over the shortcake and top with a dollop of lightly sweetened whipped cream.

rhubarb's identity crisis

Some fruits clearly fit our expectations of what a fruit should be. They have seeds and they are a product of a flower. So what's the story with rhubarb? We treat it as a fruit, all sugared up, to add it to pies, baked goods, sauces, and jams. Yet botanically speaking, rhubarb is an ornamental vegetable, of which the stalks are the only edible portions. Beware! The leaves are toxic and should never be eaten.

Rhubarb Potato Salad with Balsamic Dressing

Makes 6 to 8 servings

It's a rare moment when a recipe featuring rhubarb doesn't call for large amounts of sugar to balance the tart flavors. Here, the tart tones are encouraged to strut their stuff with just a nudge from brown sugar and balsamic vinegar.

1½ pounds small red potatoes

1 cup chopped rhubarb

2 tablespoons water

2 tablespoons brown sugar

3 tablespoons balsamic vinegar

2 tablespoons extra virgin olive oil

Salt and freshly ground black pepper

½ red onion, cut into small dice

Place the potatoes in a large pot and add water to cover one inch above the potatoes. Bring to a boil and cook for 12 to 15 minutes until fork tender. Drain, let cool enough to handle, and cut the potatoes into halves or quarters. Place in a large bowl, cover, and keep warm.

Combine the rhubarb, water, and brown sugar in a saucepan and cook over medium heat, stirring frequently, until the rhubarb breaks up and softens. Mash the softened rhubarb with a fork. Add the balsamic vinegar and olive oil. Reduce the heat to low and warm the mixture through. Season with salt and freshly ground black pepper.

While the dressing is still warm, pour it over the potatoes and toss gently. Scatter the onion over the potato salad and serve warm or at room temperature.

Grilled Rhubarb and Lemon Preserves

Makes 3 half-pint jars

A hot grill spikes sugars and tames the acids in rhubarb as well as adding a subtle smoky flavor to this jam. Can the jam in the spring and pull it from the pantry on a snowy day. It's delightful over a toasted English muffin or served over thick slices of pound cake with a dollop of lightly sweetened whipped cream.

New to making jams, jellies, and preserves? For a step-by-step guide to the basics, see "Jams, Jellies, and Preserves" on page 237.

3 pounds rhubarb stalks

Vegetable or canola oil, for brushing

1½ cups sugar

4 tablespoons fresh lemon juice

Grated zest of 1 fresh lemon

Preheat the grill or broiler to medium-high.

Lightly brush the rhubarb stalks with the oil. Grill or broil until lightly charred, about 2 to 3 minutes on each side. Smaller stalks will likely break down from the heat. Remove, let cool, and coarsely chop the stalks. Set aside.

Combine the sugar and lemon juice in a large saucepan and cook over medium heat, stirring occasionally, until sugar just begins to dissolve, about 8 to 10 minutes. Stir in the chopped rhubarb and cook over medium heat, stirring occasionally, for 15 minutes or until most of the rhubarb breaks down yet a few chunks remain. Remove from the heat and perform a gel test (see page 238). If the gel stage has not been reached, return to the heat and cook for a few minutes. Repeat the test until the gel stage has been reached. Once the mixture has gelled, skim off any foam that has developed. Stir in the lemon zest.

Ladle the jam into sterilized jars to within ¼ inch of the rim (headspace), seal, and process for 10 minutes.

spinach

One of the most welcome sights, whether in the garden or at a farmers market, is spinach in the spring . . . delicate, young, cool-weather-loving spinach. Spinach enjoys a long harvest from the spring into the early summer, takes a few months off, and shows up again at farmers markets and roadside stands in the fall, sturdier and strong-flavored but wonderful nonetheless. The main reason to seek out locally grown spinach in the spring is its tender nature, which is preferred when using it raw in salads.

Attention to the fresh flavor of locally grown foods has put some less-than-popular foods of our childhood back in the limelight. Spinach might be one, if you're willing to give it another try.

Choosing the Best. Looks are everything when it comes to choosing fresh spinach. Few vegetables are as obvious about showing their age. Spinach should be bouncy and dark green. If it shows signs of wilting or brown or yellow edges, it's past its prime and won't deliver a delicate crunch, buttery texture, or that fresh green flavor.

How to Store Fresh. Freshly picked spinach is likely to have a measure of dirt and grit. It also has a naturally high water content, which makes it highly perishable. After picking or buying, it's best to refrigerate spinach unwashed, even if some soil clings to the leaves, in a perforated sealable plastic bag or container, washing just the amount you'll need at a time.

Spinach stores best in the crisper of the refrigerator where the temperature is cool and there is just a touch of humidity. Handled correctly, it can be stored for up to five days.

To Prepare for Cooking. To clean spinach, plunge the leaves into a tub or sink of room-temperature water and drain off as much water as possible. You may have to do this a few times, using clean water each time, until a taste of a leaf reveals no grittiness. Drain off as much water as possible, then blot the excess with a paper towel or use a salad spinner to do the job.

Use whole or chop as your recipe suggests. Use spinach with the stems intact as long as they have not become tough and stringy. If that's the case, simply fold the leaf in half lengthwise with the underside of the stem facing you and pull down on the stem to remove it.

Pick or Buy Now, Enjoy Later. Fresh spinach, whole or chopped, freezes beautifully and can be used later in quiches, dips, or any recipe calling for cooked spinach like the Spinach Balls on page 204.

Freeze this season's spinach! To learn how, go to page 218.

Savory Spinach Custard

Makes 6 servings

Two pounds of spinach looks like a mountain, but as it cooks down and releases its water, you'll wonder where it went. To achieve a perfect finish on this egg-rich dish, it's necessary and worth the effort to use a bain marie, a technique that surrounds the delicate contents of the baking dish with hot water to gently cook the custard to perfection.

2 tablespoons extra virgin olive oil

1 medium onion, chopped

2 cloves garlic, minced

2 pounds fresh spinach, washed, dried, and trimmed, if necessary

4 fresh eggs

¾ cup milk or half-and-half

¾ cup Romano cheese

½ teaspoon crushed red pepper

1 teaspoon salt

Grating of nutmeg

Preheat the oven to 325°F. Lightly oil a 1½-quart baking dish.

Heat the oil in a large sauté pan over medium-high heat. Add the onion and sauté until soft and fragrant, about 5 minutes. Add the garlic and sauté for an additional minute. Add the spinach in batches, stirring occasionally, until the spinach cooks down. Add more spinach when the previous batch cooks down. When all the spinach has softened and cooked down, remove from the heat and set aside to cool slightly.

Beat the eggs in a large mixing bowl until blended. Stir in the milk. Add the spinach mixture, cheese, crushed red pepper, and salt and mix well. Transfer the mixture to the prepared baking dish. Sprinkle grated nutmeg over the top. Put the baking dish into a 9 x 13-inch pan and place on the oven rack. Carefully pour very hot water into the pan until it reaches halfway up the outside of the baking dish.

Bake until the custard is set, about 40 to 45 minutes, or until a knife inserted in the center of the custard comes out clean. Let the baking dish cool enough to handle before removing from the water bath.

To serve, cut the custard into squares or scoop out with a spoon and serve immediately.

Stir-Fried Spinach with Walnuts

Makes 4 servings

The key to winning spinach skeptics over is to pay attention to cooking times. Cooked too long or left to sit, spinach diminishes in texture, color, flavor, and nutrients. Here's where stir-frying, which calls for high heat and quick cooking, comes into play. A watchful eye is important, too. This dish can go from soft and succulent to a soggy mass in a heartbeat, and the fresh green flavor will be lost.

3 tablespoons peanut oil

2 tablespoons coarsely chopped walnuts

2 tablespoons rice wine

2 teaspoons sugar

1 teaspoon salt

2 cloves garlic, minced

1 pound fresh spinach (about 6 cups packed), washed and dried

Dark sesame oil, to taste

Gently heat the peanut oil in a small saucepan over high heat to hot but not smoking. Add the walnuts, stir, and remove from the heat. Allow to sit for 5 minutes or until the walnuts are a golden brown. Remove the walnuts to a paper towel to drain, reserving the oil.

Combine the rice wine, sugar, and salt. Set aside.

Heat a wok or a large skillet over high heat (if the skillet is smaller than 16 inches, work in two batches). Add 2 tablespoons of the reserved oil to the wok. When it is hot, add the garlic and stir-fry for 10 seconds, then add the spinach. Cook, stirring and tossing rapidly in the pan until the spinach is coated with the oil, about 20 seconds. Add the rice wine mixture and continue to cook, tossing until the spinach begins to wilt. Remove the wok from the heat, toss again, and transfer to a warmed serving platter.

Sprinkle the walnuts and the sesame oil over the top and serve.

Spinach Salad with Strawberries, Nuts, and Blue Cheese

When spring hands you tiny, tender spinach leaves, rush them into this salad with seasonal strawberries. After a long winter, a salad of fresh tender spring spinach can really hit the spot.

Makes 4 servings

½ pound fresh baby spinach, rinsed and dried

1 to 1½ cups sliced strawberries

½ cup pecan or walnut halves, lightly toasted

3 to 4 ounces crumbled blue cheese (feta or goat cheese can be substituted)

2 tablespoons balsamic vinegar or fruit vinegar

½ tablespoon minced shallot

1 tablespoon honey

1 teaspoon fresh thyme leaves

⅛ teaspoon dry mustard

¼ cup mild salad oil

Salt and freshly ground black pepper, to taste

Toss spinach with sliced strawberries, pecans, and cheese in a large salad bowl.

Combine the vinegar, shallot, honey, thyme, and mustard in a blender. Blend for 30 seconds. Add the oil, salt, and pepper and blend for another 30 seconds. Drizzle over the salad and toss until the leaves are coated. Serve immediately.

Creamed Spinach with a
Buttered Breadcrumb Crust

Makes 8 to 10 servings

This recipe bathes tender spinach in a silky combination of eggs, milk, and sour cream for a rich, heavenly effect, and the buttery crumb topping brings a welcome crunchy contrast to the smooth, velvety spinach.

¼ cup unsalted butter

2 cups fresh breadcrumbs

3 pounds young fresh spinach

1 cup whole milk

2 cups sour cream

1 cup grated Parmesan cheese

1 small onion, minced

Freshly grated nutmeg

2 large eggs, beaten

Salt and freshly ground black pepper, to taste

Melt the butter in a large skillet over medium heat. Add the breadcrumbs and sauté until golden, about 3 to 4 minutes. Set aside to cool.

Cook the spinach in 2 batches in a large pot of boiling salted water, stirring constantly until wilted, about 2 minutes. Drain in a colander and rinse with cold water to halt the cooking. Squeeze the spinach to remove as much moisture as possible. Coarsely chop.

Preheat the oven to 350°F. Butter an 8-inch square baking dish.

In a large bowl, mix the spinach, milk, sour cream, cheese, onion, and nutmeg. Add the eggs and stir until combined. Season with salt and pepper. Pour the mixture into the prepared baking dish. Top with the breadcrumb mixture and bake until set, about 30 minutes.

Making Your Own: Whole Wheat Bread

Before jam and jelly season arrives, make sure you're ready with one reliable recipe for a hardy sandwich loaf worthy of any fruit spread made with perfect, in-season local fruits. It should be a recipe you look forward to making at the beginning of the week and watching disappear in sandwiches, as breakfast toast, or grilled with some fresh locally produced cheese together with a cup of homemade tomato soup for lunch.

If you're fortunate enough to find locally grown and milled flours at farmers markets, buy them in quantities you'll use within 6 to 8 weeks. Freshly milled whole wheat flours have shorter shelf lives than refined flours. The wonderful wheat germ, bran, and middling that account for most of its nutritional value can turn rancid when the oils from these components begin to break down, leaving a bitter taste in the finished loaf.

Everyday Whole Wheat Bread

While this recipe works perfectly in a heavy-duty stand mixer, there's some satisfaction in crafting it by hand, familiarizing yourself with the way the dough looks, feels, and smells as the recipe moves along.

Variations: To give this bread some added texture and nutritional benefits, experiment by adding up to ½ cup of coarse seeds or grains such as flax seeds, wheat berries, or wheat kernels.

Finished dough is tacky, not sticky. The difference? Sticky dough comes away from the dough mass and sticks to your hands. Tacky dough is cool but not dry and won't leave traces on your hands when kneading.

Yields 2 loaves

2⅓ cups warm water (about 110°F)

1½ tablespoons active dry yeast

¼ cup local honey

4 tablespoons unsalted butter, melted and cooled

2½ teaspoons salt

¼ cup rye flour

½ cup cracked wheat flour

3 cups whole wheat flour

2¾ cups all-purpose flour, plus extra for kneading, if necessary

Mix the water, yeast, honey, and butter in a large bowl. Let stand for 10 minutes until foamy. Add the salt, rye flour, cracked wheat flour, and one cup each of the whole wheat and all-purpose flour until the mixture resembles a batter. Combine the remaining flours in a separate bowl.

Using a wooden spoon, mix in some of the remaining flour mixture, bit by bit, until the dough becomes too stiff to stir. Turn the dough out onto a surface floured with the some of the remaining flour mixture. Knead in the remaining flours, a little at a time. Continue kneading the dough for 8 to 10 minutes until it is smooth and elastic, cool to the touch, tacky but not sticky.

Place the dough in a lightly oiled bowl. Cover with plastic wrap or a damp towel and let rise in a warm, draft-free area until the dough has doubled in volume, about one hour.

Preheat the oven to 375°F.

Gently press down on the dough and divide into two equal pieces. Press and shape each into a rectangle, 1 inch thick and about 9 inches long.

Roll the dough into a cylinder, pressing down gently. Pinch the seam side closed. Place each loaf in a lightly greased 9 x 5-inch loaf pan, seam side down. Cover and let rise until doubled in volume, 35 to 40 minutes.

Bake for 35 to 40 minutes or until browned on the top. (An instant-read thermometer inserted into the center should read 205°F.) Remove from the loaf pans and transfer to a baking rack. Cool to room temperature.

milk

If you've heard the phrase "the cream rises to the top," take it as a compliment. But if you've never experienced that particular quality in milk, start looking for the return of milk and dairy products from local and regional dairies, and the origin of this popular expression will become apparent.

Midsized or micro dairies, those that keep smaller herds on lush green pastures, are part of the local food culture in many regions throughout the country. Committed to keeping a closer connection to the finished product, they enjoy a strong following of local and loyal customers who care about quality and animal welfare, appreciate the value of a local milk supply, and savor the genuine taste of milk—full, creamy, and sweet—where the cream did indeed rise to the top.

Many dairies, regardless of size and whether they produce milk organically or otherwise, now produce milk free of antibiotics and growth hormones, and that's good for all. Smaller dairies capture locavores' attention to flavor.

Some dairies milk only one breed of cows prized for specific milk qualities, while others keep diversified herds and blend the milk to achieve a uniquely rich flavor. The milk may be from Holsteins, prolific milk producers, or the familiar brown-eyed Jerseys that yield milk high in butterfat. Milk from Guernseys is richly flavored milk, while Brown Swiss milk has a desirable ratio of butterfat to protein.

Most of the milk you'll find in the grocery's dairy case is ultrapasteurized, meaning the milk is sterilized at 280°F, a process that trades flavor for long-distance marketing and a long shelf life. Smaller dairies use slower, more deliberate methods to preserve the genuine taste and nutritional value of the milk. They lightly pasteurize, heating the milk to a lower temperature for a longer period of times to eliminate harmful bacteria, then cooling it quickly to maintain the genuine flavor of the milk. Most do not homogenize their milk, which means the cream remains and rises to the top, a prize for the first to uncap the bottle or open the container. From the cow to the dairy case—and into your glass—it can be a matter of twenty-four hours.

Hot Milk Cakes with Peaches and Cream

Makes 6 servings

Any type of milk will work in this recipe, but the richer the milk, the richer the cake. This cake can follow you throughout the year using any seasonal berry or simply enjoyed plain.

5 tablespoons unsalted butter

⅔ cup whole milk

2 eggs

1 cup sugar

1 cup plus 2 tablespoons all-purpose flour

1¼ teaspoons baking powder

½ teaspoon vanilla

4 ripe peaches, peeled, pitted, and sliced

Lightly sweetened whipped cream

Preheat the oven to 425°F. Butter and flour six ¾-cup ramekins or 6 muffin tin cups.

In a small saucepan, gently warm the butter and milk until the butter is melted. Set aside.

Using an electric mixer, beat the eggs on high speed until thick, about 5 minutes. Gradually add the sugar and beat an additional 2 minutes. In a separate bowl, combine the flour and baking powder. Add to the egg mixture and beat until smooth, about 2 minutes. Add the milk mixture and vanilla and beat an additional 2 minutes.

Divide between the prepared ramekins. Bake for 16 to 18 minutes, until pale gold and firm to the touch.

Cool for 20 minutes before removing from the ramekins.

To serve, split the cakes in half horizontally. Place the bottom half in a shallow bowl or plate and spoon peaches over the top with a dollop of the whipped cream. Top with the remaining cake and a dollop of whipped cream. Serve immediately.

shake things up

Nonhomogenized milk might look strange at first, but one taste can lead to a seriously wonderful addiction. Shake the milk before each serving to disperse the cream. While the little flecks of butterfat never quite disappear, the taste it delivers is smooth, creamy, and flavorful. The plug of cream that rises to the top? Shake it to blend or scoop it off and stir it into hot coffee or lightly whip to top off a serving or two of fresh berries.

about raw milk

All over the United States, there has been a renewed interest in raw milk, unprocessed milk straight from the source. Raw milk was made illegal through much of the country in the days when cows frequently had tuberculosis. Today's raw milk enthusiasts believe that knowing the source, the dairyman, the farming methods, and the care the herd receives makes the risk minimal or nonexistent. The taste and desire for raw milk are back, and it is legal in some states. How about where you live? If you're not sure about the regulations, go to realmilk.com to find out.

in season ...
radishes

The radish is a zesty, often harsh, little number that often gets passed up or dismissed as disagreeable. That's a shame, because a properly harvested radish delivers a wonderful peppery sensation that spices up a recipe without much outside help. Radishes are a cool-weather vegetable and one of the first to green up the garden or appear at farmers markets in the spring.

Radishes come in a number of varieties ranging in color from red to purple, pink to white and in shapes from small and round to long and oval. The most common radishes are the round, intensely flavored, red-skinned variety, about the size of a cherry tomato. A milder option is the distinctive Daikon, a long, white, cylindrical Japanese variety. For the most part, depending on the desired results, varieties can be swapped out in any recipe.

Choosing the Best. Smaller—about an inch in diameter—is better when it comes to choosing radishes, but size is not the only indicator of good taste. A gentle squeeze should find them firm and sturdy, and the roots should be crisp and no more than an inch long. The skin should be smooth and free of cracks, and the leaves should be intact, bright green, and fresh looking. Radishes that are too big or too old have a pithy texture and a bitter, hot taste.

How to Store Fresh. Radishes are best when used within two weeks of harvest. Rinse off any dirt and remove the leafy tops but keep the roots intact, removing when ready to use. Blot dry before storing in a sealable plastic bag. If using the tops, store separately.

To Prepare for Cooking. Cooking or roasting will mellow out the peppery flavor of radishes. If using raw, an hour's soak in lightly salted water also draws out some of the spiciness. Drain, rinse, and pat dry before using. Typically, radishes are not peeled, but both the roots and leaves should be removed before cooking.

Pick or Buy Now, Enjoy Later. Because of their high water content, radishes will not retain their classic crunch once frozen and thawed. To enjoy them out of season, consider recipes that preserve the vegetable's satisfying crunch by pickling and refrigerating. Subjecting radishes to canning methods will void the expected crunch.

Preserve the seasonal flavor of radishes with Gingery Pickled Radishes on page 21.

Minty Radish Tea Sandwiches

Makes 24 sandwiches

Cooling mint is the perfect counterbalance to the peppery radish … and on a warm day, this dainty sandwich and a tall glass of iced tea make a delightful way to cool off.

1 cup mayonnaise

2 tablespoons sour cream

1 tablespoon freshly grated lemon zest

2 teaspoons fresh lemon juice, more or less to taste

2 teaspoons grainy mustard

Salt and freshly ground black pepper, to taste

24 thin slices of white bread

1 cup fresh mint leaves

16 radishes, trimmed and thinly sliced

In a small bowl, combine the mayonnaise, sour cream, lemon zest, lemon juice, and mustard. Season with salt and pepper, to taste.

Spread each of the bread slices with a thin layer of the mayonnaise mixture. Top with a layer of the mint leaves and a layer of the sliced radishes. Top with the remaining bread slice and press gently together. Trim the crusts and cut the sandwiches in half diagonally.

Wrap in plastic wrap and refrigerate for at least 2 hours before serving.

Radishes with Goat Cheese and Honey

Makes 24 appetizers

Easy to make, complex in flavor, this appetizer features three wonderful sensations in each bite: spicy (radish), tangy (goat cheese), and sweet (honey). If the green tops are tiny and in perfect condition, leave them attached to the radish.

½ cup soft, mild goat cheese, softened

3 tablespoons honey

Salt and freshly ground black pepper

12 large radishes, leafy greens trimmed to ½ inch and halved

3 tablespoons chopped fresh chives or flat-leaf parsley

In a small bowl, stir together the goat cheese and honey. Season to taste with salt and pepper. (Can be made 2 days ahead of time. Bring to room temperature before using.)

Arrange the radishes cut side up on a large platter and spoon a small dollop of the goat cheese mixture on the top of each. Garnish with the chopped chives before serving.

Radish Salad with Feta and Pickled Red Spring Onions

Makes 6 servings

This peppery salad is a variation on a classic Greek radish salad. Add pitted olives, if you like ... either way, the taste is fresh and evocative of spring. Freshly chopped flat-leaf parsley can be substituted for the radish greens, too.

4 bunches fresh young radishes, leaves intact

½ teaspoon salt

½ teaspoon freshly ground black pepper

½ teaspoon sugar

½ cup crumbled feta cheese

½ cup pickled red spring onions (recipe on page 43)

1 tablespoon red wine vinegar

3 tablespoons extra virgin olive oil

Trim the tops and roots from the radishes, reserving the leaves. Thinly slice the radishes and set aside. Wash and dry the leaves, removing any that appear damaged or wilted, and tear them into bite-sized pieces.

Toss the radishes and leaves together in a salad bowl. Season with salt, pepper, and sugar. Toss in the cheese. Top with the pickled red onions, sprinkle with the vinegar, and drizzle the olive oil over the top. Serve immediately.

Soy Roasted Radishes

Makes 4 servings

All root vegetables benefit from a little roasting time, so why not radishes? The oven's heat will mellow the sharp tones and soften the crunchy orbs to a buttery texture. Forget the salt ... the soy sauce will do the honors.

2 bunches radishes, cleaned, trimmed, and halved

1½ tablespoons canola oil

2 tablespoons soy sauce

2 scallions, thinly sliced

1 tablespoon sesame seeds, toasted

Preheat the oven to 425°F.

Toss the radishes with the oil to coat. Spread the radishes in a single layer on a sturdy baking sheet. Roast, turning once or twice, until the radishes are tender and just beginning to brown, about 20 to 25 minutes.

Sprinkle with the soy sauce and scatter the scallions over the radishes. Roast for an additional 3 to 5 minutes.

Transfer the radishes and any liquid to a serving bowl and sprinkle with the sesame seeds.

To toast sesame seeds: Place the sesame seeds in a large frying pan. Heat the seeds over medium heat, shaking the pan frequently to prevent burning. When the seeds begin to darken and become fragrant, remove from the heat. Immediately transfer the seeds to a bowl and cool.

Gingery Pickled Radishes

Makes 3 cups

1½ pounds Daikon radish, peeled, halved vertically, and cut crosswise into thin slices

10 red radishes, thinly sliced

1 tablespoon kosher salt

¼ cup rice vinegar

¼ cup sugar

1-inch knob ginger, peeled and thinly sliced

In a large bowl, toss the radish slices with the salt. Let stand at room temperature for 1 hour. Drain, rinse, and return to the bowl.

In a small saucepan, combine the vinegar, sugar, and ginger. Place over low heat and stir occasionally until the sugar has dissolved. Remove from heat and cool to room temperature.

Place the radishes in a container, preferably a large jar that has a tight-fitting lid. (Radishes and vinegar can also be divided between smaller jars.) Add the vinegar mixture. Chill for a minimum of 12 hours, shaking occasionally. This will keep for 2 months refrigerated.

Daikon radishes are a good choice for this tangy relish. Long, white, and carrot shaped, they are crisper, juicier, and milder than their ruby-hued cousins. This relish is a delicious companion to thin slices of grilled rare beef. A friendly warning: the aroma when opening the container can be quite sharp. Sniff with caution!

radishes: now and later

As a cool-weather vegetable, radishes appear in both the spring and the fall, but there is a difference to note. Spring radishes are mild and enjoyed as a raw ingredient in recipes. The fall or winter varieties are stronger tasting and are better prepared cooked, either braised or roasted, to mellow the flavor.

Local Flavor

pastured lamb

There's a legion of cooks and locavores armed with an adventurous nature and a commitment to locally grown food, yet when it comes to lamb, some harbor old and outdated misconceptions. Many have neither cooked nor tasted lamb, and their reasons include thinking that lamb and mutton are one and the same or that lamb is gamey and hard to prepare. In many cases their experience has been limited to commercially raised lamb, which sometimes can be fatty and strongly flavored. Among their many jobs on the farm, local lamb producers gladly take on one more—that of "educator," unraveling long-standing notions about the tender and richly flavored lamb they take great care to raise.

As some of the best and most dedicated stewards of our farmlands, lamb producers know that raising flocks on pasture is better for the environment and the animal. These farmers manage their pastures as a sustainable resource, using rotational grazing practices so that the land can constantly renew itself and provide the best possible nutrition source for the animal. Maintaining high-quality natural resources results in a healthier animal and better-tasting, more nutritious lamb. While a lamb's life is short, it is well lived.

The label "grass-fed" is an increasingly familiar one that requires a bit of explanation, since there exists no official regulation for what it really means. Some producers raise their flocks strictly on a "pasture salad"—grazing on natural grasses, legumes, and herbs. The result is an animal whose lean meat will have a pleasant "grassy" aroma and will be lower in fat, saturated fat, cholesterol, and calories. Some producers supplement the grazing with grain or finish the

lambs on grains like corn and alfalfa, which will add marbling and create a more subtle flavor and a mild aroma, one that appeals to a different palate. It's both a matter of preference for the producer and a matter of taste for the customer.

Producers also choose heritage breeds specifically suited to the local palate as well as to the agricultural personality of the region. For example, Cotswolds are efficient grazers and excellent foragers, while Poll Dorsets grow rapidly, adapt well to seasonal conditions, and are highly suited for meat production. Southdowns are hardy under all conditions, do well in large or small flocks, and have high meat-to-bone and flesh-to-fat ratios, which means less waste.

Lamb is meat from sheep that have reached 120 to 135 pounds and are butchered before their first year. This is when the animal develops a high ratio of meat to bone and yields cuts that are substantial, meatier, mildly flavored, and still tender because the lamb hasn't developed much muscle or an excess of fat. Mutton, on the other hand, is meat harvested from sheep older than a year. It has a stronger flavor, darker color, and a tougher texture. Inexpensive and available in great quantity a half-century ago, its less than optimal taste was compounded by overcooking in the hope of making it more tender.

If you're thinking about giving lamb a chance or another try (and you should be), find local lamb producers at farmers markets, a great "classroom" for enlightening potential customers about the ways lamb is raised and why it makes a difference in each wonderful bite.

Rosemary and Mint Lamb Chops

Makes 6 servings

12 lamb loin chops, cut 1½ inches thick

Salt and freshly ground black pepper, to season

1 cup red wine

½ cup balsamic vinegar

½ cup hot pepper jelly

½ cup freshly chopped rosemary

¼ cup freshly chopped mint

Extra virgin olive oil, for brushing

Season both sides of the chops liberally with salt and pepper. Set aside.

In a large mixing bowl (large enough to hold the chops), combine the red wine, balsamic vinegar, jelly, and chopped herbs, stirring to dissolve the jelly. Add the chops, turning to coat with the mixture. Set aside at room temperature for 1 hour. (The chops can also be refrigerated for up to 8 hours).

Preheat the broiler to high.

Remove the chops from the marinade, reserving the marinade. Use a paper towel to blot the surface of the chops dry. Lightly brush both sides of the chops with the olive oil. Arrange the chops on the rack of a broiler pan about 3 inches from the heat source and broil until well seared on both sides, about 4 minutes per side, and done to medium rare (130°F internal temperature). For a medium finish, broil the chops 5 to 6 minutes per side (135°F internal temperature). Remove from the broiler and set aside to rest for 5 minutes.

Meanwhile, pour about a cup of the reserved marinade into a saucepan and bring to a boil. Boil for 5 minutes or until reduced and slightly syrupy. Brush on the chops before serving.

This recipe assumes that the chops are small and that 2 (about 8 ounces) will serve 1 guest. Use your own judgment. If the chops are on the hefty side, 1 per guest will be sufficient.

tips for cooking pastured lamb

- Don't overcook. Grass-fed meats are lean and usually don't have too much fat, so they will cook faster. Lower heat, such as roasting at 325°F for cuts like a leg of lamb, and longer cooking times are recommended.

- Remove the lamb from the oven or grill just before it reaches the desired internal temperature, usually between 125°F and 135°F for most cuts of lamb. As it rests, it will continue to cook. Lamb achieves its fullest flavor when cooked to medium rare.

- Use a meat thermometer to test the internal temperature on thick cuts of lamb such as the leg and thick-cut chops, inserting it into the thickest part.

- Allow the meat to rest (10 to 15 minutes for thicker cuts) after cooking before serving to give the natural juices a chance to redistribute throughout the meat.

Internal Temperatures for Leg of Lamb (Bone in or Boneless) and Thick Chops

Rare	125°F
Medium Rare	130°F
Medium	135°F

in season ...
strawberries

When it comes to homegrown strawberries, there is no equal, no match, and certainly no substitute. When strawberries come on in the garden or come in from the fields, we rush to add them to salads, cobbler, pies, and parfaits; blend them into smoothies, shakes, and ice cream; top off shortcake, roll into a crepe, spoon over pancakes ... the possibilities are endless and delicious.

Although you'll find lots of recipes that essentially "gild the lily," fresh local berries need little embellishment to be spectacular. Isn't this what you expect of homegrown, locally grown foods?

Choosing the Best. To tell how a strawberry will taste, follow your nose. If it smells like a delicious strawberry, it's going to taste like a delicious strawberry. As a general rule of thumb, choose smaller berries rather than overly large ones that have a tendency to be dry and hollow inside. Look for an all-over, perfectly glossy red color and fresh, bright green hulls. Berries with white patches were picked underripe, and once picked, berries do not continue to ripen.

How to Store Fresh. Excess moisture is a strawberry's biggest foe, so store them unwashed with the caps intact. Place the strawberries in single layers separated by paper towels in a plastic container or a sealable plastic bag and refrigerate for 3 to 5 days. Bruised, moldy, or crushed fruit will spoil an entire batch, so remove them before storing.

To Prepare for Cooking. Rinse strawberries with a shower of cool water just before using. Remove the hulls and the pale flesh just underneath with the tip of a sharp paring knife. Blot dry with a paper towel, then halve, slice, or crush.

Pick or Buy Now, Enjoy Later. Freezing is the best way to preserve cleaned and trimmed whole or sliced strawberries, but because of the high water content they won't hold their shape or have the same texture as fresh when they are thawed. The upside is that the flavor is still there, and you'll swear you're in the middle of the real strawberry season. Another delicious way to preserve strawberries and capture the flavor and color is in jams, great with the "Bring on the Jam" Muffins on page 209.

Freeze this season's strawberries! To learn how, go to page 221. Or preserve the seasonal flavor of strawberries with Strawberry Preserves on page 28.

Roasted Strawberries with Cornmeal Pound Cake

Makes 8 to 10 servings

Fresh strawberries are wonderful. Roasted strawberries? Outstanding! The sweet, warm fruit is the perfect adornment for this coarse-textured cornmeal pound cake that soaks up the syrupy juice so not a single delicious drop goes to waste.

1 cup all-purpose flour

1 cup medium grind yellow cornmeal

½ teaspoon salt

1 cup unsalted butter, room temperature

1⅓ cups sugar

5 large eggs at room temperature, lightly beaten to combine

1 teaspoon pure vanilla extract

2 quarts fresh strawberries, washed, patted dry, and hulled

¼ to ½ cup sugar

Sweetened whipped cream, to accompany

Fresh mint leaves, as garnish

Preheat the oven to 325°F. Butter and flour a 9 x 5 x 3-inch loaf pan.

Whisk the flour, cornmeal, and salt together in a medium bowl to blend. Using an electric mixer, beat the butter in a large bowl until light and fluffy, about 3 minutes. Gradually add the 1⅓ cups sugar and beat for an additional 3 minutes. Add the eggs, a little at a time, to combine. Stir in the vanilla. Add the dry ingredients, a third at a time, beating until just blended after each addition. Scrape the batter into the prepared pan and bake for about 1 hour and 15 minutes or until a tester inserted into the center comes out clean.

Let the cake cool for 15 minutes before turning out onto a cake rack. Let cool completely. (This cake can be wrapped tightly and frozen for up to two months.)

While the cake is baking, toss the strawberries with the ¼ to ½ cup sugar to coat. Arrange in a single layer in a shallow baking dish. When the cake is out of the oven, increase the temperature to 400°F. Roast the strawberries for 15 minutes, shaking the pan halfway through the roasting time. Remove from the oven and let sit at room temperature.

To serve, cut the cake into wedges and spoon roasted berries and some of the syrup that has collected in the baking dish over the top. Garnish with a fresh mint leaf or sweetened whipped cream.

• •

quick fix for cleaning strawberries!

If the season hands you—or blesses you with—a load of strawberries to clean, here's a simple way to get the job done. Take a sturdy plastic straw and push it through the bottom of the strawberry. The straw easily tunnels through the fruit, removing the hull as well as the cap. Clean the shaft of the straw after every fifth or sixth strawberry and continue on.

Fresh Strawberry Pie

Makes one 9-inch pie

The first-of-the-season strawberries, sweet, tiny, and juicy, belong on this pie. Make your own homemade piecrust (page 128) for an extra-special pie that will make you wish strawberry season would never end.

1 prebaked 9-inch pie shell

5 cups strawberries, washed and hulled; left whole if small, halved if larger

¾ cup sugar

3 tablespoons cornstarch

½ cup water

⅓ cup cream cheese, softened

Mash enough strawberries to measure ¾ cup. Mix the sugar and cornstarch in a large saucepan. Gradually stir in the water and mashed berries. Cook over medium heat, stirring constantly until the mixture thickens and boils. Boil and stir for one minute. Remove from the heat and set aside to cool for 20 to 30 minutes.

Beat the softened cream cheese until smooth; spread in the bottom of the pie shell. Place the remaining strawberries in a large bowl. Add the cooled glaze and gently toss to combine. Fill the shell with the berry mixture. Refrigerate until set, at least 3 hours.

Strawberry Frozen Yogurt

Makes 6 servings

Let the season for frozen treats begin right in your own kitchen with this recipe that takes sweet red berries and turns them into a chilly dessert— without an ice cream maker. To really make this a local treat, use your own homemade yogurt (see page 29).

1 quart fresh strawberries, hulled and halved, divided use

½ cup sugar

Freshly squeezed juice of one lemon

1 cup yogurt

¼ cup milk (approximate), if needed to thin

Combine 2 cups of the berries with the sugar in a medium saucepan. Bring to a simmer over low heat, stirring occasionally until the sugar is dissolved and the berries have released some of their juice, about 5 minutes. Transfer the mixture to a blender or food processor along with the remaining berries, lemon juice, and yogurt. Process to a smooth puree.

Transfer the mixture to a shallow baking dish or bowl. Place in the freezer. Stir every 30 minutes. The mixture will freeze solid in about 3 hours.

When ready to serve, transfer the mixture to the blender or food processor and pulse for 5-second intervals, adding a little milk if necessary until the mixture is smooth. Serve immediately.

Chocolate Oven Pancake with Strawberries

This pancake emerges from the oven big and fluffy, almost bowl shaped, ready to fill with sweet, succulent strawberries. Homegrown only, please.

Makes 8 servings

4 eggs

1 cup whole milk

1 cup all-purpose flour

¼ cup unsalted butter

1 cup semisweet or bittersweet chocolate pieces

1 quart fresh strawberries, washed, hulled, and sliced

Confectioners' sugar

Preheat the oven to 425°F.

Place the eggs, milk, and flour in a blender or food processor. Blend until smooth. Melt the butter in a 10-inch ovenproof skillet. Pour the batter into the hot skillet and bake for 4 minutes. Scatter the chocolate pieces over the pancake. Bake for an additional 15 to 20 minutes until puffed and golden brown. Top with fresh strawberries and dust with confectioners' sugar. Cut into wedges and serve immediately.

Strawberries in Balsamic with Black Pepper

Here is a simple take on dessert for fresh strawberries. Balsamic vinegar not only plays up the color of the fruit, it also creates exciting contrast between sweet and tart. For the prettiest presentation, use petite-sized berries bursting with flavor.

The balsamic-steeped strawberries are also delicious spooned over vanilla ice cream or served with a dollop of crème fraîche.

Makes 4 servings

2 cups small fresh strawberries, washed, hulled, and halved

2 tablespoons dark brown sugar

1 tablespoon balsamic vinegar

Grinding of coarse black pepper

Fresh mint leaves, optional

Place the strawberries in a medium bowl. Sprinkle with the brown sugar and the vinegar. Stir gently to combine. Let sit for 1 hour at room temperature. Grind a small amount of black pepper over the berries. Spoon into small dessert bowls, pouring some of the juice from the bowl over the berries. Garnish with mint leaves, if desired.

Strawberry and Feta Salad

Makes 4 servings

Sweet strawberries, salty feta, and peppery watercress are unique flavors on their own but work together harmoniously in this easy-to-create salad. If watercress is not available, arugula is a suitable substitute.

2 tablespoons balsamic vinegar, preferably white balsamic

2 tablespoons fruit-flavored vinegar or cider vinegar

⅓ cup extra virgin olive oil

Salt and freshly ground black pepper, to taste

4 cups watercress, washed, dried, and trimmed

1 pint fresh strawberries, washed, hulled, and sliced

½ cup crumbled feta cheese or blue cheese

In a small bowl, combine the vinegars. In a thin stream, whisk in the oil until blended. Season to taste with salt and black pepper.

Place the watercress in a large bowl. Add half the vinaigrette and toss until coated. Divide among chilled salad plates. Place the strawberries in the same bowl and toss with the remaining vinaigrette. Divide among the salad plates, arranging on top of the watercress. Top each salad with 2 tablespoons of feta and a grinding of black pepper and serve immediately.

Strawberry Preserves

Makes 3 half-pint jars

There are a few goals to reach for when making strawberry preserves. One is to keep the brilliant red color of truly ripe and wonderful strawberries. Another is to maintain the genuine flavor. Ultimately it's nice to see big pieces of fruit in any jam. This pectin-free method delivers those results in a recipe that is prepared over 24 hours, which seems like a long time, but the actual time spent over the stove is minimal.

New to making jams, jellies, and preserves? For a step-by-step guide to the basics, see "Jams, Jellies, and Preserves" on page 237.

5 heaping cups fresh, firm strawberries, washed, hulled, and halved

2 cups sugar

½ cup freshly squeezed lemon juice

Place the berries and sugar in a large bowl. Stir until the berries are coated in sugar. Cover and let stand at room temperature overnight.

Transfer the berries and any juices to a large heavy pot or Dutch oven. Bring to a boil over medium heat, stirring occasionally, until sugar is dissolved. Stir in the lemon juice. Return to a rapid boil and cook for 5 minutes, stirring occasionally. Remove from the heat and let stand for 24 hours.

Bring berries to a full boil over high heat and boil rapidly for 5 minutes, stirring constantly. Remove from the heat and perform a gel test (see page 238). If the gel stage has not been reached, return to the heat and cook for a few additional minutes, repeating until the gel stage has been reached. Once the mixture has gelled, skim off any foam that may have developed. Remove from heat.

Ladle the jam into sterilized jars to within ¼ inch of the rim (headspace), seal, and process for 10 minutes.

Variation: If you liked the combination of flavors in Strawberries in Balsamic with Black Pepper (page 27), translate it to your strawberry jam by reducing the amount of lemon juice to 4 tablespoons and adding 4 tablespoons of good-quality balsamic vinegar. Add pepper to taste just before ladling into jars, if desired.

What's the difference between jams, jellies, and preserves? Find out on page 237.

Making Your Own: Yogurt

Locally sourced dairy products such as milk and heavy cream are great finds at farmers markets. Drink them or whip them, but start thinking outside the carton (or glass bottle) and you'll discover that it's easy to transform the rich flavor of local dairy products into other wonderful foods and ingredients like yogurt. The advantage of making your own yogurt? There's more than one.

Homemade yogurt simply tastes better than commercial yogurts. It's lively, tangy, and silky, contains no added sugars or thickeners, and is delicious drizzled with honey or topped with a jumble of fresh seasonal fruits. There's also the comfort of knowing that it's wholesome as well.

As an added bonus, homemade yogurt is typically less expensive than grocery-store varieties and there's no packaging waste. Not convinced? All it takes is one batch.

Homemade Yogurt

Makes 8 cups or 2 quarts

Make sure that all the equipment used to make and store your yogurt has been washed with very hot water, completely rinsed, and dried.

If you want to thicken the yogurt to use for a sauce, drain a portion in a fine mesh sieve lined with a coffee filter for a few hours.

½ gallon good-quality cow's milk, any variety
1 6-ounce carton good-quality plain yogurt that contains active cultures

Pour the milk into a large stainless steel pot. Place over medium to medium-low heat and gently heat until the milk is frothy. This will take about 15 to 20 minutes. Use a reliable instant-read thermometer to check the temperature occasionally. When the temperature reaches 185°F, remove the pot from the heat and set aside to cool. (Heating the milk to 185°F destroys any of the bacteria that prevent the yogurt cultures from doing their work.)

After about 30 minutes, check the temperature of the milk with the thermometer. When the temperature has dropped to between 110°F and 115°F, stir in the plain yogurt until completely blended.

Pour the mixture into two clean, sterilized quart jars or two 16-ounce plastic yogurt containers. Seal with tight-fitting lids.

Cover the jars or containers with a heavy towel and let sit undisturbed in a warm part of the kitchen for 8 hours or overnight. The yogurt will have thickened. Place in the refrigerator to chill. Before using, give the yogurt a good stir. This yogurt will keep in the refrigerator for 2 weeks.

Add yogurt to smoothies, chilled fruit soups, and salad dressings and use in baking, too. Use it for the Cucumber Sauce on page 53 that accompanies the Lamb Burgers, blend it into the chilly Strawberry Frozen Yogurt on page 26, or try it as the base for the Yogurt Sauce that tops the Sweet Pumpkin on page 200. You can also just get a spoon and prepare to be delighted!

get a head start!

Besides having just created a batch of great-tasting yogurt at less than the cost of commercial varieties, you've also created the starter for your next batch and any to follow. Remove 6 tablespoons to launch your next batch and store in a small freezer bag or freezer-proof container with a tight-fitting lid. Thaw the starter in the refrigerator before adding to a new batch. Starters can be frozen for several months.

in season ... peas

Sweet and tender peas are the green candy of the garden. While the vast majority of peas in the world are sold either canned or frozen, the taste of peas picked and enjoyed in season has no rival.

Whether you choose the shelled or the edible pod varieties, you owe it to yourself to either grow peas or be the first at the farmers market or roadside stand to buy them shortly after they are harvested. As with corn, once peas are picked, the sugars begin to turn to starch and with that, the sweetness wanes and the texture toughens. Making them part of your dinner plan that day is smart (and delicious) thinking.

Choosing the Best. Color is key when it comes to choosing any variety of peas. Look for firm, lustrous green pods that snap instantly when bent. Pass on pea pods that look spotted, limp, or just plain tired—and never buy shelled peas where the work has been done for you. Ideal sugar snap and snow pea pods should be about three inches long, and garden pea pods should be full and plump, signs that the peas inside are fully developed and will be easier to shell.

How to Store Fresh. It's to the cook's advantage to cook peas the same day they are picked or purchased, but if you do need to keep them for a day or two, store the unwashed pods in a sealable, perforated plastic bag or container. Garden peas should be left in their shells until needed.

To Prepare for Cooking. Garden peas have to be removed from the pod, which, although laborious, rewards the worker with a taste unique to fresh peas. Simply snap the top of the pod and pull the string that runs down the side. That will open up the pod, and peas will spill out with a gentle nudge.

Sugar snap peas' edible pods still require stringing. Simply snap the top down toward the flat side of the pod and pull down, simultaneously removing the strings down both seams. Snow peas generally only need the stem tip removed.

Whoever came up with the color "pea green" might have been overcooking their peas. Peas, picked or cooked, should never have the washed-out yellow tones of the infamous crayon color. Heat destroys their character and color, so the trick is to be quick! Fresh peas cook in minutes.

Pick or Buy Now, Enjoy Later. Blanching and freezing shelled garden peas and sugar snap or snow pea varieties is the best way to preserve the beautiful color and some of the texture. Still, once thawed they will lose the characteristic crunch reserved for fresh, but the flavor will still make you think of spring.

Snow and snap peas can be used for sautés and stir-fries. Frozen shelled peas can be added to quick-cooking side dishes and soups and can be used to make the Green Pea Hummus on page 34 all year long.

Freeze this season's peas. To learn how, go to page 218.

Peppered Peas and Garlic

Makes 4 servings

Whether your preference is for shelled peas or for snow or sugar snap varieties, this recipe is very accommodating. Simply substitute about 1 pound of the edible pods for the shelled peas and lengthen the cooking times a bit.

1 tablespoon extra virgin olive oil

2 cloves garlic, crushed

1 teaspoon freshly cracked black pepper

2 cups freshly shelled peas

1 teaspoon dark brown sugar

1 teaspoon balsamic vinegar

Heat the oil in a large, heavy, nonstick skillet over medium heat. Add the garlic and pepper and sauté for about 30 seconds, until the garlic softens and the pepper is fragrant. Add the peas and the brown sugar and cook for 2 to 3 minutes or until the peas are tender. Drizzle with the balsamic. Season with salt to taste and serve immediately.

Pea Shooters

Makes 12 shooter servings or 6 servings of chilled soup

When spring yields sweet peas and fresh mint, they make for good companions in this simple soup that should be enjoyed chilled on a hot day. Serve these as an appetizer in tall "shooter" glasses or in small chilled bowls as a little something before supper.

2 tablespoons unsalted butter

1 medium onion, chopped

1 small leek, white and light green parts only, thinly sliced

1 stalk celery, chopped

4 cups chicken or vegetable stock

4 cups fresh peas*

Salt and freshly ground white pepper to taste

Crème fraîche, to accompany

Fresh mint, finely chopped

Melt the butter in a large pan over medium heat. Add the onion, leek, and celery. Cook, stirring, until soft and fragrant, about 8 to 10 minutes (avoid browning the vegetables). Add the stock and raise the heat to high. When it reaches a boil, reduce the heat to low and simmer 5 minutes. Add the peas and cook 5 minutes.

Transfer the mixture to a blender and working in small batches, puree the soup. Transfer the puree to a tall pitcher or medium bowl.

Partially fill a large bowl with ice and water. Place the pitcher in the ice water to cool the puree to room temperature, stirring occasionally. This will help the puree maintain its vibrant color. Taste and season with salt and pepper.

Cover the pitcher and refrigerate the soup until chilled.

To serve, pour the soup from the pitcher into shooter glasses or divide between chilled soup bowls. Add a tiny dollop of crème fraîche. Garnish with a little finely chopped mint and serve.

*Frozen peas may be substituted for fresh. Adjust the cooking time to 2 minutes.

Chilled Pea Salad with Dill

Full of fresh peas, scallions, and dill, this chilled salad is a lovely way to begin a spring brunch, lunch, or light dinner and a perfect companion to the Chard Pancakes on page 36.

Makes 4 servings

4 cups freshly shelled peas
½ cup crème fraîche or sour cream
2 teaspoons freshly squeezed lemon juice
1 scallion, thinly sliced
1 teaspoon sugar
2 teaspoons fresh dill or 1 teaspoon dried
Pinch of cayenne pepper
½ teaspoon salt
¼ teaspoon freshly ground black pepper
4 cups fresh salad greens, optional

Cook the peas in a large saucepan of boiling water for 3 to 4 minutes until tender. Drain and set aside to cool completely.

In a medium bowl, whisk together all the remaining ingredients. When combined, add the peas and toss gently to coat. Refrigerate until chilled, at least 2 hours or up to 6. Serve on a small bed of greens or in small chilled bowls.

Stir-Fried Snow Peas

Quick is the trick when it comes to stir-frying . . . and that's why snow peas are the perfect ingredient for this cooking technique that demands high heat and short cooking times to maintain the color and integrity of fresh ingredients.

Makes 4 servings

1 tablespoon peanut oil or canola oil
1 pound snow peas, trimmed and rinsed
3 scallions, cut into 1-inch pieces
1 clove garlic, minced
1 tablespoon chopped fresh mint or more to taste
Salt and freshly ground black pepper

Heat the oil in a large frying pan or wok over high heat. Add the peas and stir-fry, tossing often, for 3 minutes. Add the scallions and garlic and toss for an additional minute or until the peas are crisp-tender and bright green. Remove from the heat and toss with chopped mint. Season to taste with salt and pepper.

• •

mind your peas

Peas come in a few varieties, each with unique features. It's important to know the differences before choosing one for a particular recipe.

snow peas: Sweet, tender, edible flat pods with tiny peas that cook quickly and are often used for stir-fry dishes.

sugar snap peas: These bear a strong resemblance to shelling peas but have smaller, curvy pods that, cooked or raw, are sweet and edible.

shelling peas: Plump garden or English peas grow in a stringy, tough, inedible pod. Peas in a pod must be removed before cooking.

Sugar Snap Peas with Sage and Nut Butter

Makes 6 servings

The added step of blanching the plump pods of sugar snap peas helps seal in the bright green color and fresh flavor of the peas as well as reducing the amount of time the peas spend over the heat. This is an excellent technique to use for thicker vegetables tossed into stir-fries.

1 pound sugar snap peas, rinsed and dried

2 tablespoons chopped nuts (walnuts, hazelnuts, or pecans)

3 tablespoons unsalted butter

2 tablespoons chopped sage

Salt and freshly ground black pepper

Blanch the peas in a large pot of boiling salted water for 3 to 4 minutes or until bright green. Transfer peas to a bowl of ice water to stop the cooking. Drain well and set aside.

Toast the nuts in a large skillet over medium heat, stirring frequently, about 5 minutes. When the nuts are fragrant and lightly browned, remove from the pan and set aside to cool.

Add the butter to the hot skillet and cook until it turns a light brown color (similar to light brown sugar) and has a nutty, not burnt, fragrance. Add the peas, chopped sage, and nuts to the skillet and toss to combine. Cook until heated through, about 2 minutes. Season with salt and pepper to taste and serve immediately.

Roasted Sugar Snap Peas

Makes 4 servings

Roasting has a way of bringing out the best flavor in most fruits and vegetables, including fresh sugar snap peas. It's a simple, hands-off cooking technique that brings this side dish to the table in less than 10 minutes.

1 pound fresh sugar snap peas, rinsed and dried

1 tablespoon extra virgin olive oil

Coarse sea salt, to taste

Cracked black pepper, to taste

2 tablespoons chopped fresh chives

Preheat the oven to 450°F.

Toss the peas with the olive oil and spread in a single layer on a rimmed baking sheet. Roast for 5 minutes before stirring. Continue roasting for a few additional minutes or until brown spots begin to appear on the pods. Remove from the oven and transfer to a serving dish. Season to taste with salt and pepper and sprinkle with fresh chives. Serve immediately.

Green Pea Hummus

In this recipe, all of the classic ingredients that go into a creamy hummus revolve around fresh seasonal green peas instead of the traditional chickpeas. The result is a fresh, sweet flavor and beautiful, bright color. Use it as a dip or as a spread for sandwiches. If you have frozen peas, call them into service in the winter.

Makes 6 to 8 appetizer servings

3 cups freshly shelled peas

3 cloves garlic, peeled

3 tablespoons tahini

Juice of 1 large lemon

1 teaspoon ground cumin

½ teaspoon salt

1 tablespoon extra virgin olive oil, more or less to taste

Freshly ground black pepper

Pinch of chili powder or chipotle powder

4 8-inch pita rounds

Extra virgin olive oil

Place the peas in a large saucepan of boiling water. Cook for 3 to 4 minutes until tender. Drain and set aside to cool slightly.

Place the garlic, tahini, and lemon juice in the work bowl of a food processor. Add the peas and process for about 30 seconds. Add the cumin, salt, olive oil, pepper, and chili powder and process until smooth, scraping down the sides of the work bowl once or twice. Transfer to a bowl, cover, and refrigerate for at least 2 hours or overnight. Serve with baked pita chips.

To prepare the pitas, preheat the oven to 375°F. Cut each of the rounds into eight wedges. Brush both sides lightly with olive oil and arrange in a single layer on a baking sheet. Bake for 12 to 15 minutes or until golden and slightly crispy. Remove from oven and allow to cool before serving with the hummus. Chips may be stored in a container with a tight-fitting lid for up to a week.

• •

easy tahini

Tahini is ground sesame paste, typically found in classic hummus recipes. You can make your own tahini by placing 1½ cups untoasted sesame seeds in the work bowl of a food processor. With the motor running, add ½ cup olive oil and process into a coarse paste, scraping the sides of the bowl occasionally, about 2 minutes. Add up to ¼ cup additional oil and process for up to an additional 2 minutes until it becomes a smooth paste with a slightly grainy texture. Store in a well-sealed jar in the refrigerator for up to 3 months. This will make about 1½ cups of tahini.

Chard or Swiss chard (although there's nothing really *Swiss* about it) arrives at the farmers

markets in unexplained bundles. Deeply creased, fanlike leaves wave from the tops of intensely colored stalks in crimson orange, gold, or cream tones, vying for some long-overdue attention yet often passed up for more familiar choices in greens.

Ask longtime fans about the often underutilized vegetable and they'll attest to the earthy, robust taste of the leaves, often compared to and used as a substitute in recipes calling for spinach. Thin slivers of the raw leaf look and taste wonderful in fresh salads. The stalks, when featured on their own, are reminiscent of beets—not surprising, since chard is a member of the beet family.

Chard is the garden's two-for-the-price-of-one special. From the ground up, every bit of it is used.

Choosing the Best. Young chard is the preferred choice, mild and tender when the leaves are crisp and

glossy green and measure no more than 6 inches high. The ribs, no matter what color, should be bright and firm. Mix them up in your cooking, because there is little difference in flavor between colors. Don't feel you have to pass up chard when the leaves are bigger. Larger leaves may need a little more cooking time to soften but make a great wrap for savory meat and rice fillings, and the stalk can be chopped and tossed into vegetable soups.

How to Store Fresh. There is a lot of water in chard, so buying or picking fresh and using it the same day

is preferred, but unwashed chard, refrigerated in a perforated plastic bag, will hold for a few days. Once cooked, chard does not store well in the refrigerator, turning an unpleasant color with a tart taste.

To Prepare for Cooking. Harvested young, the tender leaves and slim stalks can be chopped and cooked

together, softening to perfection at the same rate. Clean the chard by swishing the leaves and stems in a large bowl or sink filled with cool water. Shake off the excess water and blot dry before proceeding with the recipe.

Larger plants are certainly usable, but take more work. The stalk, as thick as celery, has strings running up the back that should be removed. The leaf becomes a bit tougher. Leaves and stalks will now cook at different rates, so they have to be separated, giving the stalks a head start in the pan before adding the leaves.

Pick or Buy Now, Enjoy Later. Whole chard leaves can be blanched and frozen, but the same is not

true of the stems, which will discolor and turn mushy when thawed. Thawed leaves can be stirred into soups and stews and used to make Chard Pancakes (page 36) all year round.

Freeze this season's chard! To learn how, go to page 218.

Chard Pancakes

Makes 6 servings

These fluffy pancakes make dinner out of a breakfast favorite by adding sautéed chard, onions, and garlic. Pass the sour cream with each stack or top with some warm Chunky All-Purpose Tomato Sauce from the pantry (page 121) for an unusual twist.

....

If using frozen chard leaves, thaw, drain, and squeeze as much liquid as possible from the leaves before adding to the recipe.

2 tablespoons unsalted butter
1 medium onion, diced
2 cloves garlic, minced
1 bunch chard, stalks and leaves separated, rinsed and dried, about 8 to 10 ounces
Salt and freshly ground black pepper, to taste

2 cups all-purpose flour
1 tablespoon baking powder
1 teaspoon sugar
1½ cups buttermilk, plus extra to thin
Oil for the griddle
Sour cream, to accompany

Melt the butter in a large skillet over medium heat. Add the onion and sauté until soft and fragrant, about 6 minutes. Add the garlic and sauté a minute longer. Add the chard stalks and cook for 2 minutes before adding the leaves. Cook until both are soft and limp, about 5 minutes total. Season with salt and pepper. Remove from the heat and set aside to cool.

In a large mixing bowl, combine the flour, baking powder, and sugar. Stir in 1½ cups buttermilk until all the dry ingredients are moistened. Add the chard mixture, stirring until combined. Add enough additional buttermilk that the batter is thick but pourable.

Heat a griddle over medium heat. When the griddle is hot, brush with the oil. Pour or scoop the batter onto the griddle, using approximately ¼ cup for each pancake. Let cook until bubbles appear on the surface and the edges of the pancake look lightly browned, about 4 minutes. Flip the pancake over and cook an additional minute. Oil the grill for every batch of pancakes.

Serve hot with a dollop of sour cream.

Linguine with Chard and Bacon

Makes 6 servings

In this rustic pasta dish, only the leaves of the chard are called into service. Save the stalks and toss them the next day into a soup or stew or simply sauté them in some olive oil and garlic and finish with a splash of vinegar.

1 pound dried linguine
12 to 15 slices thick-sliced bacon (about ¾ pound), cut into ½-inch pieces
1 large red onion, thinly sliced
2 cloves garlic, coarsely chopped
2 bunches chard, stems removed, cut into thin ribbons

1 to 2 tablespoons balsamic vinegar
1 tablespoon extra virgin olive oil
1 cup grated Parmesan cheese
Salt and freshly ground black pepper, to taste

Cook the pasta in a large pot of boiling salted water, stirring occasionally, until al dente (tender with a firm bite), about 12 to 14 minutes. Drain, reserving 1 cup of the cooking liquid. Cover the pasta with a sheet of plastic wrap to keep it warm.

Return the pot to the stove over medium heat. Add the bacon and cook until crisp, stirring occasionally, about 10 minutes. Remove the bacon with a slotted spoon and transfer to paper towels to drain.

Remove all but 2 tablespoons of the bacon drippings. Add the onion and sauté over medium-high heat until softened, about 5 minutes. Add the garlic and sauté for an additional minute. Add the chard and the reserved pasta liquid and toss until the chard is wilted and tender, about 4 to 5 minutes. Sprinkle the vinegar over the chard and toss for an additional minute.

Add the linguine back to the pot. Add the olive oil and toss to coat. Add the bacon and cheese and toss until combined. Taste and season with salt and pepper as needed. Transfer to a serving bowl. Serve immediately.

Chard and Egg Ribbon Soup

Makes 6 servings

You can substitute a variety of seasonal hardy greens, like spinach, deep green lettuces, and kale, in this classic soup to give it a different character, but be sure to try it with fresh, leafy chard. It will take the chill out of a cold spring day.

6 cups rich chicken stock

2 cloves garlic, minced

1 pound chard, leaves and stems separated, leaves cut into thin ribbons
   (stems reserved for another use)

¼ cup freshly grated Parmesan cheese, plus extra for serving

3 large eggs

½ tablespoon freshly squeezed lemon juice

Salt and freshly ground black pepper, to taste

Combine the stock and garlic in a large pot. Bring to a boil over high heat. Add the chard, cover, and reduce the heat to low. Cook until the chard is tender, about 10 to 12 minutes. Stir in the cheese.

Lightly beat the eggs with the lemon juice in a small bowl. Return the soup to a boil. Using a fork, gradually stir the eggs into the soup until they appear thin and "thread"-like, about 30 seconds. Season to taste with salt and pepper.

Serve immediately with extra cheese, if desired.

Sweet and Spicy Chard

Makes 4 servings

Brightly colored chard finds a perfect home in this recipe that uses both stems and leaves. It's cooked just enough to keep the bright colors and the texture interesting. Local maple syrup adds a delightful burst of sweet flavor.

1 pound chard, rinsed and patted dry

1 tablespoon extra virgin olive oil

1 small onion, chopped

1-inch piece ginger root, peeled and grated

Salt and freshly ground black pepper, to taste

2 tablespoons real maple syrup

Separate the stems and leaves of the chard. Slice the stems into ¼-inch pieces. Stack the leaves, roll up and slice crosswise into 1-inch strips. Set both aside.

Heat the olive oil in a large skillet over medium heat. Sauté the chard stems, onion, and ginger until soft and fragrant, about 5 minutes. Season with salt and pepper. Add the leaves to the skillet and reduce the heat to low. Continue cooking until the leaves have wilted, about 2 additional minutes. Drizzle the maple syrup over the mixture and stir to coat evenly. Remove from the heat and serve immediately.

edible landscapes

Experienced gardeners know and appreciate chard not only for its delicious and sturdy nature but also as a decorative plant that can be used as an ornamental in the flower garden, pretty to look at both in the garden and on the plate. Chard grows well regardless of soil type and tolerates partial shade. It can be easily started from seed in early spring. You can begin harvesting the leaves when they are 3 inches long, and providing that you continue to remove them, the plant will keep producing. The heat of the summer turns the leaves bitter, but if you continue to remove the older leaves, the plant will produce into the fall.

maple syrup

If you live in a region of the country where cold weather is a natural fact, one of your rewards for enduring it is the arrival of spring and another is the promise of local maple syrup. The work of nature and skilled maple syrup producers, it's worthy of a locavore's attention.

True maple syrup is a product of maple sap, tasteless and watery when collected in the spring and boiled down typically over a wood fire to drive off the water. It takes about forty gallons of sap and a lot of time to make one gallon of syrup. The labor-intensive process accounts for what might at first blush seem a steep price, but it's a singular taste that has no equal. "Imitation" syrups, a distinction confirmed by taste, is overly thick and cloyingly sweet and nothing like the original it desperately seeks to imitate. Real maple syrup can have a consistency that ranges from somewhat thin to thick (like honey) and a natural earthy sweet taste with undertones of smoke and minerals.

Maple syrup can be poured onto oatmeal topped with chopped apples, added along with cinnamon to pureed sweet potatoes, or used to sweeten freshly made applesauce (page 135)—and of course poured over the ubiquitous short stack dripping with butter, the ultimate platform for maple syrup.

grades of maple syrup

The United States Department of Agriculture has assigned grades to maple syrup based on flavor and color. Which grade you prefer is a matter of personal taste.

grade light amber: Harvested early in the season when the weather is cold; light in color with a delicate maple flavor; enjoy as pancake and waffle syrup.

grade medium amber: Darker and with a more pronounced maple flavor; use as syrup and in baking.

grade dark amber: Very dark and with a strong maple flavor; better for cooking and baking although some like to use it as syrup.

grade b or cooking syrup: Extremely dark in color with a strong maple taste and a hint of caramel; mostly used in baked goods.

Baked Eggs in Maple Toast Cups

Eggs, maple syrup, butter, bread, bacon ... sounds like a trip to the farmers market. There's lots of satisfaction to be had when the majority of ingredients in a recipe can be locally sourced.

Makes 3 to 6 servings

2 tablespoons unsalted butter, plus extra for muffin cups
2 tablespoons pure maple syrup, plus extra to accompany
6 slices white bread, sandwich style, crusts trimmed
3 slices bacon, cooked and crumbled
6 large fresh eggs

Preheat the oven to 400°F. Butter 6 muffin cups or 6 4-ounce ramekins. Melt the butter with the syrup.

Flatten each slice of bread with a rolling pin. Brush both sides with the butter-maple mixture and tuck each slice into a muffin cup. Divide the crumbled bacon between the cups. Crack an egg into each cup. Bake until the eggs are set and opaque and the yolks are still soft, about 14 minutes. Check the eggs after 10 minutes. Let cool for just a few minutes before removing from the muffin cups. Serve, passing additional warmed maple syrup.

Collectively, the first onions to arrive at farmers markets are called spring onions. While there are differences among varieties, spring onions are generally intended to be enjoyed soon after harvesting.

Technically, spring onions are younger, more tender versions of themselves before they swell to the papery-skinned storing onions harvested in the fall. They'll have a slightly swollen bulb and perky green leaves (or stalks) and come in either white or purple, with little difference in flavor between the two. Spring onions are zippier and sweeter than green onions, yet milder than regular onions.

Green onions, often called scallions, are actually two different types of onions but so close in looks and taste that they can be used interchangeably in most recipes. Both are tall and slim with an undeveloped bulb, but true scallions are a bit milder than green onions.

Choosing the Best. On any spring variety, the stiff, green, and edible stalks (which are the leaves) should show no signs of wilting, yellowing, or slime and should be vividly green. If they look pale or faded, they've been harvested too soon and won't keep very long or well. The bulb on any spring onion, whether green, white, red, or purple, should be bright and shiny.

How to Store Fresh. Store unwashed onions in the refrigerator, wrapped in plastic or placed in a sealable storage bag. Leave behind any limp or faded stalks. Thinner onions will keep up to three days, while those with a more developed bulb will hold for a few days more.

To Prepare for Cooking. For thinner green onions, trim just above the root and halfway up the green stalk. They can be sliced in any number of ways, from cutting the tubular leaves into thin slivers for salads to slicing larger pieces for stir-fries, or left whole to use as crudités.

For spring onions with a more developed bulb, trim off the root end and slip off a layer or two of the onionskin, as needed. Trim up the stalk just an inch or two. You can use these onions for roasting, chop the stalks for salads and stir fries, or thinly slice and sauté them.

Pick or Buy Now, Enjoy Later. Chopped or sliced fresh onions can be packaged in smaller plastic bags for the freezer. Once thawed, they will be limp and will not resemble their fresh selves, which is fine if you're planning on using them in soups, stews, chilis, or chowders. To stretch their taste and beautiful color beyond the spring, pickle them in a brine and refrigerate. Use them as a condiment or toss them into salads all year long.

Preserve the seasonal flavor of spring onions with the Pickled Red Spring Onions on page 43.

Scallion Skillet Breads

Makes 8 servings

The absence of yeast in this bread recipe may make you wonder about the texture, but you'll be surprised at the tender and delicious results. Every bite features a little burst of spring green onion flavor.

4 cups all-purpose flour

1½ cups boiling water

¼ cup toasted sesame oil

2 teaspoons salt

½ cup minced scallions

¼ cup coarsely chopped cilantro

¼ cup sesame seeds, toasted

Vegetable oil, for frying

Put the flour in a large bowl and add the boiling water. Stir until a rough, shaggy dough forms. Gather the scraps together and form a dough ball. Turn the dough out onto a work surface and knead until the dough is soft and smooth, but not sticky, about 10 minutes. (Flour the work surface only if the dough is sticking.) Cover the dough with the bowl and let rest 20 minutes.

Knead the dough for another 3 minutes, then shape it into a cylinder, about 8 inches long. Divide the dough into 8 pieces. Use a rolling pin to roll one piece of dough into a 6-inch round, about ¼ inch thick. Brush the top of the round with sesame oil and sprinkle lightly with ¼ teaspoon salt, 1 tablespoon scallions, ½ tablespoon cilantro, and ½ tablespoon sesame seeds. Roll the pancake up into a tight cylinder. Twist it into a knot and flatten with the palm of your hand. Roll the dough out again into a 6-inch round. Repeat with the remaining pieces of dough.

Place a heavy nonstick skillet over medium heat. Add about a tablespoon of vegetable oil. When the oil is hot, fry the breads, one at a time, on both sides for about 3 minutes per side until golden and crispy. Drain on paper towels and sprinkle with additional salt, if desired. Serve warm.

Roasted Spring Onions

Makes 4 servings

Quick, simple, and delicious, roasting brings out the sweetness in spring onions. Depending on the size of the onions, adjust the cooking time— less for smaller onions, perhaps a bit more for larger. You can also repeat this recipe in the fall with red storage onions.

4 red spring onions, on the larger side

2 tablespoons unsalted butter, cut into 8 pieces

Extra virgin olive oil, for drizzling

Coarse sea salt

Coarsely ground black pepper

Balsamic vinegar, for drizzling (optional)

2 teaspoons freshly chopped thyme

Preheat the oven to 425°F.

Split the onions in half at the equator. On the cut side of each onion, cut a shallow X in the tops. Trim the root end so the onion sits flat in the baking dish. Arrange cut side up in a shallow baking pan. Place a knob of butter on top of each, followed by a drizzling of olive oil. Sprinkle with salt and pepper. Roast for 20 to 25 minutes or until tender and lightly browned.

Lightly drizzle balsamic vinegar over the top of the onions and sprinkle with thyme. Serve warm or at room temperature.

Savory Cheese and Scallion Scones

Makes 8 scones

Studded with green, these scones are nice companions to other fresh flavors of the season you'll find in soups and salads. The trick to getting buttery, tender results is to handle the dough as little as possible.

2½ to 3 cups all-purpose flour

1 tablespoon baking powder

½ teaspoon baking soda

1 teaspoon salt

4 ounces crumbled feta cheese

4 ounces cream cheese, softened

6 scallions, green and white sections, sliced

1 cup buttermilk

2 eggs, divided use

2 tablespoons milk

Preheat the oven to 425°F. Line a baking sheet with parchment paper and dust lightly with flour.

Combine 2½ cups flour, baking powder, soda, and salt in a large bowl. Add the cheeses and scallions, tossing gently with a fork until combined.

In a separate small bowl, beat the buttermilk with 1 egg until blended. Gently fold into the dry ingredients until a soft dough forms. (Add up to ½ cup additional flour if the dough is too sticky.)

Turn the dough out onto a floured surface and gently pat into a 1-inch-thick circle. Transfer to the baking sheet. Using a serrated knife rubbed with flour, cut the circle into 8 wedges. Using a fork, blend the remaining egg with the milk in a small bowl. Brush this mixture over the wedges.

Bake until the scones are golden on top and a tester inserted in the center comes out clean, about 15 minutes. Cool for 5 minutes on the tray. Serve warm.

Spring Onion Puddings

Makes 8 servings

1 tablespoon extra virgin olive oil

3 cups coarsely chopped spring onions

1 teaspoon fresh thyme

1 tablespoon chopped fresh parsley, plus extra for garnish

½ teaspoon chopped fresh rosemary

3 tablespoons unsalted butter, divided use

2 tablespoons all-purpose flour

1½ cups whole milk

1 cup fresh soft breadcrumbs, divided use

3 eggs, lightly beaten

½ teaspoon salt

Freshly ground black pepper

Grated nutmeg

Preheat the oven to 350°F. Butter 8 4-ounce ramekins.

Heat the olive oil in a large saucepan. Add the onions, thyme, parsley, and rosemary and cook until soft and tender, about 8 to 10 minutes. Divide the onion mixture between the ramekins.

In the same saucepan, melt 2 tablespoons of the butter and whisk in the flour until smooth and bubbly. Gradually add the milk, whisking constantly until blended. Cook over medium-low heat, whisking constantly, until thick and bubbly. Remove from the heat and stir in half of the breadcrumbs with the eggs, salt, pepper, and a grating of nutmeg. Ladle the mixture over the onions in the ramekins.

Melt the remaining tablespoon of butter and toss the remaining breadcrumbs and the extra parsley with the melted butter. Distribute over the top of the onion mixture. Bake for 35 to 40 minutes or until a knife inserted in the center comes out clean.

Pickled Red Spring Onions

Makes about 4 cups

1 pound red spring onions, peeled and thinly sliced

4 cups boiling water

½ cup cider vinegar or red wine vinegar

½ cup water

3 tablespoons local honey

1 teaspoon salt

1 teaspoon peppercorns, crushed

You'll love the bright magenta color of these onions both in the jar and on a salad or toasted baguettes. They're also great mixed into bean dishes, chilled asparagus spears, and more. This is a great condiment that will keep for four months in a tightly sealed jar in the refrigerator. Repeat this recipe when red onions, the larger storage versions, show up in the fall.

Place the sliced onions in a large bowl and pour the boiling water over the top. Let them sit for 5 minutes and then drain thoroughly in a colander.

In a separate bowl, combine the vinegar, water, honey, salt, and peppercorns for the pickling liquid, stirring until the honey is dissolved. Pour into the bowl with the onions and let sit for about 30 minutes. Transfer the onions and enough liquid to cover to a large quart jar with a tight-fitting lid. Store in the refrigerator for up to 3 months.

fresh eggs

There's an old proverb that goes, "Love and eggs are best when they are fresh." Love, maybe, but eggs? Definitely.

You've probably noticed that eggs, by the dozens, are getting more attention as locavores and cooks get hooked on the fresh taste and nutritional quality of eggs from "free-range" or "pastured" chickens, flocks that spend their lifetime on pasture, moving about on grass and enjoying fresh air and clean water, foraging for greens and clover, eating all the worms and insects they want—in short, living the life intended for chickens. Diligent farmers and those who tend backyard flocks balance this free-ranging lifestyle with healthy feeds rich in calcium, protein, and carbohydrates from wheat and barley, plus minerals and vitamins. This natural and diverse diet translates in wonderful and delicious ways to the eggs you bring into your kitchen.

Finding fresh eggs at farmers markets is fairly common, and increasing numbers of small independent grocers also include fresh free-range and organic eggs in their dairy cases. Free-range and organic eggs are usually more expensive than factory-produced eggs, but typically better tasting and better performers when used in baking and cooking.

Fresh eggs work as a superior leavening agent in batters and thicken and add body to custards and creams. Meringues made with fresh egg whites reach new heights. Wherever they are used, fresh eggs enhance color, texture, flavor, and richness.

With more and more communities hosting winter farmers markets, finding truly fresh eggs year round is easy. Lucky for us, because if you've grown accustomed to the taste and performance of fresh eggs, a season without them is a long one indeed.

don't judge an egg by its color

It's not unusual to find a multitude of multicolored eggs for sale at farmers markets—shells of creamy white, pink, blues, greens, buff, and cinnamon and others lightly freckled. Fun for their novelty and pretty to behold, but shell color does not reflect better quality or nutritional value of the eggs. Certain breeds lay certain colors of eggs. Golden Comets lay brown eggs; Leghorns, prolific layers, produce white-shelled eggs; Araucanas lay the beautiful blue eggs. It's not about the shell, it's about what's inside.

Chive and Goat Cheese Omelet

This recipe takes a little effort on your part. The chickens that laid the eggs with the bright beautiful yolks really deserve most of the credit. Yes, it only serves one or two, but omelets should be made in small measure for the best results.

Makes 1 to 2 servings

2 fresh eggs
2 tablespoons finely chopped chives, plus extra for garnish
Splash of water
Salt and freshly ground black pepper, to taste
½ tablespoon unsalted butter
2 tablespoons softened goat cheese

In a small bowl, whisk together the eggs, chives, water, and a pinch each of salt and pepper.

Melt the butter in an 8-inch nonstick skillet over medium heat. Add the egg mixture and stir until the eggs just begin to set but the center is still moist, about 1 minute. Use the spatula to smooth the top of the omelet. Dollop the goat cheese down the center. Use the spatula to fold one edge to the center of the omelet, then the opposite edge, covering the filling.

Slide the omelet onto a plate and garnish with additional chives. Serve immediately.

perfectly poached eggs

Fill a medium-sized nonstick skillet with 2 cups of water. Add 1 teaspoon vinegar and ½ teaspoon salt and bring to a slow boil. Break an egg into a small glass bowl and gently let it slip into the water. Let the water return to a boil, then reduce the heat to a simmer.

Once the egg begins to set, run a heatproof spatula underneath to free it from the bottom of the skillet. Cook until the white is firm. Remove the egg with a slotted spoon. Drain well and serve with toast or on top of the Arugula and Frisée Salad on page 58.

Summer

Summer is when Mother Nature hands us some of her best work in great quantity. It feels almost effortless to fill our plates with the bounty of fruits and vegetables found at farmers markets and roadside stands and coming from our own gardens. We live for the moment, eating plump blueberries by the handful or biting into a perfectly ripe, juicy peach. It's easy to forget that only six months before, we were hungry for the same flavors.

Summer is certainly the time to savor the season and embrace being a locavore, but it's also the perfect time to act on preserving those same flavors for the winter. So while the juice from that peach dribbles down your chin, do something to ensure that you'll have the same sweet, summery flavor on hand later this year.

in season ...
green beans

When spring slips into summer, green (and yellow and purple) beans begin to appear. Whether they are called string, snap, or green beans, the beans you pluck from the garden now or find on farm stands are best enjoyed fresh and can often be swapped for one another in recipes. These beans are picked young, at their tenderest, before the seeds have a chance to swell in the pods.

You're likely to come across two varieties during the growing season: pole beans and bush beans. Pole beans grow on vines and yield beans all summer long, while bush beans grow on small compact bushes, ripening all at the same time, making them the beans of choice for canning.

Choosing the Best. Bean pods should be smooth, bright green, and lacking any brown or yellow spots. The beans or seeds inside should be inconspicuous. You should see and feel only a small bump under the pod. Finally, look, or rather listen, for the "snap" when you bend them . . . beans that simply curve when bent are beyond fresh.

How to Store Fresh. Store freshly picked or purchased beans unwashed in a sealable perforated plastic bag for three to five days. Rinse and trim the beans just before using.

To Prepare for Cooking. Classic string beans need to have the fibrous string removed from the seam that runs along one side, easy to do with a snap at the stem end and a gentle tug downward. You're more likely to come across stringless varieties for which this step is unnecessary. Then your only decision is whether or not to snap off the caps; although the caps are not palatable, they add some visual interest to the plate, so some cooks leave them on.

It's also helpful to know that purple beans, although beautiful, lose their color when cooked even for short periods of time. Use them raw for pickling or as crudités.

Pick or Buy Now, Enjoy Later. Pickling is a good way to keep the colors of beans vibrant and the texture close to genuine. Blanching and freezing beans is also a good way to preserve the harvest. Beans snagged from the freezer can be used in most recipes calling for fresh simply by reducing the cooking time to keep a bite to the texture.

Freeze this season's beans! To learn how, go to page 218.
Or preserve the seasonal flavor of beans with the Lemon Dill Beans on page 49.

Green Bean Salad with Caramelized Red Onion and Mustard Seed Vinaigrette

There are a few simple steps to preparing this beautiful salad, but when the colors and textures all come together in the serving bowl, you'll appreciate your efforts. One bite and you'll pat yourself on the back.

Tip: To help blanched green beans stay green, add a pinch of baking soda to the cooking water.

Makes 6 to 8 servings

3 tablespoons extra virgin olive oil, divided use
2 tablespoons mustard seeds
1/3 cup red wine vinegar
1 tablespoon sugar
1 large red onion, thinly sliced
2 pounds fresh green beans, rinsed and trimmed
Salt and freshly ground black pepper, to taste

Heat 1 tablespoon of the oil in a large skillet over medium heat. Add the mustard seeds and cook, stirring constantly, until they begin to "pop" and are a shade darker, about 2 to 3 minutes (use a splatter screen over the skillet to keep the seeds from popping out of the skillet). Transfer the seeds and oil to a small bowl.

Combine the vinegar and sugar in a small saucepan and cook over medium heat, stirring, until the sugar dissolves. Set aside to cool.

Heat the remaining oil in the skillet over medium-high heat. Add the onions and stir until coated with oil. Cook for 5 minutes until the onions just begin to soften and then reduce the heat to low and cook for an additional 15 to 20 minutes until the onions are soft and fragrant but still brightly colored. Remove from the heat and stir in the vinegar mixture and the mustard seed mixture.

Prepare a large bowl of ice water. Cook the beans in a large pot of salted water until crisp-tender and bright green, about 4 to 5 minutes. Drain beans in a colander and then plunge them into the ice water to halt the cooking. Let sit for 2 minutes, then drain well.

Toss the beans with the onion mixture in a large bowl, season with salt and pepper, and serve at room temperature or chill for at least 4 hours or overnight.

Green Beans with Lemon

It's all about fresh in this recipe. A few simple ingredients complement the taste of freshly picked green beans, rather than standing between it and your taste buds. So easy, you'll make this side dish once and then from memory the rest of the season.

Makes 4 to 6 servings

1 pound fresh green beans, rinsed and trimmed
2 teaspoons freshly squeezed lemon juice
2 teaspoons finely chopped Italian parsley
2 teaspoons grated lemon zest or more to taste
Good-quality extra virgin olive oil, for drizzling
Sea salt and freshly ground black pepper

Cook the beans in a large pot of boiling salted water until crisp-tender and bright green, about 3 to 4 minutes. Drain in a colander.

Transfer the beans to a large bowl and toss with the lemon juice, parsley, and lemon zest. Taste and season with salt and pepper and serve with a fine drizzle of olive oil.

Butter-Basted Green Beans

Makes 6 servings

Butter basting is a great way to help beans retain their beautiful hues, and browning the butter adds a delightfully nutty flavor. When using frozen green beans straight from the freezer in this recipe, reduce the time they spend in the steaming basket to about 3 minutes, just enough to thaw and warm the beans before buttering.

1 ½ pounds green string beans, rinsed and trimmed
2 tablespoons unsalted butter, at room temperature
2 tablespoons freshly squeezed lemon juice
Salt and freshly ground black pepper

Partially fill a stockpot with 2 inches of water and place a steamer basket inside. (If you don't have a steamer, simply reduce the cooking time by a minute.) Bring the water to a boil. Add the beans, cover, and steam for 4 to 5 minutes until the beans are bright green, cooked through, and crisp-tender.

Thoroughly drain the beans. Return them to the pot and let sit, uncovered, for a few minutes to allow any remaining water to evaporate. Drain any excess water that accumulates.

Place a small saucepan over medium heat. Add the butter and cook for about 2 to 3 minutes until the butter turns a golden brown and has a pleasant, nutty fragrance. Watch carefully so the butter does not burn. Remove from the heat and pour over the beans. Add the lemon juice and toss thoroughly. Season with salt and pepper and toss again. Serve immediately.

Green Beans with Crème Fraîche and Chives

Makes 4 servings

When green beans are really fresh, there's reason to adore rather than adorn them. Why overwhelm what nature delivers best—flavor! Here's a dish that comes to the table quickly accompanied by tangy crème fraîche—one of the best condiments in the locavore's kitchen—and a sprinkling of fresh chives or dill. Learn how to make your own crème fraîche, a valuable ingredient, on page 50. Serve chilled for a great cold salad.

1 pound fresh green beans, rinsed and trimmed
Juice of one lemon
½ cup crème fraîche
1 shallot, minced
3 tablespoons chopped fresh chives or chopped fresh dill
Freshly ground black pepper

Bring a large pot of salted water to a boil. Add the green beans and cook until crisp-tender, about 3 minutes. Drain and plunge the beans into a bowl filled with ice water to stop the cooking. Drain again and pat dry to remove as much water as possible. Sprinkle the lemon juice over the beans. Transfer to a large bowl.

To make the sauce, mix the prepared crème fraîche with the minced shallot. Add the crème fraîche mixture to the beans and toss until coated. Scatter the chopped chives over the top, season with pepper, and serve immediately or chill for up to 6 hours.

Substitute ½ cup of sour cream thinned with a little milk for the crème fraîche, if desired.

Green Bean and Walnut Sauté

Makes 6 to 8 servings

This recipe works equally well with fresh green beans or those frozen from a bumper crop. If using frozen beans, reduce the cooking time to only a few minutes to retain the crisp texture and the vibrant color.

1 cup walnuts

2 pounds fresh green beans, rinsed and trimmed

2 tablespoons unsalted butter

2 tablespoons walnut oil or canola oil

2 tablespoons minced fresh parsley

Salt and freshly ground black pepper, to taste

Preheat the oven to 350°F.

Spread the walnuts on a rimmed baking sheet and toast for 5 to 8 minutes until lightly browned and fragrant. Watch carefully so the nuts don't burn. Remove from baking sheet into a bowl, let cool, and coarsely chop.

Cook the beans in a large pot of boiling salted water until just tender, about 3 to 4 minutes. Drain and rinse with cold water. Drain well. (This step can be done up to 6 hours ahead of time and the beans held at room temperature.)

Melt the butter with the oil in a large, heavy skillet over medium-high heat. Add the beans and toss until coated and heated through, about 4 to 5 minutes. Season to taste with salt and pepper. Add the walnuts and parsley and toss. Transfer to a serving bowl and serve immediately.

Lemon Dill Beans

Makes 3 pint jars

Part of the pleasure of canning anything lies in admiring your work lined up on the pantry shelves and waiting for the right moment to pop open a jar and enjoy the preserved flavors. Imagine the beauty of jars filled with slender yellow and green beans. If the image makes you want to fire up the canner, then do it for this recipe that puts up beans with their classic companions: lemon and dill. Use widemouthed jars for this recipe.

1 pound green beans, rinsed and trimmed

1 pound yellow beans, rinsed and trimmed

2½ cups cider vinegar

1¼ cups water

1 tablespoon pickling salt

1 tablespoon sugar

3 teaspoons pickling spice

3 large strips of lemon zest

Trim the beans into 4-inch lengths to fit into one-pint glass canning jars.

Combine the vinegar, water, pickling salt, and sugar in a large saucepan and bring to a boil over high heat.

Add 1 teaspoon pickling spice and 1 strip of lemon zest to each pint jar. Tightly pack the green beans into the jars. (Laying the jar on its side to do this is helpful.) Pour the boiling pickling liquid into the jars to within ½ inch of the rim (headspace), seal, and process for 5 minutes.

New to pickling? For a step-by-step guide to the basics, see "Pickled Vegetables, Relishes, and Salsas" on page 239.

Learn to make your own pickling spice on page 55.

pickling salt

Fine-grained, like table salt, pickling salt is the purest of salts, highly concentrated and the choice for canning. It contains no anticaking chemicals, which can turn preserved foods unappetizing colors. Use it for pickling vegetables or making sauerkraut.

SUMMER

Making Your Own: Crème Fraîche

Creating the locavore's kitchen is a culinary journey filled with delightful experimentation and clever kitchen projects. Some are simple, others more involved, yet all are delicious and satisfying in a "did it myself" kind of way. One of the simplest projects is to create your own crème fraîche, a velvety version of sour cream that can serve as a base for dips, thicken soups and stews, finish sauces, or be sweetened with a little sugar and vanilla to top off freshly picked berries.

Crème fraîche uses common, locally produced and pasteurized dairy products—buttermilk and heavy cream—to make a wonderfully creamy, tangy, slightly nutty-tasting ingredient. Experienced cooks love crème fraîche because it doesn't "break" or curdle like other dairy additions when stirred into hot liquids. Where sour cream is used, crème fraîche can be substituted. Don't be surprised if you discover this is one ingredient you can't cook without.

Crème Fraîche

Good crème fraîche is full of body and complex flavor, and a simple dollop is a nice complement to naturally sweet, seasonal fruits. To balance tartness in dishes like Strawberries in Balsamic with Black Pepper on page 27, lightly sweeten the crème fraîche by adding powdered sugar to taste.

1 cup good-quality heavy cream
1 cup cultured buttermilk, at room temperature

Heat the cup of heavy cream in a small saucepan over medium-low heat for 3 to 5 minutes until the temperature registers between 80°F and 85°F when tested with an instant-read thermometer. Transfer to a clean container such as a glass pint jar. Add the cup of cultured buttermilk, shaking to combine. (The bacterial culture in buttermilk is what will slightly sour and thicken the heavy cream.)

Cover loosely with plastic wrap. Place the jar in a warm spot for 24 hours until the crème fraîche is slightly thickened. Stir before sealing with a tight-fitting lid and storing in the refrigerator for up to 10 days. As the crème fraîche ages, it will continue to thicken to the consistency of loose yogurt and develop an even tangier flavor.

in season ...
cucumbers

Slicing Cucumbers and Pickling Cucumbers.
Cucumbers are the "cool" we relish during the summer months. Whether thinly sliced and splashed with vinegar, pureed into a base for a chilled soup, or pickled in a jar, it's a taste so closely connected to summer that to do without would just be wrong.

You're apt to come across two different kinds of cucumbers or cukes at farmers markets or roadside stands: slicing and pickling. We expect to use slicing cukes in our salads, while pickling cukes fit neatly in a jar. You can substitute pickling cukes for slicers and slicing cukes for picklers—it's a matter of preference. Slicing cukes are larger and thick-skinned and have far more seeds than their pickling cousins, so there's work behind preparing them for a pickling jar.

Many of the slicers you'll find today are touted as "burpless" varieties, mild, sweeter, and crisper, with thin, edible skins. However, a stressful growing season can add a bitter taste to any variety, usually concentrated in the skin and about an inch from the stem end. Removing these as well as any large seeds will help tame the backlash.

Choosing the Best.
Among cucumber varieties the taste and the art of choosing are basically the same. Slicing cucumbers should be 6 to 8 inches long, uniformly green, firm, and crisp. The narrower the cuke, the smaller the seed chamber and the fewer the seeds to contend with.

Pickling cucumbers are usually 3 to 4 inches long and have a thinner, lighter green skin. For the best quality and results, try to buy these the same day you plan to pickle. Never use for pickling any cucumber that has been waxed—the two do not mix.

Signs of yellowing mean the cucumbers are old; shriveling means they have lost precious moisture; and pitting means they've been refrigerated too long.

How to Store Fresh.
Cucumbers are mainly water, and once separated from the vine, they begin a journey to shriveling. Work with pickling cucumbers the same day they are bought or picked or store them in a cool part of the house overnight. Slicing cucumbers can spend a couple of days in the crisper of the refrigerator.

To Prepare for Cooking.
Because of their petite size, pickling cucumbers do not need to be peeled or seeded. Use them whole or cut into halves, spears, or chunks for canning.

Whether to peel or seed slicing cucumbers is a matter of preference and comes down to how thick the skin is and how large and numerous the seeds are. Remove the skin with a vegetable peeler. To easily remove the seeds, cut the cucumber in half lengthwise, from stem to blossom end, and use a spoon to scrape the seeds from the chamber.

Pick or Buy Now, Enjoy Later.
Pickling is the only method for keeping cucumbers at the table in some form from season to season. From dills to sweet pickles and relishes, it's work with delicious rewards. Enjoy pickled relishes on sausages and hamburgers or with grilled meats, or simply eat pickles straight from the jar.

Preserve the seasonal flavor of cucumbers with Classic Garlic Dill Pickles on page 54, Classic Bread and Butter Pickle Chips on page 55, or the Sweet Garlic Dills on page 54.

Cucumber Salad with Cilantro and Peanuts

This salad has an Asian flair, delivering a range of flavors including sweet, sour, spicy, and salty. Be sure to use the thin-skinned "burpless" variety of cucumber, which adds color to this dish and saves you the job of peeling. Serve it with spicy grilled chicken or beef.

Makes 6 servings

3 tablespoons water
3 tablespoons distilled white vinegar
3 tablespoons sugar
1 clove garlic, crushed
Dash of salt
1 or 2 whole, small chile peppers, optional
1 large cucumber, seeded, if necessary, thinly sliced
½ cup freshly chopped cilantro
½ cup roasted, unsalted peanuts, coarsely chopped
Sprigs of cilantro for garnish

Combine water, vinegar, sugar, garlic, salt, and chile pepper in a small saucepan. Place over medium heat and stir occasionally until sugar dissolves. Let cool at room temperature.

Combine the sliced cucumbers and cilantro in a large bowl. Pour the vinegar dressing over and toss until combined. Let sit for a few minutes before serving. Top with chopped peanuts and sprigs of cilantro for garnish.

Cucumber and Watermelon Salad

Two of the freshest, coolest flavors of summer team up in this pretty and simple salad. It's an unusual combination with a refreshing sweet and sour delivery.

Makes 8 servings

¼ cup distilled white vinegar
¼ cup sugar
½ teaspoon crushed red pepper flakes
2 fresh cucumbers, peeled, seeded, and thinly sliced
4 cups seeded and cubed watermelon
2 teaspoons salt, divided use
¼ cup thinly sliced red onion

Combine the vinegar, sugar, and red pepper flakes in a small saucepan. Bring to a boil and cook for 1 minute. Remove from heat and cool.

Place the sliced cucumbers in a colander, toss with 1 teaspoon salt, and let sit for 30 minutes. Rinse and pat dry. When ready to serve, toss the watermelon with the remaining teaspoon salt, add the cucumbers and red onion, and dress with the vinegar mixture. Toss until combined. Serve at room temperature or chill for a few hours before serving.

Cucumber and Mint Soup

Makes 6 servings

When the heat of summer climbs, you'll be "cool as a cucumber" sipping this delicious soup—chilled, of course. The popular phrase is an apt one. When a cucumber is on the vine, even on the hottest of days, its internal temperature can be about 10 degrees lower than the air temperature.

3 fresh cucumbers, peeled, seeded, and coarsely chopped
1 cup plain yogurt
½ cup sour cream or crème fraîche (page 50)
½ teaspoon dry mustard
½ teaspoon salt
¼ cup chopped fresh mint leaves
Thin slices of cucumber and mint sprigs for garnish

Puree the cucumbers, yogurt, sour cream, mustard, and salt in a blender for 1 minute. Transfer to a bowl or pitcher. Cover and chill at least 6 hours or overnight.

Just before serving, stir in the chopped mint leaves. Ladle the soup into chilled soup bowls and garnish each bowl with a thin slice of cucumber and a sprig of mint.

Lamb Burgers with Cucumber Sauce

Makes 4 burgers and 1 cup of sauce

Juicy lamb burgers are a welcome departure from typical beef burgers as the summer grilling season moves on. The smoky taste of the grilled lamb pairs perfectly with the cool cucumber sauce.

Sauce:
½ cup diced peeled and seeded cucumber
½ cup plain yogurt
2 teaspoons chopped fresh parsley

2 cloves garlic, minced
⅛ teaspoon ground cumin
⅛ teaspoon freshly ground black pepper

Burgers:
1½ pounds ground lamb
½ cup fresh breadcrumbs
1 small red onion, minced
1 clove garlic, minced
3 tablespoons chopped fresh mint
3 tablespoons chopped fresh parsley
Zest from two fresh lemons

½ teaspoon salt
¼ teaspoon cayenne pepper
Extra virgin olive oil, for brushing
4 8-inch flat rounds of pita bread
Chopped tomatoes, to accompany
Thin slices of red onion, to accompany

Sauce:
In a small bowl, stir together the diced cucumber, yogurt, parsley, 2 cloves garlic, cumin, and black pepper. Cover and refrigerate until needed.

Burgers:
Preheat the grill to medium-high.

In a medium bowl, lightly mix the ground lamb with the breadcrumbs, onions, 1 clove garlic, mint, parsley, lemon zest, salt, and pepper. Shape the meat mixture into 4 oval patties one-half inch thick and transfer to a platter lined with plastic wrap. Brush the burgers with olive oil.

Grill the burgers for 6 minutes on each side until cooked through and the internal temperature registers 160°F when tested with a meat thermometer. Move to the cooler part of the grill.

Quickly warm the pitas on the grill. Fold the pitas over the burgers and serve with cucumber sauce, chopped tomato, and red onion slices.

A Trio of Pickled Classics

Cooks who "put up" pickles, whether chips or spears or whole, do so because the flavor and the crunch is far superior to those that come from a grocery store shelf. Prove it to yourself by taking a jar of your own home-canned pickles to a potluck. Chances are very good it will return home—empty.

"Canning" on page 227 and "Pickled Vegetables, Relishes, and Salsas" on page 239 provide a step-by-step guide to the basics of canning and pickling. Once you're familiar with the process, try any of these classic pickle recipes. Before you get started, here are a few more helpful tips related to canning pickles.

- Soak fresh, uncut cucumbers in ice-cold water for 2 hours before canning to ensure crispness.
- Use widemouthed jars for canning pickles. The wide opening makes it easier to pack pickles in—and take them out.
- In recipes calling for garlic, gently crush the cloves, enough that they release their flavor yet still hold their shape.
- Use the flower heads of dill just beginning to go to seed. They deliver the most potent dill flavor.

Classic Garlic Dill Pickles

Pucker up and enjoy! This is your traditional sour pickle with a blast of garlic flavor. You'll love how it tastes and how it holds its crunch.

Makes 4 pint jars

3 pounds pickling cucumbers
2 cups distilled white vinegar
2 cups water
2 tablespoons pickling salt
4 fresh dill flower heads
4 small cloves garlic

Trim the cucumbers to 4-inch lengths to fit in one-pint jars. Slice in half lengthwise. If the cucumbers are particularly thick, quarter them.

Combine the vinegar, water, and pickling salt in a nonreactive saucepan and bring to a boil.

Place a dill flower head and a clove of garlic in each of the widemouthed pint jars. Tightly pack the cucumbers in the jars. Ladle the hot liquid over the cucumbers to within ½ inch of the rim (headspace). Seal and process for 10 minutes.

Sweet Garlic Dills

If you like the taste of garlic and the taste of sweet pickles, then you'll really like this recipe, which combines both for an outstanding pickle.

Makes 4 pint jars

4 pounds pickling cucumbers
2 cups distilled white vinegar
⅔ cup water
1 cup sugar
3 tablespoons pickling salt
4 cloves garlic
4 fresh dill flower heads
1 teaspoon celery seeds
2 teaspoons black peppercorns, cracked

Trim the cucumbers to 4-inch lengths to fit in the jars. Slice in half lengthwise.

Combine the vinegar, water, sugar, and pickling salt in a small saucepan and bring to a boil.

Place 1 clove of garlic, 1 dill seed head, ¼ teaspoon celery seeds, and ½ teaspoon peppercorns in each of the widemouthed pint jars. Tightly pack the cucumbers in the jars. Ladle the hot liquid over the cucumbers to within ½ inch of the rim (headspace). Seal and process for 10 minutes.

Classic Bread and Butter Pickle Chips

Bread and butter pickles are on the sweeter end of the pickle spectrum. Serve them with cold meat and pasta salads or chop up as a relish and use for burgers.

Makes 6 pint jars

4 pounds pickling cucumbers
4 small onions, cut into large dice
1 green bell pepper, cut into large dice
1 red bell pepper, cut into large dice
2 tablespoons pickling salt
4 cups cider vinegar
3 cups sugar
2 tablespoons mustard seeds
1 teaspoon celery seeds
½ teaspoon turmeric
¼ teaspoon ground cloves

Trim the ends of the cucumbers and cut into slices about ¼ to ½ inch thick. Combine the cucumber slices, onion, and peppers in a large colander. Sprinkle with the pickling salt and let drain for 3 hours. Rinse thoroughly before proceeding.

Combine the vinegar, sugar, mustard seeds, celery seeds, turmeric, and cloves in a large nonreactive pot. Bring to a boil over high heat. Add the cucumber mixture. Return to a boil for 30 seconds.

Using a slotted spoon, pack the hot cucumber mixture into widemouthed jars to within ½ inch of the rim (headspace). Add enough hot liquid to cover the contents. Seal and process for 10 minutes.

a season for all pickling

Pickling Spice

Pickling spice is a mixture of spices that add flavor to canned beans, pickles, beets, zucchini, and more. You can find ready-made versions in the grocery, but making your own gives you the freedom to adjust flavors to suit your tastes. Pickling spices are best left whole in canning recipes so that the flavor is released without any powdery residue to cloud the jar.

Makes about ½ cup

4 tablespoons mustard seeds
2 tablespoons whole allspice
4 teaspoons black peppercorns
2 teaspoons dried chopped ginger root
2 teaspoons hot red pepper flakes
4 small bay leaves, broken up
4-inch piece of cinnamon stick, cracked into small pieces
2 teaspoons cardamom pods 4 teaspoons whole cloves

Combine all the ingredients and store in an airtight container.

in season ...
salad greens

Truly fresh salad greens are one of the greatest advantages to eating locally, whether from the farmers market or your own garden. Frilly bouquets of ruby and green leaf lettuces; sturdy, crisp romaines; crunchy butterheads; pleasantly bitter radicchios, endives, and escaroles; spicy cresses; tart arugulas . . . the list goes on, as does the harvest.

For the most part, lettuces are enjoyed raw in salads. In fact, their name is almost synonymous with salads, but they do have a place in soups and, of course, as part of a sandwich. While fresh green salad often ushers in a dinner, there is no rule saying it can't be a refreshing pause between the main course and dessert.

Choosing the Best. Firm green heads and crisp, fresh-looking leaves are signs of just-picked lettuce. Where the lettuce has been cut from the plant, it should be clean and fresh-looking, not rusty and dried out.

How to Store Fresh. Put off washing freshly bought or harvested greens, whether in heads or loose leaf, until needed. If they harbor a little dirt or sand, shake off as much as possible and blot away excessive moisture with a towel. Roll the greens in a layer of paper towels or a thin lint-free cotton towel, which will wick the water from the greens and supply the humidity necessary to keep them fresh. Place the towel-wrapped greens in a perforated plastic bag, seal, and store in the refrigerator's crisper drawer for 4 to 7 days.

To Prepare for Cooking. Tear salad greens into bite-sized pieces by hand. Cutting greens with a knife often leaves bruised and discolored edges, especially if the salad is not being served immediately. Swish the prepared greens in a bowl of water to clean, drain well in a colander, and dry in a salad spinner.

Pick or Buy Now, Enjoy Later. Summer salad greens are to be picked or bought and enjoyed in short order. There is no effective way to preserve salad greens for much longer than a week. When summer's salad harvest is over, move on to heartier fall greens such as kale and fall spinach for salads and cooking. There are other fresh, seasonal foods that can be served as the salad course, too. Serve the Chilled Asparagus and Red Onion Salad on page 5 in the spring or the Grilled Eggplant Salad on page 81 when fall rolls around.

Bibb and Spinach Salad with Fresh Strawberries

Serve this salad in early summer when spinach and Bibb lettuce, both cool-weather greens, are sweet and tender, and strawberries are at their peak of flavor. The creamy salad dressing does its job of uniting all the fresh ingredients without overpowering a single one.

Makes 6 servings

2 tablespoons mayonnaise

2 tablespoons lemon juice

4 tablespoons extra virgin olive oil

Pinch of sugar

Salt and freshly ground black pepper, to taste

1 head fresh Bibb lettuce, torn into bite-size pieces, washed and dried

4 cups fresh spinach leaves, washed and dried

1 quart fresh strawberries, cleaned, hulled, and sliced

6 tablespoons nuts (pine nuts, walnuts, or pecans), toasted

In a large bowl, whisk the mayonnaise with the lemon juice. Gradually whisk in the olive oil and season with a pinch of sugar and season with salt and pepper to taste. Add the lettuce, spinach, and strawberries. Toss gently until the leaves are coated. Divide between 6 chilled salad plates and top with a tablespoon of toasted nuts.

Simply Summer Salad

Don't be fooled by the simplicity of this salad. It relies on the sum of its ingredients to be as good as it can possibly be. Don't settle for anything less than the freshest greens and chives from your garden or the farmers market. And be gentle ... tender greens bruise easily when handled roughly.

Makes 6 servings

6 cups mixed fresh greens, gently washed and thoroughly dried

3 tablespoons good-quality extra virgin olive oil

2 tablespoons good-quality champagne vinegar or balsamic vinegar

2 tablespoons freshly chopped chives and chive blossoms, if available

Good-quality sea salt and freshly ground black pepper

Place the greens in a large bowl. Lightly drizzle the oil over the lettuces, tossing to coat. Sprinkle the vinegar over the greens and toss again. Add chives and season with salt and pepper. Toss again. Taste and adjust seasoning.

Divide between 6 chilled salad plates and serve immediately.

• •

spinning class

Water that remains on salad greens and spinach can add an undesirable sogginess to a recipe. In salads, moisture dilutes the dressing and prevents it from coating the leaves. Blotting the leaves with a paper towel is effective, but can be tedious and time consuming. This is a job for a salad spinner, a great kitchen tool that not only gently spins greens dry but also is a perfect place to store them. Keep the greens in the spinner basket and lay a wet paper towel on the bottom of the outer bowl for humidity. Give the greens an extra spin before using.

toasting nuts

Preheat the oven to 400°F. Scatter the nuts on a rimmed baking sheet and place in the oven for 7 to 10 minutes, stirring halfway through toasting, or until the nuts begin to turn golden and become fragrant. Remove from the pan and into a bowl to cool.

You can also use the stove top and a heavy skillet as another option for toasting small amounts of nuts. Heat a heavy skillet over medium-low heat. Add the nuts and toast, stirring frequently until you notice slight streaks of oil in the pan and the nuts become fragrant and lightly toasted. Remove from the pan onto a few layers of paper towels and cool.

Punchy Peppery Salad

This salad departs from the traditional pattern of mixing salad greens to achieve a balance of flavor and leans toward making a power statement of flavors in a salad that delivers a spicy punch. It pairs perfectly with a hot or cold cream-based soup.

Makes 6 to 8 servings

2 tablespoons white wine vinegar
½ teaspoon Dijon mustard
2 teaspoons freshly minced flat-leaf parsley
⅓ cup extra virgin olive oil
Salt and freshly ground black pepper
2 small heads radicchio, washed, spun dry, and torn
2 bunches watercress, washed, trimmed, and separated into sprigs
2 bunches fresh arugula, washed, spun dry, and torn, stems removed
3 scallions, thinly sliced
1 cup shaved Parmesan cheese

To make the dressing, combine the vinegar, mustard, and parsley in a small bowl. Add the oil in a thin stream, whisking constantly, and whisk until blended. Season with salt and pepper. Set aside.

Toss the greens and scallions in a large salad bowl, add the dressing, and toss to coat the leaves. Top with the cheese and serve immediately.

Arugula and Frisée Salad

Play with this salad by swapping out some of the greens with other seasonal greens like endive and radicchio. The harmony of fresh flavors in this salad will convince you that when it comes to homegrown food, fresh, flavorful ingredients rely on little more than each other for great results. To dress up this salad for a luncheon entrée, omit the nuts, top with a freshly poached egg (see page 44 for how to make the perfect one), and serve with a toasted baguette.

Makes 6 servings

4 tablespoons nuts (pine nuts, walnuts, or hazelnuts), coarsely chopped
3 tablespoons extra virgin olive oil
1 tablespoon freshly squeezed lemon juice
Sea salt and freshly ground black pepper
1 6-ounce bunch frisée, washed, dried, and torn into bite-size pieces
1 6-ounce bunch arugula, thick stems removed and discarded
1 cup ripe cherry tomatoes, halved
¼ cup shaved Parmesan cheese, plus extra for garnish

Toast the nuts in a small skillet over low heat, shaking the pan occasionally, until they are golden and fragrant. Transfer the nuts to a bowl to cool. Set aside.

In a large bowl, whisk together the olive oil and lemon juice and season with salt and pepper. Add the greens, tomatoes, and cheese, tossing gently to coat. Divide among 6 chilled salad plates. Top with the nuts and garnish with a shaving of Parmesan.

Bread Soup with Lettuce

Makes 6 servings

This is a lovely, rustic soup sweetened by tender fresh Bibb lettuce. Simplistic and easy, its success depends in part on great chicken stock, rich and flavorful. Learn to make and store Rich Chicken Stock on page 143. See if you don't notice that your soups and stews reflect the delicious difference.

2 or 3 heads Bibb lettuce
4 tablespoons extra virgin olive oil
4 cloves garlic, chopped
6 cups rich chicken stock
Salt and freshly ground black pepper, to taste
4 thick slices of coarse, rustic bread, lightly toasted, cubed

Core the lettuce heads and cut the leaves into thin strips. Warm the oil in a stockpot or Dutch oven over medium heat. Add the garlic and cook, stirring constantly, until soft, translucent, and fragrant, about 1 minute. Add the lettuce and stir until wilted, about 2 minutes. Add the stock and bring to a boil. Reduce the heat and simmer for 10 minutes to blend flavors. Season to taste with salt and pepper. Add the bread cubes to the soup or divide them among individual bowls and pour the stock over the top. Serve immediately.

Greens with Goat Cheese Croutons and Honey Thyme Vinaigrette

Makes 4 servings

Fresh salad greens are the perfect bed on which to rest these warm medallions of fresh goat cheese.

8 ounces fresh goat cheese
Salt and freshly ground black pepper
2 tablespoons fresh thyme leaves, divided use
1 cup extra virgin olive oil, divided use
1 teaspoon Dijon mustard
1 cup unseasoned dry breadcrumbs
1 tablespoon honey
¼ cup balsamic vinegar
6 cups assorted fresh salad greens, washed and dried

Divide the cheese into four 2-ounce portions, forming each into a medallion shape, about 1 inch thick. Season lightly with salt, pepper, and 1 tablespoon of the thyme leaves. In a shallow bowl, whisk together ¼ cup of the olive oil and the mustard. Dip the goat cheese in the oil mixture to coat all sides and then roll in the breadcrumbs. Place in a lightly oiled baking dish and refrigerate for at least 30 minutes or up to 2 hours before baking.

Preheat the oven to 350°F.

Bake for 12 minutes or until the center is soft to the touch. Remove from the oven and let stand for 10 minutes.

To make the vinaigrette, whisk the honey, vinegar, and remaining tablespoon of thyme together. Add the remaining ¾ cup olive oil in a thin stream, whisking constantly. Season to taste with salt and pepper.

Toss salad greens with the vinaigrette and divide between 4 salad plates. Top each salad with a warm goat cheese medallion and serve immediately.

Escarole Soup

While lettuces tend to be thought of only as a salad ingredient, heartier greens like escarole find their way into soups. Braising escarole renders it sweet and tender. The finished soup is just another fine example of how simplicity in ingredients yields complex flavors.

*Canned or frozen tomatoes with their juices may be substituted for fresh.

Making your own pesto is easy and produces a great ingredient for adding flavor to soups. Learn to make your own pestos on page 89.

Makes 6 to 8 servings

2 tablespoons extra virgin olive oil

1 large onion, diced

4 cloves garlic, minced

2 small heads escarole, washed, trimmed, sliced into strips

8 cups rich chicken stock or vegetable stock

4 cups chopped fresh ripe tomatoes*

3 tablespoons prepared pesto, more or less to taste

½ cup small pasta or spaghetti noodles broken into pieces

½ cup grated Parmesan cheese

Salt and freshly ground black pepper, to taste

Heat the olive oil in a large stockpot over medium heat. Add the onion and sauté until soft and fragrant, about 6 minutes. Add the garlic and sauté an additional minute, stirring constantly. Add the escarole and sauté until it is soft and limp. Add the chicken stock and tomatoes; bring to a boil. Reduce to a simmer and cook for 30 minutes. Stir in the pesto.

Add the pasta and cook until tender, about 15 minutes. Stir in the cheese. Taste and season with salt and pepper. Serve hot with crusty bread.

simple and seasonal, leafy greens

Here's a primer on varieties of greens you'll find popping up in gardens or at markets as early as spring and some into the fall. Remember that within each variety you'll find plenty of variations. Some work alone in a salad, but feel free to toss them together to create the balance of flavors and textures that suits your palate.

arugula: An early-season, long-leafed green, arugula has a peppery punch that adds spice to a salad mix; it's also a special treat on its own with a simple dressing and some fresh tomatoes.

butterhead lettuce: Cool-weather-loving head lettuces such as Bibb and Buttercrunch have a soft texture and a nice nutty flavor; butterhead lettuce teams well with strawberries.

dandelion greens: The buttery leaves of the backyard flower are mildly bitter and tangy and best harvested young in early summer.

endive or frisée: Same lettuce, different names. Curly and frilly, it adds a peppery, nutty bite to salads.

escarole: A close cousin to endive, escarole is milder and more lettuce-like, with broad green leaves.

green or red loose leaf: Loosely gathered leaves in colors ranging from purple to red and dark to light greens have a soft texture and mild taste. They are best mixed in with sturdy salad greens.

mâche: Also called "lambs' lettuce," mâche is fragile and velvety with a subtle flavor.

mesclun: A mix of leaf and loose-headed lettuces, mesclun may include mustards, cresses, parsley, arugula, wild greens, and more. The types of lettuces are not as important as the taste and texture sensations balanced throughout the salad: sweet, bitter, tangy, crunchy, and silky.

mizuna: The tender, jagged leaves of mizuna have a peppery flavor and offer a nice contrast to leaf lettuces.

oak leaf: In shades of green or burgundy, the leaves are notched like a common oak leaf. The flavor is sweet and the texture is tender and delicate.

radicchio: Looking like a tiny head of red cabbage but slightly bitter, radicchio adds a great crunch to salads.

romaine: A great all-around sweet-tasting salad green, romaine has plenty of crunch and crevices to hold onto salad dressing.

watercress: A special treat for salad green lovers, watercress has tiny, tender leaves and edible stems with a peppery edge.

A Trio of Dressings Using Local Ingredients

Honey and Garlic Vinaigrette

Makes 1½ cups

The personality of this dressing will change depending on the type of honey used: lighter honeys are subtle and perfect with delicate greens like leaf lettuces and Bibbs, and darker, more robust honey is a better companion to more assertive greens and salad fixings like onions and aged cheeses.

⅓ cup apple cider vinegar
3 to 4 tablespoons honey
3 cloves garlic, minced
1 cup vegetable or canola oil
Salt and freshly ground black pepper, to taste

Whisk together the vinegar, honey, and garlic in a medium bowl. Add the oil in a slow, steady stream, whisking constantly. Season with salt and pepper. Store in the refrigerator in a tightly sealed jar. Shake well before using.

Herbed Buttermilk Dressing

Makes about 2 cups

Creamy dressings are better suited for sturdy greens like romaines, escarole, and endives and are ideal for salads that include sharp, aged cheeses. Add a little less buttermilk and use as a dip with fresh vegetables.

¾ cup mayonnaise
½ cup buttermilk, plus extra to thin
2 tablespoons cider vinegar
½ teaspoon kosher salt
⅛ teaspoon freshly ground black pepper
Dash of hot sauce (optional)
1 cup freshly chopped herbs, more or less to taste

Suggested Herbs:
¼ cup freshly chopped chives
¼ cup fresh dill, minced
½ cup freshly chopped flat leaf parsley
2 tablespoons fresh thyme leaves

Combine the mayonnaise and buttermilk in a blender. Add the cider vinegar, salt, pepper, and hot sauce, if desired. If the mixture is too thick, add buttermilk to thin.

Add up to 1 cup freshly chopped herbs, ¼ cup at a time, blending and tasting before adding the next batch. Transfer the mixture to a bottle or jar with a tight-fitting lid. Refrigerate and use within 2 weeks.

Maple Vinaigrette

Makes about 1¾ cups

Any grade of maple syrup will do, but for full, robust flavor, choose darker, late-season maple syrup. This vinaigrette is perfect for salads that have slices of seasonal pears or apples—it's especially delicious on the Orchard Salad (page 133).

1 teaspoon dry mustard
1 teaspoon minced fresh basil or ¼ teaspoon dried basil, more if desired
¼ cup cider vinegar
½ cup pure maple syrup
1 tablespoon freshly squeezed lemon juice
1 clove garlic, minced
1 cup extra virgin olive oil
Salt and freshly ground black pepper, to taste

Combine the mustard, basil, vinegar, maple syrup, lemon juice, and garlic in a medium bowl. Add the oil in a slow, steady stream, whisking constantly. Season with salt and pepper. Store in the refrigerator in a tightly sealed jar. Shake well before using.

Making Your Own: Infused Vinegars

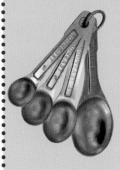

Sprigs of fresh, tender herbs infuse vinegar with local, seasonal flavors. Infused vinegars can be used all year long in salad dressings, as bases for marinades and sauces, to flavor mayonnaise, and for many other culinary purposes. A tiny bouquet of herbs may not seem very powerful. But steep it for a few weeks in vinegar, and flavors are coaxed out, offering complex undertones, seasonality, and a defining flavor in recipes.

Infused vinegars can be as simple as just a few sprigs of your favorite herb delivering a singular flavor to the vinegar, or they can be a combination of herbs with some accompanying flavors from the pantry to fashion your own signature vinegar blend.

An Infused Vinegar Sampler

Here are a few combinations of vinegar, herbs, and other flavors to get you thinking about creating your own flavored vinegars. Experiment freely and often as new herbs and local produce pops up.

Berry Vinegar

Berry-infused vinegars are good choices for dressing fruit salads or mixed green salads featuring fresh seasonal fruit.

Makes 2 cups infused vinegar

2 cups white wine vinegar
1 cup fresh berries or mixed berries, cleaned and patted dry
2 tablespoons light honey
6 sprigs thyme, gently bruised

• •

Tarragon Garlic Vinegar

Tarragon is such a potent herb that it doesn't take much more than a few sprigs to impart an anise-like flavor. Use this vinegar on salads that feature other strong flavors.

Makes 2 cups infused vinegar

2 cups white wine or cider vinegar
6 sprigs fresh tarragon, gently bruised
1 clove garlic, peeled

• •

Lemon Oregano Vinegar

This vinegar blend is especially good with salads that feature feta cheese or olives.

Makes 2 cups infused vinegar

2 cups white wine vinegar
1 bunch fresh oregano sprigs (about 10 to 15 4-inch sprigs
    with blooms, if desired), gently bruised
4 wide strips of lemon zest
1 clove garlic, peeled

Making Herbal Infused Vinegar

- Begin by gathering the herbs you want to use, whether from your own garden or from a farmers market. Rinse them thoroughly and gently pat dry. Use the sprigs intact; do not strip the leaves. For every 2 cups of vinegar, use about 1 cup of herbs, more or less according to personal taste and the desired strength of the herb flavor.

- Choose vinegars that will absorb flavor easily: white wine or red wine vinegar, cider vinegar, rice wine vinegar, or champagne vinegar. Distilled white vinegar and balsamic vinegar are strong and distinct in their own flavor and don't share the spotlight well with other flavors. Gently warm, not heat, the vinegar in a small saucepan.

- Using clean hands, bruise or lightly crush or rub the herbs to release the oils and flavors. Place them in a clean, sterilized quart jar and add the warmed vinegar. It can be as simple as that, or you can add other seasonal, local, and flavorful ingredients. Follow the suggestions below or experiment with your own preferences.

- Seal with a tight-fitting lid and shake gently to combine. Let the jar sit at room temperature for 2 weeks, shaking the contents occasionally. Taste the vinegar after that time to determine if it has the desired flavor. If not, replace the herbs with fresh ones, let steep for an additional week, and taste again. If the flavor is too strong, add more vinegar to dilute and soften the taste.

- When the vinegar has the desired flavor, strain into a clean container through several layers of cheesecloth or a coffee filter, discarding the solids. Store the strained vinegar in a clean, sterilized bottle or jar, adding a fresh herb sprig, if desired. Seal, using a cork or tight-fitting lid, label, and store in a cool part of the kitchen, away from direct sunlight.

While vinegars have an indefinite shelf life, it's best to create only what you'll use in a year's time and then repeat the process when fresh herbs are available the following season.

Consider the following suggestions for adding complex flavor:

- Herbs. Those producing especially flavorful vinegars include basil, chives, dill, fennel, garlic, lemon balm, marjoram, oregano, rosemary, tarragon, and thyme.

- Berries. Most seasonal berries such as strawberries, blueberries, raspberries, and blackberries make flavorful additions to vinegar blends, especially those used to dress fruit salads. Strain out the berries before storing.

- Edible Flowers and Blossoms. Pretty chive, oregano, or sage blossoms add flavor and beautiful color to clear vinegars. Nasturtiums add a peppery flavor, and marigolds a citrus tang, while johnny-jump-ups add a hint of mint. Bean and pea blossoms and shoots add a little sweet flavor. (Not all flowers are edible. Choose only blossoms you know are safe.)

- Fruits. Add 1 cup of peeled, chopped, ever so slightly overripe fruits such as peaches, nectarines, and apricots or pears and Asian pears to steep in the vinegar. Strain well before storing.

- Garlic. Add one or two whole, peeled cloves.

- Whole Spices (such as allspice, cloves, coriander seed, cumin seed, dill and fennel seed, and peppercorns). Do not use ground or crushed spices, which will cloud the vinegar. Thin slivers or slices of peeled fresh ginger root can also be added.

- Honey. A tablespoon or two of honey naturally complements berry vinegars.

- Lemon or Orange Peel. Add thin, wide strips of citrus zest removed from the fruit using a vegetable peeler or paring knife.

in season . . .
summer berries

To tell someone "You're the berries" is quite a compliment—if you know about berries. Raspberries, blueberries, and blackberries are the gems of summer, small in size, mighty in flavor and sweetness, delicate to behold, and so easy to be stingy with. Whether you're picking your own or happily carrying a flat away from a farmers market, fresh berries are usually not inexpensive—but then again, when they are at their peak of ripeness, full and juicy, few would question the price tag.

Choosing the Best. Any berry should be plump and free of mold, with a fruity berry aroma. Be wary of containers or flats containing crushed or moldy berries that can quickly compromise the entire lot.

Avoid raspberries and blackberries that have stems and hulls attached. They have been picked before they are fully ripened.

Raspberries, whether red or golden, should be plump and evenly colored, with a soft, hazy gloss. Pale-colored berries are underripe and not very sweet, and berries that are dark red are likely overly ripe.

Blueberries should be round and firm, with a silvery bloom over a deep purple color, a good sign that they were picked recently. Any hint of red is a sign of an underripe blueberry.

Blackberries should be large and firm, a dull black color, and lacking any tinge of red or brown spots. The taste ranges from sweet to mildly sweet, although some varietals are naturally on the sour side and best used in recipes that call for a measure of sugar.

How to Store Fresh. Always keep berries refrigerated and rinse just before using them. Fresh blueberries can keep up to five days, but raspberries and blackberries are a little more delicate and sometimes keep their looks only two days. To better your chances of extending the shelf life, spread just-bought or freshly picked berries in a single layer in a shallow dish, removing any that are crushed or show signs of age or mold, cover, and store in the refrigerator.

To Prepare for Cooking. The beauty of berries, aside from the taste, is that they usually come pretty clean with only a gentle rinsing standing between them and a great recipe. Place the berries in a colander and gently plunge or rinse in cold water a few times. Let the excess water drain off. Spread the berries on a towel and let them dry. Do not pat, toss, or squeeze the berries.

Pick or Buy Now, Enjoy Later. If you can keep yourself from eating the berries while they are fresh, freezing is the best option for extending their flavor, color, and usefulness. From the freezer, raspberries can be used in the Simple Raspberry Mousse on page 212. All berries can also be crafted into jams, jellies, and preserves and called into service later in the year to spread on toast or be used in the recipes like Chocolate Red Wine Layer Cake on page 181 or Rosemary Meatballs with Tangy Red Raspberry Glaze on page 202.

Freeze this season's berries! To learn how, go to page 221. Or for other ways to preserve the seasonal flavor of berries, try the trio of berry jams on page 71.

Mixed Berry Crumble

Makes 4 to 6 servings

For that small window of opportunity when different berry harvests overlap, here's a wonderful way to mix the flavors. Combine two or three different varieties, fresh, frozen, or a combination, or use just one berry variety.

4 cups mixed berries (raspberries, blueberries, and blackberries)
1 cup sugar, divided use
3 tablespoons balsamic vinegar
½ cup all-purpose flour
½ cup brown sugar
Pinch of salt
4 tablespoons unsalted butter, cut into small pieces
Vanilla ice cream, to accompany

Preheat the oven to 400°F. Butter a shallow 4-cup baking dish.

In a medium bowl, combine the berries, ½ cup sugar, and vinegar. Set aside for 20 minutes.

In another medium bowl, combine the flour, brown sugar, salt, and remaining ½ cup sugar. Cut the butter into the flour mixture until completely blended and sandy in texture.

Place the berry mixture in the baking dish, draining a little of the liquid if too juicy. Scatter the crumb mixture evenly over the top. Bake for 30 minutes until the crumb topping is golden and set. Serve warm or at room temperature with a scoop of vanilla ice cream.

Ultimate Blueberry Muffins

Makes 1 dozen

These are the kind of muffins you'll dream about after blueberry season winds down. Big, crunchy, sugary tops crown whole juicy berries in a tender crumb. Make your dreams come true by storing berries at their peak flavor in the freezer. Feel free to substitute blackberries or black raspberries for blueberries.

6 tablespoons unsalted butter
5 large eggs
½ cup whole milk
3½ cups sifted all-purpose flour
2 tablespoons plus 1 teaspoon baking powder
¾ cup granulated sugar
⅛ teaspoon salt
1½ cups fresh blueberries
Coarse sugar for sprinkling

Melt the butter in a small saucepan over medium heat. Set aside to cool.

In a large mixing bowl, beat the eggs until well blended, about 2 minutes. Add the melted butter and the milk.

In a separate bowl, combine the sifted flour, baking powder, sugar, and salt. Add to the egg mixture and mix until just blended, less than 1 minute. Fold in the blueberries. Cover the bowl with plastic wrap and refrigerate for 2 hours. (Do not skip this step.)

Preheat the oven to 400°F. Line a 12-cup muffin tin with paper muffin cups or coat the cups of the tin with cooking spray.

Spoon the batter into the prepared baking cups so that it mounds about ½ inch above the top of each cup. Sprinkle the tops with coarse sugar. Bake for 25 to 30 minutes or until the tops are domed and golden brown. Remove from the oven and let cool before removing from the pan.

Berry Clafouti with Crème Fraîche

Makes 6 to 8 servings

Clafouti (kla-foo-tee) has taken America by storm—possibly because it's easy, homey, and custardy and it can follow you from one berry season to the next. You can feature one berry, like raspberries, or mix it up by combining berries with overlapping seasons like raspberries and blueberries. Freeze seasonal berries and enjoy this clafouti in the winter.

Black raspberries are among the best-tasting brambles and the most elusive, not grown everywhere and with a harvest season that lasts only 4 weeks. When you find them at farmers markets or roadside stands, buy them! They have a distinct and moderately tart flavor, small seeds, and a hollow core and are wonderful in this clafouti.

2 large eggs
⅓ cup sugar
½ vanilla bean, split lengthwise (substitution: 1 teaspoon vanilla extract)
3 tablespoons all-purpose flour
Pinch of salt
⅓ cup plus 3 tablespoons homemade crème fraîche (page 50) or sour cream
⅓ cup milk
2 cups seasonal berries (blackberries, blueberries, raspberries, strawberries, or a combination)
1 ½ teaspoons confectioners' sugar

Preheat the oven to 400°F.

Whisk the eggs and sugar together in a medium bowl until frothy. Scrape the seeds from the split vanilla bean into the mixture. Add the flour and salt and whisk to combine.

In a separate bowl, whisk the ⅓ cup of crème fraîche with the milk and then whisk that into the batter.

Coat a 10-inch nonstick ovenproof skillet with melted butter or cooking spray. Pour a third of the batter into the skillet. Bake until just set, about 5 minutes. Remove from the oven and top with the berries, then the remaining batter. Return the skillet to the oven and bake for 25 to 30 minutes until the batter has puffed up.

Remove from the oven and let cool for 10 minutes. Run a flexible spatula around the edge to loosen. Slide onto a large serving plate (or if necessary, invert onto a plate and then invert again so the berry side is facing up).

Whip the remaining 3 tablespoons crème fraîche with the confectioners' sugar in a small bowl.

Cut the clafouti into 6 or 8 wedges and serve each wedge with a dollop of the crème fraîche.

Chilled Red Raspberry and Wine Soup

Makes 4 to 6 servings

Chilled soup is a lovely beginning or ending to a meal on a hot summer night. This versatile soup cools down the body with fresh local berries and local wine.

4 cups fresh raspberries (reserve a few for garnish)
¼ to ½ cup sugar or honey, more or less to taste
¼ cup dry red locally produced wine
1 cup sour cream or homemade crème fraîche (page 50)
Fresh mint leaves

Place the raspberries, sugar, and wine in a blender. Cover and blend on high speed until smooth. Strain the seeds from the mixture using a fine-mesh sieve. Discard the seeds.

Pour the raspberry mixture into a large bowl or pitcher. Stir in the sour cream or crème fraîche. Cover and refrigerate for up to 2 hours until chilled. Serve with an extra dollop of sour cream or crème fraîche, a fresh raspberry, and a mint leaf for garnish.

Blackberry Upside Down Cake

Here's a version of the familiar and traditional pineapple upside down cake that features big juicy blackberries nestled in a delightful caramelized topping. You can use a 9-inch cake pan for this recipe, but a well-seasoned cast iron skillet helps keep the sugary topping from scorching over the burner and makes it a breeze to flip the cake out when finished.

A heavy 9-inch round cake pan can be substituted for the frying pan. Make the brown sugar and nut mixture in a saucepan first and then transfer to the buttered cake pan.

Makes 8 to 10 servings

½ cup unsalted butter, divided use
½ cup packed dark brown sugar
1½ teaspoons grated lemon zest, divided use
¼ cup chopped walnuts or pecans
2 heaping cups fresh blackberries
1 cup all-purpose flour
¾ cup granulated sugar
1½ teaspoons baking powder
¼ teaspoon salt
1 egg, room temperature
½ cup milk, room temperature
1 teaspoon fresh lemon juice
1 teaspoon pure vanilla extract
Whipped cream, to accompany

Preheat the oven to 350°F.

Melt ¼ cup of the butter in a 10-inch cast iron frying pan. Stir in the brown sugar until blended, not melted. Remove from the heat and sprinkle 1 teaspoon of the zest and the chopped nuts over the sugar. Arrange the blackberries in a single layer over the nuts. Set aside.

Melt the remaining ¼ cup butter and let cool. In a large bowl, combine the flour, sugar, baking powder, and salt. In a separate bowl, combine the egg, milk, melted butter, remaining ½ teaspoon lemon zest, lemon juice, and vanilla. Add the egg mixture to the dry ingredients and beat for 2 minutes. Pour the mixture over the blackberries in the frying pan, spreading evenly.

Bake for 45 minutes or until a toothpick inserted into the center comes out clean. Remove from the oven and let cool for 5 minutes before running a knife around the edge of the pan to loosen. Invert onto a cake plate and serve warm or at room temperature with a dollop of whipped cream, if desired.

A Trio of Berry Pies

Delicious decisions can still be hard to make. To solve the question of which kind of berry pie to make, simply go with the season and worry about which is your favorite later. You'll notice that each of the fillings in these pies is simplistic in its ingredient list. That's because when it comes to ripe summer berries, there's hardly a need to embellish.

Fresh Blueberry Pie

Makes one 9-inch double-crust pie

Fresh blueberries have such distinctive flavor that the fewer ingredients to accompany them in a pie, the better. Make this pie over and over again while blueberries are in season and resist the urge to recreate this from frozen berries, which will not produce the same results.

5 to 6 cups fresh blueberries
½ cup sifted all-purpose flour
1 cup sugar
1 tablespoon unsalted butter, cut into small pieces, chilled
1 recipe pie dough for a 9-inch double-crust pie (page 128)

Place a baking stone or a heavy baking sheet on the middle rack in the oven to heat. Preheat the oven to 400°F.

In a large mixing bowl, combine the blueberries, flour, sugar, and butter. Toss gently so the blueberries are completely coated with the mixture.

Roll out half the pie dough to fit a 9-inch pie plate. Turn the blueberry filling into the bottom crust. Roll out the top crust and cover the filling and bottom crust. Trim and crimp the edges together. Cut 4 slits in the top crust. Place the pie on the baking stone and bake for 50 minutes or until the crust is golden and the juices are bubbly.

Let cool for at least 1 hour before slicing.

Fresh Raspberry Tart

Makes one 9-inch tart

When you step back and look at this finished tart, it appears complicated to make. That's the wonder of fresh, seasonal raspberries. Their complex beauty is an ingredient delivered only by nature.

1 9-inch tart shell, blind baked and cooled (directions on page 128)
¼ cup red currant jelly
6 ounces cream cheese, room temperature
⅓ cup sugar
½ cup sour cream
2 teaspoons fresh lemon juice
½ teaspoon vanilla extract
3 cups fresh raspberries
Fresh mint leaves, to garnish

Melt the jelly in a small saucepan over low heat. Use some to lightly brush the bottom and sides of the prepared tart shell.

In a large mixing bowl, beat the cream cheese and sugar together until smooth. Beat in the sour cream, lemon juice, and vanilla. Spread evenly in the bottom of the tart shell. Chill for 4 hours.

When ready to serve, arrange the raspberries on top of the filling. Gently reheat the glaze and lightly brush the tops of the raspberries. Serve immediately or chill for up to 3 hours. Garnish with fresh mint leaves before serving.

Rustic Blackberry Tart

Makes one 9-inch tart

You can make a rustic-looking tart out of any fruit, but this one looks particularly amazing. Plump, dark berries peeking out from the center beg to be admired—or eaten. You decide.

4 cups fresh blackberries
1 cup granulated sugar
¼ cup all-purpose flour
Pinch of salt
4 tablespoons unsalted butter, cut into small dice
Juice of 1 lemon
½ tablespoon grated lemon zest
½ tablespoon brown sugar
1 recipe pie dough for one 9-inch tart (directions on page 128)
Heavy cream, for brushing

Preheat the oven to 400°F.

In a large mixing bowl, combine the blackberries, sugar, flour, salt, butter, lemon juice, lemon zest, and brown sugar. Toss gently so the blackberries are completely coated with the mixture.

Roll out the dough to a 14-inch circle. Arrange in a 9-inch pie plate, letting the edges hang over the rim. Add the filling. Fold the edges of the pastry up and over the filling, leaving a gap in the middle exposing the fruit. Brush the crust edges with cream. Bake for 40 minutes or until the berries are tender, the juices are bubbly, and the pastry is golden brown.

Let cool for 1 hour before serving. Dust with confectioners' sugar, if desired.

pies: fresh fruits versus frozen

When it comes to pies, a rule of thumb is to use fresh seasonal fruit for the best baking results. Make strawberry pies in the early summer, followed by other berry pies. As summer progresses, bring peach and plum pies to the table, and when fall approaches, replace them with apple, pear, and pumpkin pies. But when you're looking at a stash of frozen berries in the freezer, sometimes you just have to buck the season.

Berry pies, in particular, are difficult to craft from frozen fruit, because frozen berries release a lot more water than their fresh versions when baking. They often leave the fillings watery, lack intense berry flavors, and render the bottom crust a soggy mess. Thawing frozen fruits overnight in the refrigerator and draining some of the liquid before combining with the remaining filling ingredients can help. Adding 2 extra tablespoons of sugar to a recipe can also help thicken the juices during baking. Some bakers like to mix a couple of tablespoons of ground tapioca into a filling recipe and let it sit for 15 minutes to soften. During baking, tapioca absorbs fruit juices without making the filling unnaturally rigid and thick.

Of all the berries, frozen blueberries in particular release a lot of water, and in a pie they often lack the amazing blueberry flavor you're after. Consider instead using frozen blueberries in recipes for muffins and bread puddings or mixed in small quantities with other berries.

Refrigerator Blueberry Jam

Makes 2 cups

If you don't have the time or enough berries to craft jars of jams and preserves but have the desire for that wonderful fruity taste on your morning toast, here's a quick recipe that you can adapt for virtually any fresh seasonal berry. Some berries, like blackberries, are particularly tart and might need more sugar.

....

*If using strawberries, hull and quarter.

4 cups fresh berries,* washed and dried
1 cup granulated sugar (up to ½ cup additional, if needed)
1 tablespoon fresh lemon juice
1 tablespoon grated lemon zest

Place the berries in a medium nonreactive saucepan and crush lightly. Stir in the sugar. Set aside for one hour.

Place the saucepan over medium-low heat. Bring the mixture to a boil, stirring occasionally. Reduce the heat to low and simmer for 15 minutes until the fruit has softened and collapsed, stirring frequently.

Use a slotted spoon to transfer the berries to a small container or jar. Simmer the remaining juices in the pan until thick and syrupy and reduced by half or more. Pour over the berries. Stir in the lemon juice and zest. Allow to cool completely before covering and refrigerating. This jam will keep for up to 3 weeks.

A Trio of Berry Jams

Here are three easy recipes that turn summer berries into wonderful, flavorful jams. The raspberry and blackberry jam recipes produce a softer set jam, relying on only the fruit, sugar, and heat to create spreads that feature genuine berry flavor. Pectin, a necessary component for setting jellies, creates jams that are thicker. Using it is a matter of personal preference. Commercial pectin, in both powdered and liquid forms, includes complete directions for how to use it in jam and jelly making. To learn how to make jams, jellies, and preserves, see page 237.

Raspberry Jam

Makes 5 to 6 half-pint jars

5 cups fresh raspberries, rinsed and dried
5 cups sugar

In a large heavy pot or Dutch oven, combine the raspberries and sugar. Bring to a boil over medium heat, stirring constantly, until sugar is dissolved. Boil for about 30 minutes until the mixture thickens, stirring frequently. Remove from the heat and perform a gel test (see page 238). If the gel stage has not been reached, return to the heat and cook for a few minutes, repeating the test until the gel stage has been reached. Once the mixture has gelled, skim off any foam that has developed.

Ladle the jam into sterilized jars to within ¼ inch of the rim (headspace), seal, and process for 10 minutes.

Blueberry Lemon Jam

Makes 8 to 9 half-pint jars

5 cups fresh blueberries, lightly crushed
7 cups sugar
2 tablespoons freshly squeezed lemon juice

½ teaspoon unsalted butter
2 (3-ounce) pouches liquid pectin
2 tablespoons grated lemon zest

Combine the berries, sugar, lemon juice, and butter in a large saucepan. Place over medium heat and stir constantly until the sugar is dissolved and the mixture is hot. Increase the heat to high and bring the mixture to a full rolling boil (one that won't stop even when stirred), stirring constantly. Stir in all of the liquid pectin. Return the mixture to a full rolling boil, stirring constantly for 1 minute. Remove the pan from the heat and skim off any foam. Stir in the lemon zest.

Ladle the jam into sterilized jars to within ¼ inch of the rim (headspace), seal, and process for 10 minutes.

Blueberries have a very low amount of natural pectin, so it is difficult to set up blueberry jam without adding commercial pectin.

Blackberry Lime Jam

Makes about 6 half-pint jars

6 cups fresh blackberries, rinsed and dried
6 cups sugar

¼ cup fresh lime juice
Grated zest from one fresh lime

In a large heavy pot or Dutch oven, combine the blackberries, sugar, and lime juice. Let stand at room temperature for 1 hour. Bring to a boil over medium heat, stirring constantly until sugar is dissolved. Boil for about 30 minutes until the mixture thickens, stirring frequently. Remove from the heat and perform a gel test (see page 238). If the gel stage has not been reached, return to the heat and cook for a few minutes, repeating the test until the gel stage has been reached. Once the mixture has gelled, skim off any foam that has developed. Stir in the lime zest.

Ladle the jam into sterilized jars to within ¼ inch of the rim (headspace), seal, and process for 10 minutes.

Making Your Own: Ricotta-Style Cheese

If you're bringing great fresh cow or goat milk into your locavore kitchen, you can also enjoy a variety of dairy products made from that same milk all year round. For the price of a half gallon of milk and really just a few minutes of your attention, you can make about a pound of fresh-tasting, still warm ricotta-style cheese with minimum effort for maximum impact in every bite your family or guests take.

Classic ricotta-style cheese is a byproduct of cheesemaking, using the whey that remains after cheese production, but this technique gets down to business using only milk and cream. It makes a wonderful base for cheesecake, ravioli fillings, and lasagna, like the Eggplant Lasagna on page 82. Warm spoonfuls served with fresh seasonal fruit accompanied by a drizzle of honey make a wonderful way to begin the day or end a meal. Later in the year, top sautéed cinnamon-spiced apples or pears with a scoop in place of ice cream. Dollops of chilled ricotta make a nice way to dress up salads, too.

The ingredient list is short, so while you spend less time gathering the necessities, you can put more thought into the quality of the ingredients. Although any milk will work in this recipe, organic milk and cream, as well as milk from herds on pasture, are the preferred ingredients. Whole milk and pasteurized but not homogenized milk lend the best flavor and texture to the finished product. Adding a cup of heavy cream to the mix contributes richness, flavor, and texture, although you can omit the heavy cream if you prefer and substitute another cup of milk. You can also blend cow's and goat's milk in this recipe and enjoy a little more tang in your cheese.

Homemade Ricotta-Style Cheese

Ricotta tastes and smells like the milk it is made from, so use the best and freshest you can find. You can control the consistency of your cheese by how long you let it drain. For a drier ricotta, drain for about 8 hours; for a ricotta that is a bit creamier, drain for 3 hours or less.

Makes about 1 pound ricotta

7 cups whole milk
1 cup heavy cream
¼ teaspoon kosher or sea salt
3 tablespoons distilled white vinegar (5% acidity)

Rinse a large, very clean, heavy nonreactive pot with cold water (this helps prevent scorching the milk). Add the milk and cream. Stir in the salt. Place the pot over medium heat and heat, stirring occasionally, until very hot but not boiling, about 180°F to 185°F. Check the temperature with a thermometer.

Remove from the heat and add the vinegar, stirring gently for 1 minute until fine grains begin forming. Cover with a dry, clean, lint-free cotton towel and allow to sit undisturbed for at least 3 hours and up to 8 hours.

Dampen a few layers of cheesecloth or a clean, lint-free cotton cloth and line the inside of a small colander or strainer suspended over the sink or a pot. Pour or ladle the ricotta into the prepared colander and let it drain freely for two hours—less if you want a creamier ricotta, more if you prefer a drier cheese.

Lift the cheesecloth up and twist gently to extract excess water (which should appear cloudy, not clear). Turn the ricotta out from the cheesecloth into a container with a tight-fitting lid and refrigerate. Ricotta is a fresh cheese and should be enjoyed within a week.

in season ... *melons*

Summer melons come in all shapes and sizes—cantaloupes small enough to hold in the palm of your hand, watermelons so big they have to be cradled like a baby—a rather large baby!

The homestretch of summer finds the aisles of farmers markets lined with unusual, exotic, and familiar varieties of melons. Each can be a wonderful taste experience—or a disappointing one. It's all in how well they were grown and when they were picked, a task traditionally entrusted to growers who understand that timing is key when it comes to harvesting the most refreshing, sweetest treats of summer.

Still, it helps to know what to look for when choosing a melon because sometimes you have to judge on looks alone.

Choosing the Best. When it comes to choosing ripe, flavorful melons, one method does not fit all. Each variety has its own subtle signal.

Watermelons respond to a good thumping. Knock a few times. If it sounds hollow, it's a keeper. If it sounds like you're knocking on solid wood, it's either underripe or overripe. The skin should also have a waxy feeling and the "belly," the spot where the watermelon lay on the ground while growing, should be a creamy yellow, not white or pale green. This above all other methods is the most reliable indicator.

For cantaloupes, it's all about the "slip"—the point where the vine was attached to the melon while growing. If any portion of the stem is still attached, the melon was picked too soon. The slip should have a slight indentation, green in color, and the melon should have an allover golden color covered by scaly netting. Unsure? Use the sniff test: if the melon smells like a sweet, ripe cantaloupe, it probably is one.

Of all melons, honeydew is the most difficult to determine ripeness. It should be smooth and firm, with an allover consistent color and a silky, velvety feel to the skin. If the skin is white, the flavor will be less sweet, almost cucumber-like, but if the skin is a creamy white, the flavor is likely to be sweet and sugary. The blossom end should give a little when pressed, and one sniff should yield a sweet, almost tropical fruit fragrance.

How to Store Fresh. Melons can be left at room temperature for a couple of days after purchasing. Once cut from the rind, slices or pieces should be covered and refrigerated for about two days. Whole melons can be chilled for a day, but longer than that and the flesh loses moisture and texture as well.

To Prepare for Cooking. Melons are meant to be eaten fresh and raw. Cooked melon turns watery and pulpy. To prepare cantaloupe or honeydew, halve the melon and scoop the seeds from the cavity. Watermelon is a little trickier in that the seeds are often dispersed throughout the melon. Seedless varieties still contain some soft, edible white seeds. The white rind on any melon can be saved for pickling.

Pick or Buy Now, Enjoy Later. Melons' high water content makes them poor choices for canning or freezing. When thawed, the fruit collapses and loses its shape and texture. To preserve a little bit of this summertime favorite, try pickling and canning the firm, thick rinds of watermelon into a tangy relish.

Preserve the seasonal flavor of watermelon with Gingered Watermelon Rind Relish on page 76.

Watermelon, Feta, and Fresh Mint Salad

Some people eat their watermelon with a sprinkling of salt. That's the whole idea behind adding feta to this watermelon salad. The saltiness of the cheese combined with cooling, fresh mint makes this the most refreshing salad of the season.

Makes 4 servings

4 cups diced seedless watermelon
1 cup diced feta cheese
½ cup mint leaves, cut into thin strips
2 tablespoons extra virgin olive oil
Freshly ground black pepper

Combine all of the ingredients. Chill to blend flavors. Taste and add salt if desired, but feta cheese serves as the salty component.

Mixed Melon in Rum Syrup

Scoop fresh melons into small balls with a melon baller or simply cube. If fresh blueberries are available, toss in a handful. This salad has it all—the best melons of the season, the best flavors, amazing color …and a little nip of rum and lime to add an exotic flair to homegrown flavors.

Makes 6 servings

¼ cup water
¼ cup sugar
½ cup light rum
⅓ cup freshly squeezed lime juice
1 teaspoon grated lime zest
2 cups cantaloupe, cut into ½-inch cubes
2 cups watermelon, cut into ½-inch cubes
2 cups honeydew melon, cut into ½-inch cubes
1 cup fresh blueberries, optional
Fresh mint leaves, for garnish

Combine the water and sugar in a saucepan. Bring to a boil. Reduce the heat to low and simmer gently, shaking (not stirring) the pan once or twice until the sugar is dissolved. Add the rum and simmer for a few more minutes until the sharp alcohol aroma has disappeared. Remove from the heat and cool for 15 minutes. Add the lime juice and zest.

Combine the melons and blueberries, if using, in a large bowl. Pour the syrup over the melon mixture and toss gently to combine. Cover and chill for up to four hours before serving. Serve as dessert in individual dessert glasses or skewer with toothpicks for appetizers or afterdinner "drinks."

Honeydew Melon Salad

Cool off at the end of a hot summer day with this refreshing salad. Chill the melon cubes for just about an hour so they are refreshing yet the taste still comes through.

Makes 4 servings

4 cups honeydew melon cubes (½-inch cubes), slightly chilled
½ cup freshly chopped mint leaves, more or less to taste
¼ cup freshly chopped cilantro leaves and stems, more or less to taste
3 tablespoons sugar, more or less to taste
1 fresh lime, finely zested and juiced

Toss all of the ingredients together. Chill for 1 hour before serving.

Chilled Cantaloupe Soup

Makes 4 servings

This creamy chilled soup is a special highlight for a summer meal on the patio. Add homemade yogurt (page 29) and crème fraîche (page 50) and some fresh garden mint and tell your guests it's the special of the day in the Locavore's Kitchen. Start the morning with this soup (minus the brandy) when summer heat descends.

1 ripe cantaloupe, skinned, seeded, and cut into ½-inch cubes
1 orange, finely zested and juiced
2 tablespoons apricot brandy or regular brandy (optional)
1 cup plain yogurt
¼ cup sugar, more if necessary
¼ cup crème fraîche
2 tablespoons chopped fresh mint

Using a blender, puree the melon cubes with the orange juice and brandy, if using. Add the yogurt and sugar. Blend until smooth. Chill for 2 hours.

To serve, divide the soup between 4 chilled soup bowls. Garnish each serving with a tablespoon of crème fraîche, a sprinkling of chopped mint, and some of the orange zest.

Melon and Red Pepper Salsa

Makes 5 cups

A trip to the farmers market during the height of the summer harvest will net you almost all of the ingredients for this refreshing salsa. Enjoy it with salty tortilla chips or as a relish to accompany grilled chicken or fish.

2 cups watermelon, cut into small dice
2 cups cantaloupe, cut into small dice
½ red bell pepper, cut into small dice
1 small sweet onion, cut into small dice
¼ cup freshly chopped cilantro
1 jalapeño pepper, minced
2 tablespoons chopped fresh mint
1 lime, finely zested and juiced
Salt, to taste

Combine all of the ingredients in a bowl. Gently toss to combine. Let sit at room temperature for an hour before serving.

Watermelon and Green Peppercorn Salsa

Makes about 4½ cups

Here's another twist on melon-based salsas you're sure to love. Sweet, cool watermelon gets a spicy, fruity kick from piquant, aromatic green peppercorns. It's a combination you wouldn't imagine would work and one you won't soon forget.

2 tablespoons minced red onion
4 cups watermelon, cut into small dice, seeds discarded
3 tablespoons freshly squeezed lime juice
1 to 2 tablespoons dried green peppercorns, coarsely crushed
3 tablespoons freshly chopped cilantro (optional)
Dash cayenne pepper
Salt, to taste

Place all of the ingredients in a medium bowl and toss to combine. Cover and refrigerate for up to three hours. Toss just before serving.

Fresh Watermelon Cooler

Makes 4 cups

What a delicious way to keep your cool on a hot summer day! Make sure that the watermelon is as sweet as can be. To save yourself the hassle of removing the seeds, use a seedless variety. The few soft seeds will disappear in the blender.

3 cups chopped watermelon, seeds removed, if necessary, and discarded
4 tablespoons sugar
3 tablespoons lime juice
2 cups water

Puree the watermelon, sugar, and lime juice in a blender, working in batches, if necessary. Stir the water with the fruit mixture (do this in a separate container if the blender is not large enough). Pour through a fine-mesh sieve to remove the pulp; discard the pulp. Cover and chill. (This juice will keep for a week in the refrigerator.) Serve in tall glasses over ice, garnishing with chunks of fresh watermelon or slices of lime.

Gingered Watermelon Rind Relish

Makes 6 half-pint jars

When you're done with the sweet flesh of the watermelon, make good use of the rinds in this sweet and spicy, hot and tangy relish. It will keep for 2 months in the refrigerator, but if you opt to can it, you'll thank yourself in the winter.

If not canning, simply transfer the relish to a container and let cool before sealing with a tight-fitting lid and refrigerating.

6 cups ½-inch cubes watermelon rind (remove the green skin before cubing)
2 cups sugar
¼ cup grated fresh ginger
4 cloves garlic, minced
1½ cups apple cider vinegar
1½ cups water
1 teaspoon crushed black peppercorns
1 jalapeño, seeded and minced
1 tablespoon kosher salt

In a large saucepan, combine all of the ingredients and bring them to a boil over medium heat, stirring occasionally. Reduce the heat to low and simmer for about one hour, stirring occasionally, until the watermelon rind is tender and translucent.

Ladle the relish into half-pint jars, to within ½ inch of the rim (headspace), and process for 10 minutes.

New to pickling? For a step-by-step guide to the basics, see "Pickled Vegetables, Relishes, and Salsas" on page 239.

Local Flavor

cheese

It's easy to find the local cheesemaker at farmers markets. Just look for the spot where people stand three deep every week, patiently waiting their turn. That's a good sign that whatever is at the front of the line is worth the wait.

Artisan and homestead cheeses are enjoying a revival all across the country, claiming space in the cheese case at specialty stores, on local restaurant menus, and at farmers markets. There's big flavor in cheeses coming out of small creameries: complex in taste, wide in variety, and completely unique from creamery to creamery, region to region, even season to season—welcome contrasts to the standardized flavors of mass-produced cheeses, shipped and sold quickly in large-scale operations.

When the word *farmstead* appears on the label, the milk used to produce the cheese comes from the cheesemaker's on-farm herd, rich milk from cows, sheep, or goats that spend their days grazing on fertile fields, natural diets that produce the purest, most wholesome milk possible and most often without the use of growth hormones or antibiotics. The label *artisan* or *artisanal* means that the milk used to produce the cheese comes from another source, no less wonderful, usually a partnership the cheesemaker forms with a local dairy farmer.

Farmstead and artisan cheeses are made by hand, using traditional and old-fashioned methods often learned at the side of world-class cheesemakers. It includes low-temperature warming of fresh milk to preserve the enzymes and fragile proteins that help form the curd. Natural cultures and rennets are used, and the curds are cut, packed, and pressed into forms by hand and turned many times to remove the whey. Some are sold fresh and others left to age or ripen to further develop flavor and textural character.

When cheesemakers are good at their craft, their work will reflect the flavor of the region in every sliver. Pay close attention to the names that cheesemakers give their cheeses. It's not surprising to find them named after ancestors, nuances of the region, or even local history, adding another important local connection.

Most creameries have signature cheeses like classic ricotta, feta, and chèvre, the tangy goat milk cheese; pressed cured cheese like cheddars or those with a soft bloomy rind; pungent cheeses like Munster and an ever-expanding selection of blue cheeses. Still, they see their craft as a constantly evolving one, creating or discovering the next new cheese for you to sample. They hope their customers come to expect—and look forward to—the unexpected.

Goat Cheesecake with Fresh Peaches

Makes 8 to 10 servings

This goat cheesecake has a tangy, fresh taste and a creamy texture and is just begging to keep company with seasonal fresh fruit like ripe, juicy peaches or other stone fruit, cherries, or seasonal berries. It's a cake for all reasons and seasons and needs no further embellishment. For another quick topping to this cheesecake, spread a cup of the Peach Ginger Jam (page 105) on top and chill before slicing.

¾ cup sugar, plus extra

¾ pound goat cheese, at room temperature

1 teaspoon grated lemon zest

2 teaspoons freshly squeezed lemon juice

1 teaspoon pure vanilla extract

6 large eggs, at room temperature, separated

3 tablespoons all-purpose flour

2 cups chopped fresh peaches (about 3 large peaches, peeled and pitted)

Cinnamon, to taste (optional)

Butter a 9-inch springform pan and sprinkle the bottom with sugar. Set aside. Position one oven rack in the middle position and one in the lowest position. Place a small ovenproof dish or pan on the bottom rack. (You'll be adding boiling water to this pan later.) Preheat the oven to 350°F. Place water on the stove to boil.

In a large mixing bowl, beat the goat cheese together with ¾ cup of sugar on medium speed until light and fluffy, about 5 minutes. Mix in the lemon zest, juice, and vanilla extract. Add the egg yolks, one at a time, beating well between each addition. Mix in the flour.

In a separate mixing bowl and using the whisk attachment, beat the egg whites on high speed until stiff peaks form. Mix ⅓ of the egg whites into the goat cheese mixture. Gently fold in the remaining egg whites. Pour the mixture into the prepared pan.

Place the pan on the middle rack. To the pan on the lowest rack, add boiling water to reach halfway up the pan.

Bake for 25 to 30 minutes or until the cake is set yet jiggles slightly in the middle. The cake will firm up as it cools. Remove to a wire rack to cool. (Cake may be made a day ahead and refrigerated in the springform pan.)

When ready to serve, remove from the springform pan.

To prepare the topping, chop the peaches into bite-size pieces. Sweeten, as needed, with sugar and season with cinnamon, if desired. Top the cheesecake just before serving.

. . . .

what are raw milk cheeses?

Raw milk cheeses, whether from goat, sheep, or cow's milk, are made from milk that has not been pasteurized or heated prior to the cheese-making process. Depending on the variety of cheese, the milk is then heated to anywhere from 90°F to 122°F, keeping alive hundreds of strains of bacteria that interact with the milk, allowing the cheese to develop greater and deeper flavors. The resulting cheese must be aged for 60 days or longer at a temperature of not less than 35°F in accordance with US FDA regulations. Raw milk cheeses prepared this way are perfectly safe to eat.

Cucumber Mint Salsa with Feta

Fresh summer flavors from the garden are right at home with the addition of fresh, salty feta. Serve this as a salsa or chop the vegetables in larger pieces for a salad course.

Makes 6 appetizer servings

1 thin-skinned, seedless cucumber, unpeeled and chopped
¼ cup freshly chopped mint
¼ cup minced red onion
1 clove garlic, minced
2 tablespoons freshly squeezed lemon juice, divided use
½ tablespoon extra virgin olive oil
½ cup crumbled feta cheese
½ cup chopped fresh tomatoes
Freshly ground black pepper, to taste
Mint leaves for garnish
Toasted pita chips, to accompany

In a medium bowl, combine the cucumber, chopped mint, onion, and garlic. Sprinkle 1 tablespoon lemon juice and the oil over the mixture and toss to combine. Season to taste with salt and pepper. Arrange in a shallow serving bowl and top with the cheese and tomatoes. Season to taste with pepper, sprinkle the remaining lemon juice over the top, garnish with mint leaves, and serve with toasted pita chips.

. . . .

storing and serving cheeses

Artisan and farmstead cheeses are treasures, fresh and full flavored, pure and a wonderful reflection of the dedication of the cheesemaker. They deserve special treatment not only on the plate but also in the refrigerator. The best place to store cheese is in the coolest part of the refrigerator, usually the bottom drawer. When you're ready to serve the cheese, let it sit at room temperature for about an hour for the best flavor. Here are some important tips and suggestions for storing specific varieties of these precious finds.

Fresh cheeses like chèvre, fromage blanc, ricotta, cottage cheese, or creamed cheese are highly perishable and should be refrigerated and used soon after buying. Keep tightly covered and well chilled.

Soft cheese such as mozzarella or feta should be stored in its whey to keep it from drying out and should be used within 4 to 5 days. Good cheesemakers know to include whey with your purchase.

Bloomy rind cheeses, including some chèvre, should be stored in a sealable container with holes punched in it for air circulation. Place a piece of parchment paper over the cut portions of the cheese. Put a clean, slightly damp towel on the bottom for added humidity.

Rindless cheeses like Gouda and Havarti, which are not aged long, can be wrapped in waxed paper and a layer of plastic wrap to help retain moisture.

Blue-veined cheeses should be wrapped tightly in plastic or aluminum foil and stored apart from other cheeses so their pungent aroma and natural molds won't be transferred.

Hard, aged cheeses like some cheddars and grating cheeses have little moisture content and are long lasting. Wrap them tightly in a layer of waxed or parchment paper and another layer of aluminum foil. Open them to the air on occasion and they will actually improve with age in the refrigerator.

in season ... eggplant

Cooks have been led to believe that eggplant is a bitter vegetable that needs extra attention—you would be, too, if you were so misunderstood. Picked at the right time and the right size, eggplant is simple to work with and eager to please. Rather than delivering big, bold flavor, cooked eggplant has a mild taste and creamy texture, serving as a blank canvas to absorb seasonings, sauces, and marinades. It lends itself to a wide repertoire of cooking techniques, including steaming, sautéing, frying, broiling, baking, grilling, and roasting.

One size or color does not fit all when it comes to varieties of eggplant. In fact, few other vegetables think so outside the box. The packaging is different, from pudgy purple ovals, to elongated lavender-colored versions, to softball-sized globes in oranges and whites, but all eggplant is similar in flavor and texture.

Choosing the Best. Regardless of color or shape, look for firm, shiny fruits, free of soft spots or wrinkles, with a fresh green cap or calyx. Needle-like spikes around the stem are a tip-off that the eggplant is fresh. It should feel heavy for its size—if it feels light, it will be pulpy. Press the eggplant with your thumb. If it doesn't give, it has been picked too early; if the indentation remains, it's overly ripe; and if it springs back, it's perfect. Fresh, ripe eggplant is not bitter, but those that are overripe and stored too long are spongy, seedy, and likely bitter.

How to Store Fresh. The best way to store eggplant is to not store it at all. Use it soon after it is picked or bought. If storing is necessary, eggplants prefer cool, not cold, temperatures. Wrap them loosely in plastic and store for a day or two in the refrigerator's crisper drawer. Much more than that and you'll notice a change in texture. Rinse under cool water and pat dry if leaving the skin on for a recipe.

To Prepare for Cooking. Picking or purchasing eggplant young and fresh solves two classic struggles: eliminating bitterness and peeling. Peeling eggplant is a matter of preference. If a recipe has a long cooking time and the eggplant is thinly sliced, it's usually enough to soften most skins, but when in doubt, remove the skin with a vegetable peeler. Bitterness comes with age, so if a recipe calls for salting and draining, skip this step when working with truly fresh eggplant. It will just add unnecessary salt.

Pick or Buy Now, Enjoy Later. Some sources offer instructions for blanching and freezing eggplant. Beware that as eggplant thaws, it releases a significant amount of water and that will change the texture and the outcome of a recipe. Therefore, it's not highly recommended.

Eggplant Caviar

Makes 4 to 6 appetizer servings

Why call this caviar? Perhaps because it's just as delicious and special as the real thing except more economical, certainly local, and definitely seasonal. Use as an appetizer at a small gathering or serve it on thicker slices of toasted bread to accompany a summer salad.

1 large eggplant (about 1½ pounds)
1 tablespoon extra virgin olive oil, plus extra for brushing
1 small onion, chopped
1 small red bell pepper, chopped
2 cloves garlic, minced
3 tablespoons freshly squeezed lemon juice
2 teaspoons dried dill weed or 4 teaspoons fresh dill
Salt and freshly ground black pepper, to taste
Toasted baguette slices, to accompany

Preheat the oven to 350°F.

Slice the eggplant in half lengthwise and brush the cut surface liberally with olive oil. Season lightly with salt and pepper and place cut side down on a rimmed baking sheet. Roast for one hour or until the eggplant is tender and collapsed. Let cool.

Meanwhile heat the tablespoon of oil in a skillet. Add the onion and red pepper and sauté until soft and fragrant, about 6 minutes. Add the garlic and sauté for an additional minute. Transfer to the bowl of a food processor.

Using a spoon, scrape the eggplant pulp into the bowl of the food processor, discarding the skin. Add the lemon juice and dill. Pulse until the vegetables are coarsely chopped, not pureed. Taste and season with salt and pepper. Serve warm or cold with toasted baguette slices.

Toasted Baguette Slices: Preheat the oven to 375°F. Cut one 10-inch baguette into ¼-inch slices. Brush the tops of the bread slices lightly with olive oil and season with salt and pepper, if desired. Arrange on a baking sheet. Bake for 10 to 12 minutes or until golden brown. Remove and let cool.

Grilled Eggplant Salad

Makes 6 servings

Out of all the cooking techniques that complement eggplant, cooking over a smoky grill has to rank number one. Choose fresh slender eggplants, round varieties, or a combination of the two. Serve as a salad or a side dish with grilled chicken.

6 to 7 slender eggplants, ends trimmed and cut crosswise into 1-inch wide slices
9 tablespoons extra virgin olive oil, divided use
4 ounces goat cheese or feta cheese, crumbled
⅓ cup fresh basil leaves, sliced into thin strips
3 tablespoons chopped fresh mint leaves
½ cup toasted nuts (pine nuts or walnuts)
3 tablespoons balsamic vinegar
½ teaspoon sea salt
½ teaspoon freshly ground black pepper

Preheat a grill to medium.

Place the eggplant slices in a large bowl. Drizzle 3 tablespoons of the oil over the top and toss to coat. Grill the eggplant on both sides, about 3 minutes per side, until tender and grill marks appear. Arrange the grilled eggplant on a serving platter. Scatter the crumbled cheese over the top, followed by the herbs and nuts.

In a small bowl, whisk together the remaining 6 tablespoons olive oil with the balsamic vinegar, salt, and pepper. Drizzle the mixture over the top of the salad and serve hot or at room temperature.

Eggplant Lasagna

Makes 6 servings

Eggplant instead of lasagna noodles makes this normally rich dish light, fresh, and great tasting. Choose the longer eggplants as opposed to the globe varieties for this recipe. If you want to add one more local component, make your own ricotta-style cheese, an easy project found on page 72.

2 large eggplants or 3 medium eggplants, peeled and top trimmed off
2 tablespoons extra virgin olive oil, plus extra for brushing
Salt and freshly ground black pepper
2 cups sliced mushrooms, any one variety or a mix
2 cloves garlic, minced
1 tablespoon freshly chopped thyme leaves
1 pound ricotta cheese
3 large eggs, lightly beaten
1 cup grated Parmesan cheese, divided use
2 tablespoons freshly chopped oregano leaves
1 teaspoon salt
½ teaspoon freshly ground black pepper
2 cups Chunky All-Purpose Tomato Sauce (page 121) or your favorite tomato sauce recipe

Preheat the oven to 400°F. Brush an 8 x 8-inch baking pan with oil. Set aside.

Slice the eggplants into ½-inch slices, lengthwise (these are your "lasagna noodles"). Brush both sides of the slices with oil. Arrange in a single layer on two rimmed baking sheets. Season with salt and pepper. Roast until the slices are soft and golden, turning once halfway through the cooking time, about 25 to 30 minutes. Remove from the oven and set aside to cool.

Heat the two 2 tablespoons of oil in a medium skillet. Add the mushrooms and sauté until soft, about 5 minutes. Add the garlic and thyme leaves and sauté an additional minute. Remove from the heat and set aside to cool slightly.

In a large bowl, mix the ricotta with the eggs, half of the Parmesan, oregano, salt, pepper, and the reserved mushrooms.

To assemble the lasagna, spread half of the tomato sauce in the bottom of the prepared baking dish. Lay half of the eggplant slices on top, overlapping as you go. Spread the ricotta mixture over the eggplant. Layer the remaining eggplant slices over the ricotta mixture. Spread the remaining tomato sauce on top. Bake for 20 minutes. Sprinkle with the remaining cheese and bake for an additional 10 minutes or until the cheese is melted and lightly browned. Let cool for 10 minutes before serving, using a serrated knife to cut through the layers.

• •

eggplant: a battle of the sexes

As long as there have been eggplants, there's been the controversy about which is better, less bitter, and contains fewer seeds—the male or the female. The answer is neither. As fruits, eggplants are neither male nor female, and spending a lot of time trying to identify the sex by dimples and rounded bottoms as a sign of seed content is . . . well, fruitless. It's more about cultivars. While there are a couple of general rules to follow—such as that slender, elongated eggplants have fewer seeds, and their rounder counterparts have more and are less meaty—this question is a good one to pose to the growers themselves who bring these eggplants to market.

Grilled Eggplant Rollups with Goat Cheese

Makes 10 to 12 appetizer servings

Using slender, young eggplants for these delightful grillable rollups will save you the step of peeling since the skins will still be tender. Eggplants about 7 inches long will roll up nicely. You can also substitute feta cheese or a well-drained ricotta for the goat cheese.

4 ounces goat cheese, at room temperature
1 tablespoon finely chopped sundried tomato
¼ cup freshly minced basil leaves
1 teaspoon extra virgin olive oil, plus extra for brushing
Salt and freshly ground black pepper, to taste
3 small eggplants, long and slender variety
2 tablespoons freshly grated Parmesan cheese

Combine the goat cheese, sundried tomatoes, basil, and the teaspoon of olive oil in a small bowl. Set aside.

Heat the grill to medium-high. Trim the stem end of the eggplants and slice each lengthwise into ¼-inch-thick slices. Brush each side of the eggplant slices with oil and season with salt and pepper. Grill the slices on both sides, about 3 to 4 minutes per side, until grill marks appear and the slices soften. Transfer to a cooling rack.

Spread a teaspoon of the filling over one side of each of the grilled eggplant slices. Roll the eggplant slices up tightly. Arrange on a foil-lined baking sheet, seam side down. (At this point, the rolls can be covered in plastic wrap and refrigerated for several hours. Bring to room temperature before proceeding.)

Heat the broiler. Sprinkle the Parmesan cheese over the rolls and brown under the broiler for one minute.

Glazed Broiled Eggplant

Makes 4 servings

Thick slices of fresh eggplant soak up this luscious glaze. When it's thrown onto the heat of the grill, the result is a slightly caramelized finish with salty undertones. This is the type of preparation that's perfect for mild, unassuming eggplant.

4 Japanese eggplants (4 to 5 ounces each), unpeeled
¼ cup honey
¼ cup vegetable or canola oil
¼ cup soy sauce
¼ cup lemon juice
1 clove garlic, crushed
¼ teaspoon crushed red pepper flakes
¼ cup chopped fresh parsley or cilantro, for garnish

Slice the eggplants crosswise into ½-inch-thick rounds. Place in a shallow baking dish.

Whisk together the remaining ingredients (except the parsley) for the glaze. Pour over the eggplant slices. Let marinate for 30 minutes, spooning the mixture over the top of the eggplant occasionally. Remove the eggplant from the marinade and arrange in a single layer on a broiler pan. Pour the marinade into a small saucepan and bring to a boil. Reduce the heat to low and simmer until reduced by half. Set aside.

Preheat the broiler. Broil the eggplant 4 inches from the heat until tender, about 4 to 6 minutes per side. Brush with the reduced marinade, sprinkle with chopped parsley, and serve.

Fresh herbs add the color, fragrance, and flavors to our food and announce the season. Tender, slender chive leaves and blossoms are a sure sign of spring—as sure as a robin's song. Feathery dill fronds and big round seed heads remind us it's time to can pickles or make potato salad for a summer potluck. Big bunches of basil tell us to start checking the garden or farmers markets for the return of tomatoes.

There are lots of fresh herbs we can plant or expect to find at farmers markets to add to our cooking, and planning ahead ensures that we'll have them beyond the harvest. Some freeze well, others are better dried. To get you in the mood, think ahead to when a taste of fresh, cool mint or pretty purple chive blossoms would add an element of surprise to winter cooking. For now, fresh herbs are a simple and delicious way to add even more character to seasonal foods.

Choosing the Best. Of course, if the herbs are growing in your garden, freshness is a given. The best time to harvest them is in the morning, before the afternoon sun has a chance to dry them out. At markets, the universal rule is to look for vibrant color and aroma when choosing fresh herbs. Simply brushing your hand over a bunch of herbs or crushing a leaf or two between your fingers should release a wave of wonderful fragrance. Black spots, yellow tired-looking leaves, and off odors signal that flavor is waning.

How to Store Fresh. Fresh herbs should be washed and blotted dry before refrigerating. Store them in an airtight container for up to 4 days. If you can devote the space, use glass jars with tight-fitting lids. Other odors in the refrigerator will not permeate the glass. You can also make a fresh cut in the bottom of the stem, place in a deep glass filled with a splash of water, and cover loosely with a plastic bag. Store in the warmest part of the refrigerator, usually the top shelf. Change the water daily and you'll extend the life (and looks) of fresh herbs for a few more days.

To Prepare for Cooking. For most herbs, stripping the leaves off thick woody stems is all that's needed before using. When it comes to cilantro, the stems carry as much taste as the leaves; and with chives, the thin leaves and blossoms can both be used. Always cut herbs with a sharp knife just before adding them to your recipe. Some recipes will call for "bruising" whole leaves—lightly crushing to release the fragrant oils—but in general most herbs prefer a gentle touch.

A Sampler of Garden Variety Herbs and How to Preserve Them

This list of herbs, describing their flavors, culinary capabilities, and how to preserve their flavor for your recipes year round, is truly a sampler. There are many other herbs to be found, cultivated, and harvested, but this list includes the herbs most frequently used, most often homegrown, and most likely to be found at farmers markets.

Basil. Basil is possibly the most widely used fresh herb in the kitchen. Fresh basil leaves have a sweet, spicy flavor and a personality that doesn't back down from garlic in pestos and sauces. Look for unusual varieties of basil, too, including purple basil, a beautiful contrast on the plate, or Thai basils, a bit spicier and perfect for Asian dishes.

Classic Basil Pesto (page 89) is a good way to use the seasonal flavor of basil, and it freezes beautifully, too.

Bay Leaves. Bay leaf has a genuine flavor that has escaped most cooks because it is primarily available in a lifeless dried form. Freshly harvested leaves are highly aromatic, sweet, and somewhat astringent. Once you've experienced fresh bay, dried will never do. Add to poaching liquids, soups, and rice, or in the recipe for Bay-Poached Pears on page 87. Remove the leaf before serving.

Preserve by storing whole leaves in an airtight container or heavy-duty plastic bag and freeze for up to 6 months.

Chives. Chives' thin leaves and pretty lilac blossoms are the first herbs to appear in the spring, and both add a pleasant, fresh onion-like flavor to cold and cooked recipes and baked goods. Sprinkle chives on soups, salads, potatoes, or spring vegetables, or mix into butters. Try the recipe for Honey and Chive Butter on page 111.

Preserve by snipping the tender leaves into small pieces or harvesting the blossoms by separating them from the stem. Store loosely in freezer containers. They won't keep their crisp texture but they will hold their taste and color.

Cilantro. Cilantro, the broad, scalloped leaves and stems of the coriander plant, is highly pungent, aromatic, and assertive, which is why you'll often find it in recipes that also feature a lot of garlic, chiles, or hot spices, like Margaret's Salsa on page 121. Once the plant flowers, it goes to seed—coriander seeds. Crushed or ground, they spice up food like the Sweet Pumpkin with Yogurt Sauce on page 200 with lemon-like flavor.

Preserve fresh cilantro leaves by packing ice cube trays with whole leaves and adding a little water. When the cubes are solid, store in a freezer bag for up to 3 months.

Coriander seeds can be air-dried and stored in an airtight container. Crush or grind just before using.

Dill. Dill's feathery bluish-green leaves have a distinct, spicy green flavor that goes well with cucumber and can be used fresh to liven up dips, fresh salads, and potato salads. Without the fresh taste of dill, pickles wouldn't be pickles or as delicious. Taste for yourself in Classic Garlic Dill Pickles or Sweet Garlic Dills on page 54.

Preserve by drying the fronds, the best way to retain dill's flavor and intensity. Harvest and dry the whole seeds from the flower heads and toss some into the jar when canning pickles or grind them to season cooked cabbage or apples.

Fennel. Fennel looks a little like dill and is harvested the same way (leaves and seeds), but the taste is remarkably different, licorice-like and highly aromatic. Chop the wispy, fresh leaves and tender stems for egg salads and soups or use the seeds in breads and baking or experience every bit in Braised Fennel on page 87.

Preserve by freezing the fronds separated from the stem in a freezer bag for up to 4 weeks. Fennel holds its flavor for a much shorter time than other herbs even when frozen. Harvest and dry the whole seeds from the flower heads and store in an airtight jar for 6 months. Crush or grind as needed.

Mints. Aromatic and refreshing, mint is a great way to trick the body into cooling down on a hot summer day. There are more than two hundred species of mint to plant, from exotic pineapple orange to chocolate mint. Good all-purpose spearmint should be used for warm dishes, including teas, and peppermint for cooling dishes, like salads and cold beverages.

Preserve the whole leaves by drying or by freezing, packed in ice cube trays. Add a little water and freeze until solid, then remove and pack in freezer bags. A better idea would be to turn a batch of mint into Mint Pesto (page 90).

Oregano and Marjoram. Oregano and marjoram are close enough in looks and flavor that you can substitute one for the other as long as you're aware of the subtle differences. Greek oregano, the preferred variety of oregano, is strong and spicy, somewhat bitter, and makes the tongue tingle. Sweet marjoram has a sweeter citrus flavor and a gentler mouth feel than oregano. Neither holds its flavor well in long-cooked sauces or soups, so add the herb, fresh or dried, toward the end of cooking.

Preserve by drying the leaves. Both oregano and marjoram also can be pureed with a bit of olive oil; place the puree in pint-sized freezer bags and smooth them flat. When frozen, break off pieces or portions as needed.

Parsley. Parsley has long been regarded as nothing more than a garnish, when in reality it can be the star ingredient of a few dishes like Gremolata on page 87. Choose the flat-leaf variety, which compared to curly parsley is more fragrant, less bitter, and has a bit of a celery-like taste.

Preserve by freezing whole sprigs to toss into stocks or by chopping the leaves, packing into ice cube trays with a little water, freezing, and then storing in freezer bags. Frozen parsley will lose its texture, but the color and flavor will prevail so it's best for soups and cooked dishes.

Rosemary. Rosemary is unique in that it does not lose its piney flavor or tea-like aroma in recipes that require long cooking. Use fresh rosemary sparingly to flavor roasted vegetables and meats. The Grilled Herb-Rubbed Flank Steak on page 93 and Rosemary and Walnut Shortbreads on page 212 are delicious ways to enjoy fresh rosemary.

Preserve by washing and drying whole sprigs and storing them in freezer bags, squeezing out most of the air. The rosemary still keeps its strong flavor and the leaves remain soft and pliable, almost like fresh. When you reach into the bag, you'll notice that after time the leaves will have fallen away from the branches.

Sage. Sage is another dominant, slightly bitter-tasting aromatic that is at its best teamed with equally strong flavors like garlic and pepper. It naturally pairs with onion and poultry stuffing and adds flavor to rich, fatty meats, including pork and sausage, or takes center stage in Fried Sage Fritters on page 87.

Preserve by freezing whole sage leaves in small freezer bags. Be aware that freezing will intensify the taste of sage, so season accordingly. Most cooks like to use sage dried and ground to a fine, velvety texture or coarse finish.

Tarragon. Tarragon has a strong flavor and aroma reminiscent of licorice and is best used as the solo herb in dishes. Cooked too long, it becomes bitter. Use the twisted, dark green leaves of the French variety sparingly to flavor cream sauces for meat, poultry, and fish or to infuse vinegar (see page 62) to use in vinaigrettes.

Preserve by chopping the leaves by hand or in a food processor and packing in small freezer bags, pressing as much air out as possible before sealing. Tarragon loses its flavor when dried.

Thyme. Thyme is most at home in slowly cooked foods, like stocks, braised meats, and roasted chicken. While there are more than 100 varieties of thyme, mild-flavored common thyme with a pungent, woody aroma and citrusy lemon thyme can be widely used in the locavore's kitchen. For making stocks (page 143), thyme is always a welcome, aromatic ingredient—or make it part of the fresh herb mix in the Fresh Herb and Cream Cheese Sampler on page 87.

Preserve by drying the leaves after they have been stripped from the branches. Thyme holds its flavor better than most herbs after drying.

. . . .

substituting dried herbs for fresh

Certain recipes, like those for pesto and gremolata, rely on fresh herbs as the central component of the dish. When it comes to soups, stews, sauces, salad dressings, or dips where the herbs are suspended in liquids to infuse their flavor throughout, feel free to substitute dried herbs for fresh.

When using dried herbs in place of fresh, remember that the water in them has evaporated, making the essential oils more concentrated—so use less. The conversion is simple: 1 tablespoon fresh = 1 teaspoon dried. And always taste as you season to achieve the correct balance and flavor in a recipe.

Bay-Poached Pears

Bay leaves are used as aromatics, enjoyed in subtle ways. To experience the taste of fresh bay leaves, try this recipe in which the flavor of fresh bay infuses local white wine and is absorbed by pears. You can also substitute fresh peaches, but keep a watchful eye on the cooking time.

Makes 4 servings

2 fresh pears, halved, and seeds scooped out
1 cup local sweet white wine
1 or 2 fresh bay leaves
2 tablespoons honey
1 teaspoon pure vanilla extract
2 tablespoons unsalted butter, cut into small dice and at room temperature
4 slices of vanilla pound cake or 4 scoops of vanilla ice cream

Preheat the oven to 325°F.
Arrange pears cut side up in an 8-inch square baking dish. Set aside.
In a small saucepan, combine the wine and bay leaf. Bring to a boil and cook for 7 to 10 minutes or until reduced by half. Stir in the honey and vanilla until blended. Whisk in the butter until smooth. Pour over the pears. Bake, uncovered, for 20 to 25 minutes or until the pears are thoroughly heated and soft but still hold their shape. Remove the bay leaf.
Serve the warm pears over pound cake or vanilla ice cream. Drizzle with the remaining poaching liquid.

Braised Fennel

Fennel is made up of the bulb, the stalks, and the fronds (or leaves)—and every bit is edible. In this recipe, the juicy bulb and feathery fronds are used to turn out a simple dish where long slow cooking brings out the sweetness.

Makes 6 servings

2 fennel bulbs (about 10 ounces each), with fronds
2 tablespoons extra virgin olive oil
Salt and freshly ground black pepper
¾ cup rich chicken stock
¼ cup grated Parmesan cheese

Preheat the oven to 350°F.
Cut off and discard the stalks from fennel bulbs, reserving fronds. Chop enough of the fronds to measure 2 tablespoons.
Cut a thick slice off the root end of the bulb. Slice the bulb in half. Remove the hard inner core and cut each half into 4 wedges.
Heat the oil in a large heavy skillet over medium-high heat. Add the fennel wedges and brown the cut sides well, about 2 minutes per side. Reduce the heat to low. Sprinkle with salt and pepper, then add the stock. Cover and cook until the fennel is tender, about 12 to 15 minutes. Remove from the heat and sprinkle with cheese and the chopped fennel fronds. Serve immediately.

Gremolata

Gremolata is a condiment with just a few simple ingredients and is a great companion to fish and meaty dishes and stews. Swirl a few tablespoons into soups and stews to brighten the taste.

Makes about ⅓ cup

1 fresh lemon
¼ cup finely chopped fresh parsley
3 garlic cloves, finely chopped

Using a vegetable peeler, remove the lemon peel in long thin strips. Finely minced the peel. Transfer to a small bowl and mix in parsley and garlic. Cover and store unused potion in the refrigerator for up to 3 days.

Fried Sage Fritters

Rarely do sage leaves get the spotlight all to themselves. This recipe turns fresh sage leaves into exciting little appetizer bites that play on the strong taste of sage.

Makes 8 or more appetizer servings

¾ cup all-purpose flour
Pinch of salt
2 tablespoons extra virgin olive oil
4 tablespoons warm water
1 large egg white
Vegetable or canola oil, for frying
20 to 30 large fresh sage leaves, rinsed and completely dried

Mix the flour, salt, oil, and water in a small bowl until smooth and creamy. Set aside for a few hours.
Beat the egg white until stiff. Fold it into the batter.
Heat 1 inch of oil in a large heavy skillet with deep sides. Holding each leaf by its stem, dip into the batter until completely coated. Fry several leaves at a time, taking care not to crowd the skillet, for 2 to 3 minutes or until golden brown.
Transfer to a paper towel–lined plate to drain.

Fresh Herb and Cream Cheese Sampler

If you want your guests to experience the fresh taste or the difference in taste between fresh garden herbs, try this simple appetizer. Experiment with mixing different herbs to come up with unexpected flavor sensations, like mint and basil. You can also roll the balls in sea salt, freshly ground black pepper, crushed red pepper, or grated lemon zest before rolling in the herbs.

Makes 16 balls

1 8-ounce package cream cheese
Finely chopped fresh herbs (dill, parsley, chives, rosemary, thyme, mint, basil, fennel)

Divide the cheese into 16 equal portions and roll into small balls. Roll each ball in either one type of herb or a combination. Arrange on a serving platter, chill for 1 hour, and serve on toothpicks.

On Drying Herbs

There's nothing complicated or magical about drying herbs. Drying gets rid of the water that otherwise would cause fresh, tender herbs to mold if you were trying to store them long-term. Slow-drying bundles of herbs preserves their essential oils, the very compounds that possess the flavor you're attempting to capture. It's a process that works best with herbs that don't have a lot of water to begin with, such as dill, oregano, marjoram, rosemary, sage, thyme, and parsley. Basil, chives, mint, cilantro, and tarragon hold their flavor and color better if frozen.

Ready to "Dry"?

- Cutting your own herbs? Do it midmorning when the dew has dried from the leaves and before the hot afternoon sun has a chance to wilt them. If you're buying them from the farmers market, make sure the bundles look and smell fresh. (See "Choosing the Best" on page 84)

- Harvest the herbs before they flower. Once they begin to flower, the plants stop leaf production. You can dry herbs anytime during the growing season. Remember that if left to flower and go to seed, herbs like dill, fennel, and coriander still have a useful culinary life. Harvest the dried seeds and use when recipes call for them, whole or crushed. There's a lot of flavor there!

- Wipe off or shake any leaves free of dirt, grit, or insects. If rinsing is necessary, swish bundles in a large bowl of water. Shake off the water and pat dry with a clean lint-free cotton towel or layers of paper towels. Be gentle. Rough treatment of herbs can bruise and damage the leaves.

- Bundle a small bouquet together and secure at the stems with a rubber band or tie with kitchen or garden twine. As they dry, they will shrink, so make sure the ties are secure. The smaller you make the bundles, the quicker the drying time.

- Using brown paper lunch bags, punch or cut several holes around the bag. Be sure to label the bag with the contents.

- Place the herb bundles in the bags, upside down so the stem ends are at the opening.

- Cinch the bag closed around the stems and tie shut with string.

- Hang the bag in a warm, airy room with good ventilation, such as an attic, linen closet, dry basement, or garden shed.

- Check bundles of thyme and dill after 5 days to see the progress they are making. At 80°F, they may already be dry. If not, check them daily for up to a few more days. Look in on thicker-leafed herbs like oregano and sage after 10 days. If any bundles are sporting mold or smell moldy and musty instead of earthy and reminiscent of their former fresh selves, discard them.

- How do you know when the herbs are dry and ready for storage? When the leaves are brittle and crumble easily, yet your fingertips carry the wonderfully heady aroma of that herb, separate the leaves from their stems and move on to storing them.

Store Dried Herbs to Last

- Store dried herbs in airtight containers such as small canning jars or small sealable plastic bags.

- Take a minute to label and date the containers so you can easily recognize them.

- Store dried herb leaves whole to retain their flavor and aroma. Crushing them releases their essential oils, so for maximum impact, crush them only when you're ready to use them.

- Watch the color of the herbs you've stored. Once the color starts to fade, so will the flavor. Discard them.

- While it's gratifying to admire your work in the kitchen, dried herbs prefer cool spots, away from heat or light. Dedicated freezer space for tightly packaged herbs would be the perfect solution, though not always practical.

Cooking with Herbs: Dried or Fresh

If you're using dried herbs in a recipe that calls for fresh, add them a bit earlier than you would fresh, crushing them with your fingertips before adding. If the dish is particularly long cooking, wait until the last hour to add the herbs.

Dried herbs develop more intense and potent flavors than fresh, so begin by using a teaspoon of dried in place of a tablespoon of the fresh, then taste and adjust to your taste from there.

Beyond stocking your kitchen with dried and frozen herbs to add to soups, stews, and other recipes, you can create vinegars (on page 62) and pestos (on page 89) or herbed butters (on page 111) for the freezer—great ways to make sure the fresh flavor of herbs finds its way to your table year round.

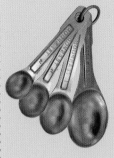

Making Your Own: **Pestos**

Pesto is that classic, vibrant sauce that has a way of enlivening soups, salads, entrees, and side dishes. So when you find yourself with a bumper crop of basil, think pesto. It's a beautiful detail in the locavore's kitchen.

You can easily double or triple recipes and freeze pesto in small batches to keep these great flavors with you throughout the winter. After you've made a batch, transfer it to a glass bowl, cover and refrigerate for eight hours to allow the mixture to firm up. Portion the pesto in one- or two-tablespoon measures onto a parchment-lined baking sheet. Freeze until solid and then transfer the portions to a freezer bag. Pull out what you need later for great dishes like Chicken Pesto Cheesecake on page 204 or Pesto-Stuffed Pork Tenderloin with Hot Pepper Jelly Glaze on page 210.

Here's a trio of easy-to-make pestos, so versatile in their application and inspiration for other pestos, too. Try spinach, parsley, or asparagus pesto (page 5).

Classic Basil Pesto

Fresh basil is the heart and soul of pesto making. Purists would blanch at the thought of preparing pesto in a food processor, but when the harvest hands you bundles instead of batches, it's the best way to get the job done. If you're making only one batch, coarsely chop the basil, nuts, and garlic beforehand, then pound away at the ingredients in the classic style, with a large mortar and pestle.

Makes 1¾ cups

2 cups packed fresh basil, stems removed, washed and dried
¾ cup freshly grated Parmesan cheese
½ cup pine nuts or walnut pieces
2 cloves garlic
¼ teaspoon salt
¼ teaspoon freshly ground black pepper
⅔ cup extra virgin olive oil

Using a food processor, combine all the ingredients except the olive oil. Process until finely chopped, stopping the machine and scraping down the sides if necessary. With the machine running, pour the olive oil through the chute in a slow, steady stream and process until the mixture is blended yet retains a coarse texture. Store in an airtight container for up to a week or freeze in small batches for up to 3 months.

To make a dipping sauce: Combine 3 tablespoons of the prepared pesto with ⅓ cup of olive oil and a pinch of crushed red pepper. Serve as a dipping sauce for crusty breads, sweet melons wrapped in ham, apples, pears, or whatever you desire.

Roasted Red Pepper Pesto

Red Pepper Pesto defies the classic definition of pesto in that there's not a speck of basil to be found, but that doesn't mean a handful wouldn't be welcome. Use this sweet pesto to top roasted potatoes, as a spread on crusty toasted breads, tossed into hot pasta for a quick meal, stirred into softened butter, or at its simple best, used as a condiment for burgers or grilled steaks. Making your own roasted red peppers is easy. See page 158 for complete instructions.

Makes about 1 cup

2 roasted bell peppers
⅓ cup chopped walnuts
2 cloves garlic
3 tablespoons extra virgin olive oil, plus extra if needed
½ teaspoon salt

Using a food processor, combine all the ingredients except the olive oil. Process until finely chopped, stopping the machine and scraping down the sides if necessary. With the machine running, pour the olive oil through the chute in a slow, steady stream and process until the mixture is smooth. Store in an airtight container for up to a week or freeze in small batches for up to 6 months.

To dress up mayonnaise for your sandwich: Mix 1 cup mayonnaise with 2 to 3 tablespoons Roasted Red Pepper Pesto and use it to dress up roast beef or turkey sandwiches. Make it better by making your own mayonnaise (page 125).

Mint Pesto

The beauty and curse of growing mint is that you can end up with a lot in one season. When the season hands you mint, grind it up into pesto. Spread this cooling condiment on grilled lamb burgers, seared lamb chops, or mild fish; toss it with steamed new potatoes; or use it to "fancy up" grilled asparagus.

Makes 1 cup

2 cups packed fresh mint leaves, stems removed, washed and dried
½ cup pine nuts or almonds, toasted
2 cloves garlic
2 tablespoons (packed) feta cheese
2 tablespoons grated Parmesan cheese
1 tablespoon coarsely chopped jalapeño (optional)
½ teaspoon salt
½ teaspoon freshly ground black pepper
2 tablespoons freshly squeezed lemon juice
⅓ cup extra virgin olive oil

Using a food processor, combine all the ingredients except the olive oil. Process until finely chopped, stopping the machine to scrape down the sides if necessary. With the machine running, pour the olive oil through the chute in a slow, steady stream and process until the mixture is blended yet retains a coarse texture. Store in an airtight container for up to a week or freeze in small batches for up to 3 months.

To make a quick, refreshing salad: Combine 2 cups of cooked orzo with one pint of ripe cherry tomatoes, halved, and mix with 3 tablespoons of mint pesto or more to taste. Top with some crumbled feta and a grinding of black pepper. Makes 4 servings.

Penne Pasta with Pesto and Goat Cheese

This is the kind of dish that makes you happy to have the batch of Classic Basil Pesto (page 89) or Roasted Red Pepper Pesto (page 89) you made this summer. Rich and creamy, it's a quick meal that seems far more special. Serve with crusty bread and a cup of homemade tomato soup.

Makes 4 servings

1 pound penne pasta
1 cup prepared pesto (thawed, if frozen)
½ cup (4 ounces) goat cheese, softened
Salt and freshly ground black pepper, to taste
Freshly grated Parmesan cheese, if desired

Cook the pasta in a large pot of boiling, salted water until al dente, firm to the bite yet cooked through. Drain in a colander, reserving 1 cup of the pasta water. Cover and keep warm.

Warm the pesto in a large sauté pan over low heat. Whisk in the goat cheese until the mixture is smooth and warm. Toss the cooked pasta into the pesto mixture and stir over very low heat 1 minute until thoroughly coated and warm. Add enough of the reserved pasta water until smooth and creamy. Taste and season with salt and freshly ground black pepper, to taste. Serve immediately with a grating of Parmesan cheese, if desired.

Local Flavor

grass-fed beef

If you've ever wanted to ask a farmer or rancher who raises grass-fed beef cattle to explain the difference between their beef and that from cattle raised in conventional ways, do it when you have a little time on your hands. The answer might not be short, but it is sure to be passionate and educational.

"Grass-fed" is not just about what the animal eats. You'll learn that allowing animals to graze naturally using rotational grazing methods is good for the environment and that growing or raising food for one's neighbors is key to developing a sustainable community. You'll hear that raising livestock this way is more humane than feedlots, that it saves energy, eliminates the farm's dependence on pesticides and chemical fertilizers, and promises better food safety, and that there's a direct connection between healthy herds and healthy food. At some point, you'll get around to the taste.

If you shop at farmers markets, you're sure to come across two types of producers: those who raise their cattle strictly on grass and those who raise beef on grass and finish on grain. You will always find farmers and locavores who prefer one over the other for taste, tenderness, and nutrition. There's no official definition for grass-fed meats, so it's important to begin a dialogue with the farmer and then do some tasting yourself.

Cattle that are 100 percent grass fed feed on live pasture spring through fall and on dry grasses when the pasture is dormant. The result is lean beef low in intramuscular fat, so it requires simple yet attentive cooking methods. Cattle finished on grain develop additional fat and marbling in the meat, combining tenderness, juiciness, and flavor.

There are a lot of variables that affect grass-fed meats in subtle ways. More than one breed of cattle thrives on grass. The popular Angus are adaptable foragers known for naturally marbled, tender beef; Herefords are efficient at converting native grasses to tasty, tender beef; Galloways forage on coarse grasses, require less food through the winter, and produce high-quality beef; and beef from Highlands is lean, flavorful, and well marbled. Where and how they are raised, even the way they are butchered, comes through in the look, texture, flavor, and smell of the meat, in ways that are both subtle and good.

Grass-fed beef gives us a reason to linger at the table or gather around the grill. It takes almost twice as long for a farmer to raise cattle on this natural diet. Shouldn't it command more of your time to savor the flavor?

Cheeseburgers

Makes 4 servings

Because grass-fed beef is so lean, adding cheese to the mix is a smart way to compensate for the lack of fat in the meat. Use hard, aged cheddars, sharp-flavored cheeses or other grating cheeses, or pungent blue cheeses.

1½ pounds lean ground beef (80% lean)
1 teaspoon kosher salt
½ teaspoon black pepper
1 cup shredded cheese or crumbled cheese, such as feta or blue cheeses
Oil for the cooking grate

Using you fingers, break up the ground chuck and place in a large bowl. Sprinkle with the salt and pepper. Add the cheese and toss lightly with your fingertips to mix, evenly distributing the cheese. Divide the mix into 4 equal portions, about 6 ounces each. Using cupped hands, toss each portion of meat back and forth to form a loose ball. Pat lightly to flatten the meat into a ¾-inch-thick burger, about 4 inches in diameter. On one side, create a divot or depression in the middle of the patty. Repeat with the remaining portions of the meat. The patties can be made earlier in the day, covered loosely with plastic wrap, and stored in the refrigerator.

Ever notice how sometimes a burger puffs up on the grill as it cooks, leaving you with a round patty, so the condiments you put on top slide off? Burgers cook from the outside in, pushing up the middle as they do. Making a divot on one side of the uncooked patty helps create a flatter surface and a better platform for mustard and ketchup.

When ready to grill the burgers, heat the grill until medium-hot, about 15 minutes. Lightly oil the grill grate with a paper towel dipped in oil and held with long-handled tongs. Grill the burgers with the lid down, divot side up, until well seared, about 3 to 4 minutes. Do not press down on the meat while cooking. Flip to the other side and continue grilling to desired doneness, about 2 minutes for rare, 3 minutes for medium rare, and 4 minutes for well done.

Serve immediately on buns with desired condiments.

Garlicky Beef Stew

Makes 4 servings

Braising and stewing are good techniques for turning muscular, tougher cuts of beef into meltingly tender, delicious dishes. Long-cooking and better reserved for weekend meals, this stew comes together quickly, spends a lot of time in the oven, and will scent the house with an amazing aroma.

2 pounds beef chuck, trimmed of fat and cut into 1½-inch cubes
¼ cup tomato paste
2 tablespoons balsamic vinegar
1 tablespoon all-purpose flour
Salt and freshly ground black pepper
1 large onion, cut into 1-inch chunks
1½ pounds potatoes, peeled and cut into 1½-inch cubes
4 to 5 medium carrots, peeled and cut into 1-inch chunks
4 cloves garlic, peeled and smashed
2 bay leaves
3 cups beef or richly flavored vegetable stock

Preheat the oven to 350°F.

In a large Dutch oven with a tight-fitting lid, combine the beef, tomato paste, vinegar, and flour. Season with salt and pepper. Add remaining ingredients. Bring to a boil over medium-high heat. Cover and transfer to the oven. Cook for 2 to 2½ hours or until the meat is very tender. Remove the bay leaves, taste, and season with salt and pepper before serving.

Grilled Herb-Rubbed Flank Steak

One of the most flavorful cuts of beef is the flank. It's a lean, flat cut that's fairly tender, but if cooked too long and at too high a temperature, it can become tough. Best finished to rare, it takes about 7 or 8 minutes per side over a nice hot fire, plus a few extra minutes of resting time, to reach perfection. One of the most important finishing steps is to cut the meat across the grain, for a nice, tender chew.

Makes 4 to 6 servings

1 flank steak, 1½ to 2 pounds
¼ cup finely chopped fresh rosemary
¼ cup finely chopped fresh parsley
2 tablespoons finely chopped fresh oregano
4 fresh sage leaves, finely chopped
4 cloves garlic, minced
2 teaspoons kosher salt
1 teaspoon cracked black pepper
¼ cup extra virgin olive oil

Using a sharp knife, score the flank steak on both sides, making long, shallow (⅛-inch-deep or less), diagonal slashes 1 inch apart and repeating at right angles to the first cuts, to create a diamond pattern. (This will help the steak stay flat during cooking.)

Combine the herbs, garlic, salt, pepper, and olive oil to make a thick paste. Rub on both sides of the steak. Let sit for 20 minutes at room temperature while you prepare the grill, or put in a sealable plastic bag and refrigerate overnight (taking the steak out of the refrigerator 20 minutes before grilling).

Prepare the grill to medium-hot. Cook the steak on each side for 5 to 6 minutes. Test for doneness by inserting an instant-read thermometer into the thickest part of the steak. It should read 125°F for medium rare or 130°F for medium. Remove from the grill, cover loosely with foil, and let rest for 10 to 15 minutes. Cut the flank steak across the grain into thin slices and serve.

- -

cooking grass-fed beef

Grass-fed beef cuts are leaner than those from cattle finished on grain. Because of their reduced levels of fat, they tend to cook faster, so it's important to check them frequently while cooking or grilling. For the best results, meat should be cooked to medium rare for the best flavor and juicy qualities. On the average, you can lower the final internal temperature of the meat by about 5 to 10 degrees, remembering that as the meat rests and the juices redistribute, the finished temperature will rise an additional 5 to 10 degrees. If you prefer beef that is well done, choose recipes that feature braising and stewing, techniques that use liquid and "low and slow" cooking temperatures and times.

Here are a few additional and important tips:

- Do not thaw grass-fed beef in the microwave. Thaw overnight in the refrigerator or in its vacuum-sealed packaging in cold water.

- Use tongs to turn steaks. Forks that pierce the meat sacrifice precious juices.

- Let the meat sit at room temperature for about an hour before cooking so it immediately gets to the business of cooking.

- Since grass-fed beef is extremely low in fat, coat with virgin olive oil or a favorite light oil for flavor enhancement and easy browning. The oil also will prevent the meat from drying and sticking to the cooking surface.

- Use a reliable instant-read thermometer to measure doneness. On cuts of meat like steak, burgers, and thinner cuts, the best reading is taken when the thermometer is inserted horizontally from the side into the center of the cut.

finish temperature for grass-fed beef

roasts and steaks

Rare . . . 120°F

Medium Rare . . . 125°F

Medium . . . 130°F

Medium Well . . . 135°F

Well Done . . . 140°F

ground meats

160°F

summer squash

Summer squash is not just zucchini—and zucchini is not the final word when it comes to summer squash. Although zucchini is the best-known, most widely available and utilized variety of summer squash, you would be depriving your recipes of some wonderful color and taste if you didn't stray from the familiar. While zucchini is subtle and light in flavor and buttery in texture, yellow and crookneck summer squash lean toward the sweet and crunchy side, saucer-like pattypan or crimped-edge green scaloppini varieties counter with interesting shapes and a slightly nutty flavor, and globe squash is really just a round version of zucchini. In recipes, one variety can typically be swapped for another with little impact on the outcome.

Regardless of shape or color or any of the other subtle nuances between varieties, there is one universal rule regarding summer squash: think small.

Choosing the Best. When zucchini or any other summer squash gets to a size that needs cradling, you'll get bogged down trying to come up with ways to improve the woody texture and bitter taste, as well as dealing with a glut of seeds and tough skin. Buy small and tender, four to six inches long for zucchini and crookneck and about the size of the palm of your hand for patty pan and scalloped. Whatever the variety, look for smooth skins with some shine, free of pitting and soft spots.

How to Store Fresh. There is about a one-week window of opportunity to maintain the taste and texture of fresh summer squash. Store dry unwashed squash in a sealable plastic bag in the refrigerator's crisper drawer. Excess moisture leads to quicker spoilage, so be sure to blot squash dry, if necessary, with a paper towel.

To Prepare for Cooking. Young, properly harvested summer squash has thin, edible skin and inconspicuous seeds, so little more than a trim of both the stem and the blossom ends is required before getting on with the recipe. Some recipes call for salting and draining whole, sliced, or grated squash before using, to purge the notoriously watery squash of excess liquid. This extra step is usually optional but will enhance the texture and flavor. Any squash should be sliced no thinner than ¼ inch. Overly thin slices will disintegrate when heated. Odd-shaped pattypan squash and scaloppini should be cut into slices vertically or into chunkier wedges pie style—or they can be parboiled, hollowed out, and stuffed.

Pick or Buy Now, Enjoy Later. Thick slices of zucchini or summer squash can be blanched and frozen with some success and perform best partially frozen in recipes that call for a quick sauté such as the Zucchini with Dill Cream on page 96. Once completely thawed, they release a lot of water and sacrifice some texture. You can also pickle them fresh as slices or a grated relish to hold the bright color of the skins.

Freeze this season's summer squash! To learn how, go to page 218.
Or preserve the seasonal flavor of zucchini with Zucchini Relish on page 97.

Grilled Zucchini and Summer Squash with Oregano and Mint

Zucchini and summer squash come on in great abundance in the summer, so you need to prepare yourself with a lot of recipes to take advantage of this versatile and prolific vegetable. In this one, the heat of the grill turns the flesh buttery and sweet, and the dried herbs add a delightful spiciness.

Makes 4 to 6 servings

2 to 3 medium zucchini (about 1 pound)
2 to 3 summer squash (about 1 pound)
3 to 4 tablespoons extra virgin olive oil
2 cloves garlic, minced
1 tablespoon dried oregano
1 tablespoon dried mint
½ teaspoon dried red pepper flakes
1 teaspoon coarse sea salt
1½ teaspoons cracked black pepper
Freshly grated Parmesan cheese, to accompany (optional)

Slice the zucchini and summer squash crosswise into ½-inch-thick slices. Place in a large bowl and drizzle with the olive oil. Toss to coat. Add the garlic, oregano, mint, pepper flakes, salt, and pepper. Toss again to coat. Let marinate for 15 minutes.

Preheat the grill to medium-high.

Arrange the zucchini and summer squash slices on the grill grate and grill until tender and nicely browned with grill marks, about 4 to 6 minutes per side. Serve warm with a grating of Parmesan cheese, if desired.

Fried Squash Blossoms with Goat Cheese

Squash blossoms are snagged from the vine before they have a chance to turn into squash—perfectly acceptable since the plants are so vigorous and productive that a few squash won't be missed. It's a small price to pay for the delicate treats that await you. Use either the male blossoms (ones that won't produce squash) or the female (those that have a little squash forming at the base). Blossoms should be picked early in the day and used the same day, as they don't keep well.

An easy way to stuff squash blossoms is to fill a small pastry bag with the goat cheese and pipe it into each blossom or fill a small plastic storage bag with the mixture, snip off one corner, and squeeze the contents into the blossom.

Makes 6 servings

1 dozen squash blossoms
6 ounces goat cheese, at room temperature
2 cloves garlic, minced (optional)
1½ cups all-purpose flour
1½ teaspoons baking powder
1 teaspoon salt
½ teaspoon freshly ground black pepper
1 cup buttermilk, plus extra to thin, if necessary
Vegetable oil, for frying

To clean the squash blossoms, soak in a large bowl filled with cold water for an hour. Rinse, gently shake off the excess water, and let dry on a layer of paper towels for about an hour.

Mix the goat cheese and garlic. Gently open the blossoms and tuck some of the goat cheese inside. Press each blossom to close the opening.

Combine the flour, baking powder, salt, and pepper in a bowl. Add the buttermilk and stir to create a batter the consistency of heavy cream.

Fill a heavy, deep skillet with an inch of oil. Heat over medium-high heat until a thermometer reads 375°F.

When the oil is hot, dip the squash blossoms in batter, coating all sides heavily. Place the blossoms in the hot oil, taking care not to crowd the pan, and fry on both sides, flipping with tongs when one side is brown. Drain finished blossoms on a paper towel–lined plate. Serve immediately.

Zucchini with Dill Cream

Makes 4 servings

Simple, humble zucchini is so easy to love. Because the flavor is mild, zucchini is the perfect place to highlight the flavors of fresh seasonal herbs. In this recipe, the zucchini soaks up some of the rich cream, giving it a silky texture.

2 tablespoons unsalted butter
2 cloves garlic, minced
3 to 4 small zucchini, trimmed and cut crosswise into ½-inch slices
¼ cup fresh dill or 2 tablespoons dried dill weed, divided use
½ cup heavy cream
Salt and freshly ground black pepper

Melt the butter in a large heavy skillet over medium heat. Add the garlic and sauté for 1 minute. Add the zucchini slices and half of the dill and sauté for 5 minutes until crisp-tender and lightly browned. Add the cream and simmer for about a minute until the sauce is thickened and has been partially absorbed by the zucchini. Season with salt and pepper and garnish with the remaining dill. Serve warm.

Zucchini Patties

Makes 10 to 12 patties

Gardeners love to share zucchini, especially the big ones that they sneak onto your porch at night when no one is looking, like an abandoned orphan. No note, no explanation. It's your problem now. Here's a great way to make decent use of some of the oversized zucchini, those maybe twice the size of the ideal pickings.

4 cups shredded zucchini (unpeeled)
1½ teaspoons salt
2 eggs
½ cup grated Parmesan cheese
½ cup shredded mozzarella cheese
¼ cup chopped onion
2 cloves garlic, minced
½ teaspoon freshly ground black pepper
½ cup all-purpose flour
Vegetable oil, for frying
Slices of fresh tomato, to accompany
Crème fraîche or sour cream, to accompany
Freshly chopped parsley, as a garnish

Put the shredded zucchini into a colander. Sprinkle with the salt and toss to combine. Let the zucchini drain for about an hour. Squeeze some of the excess water from the zucchini before proceeding.

In a large bowl, combine the zucchini with the eggs, both cheeses, onion, garlic, and pepper. Add the flour and stir to combine. Heat the oil in a large skillet over medium-high heat. Drop ½-cup measures of the batter into the hot oil, pressing down lightly with a spatula to form a patty. Cook for about 4 to 5 minutes on each side until browned and crispy. Transfer the patties to a paper towel–lined plate to drain. Repeat with remaining patties, adding oil if necessary.

To serve, sandwich a slice of fresh tomato between two zucchini patties and top with crème fraîche and a sprinkling of parsley.

Stuffed Pattypans

Makes 6 servings

Scalloped-edge pattypans are nature's ramekins, perfect little edible bowls to hold stuffing and present at the table ready to serve. Stuff them and refrigerate for up to 3 hours before baking to a buttery-textured finish.

6 pattypan squash, about 3 inches in diameter
6 slices bacon
½ cup chopped onion
1 ½ cups soft fresh breadcrumbs
½ cup freshly grated Parmesan cheese
Salt and freshly ground black pepper, to taste

Preheat the oven to 350°F.

Bring a large pot of water to a boil. Add the squash and cook for 10 minutes or until fork tender. Drain. Slice off the stem. Using a melon baller or a small scoop, remove the center of the squash, creating a cavity for the filling. Chop the removed squash pieces. Set aside.

Cook the bacon in a large skillet over medium-high heat until crisp. Transfer to paper towels to drain. Remove all but one tablespoon of the bacon fat. Reduce the heat to medium and sauté the onion until soft and tender, about 6 minutes. Add the reserved squash and sauté for an additional minute or two until soft. Remove the skillet from the heat. Crumble the bacon, adding it to the skillet along with the breadcrumbs, cheese, and salt and pepper to taste.

Divide the mixture between the prepared squash shells, stuffing generously. Place in a baking dish, cover with foil, and bake for 15 minutes or until the squash shell yields to a gentle squeeze and the stuffing is heated through. Remove the foil and bake for an additional 5 minutes to lightly brown the tops.

Zucchini Relish

Makes 4 half-pint jars

2 cups finely chopped zucchini and/or summer squash
1 large onion, finely chopped
1 green bell pepper, finely chopped
1 red bell pepper, finely chopped
2 tablespoons kosher salt
1 cup sugar
3 teaspoons celery seeds
2 teaspoons mustard seeds
½ teaspoon red pepper flakes (optional)
1 ½ cups cider vinegar
½ cup water

So many zucchini . . . so many possibilities. Whether you're in the midst of the harvest or at the tail end, this is a lovely, fresh-tasting relish that will add a little local flavor and a sweet and spicy kick to grilled sausages now and, if you preserve it by canning, later in the year.

New to pickling? For a step-by-step guide to the basics, see "Pickled Vegetables, Relishes, and Salsas" on page 239.

Combine the zucchini, onion, and peppers in a large colander. Sprinkle with salt. Mix well. Let stand for 3 hours to drain. Rinse and drain several times. Squeeze the excess water from the mixture.

Combine the remaining ingredients in a large pot. Bring to a boil. Add the zucchini mixture. Reduce the heat to low and simmer for 20 minutes.

Ladle the relish along with some of the liquid into sterilized half-pint jars to within ½ inch of the rim (headspace). Seal and process for 10 minutes.

pastured poultry

"Tastes like chicken." Isn't that what you say when trying to describe the taste of something neither here nor there, bland, nondescript, and unimpressive? This unflattering expression is an unfortunate but perhaps accurate description of how we've come to expect chicken to taste—like nothing special.

Before there were refrigerators, freezers, or large industrial poultry operations, chickens were raised on pasture, whether on a small farm pasture or in a backyard garden. Collecting eggs was a daily routine, but a chicken dinner was a special celebration. If you've discovered pastured poultry from a farmer at your local farmers market, you too might have a reason to celebrate.

Farmers who raise pastured poultry typically select heritage breeds, slow-growth birds like the Cornish, with a naturally large portion of finely textured white meat; New Hampshire, one of the "younger" breeds, just shy of 100 years old, raised for eggs and meat; or Jersey Giants, big, gentle, exceptionally slow growing and a great roaster.

Heritage breeds thrive in small flocks, making disease prevention easier and routine use of antibiotics

unnecessary. For 12 to 18 glorious weeks—more or less depending on the season, conditions, and whether a smaller bird or a larger roaster is desired—the flock has constant access to lush, grassy pasture, tasty weeds, fresh air, sunshine, and a protein-rich diet of grubs and worms, balanced by nourishing grains. The result is meat with less fat, more vitamins and nutritional value, and a texture that is silky and firm. Best of all, these chickens have rich flavor that you'll want to be sure comes through at the table. To adorn it with intense seasonings and sauces would be wrong.

One bite and you'll say, "Tastes like chicken"—because it does.

• •

free-range or pastured: what's the difference?

Pastured poultry are flocks raised on grassy pastures, fed wholesome grains and feeds, and provided access to fresh water. Free-range birds have access to the outdoors, but that doesn't always mean they spend a significant amount of time, or any, outdoors.

Perfect Roast Chicken

Makes 6 servings

Few pleasures at the table can match that of a simply prepared, perfectly roasted chicken—crispy brown on the outside, moist and juicy on the inside. Pasture-raised heritage breeds are just too precious for any old cooking method. This one will yield good results in a short amount of time.

Allowing the bird to "rest" when it comes out of the oven gives the natural juices a chance to equalize throughout the bird. The result? When the chicken is carved, you won't find puddles of juice on the cutting board—the juices remain inside the meat on your fork.

2 tablespoons fresh lemon juice
1 clove garlic, minced
½ teaspoon coarse salt
½ teaspoon freshly ground black pepper
2 tablespoons freshly minced seasonal herbs (parsley, rosemary, thyme, oregano, or sage, any combination)
¼ cup plus 1 tablespoon extra virgin olive oil, divided use
1 3- to 4-pound chicken, trimmed of excess fat, rinsed and patted dry with a paper towel

Adjust the oven rack to the middle position. Preheat the oven to 500°F.

Combine the lemon juice, garlic, salt, pepper, and minced herbs. Stir in ¼ cup of the olive oil. Set aside.

Brush the chicken with the remaining tablespoon of olive oil. Place breast side down on a rack in a shallow roasting pan. Add about ½ cup of water or chicken stock to the roasting pan, which will help keep the drippings from splattering and smoking. Roast for 20 minutes before turning breast side up. Allow to roast for a few more minutes or until the breast begins to brown. Baste with some of the herb mixture.

Reduce the heat to 350°F and roast for 30 to 35 minutes, basting 2 or 3 times, until an instant-read thermometer inserted into the thickest part of the thigh reads 160°F.

Pour the juices from the inside of the bird into the roasting pan. Place the bird on a cutting surface, cover, and let rest for 15 minutes. Meanwhile, pour the pan juices into a small saucepan and bring to a boil over medium-high heat. Season to taste with salt and pepper. When ready to serve, carve the bird and serve with the pan juices.

Variation: For a simple glaze, substitute 2 tablespoons Dijon mustard mixed with 2 tablespoons light honey for the lemon mixture. Brush on the glaze during the final 10 minutes of cooking.

in season ...
stone fruits

Few fruits can stir the senses like the deep, heady, floral perfume of stone fruits, those juicy tree fruits with a pit or "stone." These are the fruits that allow you to savor summer out-of-hand as juice trickles down your chin.

For the most part, stone fruits are interchangeable in recipes and can be tossed in with your morning cereal or yogurt, baked into a pie, and used in savory dishes and of course for a variety of desserts. But truly ripe peaches, plums, apricots, nectarines, and cherries are so full of natural sweetness and flavor that they don't require a lot of embellishment, and it would be a shame to distract attention from their natural perfection.

Choosing the Best. The best advice is to use your senses. Follow your nose. Aroma hints strongly at flavor, so when a fruit smells the way you expect it to smell, the flavor is probably at its peak. Overall color is a visual clue, but not always a reliable one. Peaches, in particular, should have a golden or soft yellow tone. Don't rely on the red blush, which is a sign of the variety, not of ripeness. Pick fruits without spots, bruises, or blemishes. Well-defined clefts in stone fruits are another clue to ripeness. Use your sense of touch, too. Rock-hard stone fruits are not ripe; those that yield to gentle palm pressure are better bets. Cherries should be clean, bright, and plump. Sweet cherries should be firm, not hard, and sour varieties should be slightly firm. The darker the color, the sweeter the cherry, and if the stems are intact, they will enjoy a longer shelf life.

How to Store Fresh. Stone fruits are delicate and highly perishable, so it's best to buy them as you plan to consume them. They will keep at room temperature for 2 or 3 days. A day or two in the coolest part of the refrigerator will extend their life, but be sure to let them return to room temperature before enjoying. And don't wash the fruit until you intend to use it. Cherries can be stored unwashed in a plastic bag.

To Prepare for Cooking. A sun-warmed peach eaten out of hand is hard to top, but when the recipe calls for a peeled peach (or nectarine or plum), refer to "Removing the Skin on Whole Tomatoes, Peaches, and Other Stone Fruits" on page 225. Apricots have such thin skins that peeling is rarely necessary. Cherries, of course, need only be pitted.

Pick or Buy Now, Enjoy Later. Peaches, nectarines, apricots, and cherries at their peak of ripeness can be frozen or canned as halves or slices or in jam and sauces. Whether freezing or preserving, packing the fruit in sugar syrup is the best way to preserve color, texture, and flavor. Plums are best used for canned jams or sauces.

Use frozen sour cherries to make the Sour Cherry Slump on page 213 in the winter. Toss frozen peach slices into a smoothie or shake. Learn to can peach slices on page 236. They can be enjoyed "straight" or drained, chopped, and used to top the Goat Cheesecake with Fresh Peaches on page 78.

Freeze this season's stone fruits! To learn how, go to page 221. Or preserve the seasonal flavor of stone fruits in the Trio of Stone Fruit Jams on page 105.

Nectarine and Blueberry Skillet Cobbler

Makes 6 servings

Plump blueberries nestled among sunny yellow slices of nectarine under a buttery cobbled topping is the kind of dish you would expect to see at a summer potluck—the kind that gets polished off first. Feel free to substitute peaches and plums for the nectarines and blackberries for the blueberries. With so many wonderful seasonal combinations, it might take all summer to find a favorite.

If you don't have a cast iron skillet, cook the fruit in a large skillet and transfer to an 8-inch square baking dish. Make the topping and bake as directed.

½ cup unsalted butter
2 to 3 cups sliced nectarines, peeled
2 to 3 cups fresh blueberries
1 cup sugar, 2 tablespoons removed, divided use
1 cup all-purpose flour
2 teaspoons baking powder
½ teaspoon salt
¾ cup half-and-half or whole milk
Whipped cream, to garnish

Preheat the oven to 400°F.

Melt the butter in a 10-inch cast iron skillet over medium heat. Add the fruit with 2 tablespoons sugar. Cook, stirring frequently, until the sugar is melted and the fruits just begin to soften and release some of their juices.

Whisk together the remaining sugar, flour, baking powder, and salt. Stir in the half-and-half to make a thick batter. Using a tablespoon, spoon dollops of the batter evenly over the fruit, creating a cobbled look. Bake for 20 minutes or until a toothpick inserted into the topping comes out clean. Serve warm with whipped cream.

Fresh Peach Pie

Makes 8 to 10 servings

Peach pie arrives at the pinnacle of summer, both juicy and delicious—and a challenge for even the veteran pie maker. Consider using cling peaches, early-season varieties in which the fruit clings to the pit. Although the slices are not perfectly neat, this type of peach is meatier and less juicy. Freestone peaches come away cleanly from the pit but release more juice. To absorb the errant juices during baking, add ground tapioca—because it's pulverized, it won't leave any lumps in the baked pie filling.

For more tips and tricks on making the perfect pie and the perfect crust, see "Make Your Own Piecrust" on page 128.

7 large, ripe peaches, peeled (see page 225), pitted, and sliced (about 7 cups)
1 tablespoon fresh lemon juice
1 cup sugar
¼ teaspoon ground cinnamon
¼ teaspoon freshly grated nutmeg
¼ teaspoon salt
4 to 5 tablespoons tapioca, ground in a spice grinder
1 recipe pie dough for 9-inch double-crust pie (page 128)

Place a baking stone or a heavy rimmed baking sheet on the middle rack in the oven to heat. Preheat the oven to 425°F.

In a large mixing bowl, combine the peaches, lemon juice, sugar, cinnamon, nutmeg, salt, and tapioca. Toss gently.

Roll out half the dough to fit a 9-inch pie plate. Turn the peach filling into the bottom crust and roll out and cover with the top crust. Trim and crimp the edges. Cut 6 slits in the top crust. Place on the baking stone and bake for 30 minutes or until the crust is set and beginning to brown. Reduce the heat to 375°F and bake for an additional 25 to 30 minutes until the crust is a deep golden brown and the juices are bubbly.

Let cool for at least 1 hour before slicing.

Peach Ginger Soup

Makes 8 servings

If you're looking to cool down on a hot day, think soup. Chilled soups are wonderfully refreshing and effective in cooling the body down. Most stone fruits as well as berries can be whipped up into a smooth, refreshing soup in no time, but peach soup is among the most delicious.

3 pounds ripe peaches, skinned (see page 225) and pitted
2 teaspoons freshly squeezed lemon juice
3 cups buttermilk or plain yogurt
1 cup apple juice or orange juice
1 teaspoon freshly grated ginger
2 teaspoons honey
1 teaspoon salt
Edible flowers, such as nasturtiums, or 8 thin slices of peach, for garnish

Puree the prepared peaches in a food processor along with the lemon juice. Transfer to a medium bowl and stir in the remaining ingredients. Taste and adjust seasonings. Refrigerate for up to 6 hours or until chilled.

Ladle the soup into shallow bowls and garnish with edible flowers or thin slices of peach, if desired.

Spiced Oven-Baked Plums

Makes 4 servings

This combination of warm spices over fresh ripe plums is unbeatable—and versatile. Try it on apricots, nectarines, or peaches, too. The result is a great side to grilled chicken or pork—or add a scoop of vanilla ice cream and a sprinkling of crushed almonds and you have dessert.

4 fresh plums, halved and pit removed
1 tablespoon unsalted butter, melted
½ cup orange juice
2 tablespoons packed brown sugar
½ teaspoon ground cinnamon
Grating of nutmeg
Pinch of cumin

Preheat the oven to 400°F. Brush a shallow baking dish or gratin pan with the melted butter. Arrange the plums cut side up in a single layer.

In a small bowl, whisk together the orange juice, brown sugar, cinnamon, nutmeg, and cumin; drizzle over the plums.

Bake for 20 minutes or until the plums are hot and the sauce is bubbly. Cool for 5 minutes before serving.

. . . .

it's the pits!

That would certainly be an accurate description of the time it takes to pit cherries, unless you have a few tricks up your sleeves. Investing in a cherry pitter is an option. A handheld version does the job one cherry at a time. A countertop pitter that feeds multiple cherries through a shoot and removes pits quickly without bruising the fruit is worth the investment if you plan to pit a lot of cherries for turning into jam or preparing for the freezer. If you just want to pit cherries for a single recipe, try this trick: Using a sturdy toothpick, a bent paper clip, or a skewer, insert the curved end into the stem end of the cherry. When it hits the pit, give it a twist and lift—out pops the pit! It may take a little practice to get a rhythm going, but this method will get the job done.

Stone Fruit Salad

Makes 4 servings

A morning trip to the farmers market can net you most of the ingredients you can quickly turn into a salad for that night's dinner. Enjoy it before the main course or between courses, or turn it into a main course itself by adding poached or grilled chicken.

3 cups arugula
3 cups red and green leaf lettuces, torn into bite-size pieces
½ cup thinly sliced red onion
2 ripe peaches, nectarines, or plums, pitted and sliced
½ cup Honey and Garlic Vinaigrette (page 61), more or less to taste
Salt and freshly ground black pepper, to taste
¼ cup crumbled blue cheese (for a milder taste, use feta cheese)
4 tablespoons toasted walnut halves

Combine the arugula, lettuces, onion, and fruit in a large bowl. Pour the prepared vinaigrette over the top and toss to coat the leaves and fruit. Taste and season lightly with salt and pepper.

Divide the dressed greens between 4 chilled salad plates. Top with the cheese and toasted walnuts. Serve immediately.

To Toast Nuts: Preheat the oven to 400°F. Scatter the nuts on a rimmed baking sheet and place in the oven for 7 to 10 minutes, stirring halfway through toasting or until the nuts begin to turn golden and become fragrant. Remove from the pan into another bowl to cool.

Sour Cherry Torte

Makes 8 servings

Juicy sour cherries ooze from a sweet buttery crust. If you can't get enough of the tart seasonal flavor of sour cherries, be sure to freeze a few batches. The same flavors that make you lick your dessert plate clean in the summer will be there for you all year round. If using cherries from the freezer, thaw and drain before using.

4 cups pitted sour cherries
2 cups sugar, divided use
3 cups all-purpose flour
1½ teaspoons baking powder
½ teaspoon salt
10 tablespoons unsalted butter, cut into small pieces, at room temperature
2 eggs, lightly beaten
Confectioners' sugar, to dust

Preheat the oven to 375°F.

In a large bowl, combine the cherries and 1 cup of sugar. Set aside, stirring occasionally until the sugar is dissolved.

In a separate bowl, combine the remaining sugar, flour, baking powder, and salt.

Cut in the butter until the mixture is coarse and crumbly. Add the eggs, mixing until just combined. Press half the mixture into a 9-inch springform pan with a removable bottom. Using a slotted spoon, spoon the cherries on top. Sprinkle the remaining crumb mixture over the top of the cherries and press down lightly to even the surface.

Bake 45 minutes or until the top is golden and the torte shrinks from the sides of the pan. Let cool for at least 1 hour before removing from the springform pan.

Dust with confectioners' sugar before slicing and serving.

Grilled Balsamic-Glazed Apricots

This apricot preparation is perfect as is for an appetizer or side dish, but try adding some crumbled blue cheese, feta, or goat cheese to the cavity and lightly drizzling with honey. It can stand alone as a dessert with a dollop of lightly sweetened ricotta cheese—and you can also substitute peaches, plums, or nectarines for the apricots.

Makes 6 servings

½ cup balsamic vinegar, preferably white balsamic
3 tablespoons brown sugar
1 teaspoon cracked black pepper
⅛ teaspoon salt
6 firm, ripe apricots, halved and pits removed
2 tablespoons vegetable oil

Combine the first 4 ingredients in a small saucepan. Bring to a boil; reduce the heat and simmer for 2 to 3 minutes. Remove from the heat and cool slightly. Place the apricots in a shallow dish and pour the vinegar mixture over the top, tossing gently to coat. Meanwhile, preheat the grill to medium.

When ready to grill, remove the apricots from the vinegar mixture, reserving 2 tablespoons of the mixture. Whisk that with the oil to make a vinaigrette, blending well. Set aside.

Lightly oil the grill grate. Brush the apricots with some of the vinaigrette. Place apricot halves cut side down and grill on each side until slightly soft to the touch.

Serve with a drizzle of the remaining vinaigrette.

Sweet Cherries in Wine

Simplicity is a friend to locally grown seasonal foods. When the ingredients are at their peak of ripeness and flavor, as cherries are in the summer, choose recipes that work with flavors, not against. Enjoy this sophisticated dessert as the sun goes down on a hot summer day—a glass of red wine in hand will complete the moment.

Makes 4 servings

1 cup water
½ cup dark brown sugar, more or less to taste
1 cup local red wine (Pinot Noir or Cabernet Franc are recommended)
2 teaspoons grated lemon zest
1 pound fresh sweet cherries, washed, stems removed, and pitted
Slices of pound cake or vanilla ice cream, to accompany, if desired

Combine the water and brown sugar in a medium saucepan. Bring to a boil over medium heat. Add the wine and lemon zest and return to a boil. Lower the heat and simmer for 5 minutes, stirring occasionally. Add the cherries and return to a simmer. Cook for an additional two minutes. Remove from the heat. (If not serving immediately, let the mixture cool before transferring to a glass bowl. Cover and refrigerate for up to 2 days. Gently reheat before serving.)

To serve, spoon the cherries and sauce over ice cream or pound cake.

Plum Dipping Sauce

Sweet and delicious, this pretty purple sauce makes a great dip for egg rolls or potstickers. It also works well as an accompaniment to the Scallion Skillet Breads on page 40.

Makes 1½ cups

1 cup plum jam
½ cup dry sherry
½ teaspoon ground cloves
½ teaspoon ground anise seed
½ teaspoon ground fennel seed
3 tablespoons dry mustard, more if a hotter sauce is desired

Combine all the ingredients except the mustard in a blender. Add the mustard, a tablespoon at a time, until the sauce has the taste and tang desired. Transfer to a container with a tight-fitting lid and refrigerate for up to a month.

A Trio of Stone Fruit Jams

Picture this: It's the dead of winter. You open your cupboards and there to greet you are all of the jams, jellies, and sauces you put up over the spring, summer, and fall: glistening jars of bright red strawberry and raspberry jams, dark blackberry and golden yellow peach jams, purple plum jam and grape jelly. The sense of satisfaction you get from extending the season by canning and preserving is second only to the flavors—real, homegrown flavors. These recipes produce a softer set jam, relying primarily on the fruit, sugar, citrus juice, the fruit's natural pectin, and heat to create spreads that feature genuine flavors.

Peach Ginger Jam

Makes 4 half-pint jars

3 pounds peaches, skinned (see page 225), pitted,
    and coarsely chopped
5 cups sugar
3 tablespoons chopped fresh ginger
2 teaspoons lemon juice
Grating of fresh nutmeg

In a large heavy pot or Dutch oven, combine the peaches, sugar, ginger, and lemon juice. Bring to a boil over medium heat, stirring constantly, until the sugar is dissolved. Cook for about 35 minutes until the mixture thickens, stirring frequently. Remove from the heat and perform the gel test (see page 238). If the gel stage has not been reached, return to the heat and cook for a few minutes, repeating the test until the gel stage has been reached. Once the mixture has gelled, skim off any foam that has developed. Add the grated nutmeg.

    Ladle the jam into sterilized jars to within ¼ inch of the rim (headspace), seal, and process for 10 minutes.

Sour Cherry Jam

Makes 4 half-pint jars

8 cups sour cherries, stemmed and pitted
5 cups sugar
2 tablespoons freshly squeezed lemon juice

In a large heavy pot or Dutch oven, combine the cherries, sugar, and lemon juice. Bring to a boil over medium heat, stirring constantly, until the sugar is dissolved. Cook for about 30 minutes until the mixture thickens, stirring frequently. Remove from the heat and perform the gel test (see page 238). If the gel stage has not been reached, return to the heat and cook for a few minutes, repeating the test until the gel stage has been reached. Once the mixture has gelled, skim off any foam that has developed.

    Ladle the jam into sterilized jars to within ¼ inch of the rim (headspace), seal, and process for 10 minutes.

It's best to halve or coarsely chop about a third of the cherries to keep the finished jam from tumbling off your toast.

Plum Jam

Makes 2 pint jars

3 pounds plums
1 cup water
2½ cups sugar
Freshly squeezed juice from 1 lemon

In a large heavy pot, cook the plums in the water until the skins pop and the pulp is tender, about 20 minutes. Remove from the heat and let cool. Run the mixture through a food mill or press through a colander to remove the skins and pits.

    Place the plum pulp in a large heavy pot or Dutch oven. Stir in the sugar and lemon juice. Bring to a boil over medium heat, stirring constantly until the sugar is dissolved. Cook for about 15 to 20 minutes until the mixture thickens, stirring frequently. Remove from the heat and perform the gel test (see page 238). If the gel stage has not been reached, return to the heat and cook for a few minutes, repeating the test until the gel stage has been reached. Once the mixture has gelled, skim off any foam that has developed.

    Ladle the jam into sterilized jars to within ¼ inch of the rim (headspace), seal, and process for 5 minutes.

Firing up the canner for this small amount of jam is impractical unless you have other canning projects going on at the same time. Don't miss out on the taste, though. Consider refrigerating this jam and enjoying it over the next few weeks, or use a portion of it to make the fabulous Plum Dipping Sauce (page 104) for egg rolls, shrimp, or beef.

Local Flavor

honey

Wherever you find locally grown fruits and vegetables, you'll find honey bees. They are the original *locavores*, traveling up to five miles to collect their food. When one particular type of flower or tree where you live is in bloom, bees will work it until all the nectar is collected before moving on to the next variety of bloom. Honey produced from their seasonal work possesses "terroir"—a particular sense of place and season that is reflected in the color, aroma, and taste, sometimes subtle between varieties, other times extreme.

Honey bottled by large commercial producers is often blended to ensure flavor consistency from one bottle to the next, thus depriving the user of the experience of the subtleties or extremes in flavor between bloom-specific honeys. Smaller apiaries and beekeepers, those who sell their honey at local farmers markets, typically harvest and bottle honey to capture particular nuances of seasonal blooms. This is your chance to experience for yourself whether you're drawn to the mild and delicate flavors or to brawny, slightly bitter tasting honey.

Here's a short list of commonly found honey varieties, their particular color and flavor nuances, and suggested uses.

Apple Blossom: Sweet floral aroma, light amber in color, and very sweet; good for a variety of uses, including dressing fruit salads.

Black Locust: An early spring honey; pale amber in color, mild, and floral; use in recipes with fish and seafood.

Alfalfa: Light, pale-colored honey with a subtle spicy profile and floral tones; good choice to use in baking.

Clover: Light-colored, pleasingly mild and sweet, with broad appeal. Use to sweeten coffee or tea.

Wildflower: Honey blended from a variety of field flowers; usually pleasantly floral and sweet and has wide appeal; perfect for dessert applications.

Goldenrod: Light to medium color with a bit of a "bite"; quick to crystallize; use in baking or cooking.

Buckwheat: Full and dark-bodied and a favorite to use for baking; use to replace molasses and maple syrup in recipes.

let it flow!

Some honeys, like Goldenrod, crystallize or harden faster than others. That doesn't mean the honey has gone bad, it just means there's more pollen in that particular variety. To loosen it, put it in the microwave (plastic or glass bottles only, with the metal caps removed) for 5- to 10-second blasts until the honey returns to a flowing consistency.

Berry-Infused Honey

Local honey and fresh local berries come together as a special sweetener for tea, to top yogurt or ice cream, to spread on a toasted muffin, even to sweeten up a salad dressing. Be sure to use a lighter variety of honey to complement, not compete with, the flavor of the berries.

Makes about 2 cups

1 cup fresh berries
1½ cups honey, divided use
2 tablespoons water
1 teaspoon grated lemon rind (optional)

Place the berries in a small saucepan and use a potato masher to lightly crush the berries. Mix in ½ cup of honey and the water. Place over low heat and bring to a simmer. Allow to simmer for 10 minutes. Stir in the remaining honey. Allow to cool. Add the lemon zest, if desired. Pour into a container, cover, and refrigerate. Use within 2 weeks.

in season ...
sweet corn

Among dedicated fans of fresh produce, there's only one sure way to capture the genuine taste of fresh sweet corn: bring a large pot full of water to a boil, go out to the field and pick the corn, then run, don't walk, back to the kitchen and get the corn into the pot. If you have ever compared the taste of an ear of corn straight off the stalk to one that is a couple of days old, you already understand that a mere 24 hours in the life of freshly picked corn can change the taste from sweet to starchy and the texture from naturally buttery to tough. There are plenty of methods and recipes for enjoying fresh locally grown or homegrown sweet corn, but the key to success begins with frequent trips to field or farmers market to get the freshest corn possible.

Choosing the Best. Peeling back the husk on an ear of corn for a closer look is a typical method to choose ears of corn, yet there are better signs that an ear of corn is freshly picked. Is the ear full, fat, and heavy for its size? Feel it with your fingers. The kernels should be plump and developed all the way to the tip. Does it feel cool? If it has been exposed to sun or heat, the texture is likely deteriorating. The husks should be soft, supple, a grassy green color, and free of worm holes or imperfections. Fresh-picked corn has a light green stem, not yellow and dry, and the silks should be pale in color and dry, but not brittle.

How to Store Fresh. Ideally, sweet corn should be cooked the same hour it is bought, certainly the same day. If it must be held, do so for no more than a day, refrigerated, husks and all, in a perforated plastic bag.

To Prepare for Cooking. Just before cooking, peel the husks down around the ear then snap at the stem. Remove the silks that cling with a dry vegetable brush or with a slightly damp paper towel, wiping from the stem end to the tip. If the recipe calls for stripping the kernels from the cob, run a sharp knife under the kernels, working from the tip to the stem end, taking care not to cut off the tough cob. Work over a bowl to catch the kernels and any of the precious, sweet liquid, a natural thickener that comes off the cob.

Pick or Buy Now, Enjoy Later. Freezing is the method of choice for preserving sweet corn. Fresh, cleaned ears should be blanched and cooled before packaging whole or stripping the kernels off for freezing. Later in the year they can be pulled from the freezer and used to make the Farmhouse Chowder on page 206 or the Cream of Corn Soup with Rosemary on page 205. Toss kernels into cornbread and custards, too.

Freeze this season's sweet corn! To learn how, go to page 218.

Corn on the Cob ... Three Ways

Here are three simple techniques for preparing corn on the cob that as you'll see can easily accommodate the number of ears you want to cook. Each cooking method has its own advantage.

Grilled Corn

Grilled corn has a smoky, almost caramelized flavor. Grilling keeps the heat out of the kitchen and eliminates the need to strip the husks before cooking.

If you are making a large quantity for a summer gathering, use a cooler to keep the corn warm as it comes off the grill.

Leaving the husks and silks intact, submerge the corn in a bucket or sink filled with water. Soak for at least 2 hours or up to 6. When ready to cook, preheat the grill to medium-high. Place the corn in a single layer on the grill grate. Cook with the lid lowered for 15 to 20 minutes, turning every 5 minutes until the husks are dried and charred in spots. To test for doneness, peel back the husk on one ear and press on a kernel. If it yields to pressure, the corn is done. Remove from the grill. When you're ready to eat, the husks and silks will peel back easily.

Microwaved Corn

Microwaving corn is a great option when you need to cook only one or two ears. Because microwaves cook food from the inside out, the corn will stay hotter longer than corn cooked with other methods.

Makes anywhere from 1 ear of corn to 6. Remove the husks and silks. Place the cleaned cobs in a sealable gallon-size plastic bag, no more than 6 ears per bag. Partially seal the bag. Place the bag on a plate in the microwave and set the timer for 2 minutes per ear. For example, if you have 4 ears, set the timer for 8 minutes; for 6 ears, 12 minutes. When done cooking, carefully remove the corn.

Steamed Corn

This method for steaming corn uses a small amount of water and is a good alternative to the traditional method of filling a pot with water, waiting for it to boil and then having to take it from the stove to the sink—and there's no worry about the pot boiling over.

Clean the husks and silks from the desired number of ears of corn. Add water to a large stockpot to a depth of about an inch and bring to a boil. Add the ears to the pot, cover, and cook for about 3 to 4 minutes for 6 ears, a bit longer if there are more ears in the pot. Remove and let cool slightly before serving.

reheating frozen ears of corn

The rules for cooking frozen, unthawed ears of corn are not substantially different from those used for cooking fresh ears. Use the same method and times to microwave frozen ears as you would for fresh. To grill frozen corn, butter the ears and wrap in foil. Grill over medium-high heat, turning frequently, about 30 minutes. Steaming or boiling frozen ears is not recommended. Frozen ears of corn cause the temperature of the boiling water to drop significantly, causing the corn to be overcooked and ruining the taste and texture you worked hard to preserve.

save the cobs

Don't toss the stripped cobs ... there's a lot of serious flavor hidden there. Use them to make a wonderful broth for any soup that features corn, like the Corn and Red Pepper Bisque on page 109. Simply take 6 to 8 cobs, crack them in half, and place in a large stockpot. Add 8 cups of water, just enough to cover the cobs, and bring to a boil over medium-high heat. Reduce the heat to low and simmer 30 minutes. Stir in ½ teaspoon of salt, then strain the broth through a fine-mesh strainer into a large bowl. Discard the cobs and pulp. Let the broth cool to room temperature, then store in an airtight container in the refrigerator for up to a week or freeze for up to 3 months.

Grilled Corn Custards

Makes 6 servings

If you're grilling corn, toss an additional half dozen ears onto the flame to add to this recipe the next day. The smoky kernels are perfectly at home in the rich, creamy custard. Freeze a batch of kernels for when you get a taste for these custards in the winter. If you would prefer to use steamed or microwaved corn, feel free to substitute.

6 to 8 ears fresh sweet corn (about 3 cups kernels), grilled or steamed
4 tablespoons unsalted butter, divided use
1 medium onion, diced
4 whole eggs
1 cup half-and-half
½ cup milk
Freshly grated nutmeg, to taste
Salt and freshly ground black pepper, to taste
2 tablespoons chopped fresh chives, for garnish

Strip the kernels from the cooked corn. Set aside.

Preheat the oven to 350°F. Melt 1 tablespoon of butter and brush the insides of 6 4-ounce ramekins.

Melt the remaining butter in a large skillet over medium heat. Add the onions and cook until soft and translucent, about 6 minutes. Set aside.

Lightly beat the eggs in a large mixing bowl. Stir in the half-and-half, milk, nutmeg, and salt and pepper to taste. Stir in the corn. Divide the mixture between the prepared ramekins. Top each ramekin with onions.

Bake the custards until set, about 30 minutes. The center may appear soft but will firm up quickly as the custard cools. Allow to cool for 10 to 15 minutes before garnishing with chives and serving.

Corn and Red Pepper Bisque

Makes 6 servings

Make this soup with fresh sweet corn stripped from the cobs or wait until the snow flies and reach into the freezer for your stash of summer corn. You did freeze some just for this moment, didn't you? Feel free to substitute a finely chopped roasted red bell pepper, freshly prepared or from the freezer, for a hint of smoky flavor. When this soup is finished, you'll forget it's winter.

2 tablespoons unsalted butter
1 medium onion, diced
1 red bell pepper, diced
1 large clove garlic, minced
3 cups fresh or frozen corn kernels (from about 6 ears)
4 cups rich chicken stock
Salt and freshly ground black pepper, to taste
½ cup crème fraîche or sour cream
1 tablespoon yellow cornmeal
2 tablespoons freshly chopped parsley
Dash of Tabasco sauce, more or less to taste

Melt the butter in a stockpot over medium-high heat. Add the onion and bell pepper and sauté for 8 minutes or until soft and fragrant. Add the garlic and sauté for another 30 seconds. Stir in the corn. Add the chicken stock and bring to a boil. Reduce the heat to a simmer and cook for 15 to 20 minutes or until the corn is very tender. Season with salt and pepper, to taste.

Using a slotted spoon, transfer 2 cups of the corn mixture to a blender. Add the crème fraîche and blend until the mixture is smooth, about 1 minute.

Stir the puree back into the pot. Increase the heat to medium-high and whisk in the cornmeal, whisking constantly, until the soup thickens, about 2 to 3 minutes.

Add the parsley and Tabasco sauce, to taste. Heat through. Serve hot.

Grilled Honey-Roasted Sweet Corn

Makes 6 servings

Save this technique for truly fresh ears of corn, at the beginning or end of the local harvest. It takes a few more steps, but the heat and smoke of the grill and the smell of the roasting corn and the honey caramelizing under the husks is a fitting tribute to the first ears, or the last, to come out of the fields.

6 ears fresh sweet corn
⅓ cup honey
⅓ cup water
Salt and freshly ground black pepper, to taste

Preheat the grill to medium-high.

Pull the husks back on each ear of corn and remove the silks. Bring the honey and water to a boil in a small saucepan. Reduce the heat to low and simmer until the mixture thickens, about 5 minutes. Brush the corn with the honey mixture and season with salt and pepper. Pull the husks back up over the corn. Wrap each ear in aluminum foil. Place on the grill and cook for 15 minutes, turning frequently. Let cool slightly before pulling the husks back and serving.

Sweet Corn and Poppyseed Cornbread

Makes 8 to 10 servings

Freshly cut kernels of corn and locally produced cornmeal give this moist, delicious cornbread great flavor and wonderful texture. Fresh eggs and local buttermilk really ramp up its local flavor profile. Be sure to freeze a batch of sweet corn kernels for the winter, when a slice of this cornbread would taste great with Local Chili (page 211).

For a special treat or even for dessert, serve still-warm pieces of this cornbread with a drizzle of warm maple syrup.

1½ cups buttermilk
3 large eggs
2 cups coarse-ground cornmeal
1 cup all-purpose flour
½ cup sugar
3 tablespoons poppyseeds
4 teaspoons baking powder
1 teaspoon salt
½ cup unsalted butter, diced and chilled
1½ cups fresh corn kernels (from about 3 ears of corn)

Preheat the oven to 400°F. Butter a 9-inch square metal baking pan.

Mix the buttermilk and eggs in a medium bowl until combined. Set aside.

Blend the cornmeal, flour, sugar, poppyseeds, baking powder, and salt in a large bowl. Add the butter and work it in with a pastry blender or your fingertips until the mixture resembles coarse meal. Mix in the corn kernels. Add the buttermilk mixture and stir until just combined. Pour the batter into the prepared pan. Bake for 45 minutes or until a toothpick inserted in the center comes out clean. Cool for 15 minutes before cutting. Serve warm or at room temperature.

corn off the cob

Stripping corn kernels from cooked or uncooked corn is not hard, but it could be easier. Here's an easy method that uses an angel food or bundt cake pan. Try it when you're determined to reap the most from this year's corn harvest or when a recipe calls for stripping just a half-dozen ears. Stand the tip of the shucked corn in the center hole of the pan. Holding the cob steady, use a sharp knife to make long, downward strokes on the cob to separate the kernels. The hole in the pan helps keeps the cob steady and the interior of the pan neatly collects the kernels.

Making Your Own: Butter

The taste of fresh butter is unlike most butter you've ever bought, full of fresh flavor, rich texture, and wonderfully aromatic. The only taste better than fresh butter is fresh butter in various stages of melting on freshly baked rolls or breads.

The only and all-important ingredient is heavy cream—good heavy cream. The taste of your butter will be a direct reflection of the richness of the butterfat content in the cream, and that is a direct result of the breed of cow, the cow's diet, and the season. The creams you'll find in summer from herds raised on fresh green pasture will be richer than those in the spring and winter. The better the cream, the better the butter.

If you can buy organic cream that has been pasteurized (not ultrapasteurized), the flavor and texture will be even better. Ready to make some butter?

Homemade Butter

Makes approximately ½ pound or 1 cup of butter

Note: This recipe calls for a food processor with a 9-cup capacity. If you are using a smaller model, adjust the amounts accordingly.

The only thing left to do is to decide what is worthy of this delicious, fresh butter. Fresh corn on the cob on page 108 would certainly deserve to be slathered in fresh butter, as would the Pumpkin Pancakes with Cider Syrup on page 208. Then there's the "Bring on the Jam" Muffins on page 209 and the Everyday Whole Wheat Bread on page 15.

4 cups good-quality heavy cream, chilled
1 teaspoon kosher salt (optional)
Iced water

Fit the work bowl of a food processor with a serrated or smooth blade. Pour enough cream into the work bowl to reach about halfway up the side of the bowl. Process for about 2 minutes. The mixture will begin to look like whipped cream. (It is, because the butter has not yet separated from the buttermilk.) Continue processing another few minutes until the mixture "breaks," looking rough and curdled.

Pour off the buttermilk (the liquid that pools at the bottom), leaving the butter mass. (Save the buttermilk and use to add to pancakes, blend into smoothies, or drink as is.) Add the salt at this point, if desired.

Wash the butter to extend the storage life by getting rid of traces of buttermilk, which will cause the butter to spoil more quickly and take on the taste of sour milk. To wash the butter, pour ½ cup of ice water into the food processor bowl. Process for 5 to 10 seconds and then pour off the water. Keep repeating this process with fresh ice water until the water is no longer cloudy but clear.

Transfer the butter to a jar with a tight-fitting lid. Shake vigorously for a few seconds. Pour off any liquid that has accumulated. Repeat this process until there is no water left.

Store the butter in the jar and refrigerate for up to 10 days. For longer storage, form the butter into a log or rounds, wrap in waxed paper, place in an airtight container, and freeze for up to 3 months.

Fresh butter all by itself is a treat, but if you feel the need to embellish a bit, mix one cup of softened butter with any of these combinations. Use immediately, within a week, or wrap tightly in plastic wrap and freeze, stored in a small freezer bag, for up to 4 months.

Pepper and Garlic Butter

Mix 1 cup unsalted butter + 2 cloves garlic, minced + 1 teaspoon cracked black pepper. Place a tablespoon of this butter on a freshly grilled steak or use to finish steamed vegetables.

Honey and Chive Butter

Mix 1 cup unsalted butter + 2 tablespoons honey + 2 tablespoons freshly snipped chives. Spread on hot dinner rolls or crusty, rustic-style breads.

Fruit Butter

Mix 1 cup unsalted butter + 1 cup chopped fresh strawberries + ¼ cup powdered sugar. Spread on English muffins or thick slices of bread.

Local Flavor

specialty grains

One of the locavore's biggest challenges has to be finding sources for locally grown and milled flours and grains, the foundations for great homemade breads and baking. While more and more locavores seek out locally grown foods and farmers respond with grass-fed meats from heritage breeds, artisan cheeses, and heirloom fruits and vegetables, most flours and grains remain a product of big industry, blends of various cultivars that arrive in our kitchens from large, distant corporate mills. They are reliable, predictable, limited in variety, and tend to homogenize bread making and baking.

While a trip to the local farmers market probably won't net you a 50-pound sack of locally grown and milled flour to round out your locavore's kitchen, it's not uncommon to find wholesome specialty grains, milled meals, and seeds that are part of the local landscape. These *landrace* grains, such as millet, spelt, and buckwheat, evolved over time to adapt to the climate and growing conditions in a specific geographical region and reflect the culinary heritage of the local people. They are the same grains our ancestors cultivated, harvested, and ground by hand or took to the local gristmills and used for their own baking needs.

Tougher, resistant to disease, and not dependent on synthetic chemical fertilizers to survive, landrace grains are typically fiber rich, nutritious, and delicious. Growing, seeking out, and using these grains are ways to help preserve diversity in our food choices.

Serious bread bakers and cooks might go the distance to find these locally grown grains, often grinding them into flour and using them quickly because they still contain the delicate and perishable bran and germ. If you're new to using these grains, success requires a sense of adventure and a bit of experimentation. Ask the growers about the specific qualities of the unique grains they sell. Can't find locally grown grain in your area? Not surprising. So let your favorite farmers know you would be a regular buyer if they grew it.

specialty grains

There's no telling what types of specialty grains you'll come across close to home—and that's where the adventuresome side of a locavore comes out. It might be *amaranth*, an herbal plant that can be cooked as a cereal, ground into flour, or used to thicken soups; or *buckwheat*, a gluten-free flour with a rich and nutty flavor and a favorite ingredient in pancakes; or *kamut*, an ancient form of wheat, yellow in color, high in protein, rich and buttery in taste, and great for bread making.

Chocolate Spelt Cake

Makes one 8-inch cake

Spelt is a nutritious, nutty-flavored ancient grain closely related to wheat that's getting a closer look these days. Not only is it nutritious and high in protein, for some with wheat allergies it's a tolerable alternative to wheat as it contains lesser gluten. In this eggless recipe, the spelt complements the flavor of chocolate in a moist, sweet cake.

1½ cups spelt flour
1 cup sugar
4 tablespoons cocoa
½ teaspoon salt
1 teaspoon baking soda
6 tablespoons vegetable oil
1 tablespoon distilled vinegar
1 teaspoon vanilla extract
1 cup cold water
Confectioners' sugar, for dusting
Raspberries or sliced strawberries, optional
Lightly sweetened whipped cream, optional

Preheat the oven to 350°F.

Sift the flour, sugar, cocoa, salt, and soda into an ungreased 8-inch square baking pan. Using the back of a large spoon, make 3 indentations in the flour mixture. In one, add the vegetable oil; in the second, add the vinegar; and in the third, add the vanilla. Pour the cold water over the entire mixture and mix thoroughly with a rubber spatula until all the ingredients are well blended. Bake for 30 to 35 minutes. The cake is done when a toothpick inserted into the center comes out clean. Cool completely. Serve with a dusting of powdered sugar or split the cake horizontally into two layers and fill with freshly whipped cream and seasonal berries.

Buckwheat Crepes

Makes about 1 dozen crepes

Buckwheat is actually a grass, high in fiber and full of great nutritional value. Ground into a flour, it has a rich, nutty flavor and can be used in baking, for pancakes, and in this recipe for crepes. Think creatively when topping. How about some lightly sautéed spinach topped by a fried egg? For your sweet tooth, try them with a scoop of ice cream, a drizzle of honey, and some fresh-picked seasonal berries.

Crepes can be made and refrigerated a day ahead of using. Freeze by stacking them with sheets of waxed paper between crepes and placing in an airtight freezer bag. The crepes will keep up to one month.

1 cup whole milk, plus extra to thin, if necessary
¼ cup water
3 large eggs
½ teaspoon salt
⅔ cup buckwheat flour
½ cup all-purpose flour
3 tablespoons vegetable or canola oil
Unsalted butter, melted, to coat the pan

Place the milk, water, eggs, and salt in a blender. Blend at low speed until combined. Add the flours and oil and blend at high speed for 1 minute to combine. Transfer to a bowl, cover, and refrigerate for one hour.

Place a small nonstick skillet or crepe pan over medium heat. Brush with butter. To add the batter, remove the pan from the stove and ladle in about 3 tablespoons of the batter, swirling to distribute evenly. Return to the heat. Cook for 1 minute until the edges appear dry and loosen easily from the pan. Turn and cook on the other side for about 30 seconds. Remove from the pan to a plate. Repeat with the remaining batter, brushing the pan with butter before adding more batter.

Cornmeal Cookies

Makes 2 dozen cookies

Cornmeal is dried and ground sweet corn and you're likely to find it in a variety of grinds, from fine to coarse, which adds a delightful gritty texture to breads and cookies. Coarse-ground cornmeal provides the crunch in these cookies and in the Sweet Corn and Poppyseed Cornbread on page 110.

¾ cup unsalted butter, at room temperature
¾ cup sugar
1 egg
1 teaspoon vanilla extract
1 tablespoon grated lemon zest (optional)
1½ cups all-purpose flour
½ cup coarse-ground cornmeal
1 teaspoon baking powder
¼ teaspoon salt

In a large bowl, blend the butter and sugar together with an electric mixer until light and fluffy, about 5 minutes. Add the egg and beat until combined. Stir in the vanilla and lemon zest, if desired.

In a separate bowl, combine the flour, cornmeal, baking powder, and salt. Gradually add to the butter mixture.

Form the dough into a ball and flatten into a disk. Wrap tightly in plastic wrap and chill for 1 hour.

Preheat the oven to 350°F.

Roll the dough out onto a lightly floured surface to a ¼-inch thickness. Cut into cookies using a 2½-inch cookie cutter. Place an inch apart on a lightly greased cookie sheet.

Bake for 10 to 12 minutes or until the edges are golden. Let cool on a wire rack before storing in an airtight container.

Making Your Own: Pizza Crust

If the locavore's kitchen is filled with the best and freshest pizza toppings, why settle for anything less than the best pizza crust? Whole wheat flour adds some fabulous texture and earthy color to this pizza crust. It also stands up to anything you decide to top it with. This is a great choice for Asparagus Pesto Pizza (on page 5), Chicken and Roasted Red Pepper Pizza (on page 203), or the classic Pizza Margherita (on page 117).

Whole Wheat Pizza Crust

Makes 2 large 10-inch pizza shells or 4 small 6-inch pizza shells

A heavy-duty stand mixer can be used to prepare this dough. After the flour has been added, replace the paddle attachment with the dough hook and knead on low speed for about 6 minutes until smooth and elastic.

1½ cups warm water (105°F to 115°F)
1.25-ounce package active dry yeast
1 teaspoon sugar
1 tablespoon olive oil
1 teaspoon kosher salt
2 cups whole wheat flour
1½ cups bread flour, plus extra for kneading
Extra virgin olive oil, for brushing

In a large bowl, combine the water, yeast, and sugar. Let stand until the mixture is foamy, about 10 minutes. Stir in the oil and salt. In a separate bowl, combine the flours. Stir in all but ½ cup of the flour and mix until the dough comes together.

Turn the dough out onto a lightly floured surface and knead until smooth and elastic, about 8 to 10 minutes. (If the dough appears too sticky, add the extra flour, a tablespoon at a time.)

Place the dough in an oiled bowl, cover with a damp towel, and let rise in a warm place until doubled in size, about 1 hour.

Punch the dough down and divide it into 2 or 4 portions. Form the pieces into balls, cover lightly with the damp towel, and let rise for 45 minutes or until doubled.

Meanwhile, preheat the oven to 425°F.

Use a rolling pin or simply hand-stretch the dough to form the crusts. Brush with oil and bake on a pizza stone or baking sheet for 5 minutes. Remove and add toppings, as desired, and bake for an additional 10 to 12 minutes or until cheeses are melted.

Freezing pizza dough: This pizza dough freezes well. After the first rise, punch the dough down and separate it into 2 or 4 portions (for individual serving pizzas). Lightly brush the dough you are freezing with a little olive oil. Store each portion in a sealable freezer bag, pressing out as much air as possible; seal and freeze for up to three months. Thaw in the refrigerator overnight. Remove from the bag and place in a lightly oiled bowl. Cover with a damp towel and let rise for the second time at room temperature. This may take 2 hours. Roll out and proceed with the recipe.

in season ... *tomatoes*

There's more than one way to enjoy a homegrown tomato, but the best way is to pick it from the vine, fully ripe and still warm from the sun, and eat it out of hand, letting the juice trickle down your chin. When it comes to homegrown tomatoes, little should stand between you and the genuine flavor of the world's favorite fruit. Look for recipes that put the spotlight on the color and flavor rather than burying it under heavy sauces and lots of cheese.

There are a handful of tomato types, including beefsteak, salad, paste, and cherry tomatoes. Each type has distinct characteristics that make it a good choice either for eating fresh or for using in cooked dishes or sauces. Tomatoes come in an array of colors from pale yellow to bright orange and fire engine red to a deep smoky purple, and their flavor can range from tart and highly acidic to sweet and fruity. Finding one that is pleasing to the eye and palate promises to be a gustatory adventure.

Choosing the Best. Tomatoes in season and harvested perfectly ripe have fully developed flavor and aroma. Whether you are picking them straight off the vine or shopping at a farmers market, look for tomatoes that are firm, not hard, and yield easily to the gentlest squeeze. The skin should have a shiny finish and be free of blemishes, soft spots, and tears. If visual cues aren't enough, trust your sense of smell. A fully ripe tomato should smell sweet and aromatic, not "green" and grassy.

How to Store Fresh. Tomatoes, like people, prefer temperatures that are not too cold and not too hot. Anywhere between 55°F and 80°F away from direct light is ideal. Chilly refrigerator temperatures put the brakes on any further ripening. While this is a good stall tactic for slightly overripe tomatoes awaiting a sauce recipe, cold will deaden the taste of a tomato headed for a salad. If refrigeration is a must, let tomatoes return to room temperature before using.

To Prepare for Cooking. Tomatoes lend themselves to many cooking techniques, including roasting, grilling, baking, stewing, pureeing for a sauce, and juicing. Often all that's needed to get on with a recipe is chopping, dicing, or slicing. To learn how to peel tomatoes, refer to "Removing the Skin on Whole Tomatoes, Peaches, and Other Stone Fruits" on page 225.

Pick or Buy Now, Enjoy Later. Tomatoes can be canned, frozen, or oven dried with good results. If you're new to preserving, canning whole tomatoes should be your first choice for learning these techniques. From there, move on to putting up tomatoes chopped, stewed, pureed, or made into a simple sauce, zesty salsa, or delicious juice—there's a long list of ways to bring homegrown tomatoes to the table year round.

Freeze this season's tomatoes! To learn about freezing whole tomatoes, go to page 224. Or preserve the seasonal flavor of tomatoes with Margaret's Salsa (page 121), Chunky All-Purpose Tomato Sauce (page 121), or Canned Whole Tomatoes (page 235).

Roasted Cherry Tomatoes with Basil Ribbons

Makes 6 to 8 servings

As if ripe cherry tomatoes weren't sweet enough, here comes a quick and simple idea that makes them even sweeter— roasting! This technique lets you rely on the natural sugars in the tomatoes to carry the flavor. "Gild the lily" with some fresh basil. For a colorful presentation, mix yellow and red cherry tomato varieties.

2 pints cherry tomatoes, washed, dried, stems removed, if necessary
Extra virgin olive oil
¼ cup basil leaves, cut into thin strips
Coarse sea salt and freshly cracked black pepper

Preheat the oven to 400°F.

Place the cherry tomatoes in a large bowl and drizzle with olive oil. Toss to coat, adding more oil if necessary to coat them well. Season with salt and pepper and toss again.

Spread the tomatoes on a baking sheet and roast about 20 to 30 minutes or until the tomatoes begin to shrivel and release some juice. Check often. As the juice begins to run, they will quickly burn.

Transfer from the baking sheet to a small bowl. Taste, season with additional salt and pepper, if necessary, toss with basil, drizzle with a little olive oil, and serve immediately.

Pizza Margherita

Makes 6 to 8 servings

What a delicious tribute to ripe tomatoes and fresh basil! While you can prepare this recipe using a large prepared pizza shell, the Whole Wheat Pizza Crust on page 115 adds an earthy and rustic flavor.

One recipe Whole Wheat Pizza Crust (page 115)
Extra virgin olive oil, for brushing and drizzling
Sea salt, to taste
2 cloves garlic, minced
1 pound ripe, meaty tomatoes, thinly sliced (plum tomatoes preferred)
12 ounces fresh mozzarella cheese, cut into ½-inch cubes or thinly sliced
12 large fresh basil leaves, cut into thin strips
½ to ¾ cup freshly grated Parmesan cheese

Preheat the oven to 425°F.

Stretch or roll the prepared dough to fit a rimmed 13 x 18-inch baking sheet. Lightly brush the surface with olive oil and sprinkle with the chopped garlic and salt. Arrange the tomatoes on the dough. Bake for 10 minutes. Scatter the mozzarella and basil over the surface. Drizzle with a little more olive oil, sprinkle the Parmesan cheese over the top, and bake for an additional 5 to 8 minutes or until the cheese has melted. Serve immediately.

heirloom tomatoes: culinary treasures

Farmers markets and a return to home gardening have done wonders for bringing heirloom tomatoes as well as other obscure varieties of vegetables back into the limelight and the locavore's kitchen. Heirlooms are true treasures in terms of taste and culinary history.

They are the result of seeds that have been passed down through generations of farming and gardening families, valued for outstanding flavor or particular culinary characteristics.

You've probably noticed a seemingly unlimited choice of heirloom tomatoes to plant or buy. There are in fact thousands of known varieties of heirlooms, and plenty more remain closely held secrets in families. When it comes to heirloom tomatoes, it's important to remember that beauty is skin deep—and it's beneath the skin where the best tomato flavor lies. Some varieties are naturally thin-skinned and prone to developing little flaws and blemishes, like cracks and scarring, which can simply be trimmed away.

Classic Bruschetta

Makes 6 appetizer servings

There's only one way to make bruschetta—with perfectly ripe, fresh tomatoes. It's a wonderful way to capture the fresh flavor of everyone's favorite summertime fruit. This basic recipe is open to your own adaptations: add diced red onion, use balsamic instead of red wine vinegar, replace the chopped basil with fresh chopped oregano or parsley, top with cheese—or don't.

2 cloves garlic, minced
8 large plum tomatoes, cored and coarsely chopped
2 tablespoons freshly chopped basil
2 teaspoons extra virgin olive oil, plus extra for brushing
Splash of red wine vinegar
Salt and freshly ground black pepper, to taste
2 small baguettes, cut into ¼-inch slices

Combine the garlic, tomatoes, basil, oil, and red wine vinegar in a medium glass bowl. Season with salt and pepper, to taste. Set aside at room temperature for at least an hour to allow flavors to meld.

Meanwhile, preheat the oven to 375°F. Brush the bread slices on both sides with olive oil. Arrange in a single layer on a baking sheet and place on the middle rack of the oven. Bake for 12 minutes or until golden brown. Remove and let cool.

To serve, top the bread slices with about a tablespoon of the tomato mixture.

Heirloom Pasta Sauce with Maple Syrup

Makes about 8 cups

So many local ingredients can only add up to fabulous local flavor in this sauce. Mix up not only the varieties and colors of heirlooms but the types of tomatoes, too. Plum and paste tomatoes will add some body. This sauce freezes beautifully for up to six months.

¼ cup extra virgin olive oil
2 medium yellow onions, chopped
2 cloves garlic, minced
5 pounds heirloom tomatoes, chopped, juices reserved
¼ cup pure maple syrup
Salt and freshly ground black pepper, to taste

Heat the oil in a large heavy skillet over medium heat. Add the onions and sauté until soft and transparent, about 8 minutes. Add the garlic and sauté for an additional minute. Add the tomatoes and any juices that have accumulated and stir to combine. Bring the mixture to a boil then reduce the heat to low and simmer for 45 minutes or until the mixture has thickened and reduced in volume. Add the maple syrup and cook an additional 10 minutes. Season with salt and pepper. Toss with hot, thick pasta noodles.

Baked Tomatoes Topped with Ricotta and Basil

Fresh, vine-ripened tomatoes deserve a crowning touch like the one in this recipe. Be sure to use fresh ricotta (or make your own) and sweet basil—out of respect for the tomato, of course!

Learn to make your own ricotta-style cheese on page 72. It's easy.

Makes 8 servings

4 ripe tomatoes (salad tomatoes preferred)
½ cup ricotta cheese
¼ cup chopped fresh basil
2 cloves garlic, minced
1 teaspoon fresh thyme
4 tablespoons grated Parmesan cheese
½ teaspoon freshly ground black pepper
Salt, to taste
Extra virgin olive oil, to drizzle

Preheat the oven to 400°F.

Cut the tomatoes in half crosswise. Arrange cut side up in a shallow baking dish. In a medium bowl, combine the ricotta, basil, garlic, thyme, Parmesan, and pepper. Taste and season with salt, to taste. Top each tomato with about 2 tablespoons of the ricotta mixture. Drizzle lightly with the olive oil. Bake 15 to 20 minutes or until the cheese mixture is lightly browned. Serve immediately.

Honey Baked Tomatoes

The pairing of two naturally sweet local finds—tomatoes and honey—results in a fresh and sophisticated side dish. This recipe is perfect for end-of-the-season tomatoes that might need a boost of sweetness.

Makes 8 servings

8 ripe medium tomatoes, cut into 1-inch slices
2 tablespoons honey
2 slices bread
2 tablespoons freshly minced tarragon
1½ teaspoons salt
2 teaspoons freshly ground black pepper
4 teaspoons unsalted butter

Preheat the oven to 350°F.

Arrange the tomatoes in a single layer on a lightly greased foil-lined rimmed baking sheet. Drizzle with the honey.

Place the bread in a food processor or blender and process until finely chopped. Transfer to a medium bowl and mix with the tarragon, salt, and pepper. Sprinkle the mixture over the tomato slices. Place a dot of butter on top of each.

Bake for 20 minutes. Remove and set aside.

Turn the oven to broil. When heated, broil the tomatoes 5 inches from the heating element for 5 minutes or until the tops are golden. Serve warm.

Heirloom Tomato Bisque

Sweet and creamy, this is a lusciously rich soup courtesy of flavorful heirloom tomatoes and cream. Make it once to enjoy the complex flavors, make it again and again because it's so easy.

....

Transform this soup into a creamy one by pureeing the mixture before adding the cream, cheese, and herbs.

Makes 4 to 6 servings

2 tablespoons olive oil
2 tablespoons unsalted butter
1 small onion, diced
1 clove garlic, minced
4 pounds mixed varieties heirloom tomatoes, seeded, chopped, juices reserved
Salt and freshly ground black pepper, to taste
1 cup heavy cream or ½ cup crème fraîche, at room temperature
½ cup freshly grated Parmesan cheese, plus extra for garnish
¼ freshly chopped basil leaves, plus extra for garnish
1 teaspoon fresh thyme leaves

Heat the oil and butter in a large stockpot over medium heat. Add the onion and cook until soft, about 6 minutes. Add the garlic and cook an additional minute. Add the tomatoes and juices to the stockpot and cook over very low heat, stirring frequently, for 15 minutes or until warm. Taste and season with salt and pepper. Remove from the heat. Slowly add the heavy cream and stir until well blended. Stir in the cheese and herbs. Ladle into bowls and garnish with extra cheese and chopped basil.

'mater matters: a tomato variety primer

Beefsteak varieties are the largest tomatoes you'll find at farmers markets but rarely in a large grocery store. In a variety of colors from white to yellow, pink to red, and burgundy to purple, they are meaty, juicy, and best eaten raw, in salads or sliced for sandwiches.

Salad tomatoes are smaller than beefsteaks and even more flavorful and juicy. You can use them in the same way, but they are better choices for filling with cold salad mix or for stuffing and baking.

Cherry tomatoes are the smallest and sweetest varieties, ranging in size from about the tip of your thumb to somewhat larger in oblong, round, and teardrop shapes. They are good in salads and appetizers, and for eating out of hand. Roasting cherry tomatoes intensifies the sweetness.

Plum or paste tomatoes are usually treated as interchangeable, but a true paste tomato is larger than a plum, even meatier, and not always the expected egg shape. Both are highly flavorful, with few seeds and less juice, making them best for cooked sauces and canning, drying, or roasting for the freezer.

simple pleasures

In the locavore's kitchen, often the simplest events bring about the greatest joy. Finding the first vine-ripened tomato would certainly have to top that list. It's one of those rare moments that make you feel secretive and greedy. After all, it's only one tomato and more will be on their way. Still ...

Here's one perfectly simple and delicious way to enjoy your find without letting too much get between you and the most anticipated taste of the growing season. Sandwich slices of the still sun-warmed tomato between two slices of soft bread, slathered with mayonnaise (homemade would be nice) and sprinkled with coarse sea salt and some freshly ground black pepper. Enjoy (alone) with a glass of cold milk or iced tea.

Learn to make homemade mayonnaise on page 125.

to seed or not to seed?

When a recipe calls for removing seeds from tomatoes, simply cut the tomato in half horizontally and gently squeeze each half into a fine mesh strainer over a bowl. The strainer catches the seeds, which can be discarded, and the bowl catches the juices, which you can return to the recipe.

Chunky All-Purpose Tomato Sauce

Makes 4 pint jars or 2 quart jars

6 pounds fresh tomatoes, plum or paste varieties preferred, peeled and coarsely
    chopped
1 cup chopped onion
3 cloves garlic, minced
¼ cup local red wine
2 tablespoons red wine or balsamic vinegar
½ cup chopped fresh basil
2 tablespoons chopped fresh oregano
2 tablespoons chopped fresh parsley
1 teaspoon sugar
1 teaspoon salt
½ teaspoon freshly ground black pepper
Tomato paste, up to 4 tablespoons, if necessary

When it comes to preparing any food for canning or preserving, flavor is everything. What you put in the jar today is what you will expect to enjoy in the months to come, so make sure that the ingredients are at their peak of ripeness and the flavor is something you would look forward to, especially when fresh tomatoes are no longer available. Taste and adjust the seasonings as you prepare this sauce, before you process it.

Combine the chopped tomatoes, onion, garlic, wine, vinegar, herbs, sugar, salt, and pepper in a large nonreactive pot. Bring to a boil, then reduce heat to a simmer. Cook, uncovered, for up to an hour or until the mixture thickens. If the mixture needs thickening, add tomato paste to your preference. Taste and adjust seasonings.

Ladle the sauce into jars to within ½ inch of the rim (headspace), seal, and process for 35 minutes for pints and 40 minutes for quarts.

Variation: To make a smooth tomato sauce, puree the mixture in batches in a blender or food processor. Return the mixture to the pot and heat until bubbling. Ladle the sauce into sterilized jars to within ½ inch of the rim (headspace), seal, and process for 30 minutes for pint jars.

See page 225 for instructions on how to remove the skins from tomatoes.

New to canning? For a step-by-step guide to the basics, see "Canning" on page 227.

Margaret's Salsa

Makes 6 pint jars or 12 half-pint jars

10 pounds tomatoes, mixed varieties, peeled and finely chopped
3 medium onions, finely chopped
12 assorted peppers, a mix of both hot varieties (such as Hungarian hot wax and
    jalapeño) and mild green and red bell peppers
2 cloves garlic, chopped
1 tablespoon salt
½ cup red wine vinegar
⅓ cup extra virgin olive oil
¼ cup freshly chopped basil
¼ cup freshly chopped cilantro
¼ cup freshly chopped parsley

One of the most satisfying home canning projects is a big batch of salsa. It calls together some of the best seasonal ingredients you'll find in abundance whether from the garden, farmers markets, or roadside stands. Salsa is easy to prepare and easy to can. A little work can put a lot of delicious snacking on your pantry shelves to carry you through the winter months.

Set a large colander over a bowl or in the sink. Place the tomatoes, onions, peppers, and garlic in the colander. Stir in the salt. Allow to rest and drain for 3 hours. Stir the salsa. Transfer to a large heavy pot and add the remaining ingredients. Cook over medium heat until the mixture is hot and begins to bubble.

Ladle the salsa into jars to within ½ inch of the rim (headspace). Seal and process for 20 minutes for pints and half pints.

New to pickling? For a step-by-step guide to the basics, see "Pickled Vegetables, Relishes, and Salsas" on page 239.

SUMMER

Making Your Own: Oven-Dried Tomatoes

Without the use of special equipment like a commercial dehydrator or a climate that cooperates with a stretch of consistently high temperatures and dry conditions, drying a wide variety of seasonal foods can pose a challenge in the locavore's kitchen.

So what do you do when the garden hands you a bumper crop of plum or paste tomatoes, perfect 'maters for "sun-drying"? First, thank your lucky stars! Then think of ways to preserve them.

While Canning Whole Tomatoes on page 235 is a great way to preserve them for the long winter ahead, oven-drying meaty varieties of tomatoes will concentrate and strengthen their flavors, delivering an intensely sweet flavor, a tender, chewy texture, and an entirely new way to savor everyone's favorite fruit. Enjoy them tossed in warm or cold salads, chopped and stirred into mashed potatoes, scattered in risotto with plenty of fresh basil, or made into the Oven-Dried Tomato Spread on page 203. Add to soups, stews, or chili or combine with fresh tomatoes for the best of both worlds—a Fresh and Oven-Dried Tomato Sauce (recipe follows).

The method for oven-drying tomatoes described here is a purposely slow process that takes a few weeks, but the reward will be obvious every time you bite into one.

Oven-Dried Tomatoes

Everyone who has an oven can use it as a dehydrator. It combines the factors of heat, low humidity, and air. An oven is slower at drying than a dehydrator because it doesn't have a fan (unless it's a convection model); in fact, it can take twice as long as a dehydrator. Admittedly, oven-drying is not always the most energy-efficient method, but it is effective for drying thick-walled, meaty tomatoes such as Roma or paste varieties. Because oven sizes and needs differ, work with enough tomatoes to fill a maximum of 3 oven racks.

To sterilize the jars and lids, wash thoroughly with hot, soapy water, rinse completely, and then submerge in boiling water for 10 minutes. Remove and dry with a clean, lint-free towel before adding tomatoes.

- Preheat the oven to its lowest setting, usually around 150°F to 175°F. Don't be tempted to increase the oven temperature at any time or you will cook or roast the tomatoes.

- Wash and dry the tomatoes. Cut them in half from stem to blossom end. Scrape out the seeds and core. Blot the interiors dry with paper towels.

- Line 2 or 3 oven racks with thin, clean lint-free cotton towels or a double layer of cheesecloth to keep the tomatoes from falling through. (As an alternative, you can arrange the tomatoes on cake cooling racks and place them on baking sheets.) Arrange the tomatoes on the racks so they are close but not touching.

- Place the racks in the oven and heat for 30 minutes. After that time, prop open the oven door using a cork or something similar to create a 2-inch gap to release the moisture that has built up. Leaving the oven on, continue to let the tomatoes dry anywhere from 4 to 8 hours, depending on the temperature of the oven and the moisture content of the tomatoes. Rotate the racks every hour or two so the tomatoes dry evenly. The tomatoes will be done when they feel soft and leathery, much like the texture of raisins. There should be no signs of moisture or a brittle texture.

- Transfer the tomatoes to a large glass or stainless steel bowl. Over the next 10 days to 2 weeks, you will "condition" the tomatoes, leaving them uncovered in a warm, dry, and airy place in the kitchen. Stir them once a day.

- The final step is to pasteurize the tomatoes, a necessary step for dried food to ensure that harmful organisms are destroyed and to allow the food to be stored for longer periods. Preheat the oven to 175°F and arrange the tomatoes in a single layer on baking sheets. Place in the oven and heat for 15 minutes. Let cool before storing in sterilized jars with tight-fitting lids or airtight plastic storage bags. Store in a cool, dry, dark place for up to 6 months.

Fresh and Oven-Dried Tomato Sauce

Makes about 3 cups

Enjoy this richly flavored uncooked sauce now or heat it up a bit in the winter when you can make good use of both canned and oven-dried tomatoes.

2 cups chopped ripe tomatoes or canned tomatoes, drained
½ cup chopped scallions or 1 large shallot, minced
¼ cup oven-dried tomatoes, rehydrated (see below), drained, and chopped
1 tablespoon chopped basil (fresh or frozen)
¼ cup flat-leaf parsley
2 cloves garlic, crushed
½ teaspoon salt
Freshly ground black pepper, to taste
¼ cup extra virgin olive oil

Combine all the ingredients. Let stand for 30 minutes. Warm gently. Toss with 1 pound cooked and drained hot pasta and serve immediately.

. . . .

rehydrating dried tomatoes

To rehydrate oven-dried tomatoes, place the amount needed in a glass bowl and cover with boiling water. In about 30 minutes, the tomatoes will have softened and will be ready to use. Drain and proceed with your recipe. Don't discard the richly flavored water; rather, save it to add to soups, stews, chili, or the Fresh and Oven-Dried Tomato Sauce.

Making Your Own: Condiments

The locavore's kitchen is full of delicious little details. Local ingredients can be incorporated in a number of unlikely but familiar places like condiments, those flavorful enhancements we pull from the refrigerator to dress up sandwiches, dunk fries, and top hot-off-the-grill burgers. These kitchen staples deserve an opportunity to be every bit as great as the foods they adorn. For locavores, they offer one more satisfying way to incorporate local ingredients like wine and tomatoes in their kitchen repertoire.

Here are three recipes for common refrigerator condiments—with results that are anything but common. Each of the three brings local flavors and ingredients into the mix and not in ways that go unnoticed.

Fresh Tomato Ketchup

This spicy tomato ketchup relies on a lot of different spices and seasonings to make it special, so make sure that the tomatoes you choose for the base are equally so. Choose absolutely ripe, aromatic, and flavorful varieties of meaty plum tomatoes.

Makes approximately 5 to 6 cups or 5 to 6 half-pint jars

3 pounds perfectly ripe plum tomatoes, peeled, cored, and seeded
2 teaspoons kosher salt
2 tablespoons extra virgin olive oil
1 medium onion, minced
2 cloves garlic, minced
½ cup red wine vinegar
½ cup packed dark brown sugar
½ cup honey
Juice of one freshly squeezed orange
Juice of one freshly squeezed lemon
2 teaspoons allspice
1 teaspoon ground ginger
½ teaspoon mustard powder
½ teaspoon freshly cracked black pepper
½ teaspoons ground cloves

Finely chop the prepared tomatoes. Place them in a large bowl and sprinkle with salt. Set aside.

Heat the olive oil in a large heavy pot over medium heat. Add the onion and sauté until soft and fragrant, about 6 minutes. Add the garlic and sauté an additional minute. Stir in the remaining ingredients, except the tomatoes. Bring to a boil. Reduce the heat and let simmer for 10 minutes, stirring frequently, until the mixture has reduced somewhat. Add the tomatoes and any juices that have accumulated and simmer for an additional 15 to 20 minutes, stirring occasionally, until the mixture has thickened and is highly flavorful. Working in batches, transfer the mixture to a blender or food processor and blend until smooth.

Cool completely before transferring to a jar with a tight-fitting lid. Store in the refrigerator for up to 8 weeks.

To prepare this ketchup for canning, return the mixture to the pot after pureeing. Reheat over medium heat, stirring occasionally until bubbling. Ladle the ketchup into sterilized half-pint jars to within ½ inch of the rim (headspace). Seal and process for 15 minutes.

Homemade Mayonnaise

Makes approximately 1 cup

Have you ever come home from the farmers market with a dozen wonderfully fresh eggs, dreaming of the numerous ways you'll enjoy them? Add homemade mayonnaise to your list. With the help of a blender or food processor it's easy to make, and the results are a smooth, creamy texture, a beautiful pale yellow color, and a bright, "eggy" flavor, unlike any you've ever found on a store shelf.

A word of advice: the goal of a great mayonnaise is to create a perfect emulsion, one where the egg and oil come together in a creamy, smooth mixture without separating into pools of oil and egg. This takes time, patience, and your full attention—for approximately two entire minutes.

....

An easy way to add oil in drops is to dip a spoon into the oil and let the drops fall from the spoon into the blender.

2 fresh egg yolks, whites reserved for another use
Pinch of salt
Fresh grinding of black pepper
1 teaspoon Dijon mustard
1 tablespoon fresh lemon juice or white wine vinegar
1 cup oil (neutral oils such as vegetable or canola or extra virgin olive oil)

Place the egg yolks, salt, pepper, mustard, and lemon juice in a blender. Blend for 15 seconds. With the blender running, begin adding the oil a few drops at a time, pausing between additions, then in a thin, threadlike stream until half of the oil has been added. (This will take up to one minute.) The mixture will have thickened, taking on the consistency of heavy cream.

At this point, the remaining oil can be added faster but still in a thin steady stream. Once all the oil has been added, the mixture will look like mayonnaise, light in color, and creamy, with a smooth, silky texture. Taste and adjust any seasonings before transferring to a container with a tight-fitting lid and refrigerate for up 10 days.

For Garlic Mayonnaise, add a clove of minced garlic to the first group of ingredients and proceed with the recipe

For Herbed Mayonnaise, add ¼ cup of chopped fresh herbs to the mixture at the midpoint, once the mayonnaise has begun to thicken but before all the oil has been added.

For Horseradish Mayonnaise, add 2 teaspoons or more of horseradish to the finished mayonnaise.

• •

pasteurizing egg yolks for mayonnaise

When a recipe like the one for Homemade Mayonnaise calls for raw egg yolks, pasteurizing them eliminates any risk of foodborne illness and ensures food safety. Pasteurizing partially sterilizes foods at a temperature that destroys harmful microorganisms without major changes in the chemistry. The choice is yours, but the process is simple and can be done with any number of egg yolks. Here's how:

In a heavy saucepan, stir together the egg yolks and liquid from the recipe. (For the mayonnaise, it would be 2 teaspoons of lemon juice or vinegar.) Cook over very low heat, stirring constantly, until the yolk mixture coats a metal spoon with a thin film, bubbles at the edges, or registers 160°F when tested with a reliable instant-read thermometer. Immediately place the saucepan in ice water and stir until the yolk mixture is cooled. Then proceed with the recipe.

Source: American Egg Board

SUMMER

Homemade Mustard

Makes approximately ¾ cup

Give one of the oft-used kitchen condiments a local connection and a boost in flavor by adding locally grown and produced wine to the ingredients list. The end result is highly flavored mustard that shares a local connection with the seasonal produce and meats it adorns. Use it in big ways, as the highlight on grilled sausage, or in little ways, such as when a salad dressing recipe calls for mustard.

¼ cup dry mustard powder
1 tablespoon light brown sugar
1 teaspoon kosher salt
¼ teaspoon turmeric (for color)
¼ teaspoon garlic powder
Dash of sweet paprika
¼ cup mustard seeds
½ cup cider vinegar
½ cup local white wine (Chardonnay preferred)

In a saucepan, whisk together the mustard powder, sugar, salt, turmeric, garlic powder, and paprika. Grind the mustard seeds in a spice grinder for 1 minute and add to the saucepan, whisking to combine. Whisk in the liquids. Bring the mixture to a boil over medium-high heat, whisking constantly. Boil for 30 seconds without whisking. Remove from heat and whisk for 10 seconds. Set aside to cool. Store in a glass jar with a tight-fitting lid in the refrigerator for up to 6 weeks.

Variation: To make Honey Mustard, place 2 tablespoons of mustard in a small bowl and whisk in 1 tablespoon of honey. Taste and adjust to your liking, adding more honey or mustard. To thin, add a little cider vinegar.

Fall

Fall is the homestretch for most homegrown foods and the locavore's last chance to capture flavors from farmers markets, roadside stands, and home gardens before they retreat for a well-earned rest. This is when nature yields some of her most intensely colored food. The color green may march in with the growing season, but reds, golds, and oranges usher it out.

Apples arrive in shades of soft golds, fiery reds, and rich burgundies. Squashes and pumpkins command attention not only by the quirkiness of their shapes but by the tones of their skins, ranging from brilliant orange to muted greens and yellows. The flesh beneath ranges in shade from soft orange to burnt umber. Clusters of grapes still clinging to the vine develop deep, dusky hues of purple as the days move along.

Dig into the flavors of this season, so uniquely fall, and remind yourself that if you've missed the opportunity to capture the flavors of the spring and summer, you still have one more chance.

Making Your Own: Piecrust

What's a pie without a tender, flaky crust? After all, it's the only thing that stands between a poised fork and the best fruit flavors of the season. If you've gone to any length to get the best fruits or vegetables for a filling, why put them in a less than worthy crust?

This recipe is perfect for berries, orchard fruits, and pumpkin. Omit the sugar and it adapts for savory fillings, including potatoes, tomatoes, quiche fillings, and more. You may find it's the one piecrust recipe that will follow you for a lifetime of pie making. Before you begin this recipe, take a look at "Tips and Tricks for Creating a Perfect Piecrust."

One Perfect Piecrust

Makes one 9-inch double-crust pie, two 9-inch single-crust pies, or two 9-inch tart shells

2¼ cups all-purpose flour
½ teaspoon salt
1 teaspoon sugar (omit when making crusts for savory fillings)
14 tablespoons unsalted butter, cut into very small pieces and thoroughly chilled
5 to 7 tablespoons ice water
1 tablespoon cider vinegar, chilled

Combine the dry ingredients in a large bowl. Cut or work the butter into the flour with a pastry blender until the mixture resembles coarse crumbs and a few remain the size of small peas, about 1 to 2 minutes. Sprinkle 5 tablespoons of ice water and the vinegar over the flour mixture. Mix with a rubber spatula until the dough begins to form clumps. Add additional water, a tablespoon at a time, as needed until the dough begins to come together.

Gather the dough into a ball and divide in half, forming each half into a round. Flatten each half and wrap tightly in plastic wrap. Refrigerate at least 2 hours or up to 3 days. (Dough can be placed in freezer bags at this point and frozen for up to 3 months. Defrost overnight in the refrigerator before using.)

When ready to roll out, remove from refrigerator and let stand at room temperature for a short while, until easy to roll. (Prepare the pie filling before rolling.)

Working with one portion of dough at a time, roll out the dough on a lightly floured work surface into a 12-inch circle, large enough to fit into a 9-inch pie plate. Roll the dough back up onto the floured rolling pin and gently unroll it into the pie plate.

Arrange the dough to fit against the bottom and sides of the pie plate with the excess hanging over the rim. For a double-crust pie, place the filling in the shell. Roll out the remaining dough and position over the top of the filling.

Using scissors or a sharp knife, trim the excess dough so that only an inch hangs over the rim of the pie plate. Fold the edge of the dough under, creating a thick ridge of dough that rests on the rim.

Using the index finger of one hand and the thumb and index finger of the other as a guide, gently crimp the edges at even intervals all around the edge of the pie, rotating the pie as you go.

For double-crust pies, cut 3 to 5 small slits or vents into the top of the crust to allow steam to escape. Glazing a top crust is optional, unless you want to add crunch with the sprinkling of sugar. To help the sugar adhere, lightly brush the crust and edges with milk or heavy cream before sprinkling with sugar. For a shiny lacquer-like glaze, mix an egg yolk with a teaspoon of heavy cream and brush over the crust.

Bake the pie according to the recipe directions.

tips and tricks for creating a perfect piecrust

One of the most important tips to remember is that making piecrust is something of an art and takes a reasonable amount of practice. Here are some important tips to consider before you begin.

- Spoon the flour into the measuring cup and level with the blunt edge of a knife for a more accurate measure.

- Flaky piecrusts begin with cold ingredients and benefit from a quick, light touch.

- Always roll from the center of the dough to the outer edges, giving the dough a quarter turn after each roll to ensure an even thickness.

- Flour the work surface and rolling pin to keep the dough from sticking to either. Avoid throwing extra flour directly onto the dough, which tends to make it tough and dry.

- Glass pie plates do the best job of absorbing heat and helping the crust bake evenly and completely.

- Baking at higher temperatures, 400°F and above, if even for part of the baking time, makes for a crisper crust.

Protecting the Edges of the Pie

If the crimped edges of the crust darken too quickly, cover them loosely with strips of foil to slow down the browning. The surface of the crust should remain exposed so it can continue to brown.

Letting the Pie Cool Off

Cool pies at room temperature before slicing so the juices can gel and come away in each slice instead of being left to pool in the pie plate.

troubleshooting a soggy bottom crust

Juicy fruits have a tendency to make the bottom crust soggy, so here are a few ways to try to prevent this from happening. Use one technique or combine two or three.

- Brush the inside of the shell with a beaten egg white or melted butter and refrigerate for 15 minutes before adding the filling. This will form a barrier between the juices and the bottom crust.

- Scatter a few tablespoons of dry breadcrumbs on the bottom to absorb excess juices.

- Place a baking stone or heavy baking sheet on the oven rack before preheating. Place the pie on the stone for the first 15 to 20 minutes of baking. This method gives the bottom crust an instant blast of heat to start baking before the juices have a chance to soak in.

single-crust pies and blind baking

Blind baking is a technique used to partially or fully bake a single-crust pie or tart shell before adding fillings. It sets the crust so that particularly juicy or moist fillings won't leave the bottom crust soggy.

To create a single crust, arrange the rolled dough in the pie plate or tart pan, letting the excess dough hang over the edges. Using scissors or a sharp knife, trim the dough so that an inch hangs over the rim of the pie plate or tart pan. If you are using a pie plate, fold the edge under, creating a thick ridge that sits on the rim, and crimp the edges. If you are making a tart shell, fold the excess inward and press to form a thick edge on the tart.

Use a fork to pierce holes in the bottom of the crust at ¼-inch intervals; this helps keep the crust from puffing up excessively during baking. Weighing the crust down is an effective measure, too. Simply line the crust with foil or parchment paper and fill with dried beans, rice, or ceramic pie weights. (Cool and store the beans in the freezer between uses. After several uses, replace the beans with a fresh batch.)

Bake in a 400°F oven for 15 minutes. Remove the foil lining and beans and return the crust to the oven. Bake 10 to 15 minutes longer or until the crust is golden and the bottom appears dry. Cool completely on a wire rack before filling and proceeding with the recipe.

Note: To keep the dough from shrinking into the pan during blind baking, place the crust-lined pie or tart pan in the freezer for at least 30 minutes before baking to help firm up the crust before it hits the oven.

in season ...
apples and pears

Apples and pears are such familiar sights in grocery stores that it's easy to forget that these fall gems do indeed have a local season. So what's the difference between Gala apples or Bartlett pears found anytime in the grocery produce section and those from the orchard close by? Freshness, for starters. There are few miles between you and the tree that bore the fruit. There are also flavor nuances that reflect the local growing season. Small but very sweet apples are the result of a dry growing season. Exceptionally tender pears speak of above-average rainfalls as the fruit swell to ripeness.

Choosing the Best. Apples should have smooth, shiny skins and good color, meaning all-over tones of red or gold. Varieties that are striped or mottled should have a golden, not green, background color. Apples should feel heavy for their size and firm to the touch. Avoid those with dull skin, bruises, or nicks. Once damaged, they will continue to deteriorate and will encourage the apples around them to do the same.

Freshly picked or purchased pears will have shiny, taut skins and should be free of bruises or blemishes. Pears are unique in that they improve in flavor, texture, and aroma after they are picked. You can tell when a pear is ready to eat because the flesh near the stem will yield to gentle pressure.

How to Store Fresh. Apples that are kept at room temperature should be eaten or used within a few days. To extend their flavor and texture for a few weeks, store them unwashed in plastic bags in the coldest part of the refrigerator, preferably the crisper drawer. Early-season apples, those harvested first, are more perishable than those that come on later in the season, so they should be used soon after picking.

Firm pears will ripen at room temperature in about 5 days. The skins will take on a matte finish and may develop a few more brown "freckles" or lenticels, a sign of ripening. With the exception of Bartletts, the color of most pears will not change as they ripen. Once ripe, pears can be refrigerated up to 3 days in a plastic bag.

To Prepare for Cooking. At their simplest, ripe apples and pears can be washed and eaten out of hand. Most cooked recipes call for apples to be peeled because the skin does not break down to the same texture as the flesh, leaving tough, chewy pieces of peel to contend with. In recipes where the apple is not cooked, such as salads, the peel is often left intact and adds color to the dish. The tough core is always removed. Some varieties quickly turn brown when cut and exposed to the air. Dip them in water mixed with a squeeze of lemon juice.

Pears have delicate, thin skins that cook to a soft finish in recipes, so often peeling is not necessary. The slender core needs to be cut away. Pears brown quickly when cut, but a quick rub or squirt of lemon juice will prevent this.

Pick or Buy Now, Enjoy Later. Apples and pears can be turned into sauces, fruit butters, and relishes for canning and preserving. Some sources recommend freezing sweet apple varieties, but the quality of frozen apples ranges from fair to poor, and is rarely good. Since some local growers can bring apples to market well beyond the season it's often not as vital to preserve them in this way.

Preserve the seasonal flavor of apples and pears with Maple Applesauce on page 135, Pear Sauce on page 136, or Orchard Chutney on page 136.

Mom's Apple Pie

Makes one 9-inch double-crust pie

Fans of classic apple pie will wonder where the cinnamon and other pie spices are in this recipe. One taste of this unadulterated pie and they will no longer care. The true, fresh, sweet taste of apples shines in this juicy, flavorful preparation. Use your favorite pie apple—but if you're new to pie making, good choices are a combination of Granny Smith and Golden Delicious or Northern Spy and Empire. Jonathan apples provide a good balance of sweet and tart all on their own.

3 pounds apples, peeled, cored, and thinly sliced (about 10 cups)
¾ cup sugar
½ cup light brown sugar
Juice of one lemon
½ teaspoon salt
4 tablespoons unsalted butter, cut into small dice
3 tablespoons all-purpose flour
1 recipe pie dough for 9-inch double-crust pie (page 128)
2 tablespoons heavy cream, for brushing

Combine all of the filling ingredients in a large nonreactive bowl. Cover and let sit at room temperature for 2 hours.

Roll out the crust to fit a 9-inch pie plate. Turn the apple filling into the bottom crust and cover with the top crust. Trim and crimp the edges. Cut 4 slits in the top crust. Refrigerate for 20 minutes.

Place a baking stone or a heavy-duty baking sheet on the middle rack in the oven to heat. Preheat the oven to 400°F.

Brush the crust with the heavy cream.

Place the pie on the baking stone or sheet and bake for 60 to 70 minutes or until the crust is golden and the juices are bubbly.

Let cool for at least 2 hours before slicing.

• •

apple primer

More than 2,500 varieties of apples are grown in the United States, and a conversation with your local fruit farmer will help you identify which varieties can be found where you live. Always be on the lookout for less-known or unknown antique varieties, those that have a history of 50 years or more and are usually specific to a particular growing region. They may not be available in great abundance, but they are delicious local treasures.

Early Season

Gala: Crisp, juicy, and sweet; excellent for applesauce.

Paula Red: Tart and juicy; crisp flesh; wonderful for sauce and for snacking.

Macintosh: Juicy, tangy, and tart; very good sauce apple.

Mid-Season

Jonathan: Spicy, tangy flavor; good pie apple.

Golden Delicious: A favorite pie or salad apple; mellow and sweet.

Cortland: Sweet, slightly tart taste; tender flesh; excellent all-purpose apple.

Red Delicious: Sweet, crisp, and juicy; best eaten fresh or tossed in a salad.

Late Season

Jonagold: Tangy, sweet flavor; firm flesh; good for sauces, pies, and salads.

Empire: Crisp and juicy, with a sweet-tart flavor; good for baking and perfect for snacking.

Rome: Mildly tart; mostly used for cooking.

Melrose: Firm, coarse flesh; superb sauce apple.

Winesap: Crisp, juicy flesh; good for salads and for snacking.

Ida Red: Tangy flavor and firm texture; good for baking.

Granny Smith: Green flesh, very tart flavor; good for pies and baking.

Fuji: Sweet and firm; excellent for salads or for eating fresh.

Northern Spy: Crisp, juicy, and aromatic; a good dessert and pie apple.

Poppyseed Apple Salad with Smoked Ham

When farmers start picking mid- and late-season apple varieties from the orchard, it's time to pull out this recipe. It blends the personalities of three varieties of apples, bringing tart, sweet, and spicy tones to the salad course.

Makes 6 servings

¼ pound thinly sliced smoked ham or prosciutto, cut into thin strips
2 Granny Smith apples, cored and julienned
2 Winesap apples, cored and julienned
2 Fuji apples, cored and julienned
2 tablespoons poppyseeds
2 tablespoons red wine vinegar or cider vinegar
¼ cup extra virgin olive oil
Sea salt, to taste
Grilled slices of bread, to accompany

Place all the ingredients, except the bread slices, in a large bowl and toss until well combined. Taste and add salt, if necessary. Serve with the bread.

Potato and Apple Galette

Warm layers of tender potato and sweet apples come together in this savory, sophisticated "cake," infused with the wonderful, piney flavor of fresh rosemary ... a lovely side dish for your fall table.

Makes 6 to 8 servings

4 tablespoons extra virgin olive oil
4 tablespoons unsalted butter, melted
4 large russet potatoes, scrubbed and thinly sliced
1 tablespoon minced fresh rosemary
2 sweet apples such as Golden Delicious, Melrose, or Cortland, peeled and thinly sliced
Salt and freshly ground black pepper, to taste

Preheat the oven to 450°F. Brush a 9-inch round cake pan with a little of the oil and line the bottom with parchment paper. Oil the top of the parchment paper.

Combine the butter with the remaining oil. Place the sliced potatoes and rosemary in a large bowl. Add half of the oil mixture and toss to coat. Season with salt and pepper and toss again. Place the apple slices in a separate bowl, drizzle with some of the oil mixture, and toss to coat. Season with salt and pepper and toss again.

Arrange half of the potato slices in a layer in the prepared pan, overlapping slices as you go. Top with the apples, then with the remaining potatoes. Pour any remaining oil mixture over the top.

Bake until the potatoes are tender and can be pierced easily with the tip of a knife, about 45 minutes. Let rest for 10 minutes before turning out onto a baking sheet. Remove the parchment paper. Place under the broiler for 3 minutes to brown the surface. Carefully transfer to a serving platter and cut into wedges. Serve immediately.

. . . .

pick your own

Apple season means apple pie, cobbler, sauces, cider—and apple picking. Spending an hour or two picking the perfect apples for your favorite recipes adds a special connection between the farm and your table. Before heading out to the orchard, you should know that there is a right way to pick apples ... and of course, a wrong way. Don't grab the apple and yank. You could knock other ripening apples off the tree, damage the branch, or pull out the stem from the fruit, which will shorten its shelf life. Grasp the apple in the palm of your hand and place your index finger on the stem where it meets the branch. Twist the apple up so that the blossom end or "eye" is pointed upward. The slight pressure of your finger will help separate the stem from the branch, and you will have picked the perfect apple. Your local fruit farmer thanks you.

Rustic Pear Tart in Cornmeal Pastry

Makes 8 servings

Fresh, ripe Bosc pears are the perfect choice for this recipe. Their firm flesh is sweet and tender, yet they hold their shape even after some time in the oven. This recipe adapts for apples, but ripe pears paired with this coarse-textured crust seem natural companions.

Pastry:
1 cup all-purpose flour
¾ cup medium-grind yellow cornmeal
1 teaspoon salt
1 teaspoon dark brown sugar
½ cup unsalted butter, diced and chilled
1 egg yolk, beaten
4 tablespoons ice water
2 tablespoons heavy cream, for brushing

Filling:
2 pounds ripe pears, cored and sliced (peeling is optional)
1 tablespoon freshly squeezed lemon juice
¼ cup sugar
3 tablespoons unsalted butter
1 teaspoon cinnamon (optional)

Lightly sweetened whipped cream or ice cream, to accompany

To make the crust, whisk together the flour, cornmeal, salt, and brown sugar. Using your fingertips, rub in the butter until the mixture resembles breadcrumbs. Combine the egg yolk and water and add to the flour mixture, mixing until the dough comes together, adding a little more water if necessary. Flatten the dough into a round, wrap in plastic, and refrigerate for 30 minutes before rolling.

Meanwhile, prepare the filling. Place the sliced pears in a large bowl and sprinkle with the lemon juice and sugar, tossing to combine. Melt the butter in a large, heavy skillet over medium heat. Add the pears and cook, stirring frequently, for about 12 minutes or until the pears have softened slightly and are golden brown. Stir in the cinnamon, if desired. Remove from the heat and set aside.

Preheat the oven to 375°F.

Roll out the crust to a 12-inch round. Transfer to a large baking sheet. Mound the pears in the center of the pastry, leaving a 3-inch border around the edges. Fold in the edges, partially covering the pears but leaving the center open. Brush the crust lightly with the cream. Bake for 35 to 40 minutes or until the pastry is lightly browned and crisp. Serve warm with lightly sweetened whipped cream or ice cream.

Orchard Salad with Maple Vinaigrette

Makes 4 servings

Plenty of local flavors come together in this versatile salad that can be used to start off a casual fall supper. Toss in some grilled or poached chicken and you have a luncheon salad. Use ripe apples or pears and pure local maple syrup in the vinaigrette for the most authentic flavor.

2 tart apples, such as Granny Smith, Rome, or Cortland, or 2 ripe pears, such as
    Comice or Asian pears (or a combination of pears and apples)
1 head romaine lettuce, washed and torn into bite-size pieces
½ red onion, sliced into thin rings
Salt and freshly ground black pepper, to taste
½ cup crumbled blue cheese or feta cheese
½ cup chopped walnuts or pecans, toasted
Maple Vinaigrette (page 61)

Core and slice the apples or pears. (Peeling is not necessary, if thinly sliced.)

In a large bowl, combine the lettuce and red onion. Season with salt and pepper. Drizzle ½ cup of the vinaigrette over the salad, tossing to coat. Divide the salad between 4 chilled salad plates. In the same bowl, toss the apples with an additional 2 tablespoons of dressing. Arrange on top of the salad mix and top with crumbled blue cheese and nuts. Serve immediately.

Pear and Red Onion Gratin

Makes 6 to 8 servings

You can tell a Bosc pear by its long, tapered neck and skin that's a shade of cinnamon brown. Dense and fragrant, the slices hold their shape in recipes that call for high heat and emerge with a honey-sweet, smooth texture, a nice contrast to the slight crunch of the onions.

3 firm, ripe pears, Bosc preferred
1 large red onion, peeled, trimmed, and cut into ½-inch wedges
1 tablespoon chopped fresh thyme
¼ teaspoon salt
Freshly ground black pepper, to taste
6 tablespoons unsalted butter or extra virgin olive oil, divided use
1 cup coarsely ground fresh whole wheat bread crumbs
½ cup grated Parmesan cheese

Preheat the oven to 425°F.

To make 1 cup of whole wheat breadcrumbs, use approximately 2 slices of bread and coarsely chop in a food processor.

Halve and core each pear. Cut each half into 6 slices. Place the slices in a large bowl along with the onion wedges, thyme, salt, and pepper. Melt four tablespoons of the butter and drizzle over the pear and onion mixture, tossing to coat. Arrange the mixture in a 9-inch square baking dish or a large gratin pan. Cover with foil and bake for 30 minutes, stirring once.

While the pears are roasting, combine the breadcrumbs and cheese in a small bowl. Melt the remaining 2 tablespoons of butter and drizzle over the mixture, tossing to combine.

Remove the pears from the oven and remove the foil. Sprinkle the crumb mixture over the top. Return to the oven and roast until the crumbs are browned, about 12 to 15 additional minutes. Cool for 10 minutes before serving.

• •

pear primer

There are more than 3,000 varieties of pears in the world and only a handful of heirloom varieties. Here are the varieties you're most likely to encounter throughout the growing season, with a description of the flavor each will bring to your baking or cooking.

Asian: Round and firm, even when ripe, it has a strong flavor and sweet aroma and holds its shape when poached. Good for salads.

Green or Red Anjou: The first variety to ripen. Egg-shaped and juicy, with a slightly spicy flavor. A good choice for baking in desserts.

Bartlett: Bell-shaped, sweet, and juicy, it's the only variety to change its color, from green to either gold or red, as it ripens. Enjoy fresh, baked, poached, or canned.

Comice: Orb-shaped with a short neck and stem and a floral fragrance. The flesh is very sweet and juicy, with a complex taste. Best for salads or eating fresh.

Bosc: Russet-colored, with a long, tapering neck. Its creamy flesh has a spicy flavor. A favorite for poaching and baking because it holds its shape.

Seckel: Tiny, almost bite-size green pear with a red blush and a pronounced sweet flavor. Holds its shape whether poached, roasted, or baked. Good for canning whole.

Wine and Honey Roasted Pears with Cinnamon Cream Cheese

Makes 6 servings

What pear wouldn't be lovely baked in sweet local honey and wine? You can use most any variety in this simple recipe, but check for tenderness as the pears roast, rather than trusting the cooking time, since size and firmness differ between varieties. If you use tiny Seckel pears, buy double the amount called for in this recipe. They are especially delicate looking and make lovely appetizers for your fall entertaining.

....

For a more savory flavor, substitute 1 tablespoon of chopped fresh rosemary for the cinnamon.

¼ cup cream cheese, softened
2 tablespoons sour cream or crème fraîche
2 tablespoons honey, plus extra to drizzle
½ teaspoon cinnamon
6 ripe but firm pears, unpeeled
2 tablespoons unsalted butter, softened
½ cup local dry white wine

In a small bowl, combine the cream cheese, sour cream, 2 tablespoons honey, and cinnamon until smooth. Cover and refrigerate until needed.

Preheat the oven to 375°F.

Cut each pear in half from the stem to the blossom end and remove the core, creating a small cavity in the pear (a melon baller is the perfect tool for this). Spread the butter in the bottom of a shallow baking dish large enough to accommodate the pears. Place the pears cut side down in the pan. Lightly drizzle each pear with the additional honey. Pour in the wine and bake for 30 minutes. Turn the pears cut side up and baste with the pan juices. Roast for an additional 10 minutes or until the pears are very tender but still hold their shape.

Remove the pears and arrange on a serving platter. Cover to keep warm.

Pour the pan juices into a small saucepan and bring to a boil. Continue to boil until very thick and syrupy and reduced to a couple of tablespoons.

To serve, spoon a dollop of the cream cheese mixture into the cavity of each pear and drizzle with the syrup. Serve warm or at room temperature.

Maple Applesauce

Makes 8 pints

Local maple syrup enhances the sweetness of this applesauce and adds a touch of smoky flavor, too. Choose a sauce apple, a variety that breaks down easily when heated, from among most early-season varieties, like Gala and Paula Red, or those that come later, such as Jonagold or Melrose.

....

This sauce can also be packed into pint containers or quart freezer bags and frozen for up to a year.

9 pounds apples, peeled, cored, and cubed
¼ cup water
2 tablespoons fresh lemon juice
½ cup pure maple syrup, more or less to taste
½ to 1 tablespoon ground cinnamon, more or less to taste (optional)

Place the apples and the water in a large, heavy-bottomed stockpot. Bring to a boil over medium-high heat, stirring frequently. Reduce the heat to low, cover, and simmer, stirring frequently, until the apples are soft, about 30 minutes. Mash with a potato masher or the back of a wooden spoon to the desired texture. Stir in the lemon juice and the maple syrup, 2 tablespoons at a time, tasting after each addition before adding more. Add the cinnamon, to taste. Return to a boil. Reduce the heat and simmer uncovered, stirring frequently, until the sauce thickens a bit.

Ladle the sauce into pint jars to within ½ inch of the rim (headspace). Seal and process for 20 minutes.

New to canning? For a step-by-step guide to the basics, see "Canning" on page 227.

Pear Sauce

Makes 6 pints

9 pounds pears, peeled, cored, and sliced
¾ cup water
2 tablespoons freshly squeezed lemon juice
1 to 1½ cups sugar (more or less, depending on sweetness of pears)
1 tablespoon ground cinnamon, more or less to taste (optional)

Pear sauce is a great addition to the locavore's pantry, and wherever applesauce is used, pear sauce can be called into service. When the harvest hands you a bushel of pears, be sure some of them go into a jar as pear sauce.

Place the pears and water in a large, heavy-bottomed stockpot. Bring to a boil over medium-high heat, stirring frequently. Reduce the heat to low, cover, and simmer, stirring frequently, until the pears are soft, about 20 minutes. Mash with a potato masher or the back of a wooden spoon to the desired texture. Stir in the lemon juice, sugar, and cinnamon, to taste. Bring to a boil. Reduce the heat and simmer uncovered, stirring frequently, until the sauce thickens a bit.

Ladle the sauce into pint jars to within ½ inch of the rim (headspace). Seal and process for 15 minutes.

New to canning? For a step-by-step guide to the basics, see "Canning" on page 227.

Orchard Chutney

Makes 4 half-pint jars

4 large tart apples (such as Granny Smith, Ida Red, or Jonathan)
  or 4 large firm pears (such as Bartletts), cored and chopped
1 large onion, chopped
½ cup red wine vinegar
½ cup packed dark brown sugar
2 tablespoons grated fresh ginger
2 tablespoons orange peel
½ teaspoon allspice
¼ teaspoon ground cloves
1 cup golden raisins

Chutney is a spicy condiment made from ripe fruits, simmered slowly to coax the flavors out of every ingredient. The result is a sweet and sour relish that is a delicious accompaniment to roasted chicken. Preserve it and enjoy in the recipe for Baked Brie with Orchard Chutney on page 202 with a glass of dry white wine.

Combine all of the ingredients in a large saucepan, stirring well. Bring to a boil. Reduce heat, cover, and simmer for 45 minutes. Uncover and simmer for 10 to 15 minutes or until the excess liquid has evaporated.

Ladle the mixture into half-pint jars to within ½ inch of the rim (headspace). Seal and process for 10 minutes.

New to pickling? For a step-by-step guide to the basics, see "Pickled Vegetables, Relishes, and Salsas" on page 239.

Local Flavor

apple cider

Apple cider lovers enjoy its unadulterated, authentic flavor that tastes of the growing season, reminding us of fall, heavy sweaters, and apple picking. But exactly what "cider" is varies from one region to another. In one corner of the world, cider or "dry cider" is an alcoholic drink made from fermented pressed apple juice. In another region, cider is the unfermented, pressed apple juice, opalescent or opaque and unfiltered, pasteurized or not, rich in apple flavor that everyone can enjoy.

You'll find some of the best cider at local orchards or small rural mills in apple-growing regions. The taste will truly reflect its locale, depending on what apple varieties thrive there and on the particulars of the past growing season. If it has been a dry summer, apples will be small and lack moisture but make up for it in sweetness—and that translates into the cider we sip cold or warmed with spices as fall slips into winter.

Cider makers typically blend cider from several different varieties of apple to achieve a balanced taste. Some cider apples are high in sugar, some in acidity, and others have desirable bitter qualities.

While you're sipping your cider, remember that apple cider also has a place as an ingredient in the locavore's kitchen. You can use it as a flavorful base for soups like the Three Onion and Cider Soup on page 139, or reduce it to a glaze to brush over sautéed chicken or pork, or add a splash or two when making applesauce, for an extra boost of flavor. Cider also freezes well and can be used throughout the winter for the same types of recipes or simply warmed and sipped when you're in the mood for the return of fall.

Apple Cider Syrup

Be prepared for an amazing and intense apple flavor in this syrup. It's simple to make and just requires a little patience while the cider reduces. A swirl of butter adds a little extra silkiness to this unique syrup that can be used to top Pumpkin Pancakes with Cider Syrup (page 208), waffles, ice cream, yogurt, and more.

Makes 1 cup

4 cups good-quality apple cider
1 tablespoon unsalted butter (optional)
Ground cinnamon, to taste (optional)

Place the cider in a large saucepan and bring to a boil. Reduce the heat so the liquid remains at a simmer. Simmer for 45 minutes to an hour or until the liquid reduces to 1 cup or less. Remove from the heat, and if desired, stir in the butter and season with cinnamon to taste. Let cool to room temperature. This syrup will be thin when warm but will thicken when refrigerated. Before serving, gently warm in a saucepan or in the microwave and drizzle over pumpkin pancakes. This syrup will store in the refrigerator for about 4 months.

···

For the best of both syrup worlds, mix equal measures of apple cider syrup and maple syrup for your next batch of pancakes.

To freeze apple cider: Fill ice cube trays or smaller containers with lids with apple cider, leaving some room for expansion.

in season ...
onions, garlic, & more

Yellow, red, and white storage onions, garlic, and shallots are close cousins with distinct personalities. Onions can be mild, strong, or sweet; shallots are delicate and tender; while garlic varieties can be meek to downright fiery. Leeks, refined and buttery, are a distant and delicious relative. Cooking mellows the natural pungency of any variety, adding aromatic undertones to a dish. Used raw, each packs a punch of varying extremes in salads or salsas.

Choosing the Best. Collectively, onions, garlic, and shallots should be firm, plump, and fill out their skins. Signs of aging include soft, wrinkly outer skins or a withered look. Any that show a sprouting green top are apt to have a bitter, unpleasant taste.

Leeks should be straight, firm, and about an inch thick, with upper leaves that are moist and green. The usable portion is the white section, from the root end up. The more white, the better.

How to Store Fresh. Onions, garlic, and shallots should be stored, skins intact, in the coolest part of the kitchen for short periods of time, about 2 weeks. To store them longer, place them in mesh bags and store in a cool, dark, and dry place, such as a cellar or attached garage. Check occasionally for signs of mold or sprouting.

Leeks, with the roots still attached, can be loosely wrapped in plastic and stored in the refrigerator crisper for about a week. Freshly harvested leeks will keep for almost 2 weeks.

To Prepare for Cooking. How you treat or cut onions, garlic, shallots, or leeks determines how strong the taste will be. The more you expose the interior by slicing, chopping, or mincing, the more intense the flavor. For example, a whole clove of garlic is quite mild, but smash it and it releases juices from exposed surfaces. Chopped onions are milder than minced onion, and sliced shallots are tamer than diced. Onions, garlic, and shallots do not need to be washed, merely peeled.

Leeks, on the other hand, tend to have a lot of dirt trapped between their layers. To remove it, discard any tired or withered-looking outer leaves. Cut off the green upper leaves at the point where the green begins to pale. Cut a slit down the leek to the center, not all the way through. Gently fan the leaves and run under lukewarm water to remove the dirt. Let drain and pat dry with a paper towel before slicing or using whole.

Pick or Buy Now, Enjoy Later. In addition to keeping a reliable stash of storage onions, garlic, and shallots, try pickling red onions as a lovely condiment for hearty roasted meats. Use the recipe for Pickled Red Spring Onions on page 43 but substitute the late-harvest onions.

Three Onion and Cider Soup

Three's a charm when it comes to this soup, loaded with sweet onion flavor. It's rich and flavorful and brings three of the season's best together in one bowl. Adding cider to this soup stock creates a sweet balance to the savory meat stocks and a mellow contrast to the sharp, strong cheese.

Makes 8 servings

1 tablespoon unsalted butter
3 tablespoons extra virgin olive oil
2 large Spanish onions (not sweet onions), thinly sliced
2 medium leeks (white and pale green parts only), thinly sliced
4 shallots, thinly sliced
2 cups apple cider
2 cups rich chicken stock
2 cups beef stock
Salt and freshly ground black pepper, to taste

Cheese Croutons:
8 (1-inch-thick) slices French-style bread
Extra virgin olive oil for brushing
1½ cups shredded strong aged cheese, such as Muenster or Gruyère
3 tablespoons chopped fresh parsley
Pinch of cayenne pepper

Melt the butter in a heavy-bottomed stockpot over medium heat. Add the oil. Stir in the onions, leeks, and shallots. Cook, stirring often, until the onions are soft and browned, about 10 to 12 minutes. Add 1 cup of the apple cider. Turn the heat to high and bring the liquid to a boil. Cook until the liquid has almost evaporated, about 3 minutes. Add the remaining cider and the beef and chicken stocks. Return to a boil. Reduce the heat and simmer for about 15 minutes. Season with salt and pepper.

Preheat the oven to 375°F.

Brush the bread slices on both sides with olive oil. Place in a single layer on a baking sheet. Bake for 10 minutes or until golden brown. Remove from the oven. Combine cheese, parsley, and cayenne. Top each bread slice with the cheese mixture. Return to the oven and bake until the cheese is melted, about 5 minutes.

Ladle the soup into individual bowls. Top each with a toasted cheese crouton. Serve immediately.

Drunken Leeks

Tender leeks bathing in luscious red wine, preferably a local find, will fill your kitchen with an amazingly heady aroma. The leeks emerge with a taste so sweet, you'll swear they're candy. Serve them as a side dish to roasted meats or chicken.

Makes 4 servings

2 tablespoons unsalted butter
8 small leeks, trimmed, washed, white parts sliced ½-inch thick
   (about 2½ to 3 cups total)
1 clove garlic, crushed
½ cup local red wine
Salt and freshly ground black pepper to taste
Splash of red wine vinegar
Chopped fresh parsley, for garnish

Melt the butter in a large skillet over medium-high heat. Add the leeks and garlic and sauté for 4 minutes. Add the wine and season lightly with salt and pepper. Reduce the heat to low, cover, and cook for 15 minutes or until the leeks are tender.

Add a splash of red wine vinegar. Season lightly again with salt and pepper. Garnish with chopped parsley. Serve immediately or at room temperature.

Leek and Tomato Tart

Makes 6 to 8 servings

*As an appetizer, a main
course, or simply a
snack, there's little room
to go wrong with this
combination of seasonal
leeks and fresh tomatoes.
Be creative and spread
a few tablespoons of
pesto on the crust before
layering the cheese or
add some thin strips of
roasted red pepper with
the leeks and tomatoes.*

1 recipe pie dough for one 9-inch tart, page 128
4 ounces shredded provolone cheese
½ pound leeks, white portion only, thinly sliced
3 medium plum tomatoes, thinly sliced
2 cloves garlic, minced
¼ cup grated Parmesan cheese
1 cup shredded mozzarella cheese
Freshly ground black pepper, to taste

Preheat the oven to 425°F.

Roll out the prepared crust to a 12-inch circle. Transfer to a heavy rimmed baking sheet.
Sprinkle the provolone cheese over the surface of the dough, leaving 2 inches around the
edges. Arrange the leeks and tomato slices over the cheese and scatter the garlic over.
Sprinkle the Parmesan and mozzarella over the top and season to taste with pepper.
Fold in the edges of the dough (a large portion of the filling will remain uncovered). Bake
for 25 minutes or until the crust is lightly browned and the cheese has melted. Cut into
wedges and serve warm.

Garlic Soup with Parsley Spaetzle

Makes 8 servings

*Four heads of garlic
in one soup sounds
daunting, but slow
cooking over a low flame
has the amazing effect of
mellowing the "stinking
rose" into something
sweet and wonderful.*

*Steer clear of garlic that
has sprouted, which can
be harsh and unpleasant
regardless of how long it is
cooked. While cooking will
tame even the strongest-
flavored garlic, the best
variety to use for this soup
is German Music, a good
all-purpose garlic.*

If peeling all this garlic
is the only thing standing
between you and this
recipe, here's an easy
way to tackle the chore.
Separate the cloves from
the bulb. Place about
a dozen at a time in
a jar with a lid. Shake
vigorously for 20 to 30
seconds and the papery
skins will have fallen away
from the cloves.

1 tablespoon extra virgin olive oil
3 or 4 heads garlic, cloves separated, peeled and coarsely chopped
8 cups vegetable stock or rich chicken stock
Salt and freshly ground black pepper, to taste

Spaetzle:
1½ cups all-purpose flour
½ teaspoon salt, plus 1 tablespoon for cooking water
½ teaspoon freshly ground black pepper
¼ teaspoon double-acting baking powder
½ cup chopped fresh parsley or cilantro
2 eggs, lightly beaten
½ cup water

Heat the oil in a large heavy-bottomed stockpot over low heat. Stir in the chopped garlic
and sauté, stirring often, until the garlic is soft and translucent, not browned. This will take
about 20 minutes. Keep the heat low and stir frequently to make sure the garlic doesn't
brown. Add the stock and bring to a boil. Reduce the heat to low and simmer, partially
covered, for about 45 minutes or until the garlic is very tender and mellow in taste.

Meanwhile, prepare the spaetzle. Whisk together flour, salt, pepper, baking powder,
and parsley in a medium bowl. In a separate bowl, combine the eggs and water. Add
this to the flour mixture, stirring to combine completely. Cover and refrigerate for 1 hour.
Bring a large pot of water to a boil. Add a tablespoon of salt. Force the dough through a
colander with large holes or through a food mill with large holes directly into the boiling
water. Cook until the spaetzle are light and delicate, about 5 minutes. Drain.

Taste the soup and season to taste with salt and pepper. Add the spaetzle to the warm
soup. Serve immediately.

Marinated and Grilled Red Onions

Make 6 to 8 servings

Nothing complements a juicy burger like grilled onions. These get an extra boost of flavor with a simple marinade. Transform this recipe into an interesting first-course salad by separating the rings after grilling, cooling to room temperature, and adding another splash of balsamic vinegar, a sprinkling of freshly chopped parsley, and some crumbled feta cheese, if desired.

2 large red onions, peeled and cut into ½-inch-thick slices, rings left intact
¼ cup fresh lemon juice
¼ cup extra virgin olive oil
¼ cup Worcestershire sauce
¼ cup balsamic vinegar
Salt and freshly ground black pepper, to taste

Pierce each onion slice horizontally with a wooden skewer to keep the rings intact. Place in a 9 x 13-inch glass baking dish (trim the ends of the skewers to fit, if necessary). Combine the lemon juice, oil, Worcestershire, and vinegar in a blender. Pour over the onions and let marinate at room temperature for at least 2 hours and up to 6 hours, basting occasionally.

Preheat the grill to medium-high. Oil the grill grate.

Remove the onions from the marinade and arrange on the grill. Cook 5 minutes on each side, until grill marks appear and the onions are tender. Remove and let cool slightly before removing the skewers.

Season to taste with salt and freshly ground black pepper and serve as a side dish with grilled steak or as a topping for hamburgers.

Roasted Garlic Cloves

Makes ½ to 1 cup

The only thing better than the house filled with the aroma of sweet garlic roasting in the oven is having a cache of roasted garlic in the refrigerator. The garlic cloves emerge soft, mellow, and spreadable and can be used as a condiment, added to soups and stews, tossed with hot vegetables, mixed into mashed potatoes, or used to top a baked potato. This technique will work with any variety of garlic and will mellow out even the ones with the most fiery disposition.

8 heads of garlic
½ cup extra virgin olive oil
½ cup balsamic vinegar
1 tablespoon fresh rosemary leaves
Pinch of salt

Remove the excess papery skin from the heads of garlic, leaving the head intact. Using a sharp knife, cut about ¼ inch or so off the tops of the garlic heads, exposing the tips of garlic.

In a small bowl, combine the oil, vinegar, and rosemary. Place the heads of garlic and the oil mixture in a resealable plastic bag. Seal, pressing out as much air as possible, and marinate at room temperature for 8 hours, shaking the bag occasionally.

Preheat the oven to 375°F.

Remove the garlic heads from the marinade and place them cut side down in a shallow baking dish. Pour the marinade into the dish. Cover tightly with foil. Bake for 45 to 50 minutes or until the garlic is soft and yields to a gentle squeeze.

Remove from the oven and cool. The garlic should slip easily from the skins with a gentle squeeze. Squeeze all the cloves into a bowl and mash with a fork, working it into a paste, adding a few drops of oil and a pinch of salt. Store in the refrigerator for up to a month.

Garlic-Rubbed Bread

This simple preparation for garlic bread delivers a lot of garlic flavor by simply exposing the clove with one simple cut. Rubbing steaks and other meats with a split garlic clove before they hit the broiler or grill also adds a lot of garlic flavor with minimal effort.

Makes 4 servings

4 1-inch-thick slices of crusty bread
Extra virgin olive oil, for brushing
Salt and freshly ground black pepper
2 cloves garlic, split in half

Preheat the oven to 375°F.

Brush one side of each bread slice with olive oil. Sprinkle with salt and pepper. Toast in the oven for 12 to 15 minutes or until golden brown.

Remove from the oven. Rub each toasted surface with a split garlic clove. Serve immediately with the garlic clove, if desired.

Roasted Potatoes and Shallots

Roasting is the perfect technique for bringing out the sweet side of shallots—or any type of onion, for that matter. Give the shallots a head start in the oven before they meet up with buttery potatoes for a simple yet highly flavorful side dish.

Makes 6 servings

6 large shallots, peeled and halved
3 tablespoons extra virgin olive oil, divided use
Salt and freshly ground black pepper, to taste
1½ pounds Yukon Gold potatoes, on the small side, peeled and quartered

Preheat the oven to 400°F.

Toss the shallots with half of the oil. Season with salt and pepper and toss again. Distribute evenly in a 9 x 13-inch baking pan. Roast for 15 minutes, stirring once or twice.

Toss the potatoes with the remaining oil. Season with salt and pepper and toss again. Add to the shallots and roast, stirring once, for an additional 35 to 40 minutes, or until the potatoes are crusty and browned on the outside and tender on the inside. Serve hot.

name that garlic

After years of buying garlic at the grocery store, the convenience store, the big box store, wherever it can be found, you may be under the impression that only one variety of garlic exists in the world—from place to place it all looks and tastes the same. The reality is that there are thousands of garlic varieties that come from every corner of the world—and the best place to find them is at your farmers market.

Garlic is divided into two broad categories: softneck and hardneck, each with very distinct characteristics. Softneck varieties are better keepers and can be stored for longer periods of time. The heads have many smaller cloves.

Hardneck garlic has a wider range of flavors and produces cloves that are big and plump, often 8 cloves or fewer to a head. They won't keep as long or as well as softneck varieties and should be used soon after purchasing. These are the varieties you're bound to come across at farmers markets.

Choosing garlic to add to a dish is a lot like choosing wine to go with dinner. Some add heat, others add sweetness, while still others are perfect for roasting and baking, and then there are those that can be enjoyed raw. Here's a sampler of popular varieties found at farmers markets. Always be open to lesser-known varieties that you're bound to come across.

Music: A good all-purpose variety with large, plump cloves and medium-hot taste; a classic garlic flavor.

Chesnok Red: Plump bulbs in a pretty purple-striped wrapper with a lingering flavor; excellent choice for roasting or baking.

Brown Tempest: Brown-skinned cloves with a fiery punch that mellows in the pan.

Italian Purple: A classic Italian garlic; peels easily, roasts to a buttery texture; versatile enough for most Italian dishes.

Persian Star: Large, fat cloves with red tips and a middle-of-the-road garlic flavor; makes the sweetest roasted garlic.

Spanish Roja: One of the best-tasting garlics around, with a piquant flavor that fades quickly; low odor and easy to peel.

Carpathian: Strong garlic flavor, hot, spicy, and pretty to behold with fat, purple-tinged cloves.

Georgian Crystal: Beautiful fat cloves with a well-rounded garlic flavor and mild enough to be enjoyed raw in salsas, bruschetta, and salads.

Siberian: A reliable all-purpose variety with a medium to strong flavor that lingers but doesn't overpower.

Making Your Own: Flavorful Stocks

In the locavore's kitchen, scraps, "throwaways," humble vegetables, and lesser cuts of poultry and meat can be the beginning of something wonderful like chicken, vegetable, or meat stock, the gold standard of cooking. It is one of the most economical and versatile ingredients you can keep on hand in the refrigerator or freezer, and it has the power to make or break a soup, a sauce, or a stew—a pretty big responsibility for something that comes from such humble beginnings.

The secret to success is in coaxing as much flavor from the key ingredients as you can. It doesn't always mean that those ingredients are the best, most expensive cuts of meat or the fresh vegetables in the refrigerator. They are actually the less desirable cuts, the bones and the vegetables that are not rotting, but have seen better days—prime choice for highly flavored stock. Carrot peelings, celery leaves, the tops of green onions, and leeks that look as if they will never amount to anything add plenty of flavor to stocks.

Wonderfully rich and flavorful, stocks can be made fresh with vegetables that define the season and will be reflected in the finished stock: chard leaves and spring onions sweeten a stock made in the spring; summer's tomatoes add color and acid in summer soups; and you'll love what the stringy interiors and seeds from squash will do for stocks simmered in the fall. Try adding any of these stocks to the cooking water for rice or beans and see what a difference they make. To brighter the flavor of chicken and vegetable stock, add a healthy squeeze of fresh lemon.

Rich Chicken Stock

Makes about 12 cups

The difference between great and mediocre stock has a lot to do with what goes into it. If you've already made friends with a farmer who raises pastured poultry, you're one step closer to a great stock. Ask him or her for necks, backs, wings, or bones saved from butchered chickens or save the bones from recipes calling for the bones to be removed or the carcass from a whole roasted chicken. "Stockpile" smaller amounts in freezer bags in the freezer until you have enough for making stock. Chicken bones are full of flavor and body and create a rich, almost creamy, stock.

5 pounds chicken parts (bones, wings, necks, and backs preferred)
3 carrots, scraped, trimmed and cut into 2-inch pieces
1 onion, peeled and quartered
3 cloves garlic, peeled and crushed
2 stalks celery, leaves attached, bottoms trimmed, cut into 2-inch pieces
1 bunch fresh parsley
3 sprigs fresh thyme
2 fresh bay leaves
1 tablespoon whole peppercorns, lightly crushed

Preheat oven to 450°F.

Place the chicken parts, carrots, onion, and garlic in a large roasting pan. Roast for 30 minutes, shaking the pan occasionally and turning the ingredients once or twice until everything is nicely browned.

Place the celery, parsley, thyme, bay leaves, and peppercorns in a large stockpot. Using a slotted spoon, transfer the roasted ingredients into the stockpot. Drain off any fat and scrape any browned bits from the bottom of the pan into the stockpot. Add cold water to cover.

Bring the contents of the stockpot to a boil, then partially cover and adjust the heat so the liquid is at a very slow simmer, sending up only a few bubbles at a time. Remove any impurities that rise to the surface. Simmer for 2 hours.

Strain through a fine-mesh strainer lined with cheesecloth. Press on the vegetables and chicken pieces to extract as much liquid as possible. Taste and season with salt. (For a more concentrated flavor, bring the stock to a full boil and let it reduce until the flavor is to your liking, tasting at frequent intervals, then salt to taste.)

Cool the stock to room temperature. Cover and place in the refrigerator for up to 48 hours. The fat from the stock will rise and congeal at the surface. Remove carefully with a slotted spoon and discard. Use stock immediately or within 5 days, storing it in the refrigerator; or freeze for up to 6 months.

Vegetable Stock

Makes about 8 cups

For some people, carrot peelings, celery leaves, corncobs, and mushroom stems are either trash or compost. It's the same dilemma with vegetables that may be a little past their prime, like celery that's a bit limp or tomatoes not pretty enough for a salad.

The resourceful cook—the locavore—knows that these are the makings of a magnificent vegetable stock, a great base for soups that feature other vegetables, like the Cabbage and Mushroom Soup on page 176, or the flavorful liquid that enhances dishes such as the creamy Pumpkin Risotto on page 196. Made correctly, rich and highly flavored, vegetable stock can often be used as a substitute for chicken stock and is helpful for converting some dishes to vegetarian options. Lighter and sweeter than meat-based stocks, it does its job quietly, but deliciously, in the background when the focus is on stronger flavors.

2 tablespoons unsalted butter or extra virgin olive oil
2 cups coarsely chopped yellow onion
2 cups chopped celery, including leaves
1½ cups chopped carrots
1 cup chopped leeks (green leaves only)
4 cloves garlic, peeled and crushed
1 bunch fresh parsley, leaves and stems, chopped
2 sprigs fresh thyme
1 fresh bay leaf
½ tablespoon peppercorns, crushed
Salt, to taste

Heat the butter or oil in a large stockpot over medium heat. Add the vegetables, herbs, and peppercorns and stir to coat. Cook, uncovered, until the vegetables have softened and released some of their liquid, about 30 minutes. Take care that the vegetables don't brown.

Add enough cold water to the pot to just cover the vegetables, about 6 cups. Bring to a gentle boil. Adjust the heat so the stock remains at a gentle simmer, cover, and cook without stirring for about an hour until the stock is flavorful and takes on some color.

Strain the stock through a fine-mesh sieve lined with cheesecloth. Press gently on the vegetables to extract as much of the liquid as possible. Taste and season with salt.

Let cool to room temperature. Use immediately, store in the refrigerator for up to a week, or freeze for up to 6 months.

● ●

customize vegetable stock

Vegetable stocks can be made all season long using sweeter, less assertive vegetables. Here are some helpful hints on how to tweak the flavor to customize it for the dish you're preparing.

- To sweeten the flavor of the stock, use vegetables like carrots, parsnips, red peppers, or celery. Add a total of 2 extra cups of those vegetables to the basic recipe.

- To make a flavorful stock for chowders, save stripped corncobs and add them to the stock. A half dozen cobs will do the trick.

- Tomatoes add great color and flavor to vegetable stocks, welcome in heartier soups but not always desired for lighter-colored cream soups.

- For a deeper, earthier stock, save mushroom stems or caps and add one to two cups to the basic recipe along with a couple of sprigs of marjoram.

- In soup recipes that feature squash or pumpkin, add any variety of winter squash, seeds and strings included, to the basic stock recipe.

- Use herbs judiciously. Strong herbs like tarragon, rosemary, oregano, and sage can overwhelm delicate vegetable stocks and turn bitter when cooked for long periods. Use sparingly, just a few sprigs, and add toward the end of the cooking time, tasting until the flavor you desire is achieved and removing the sprigs afterward.

- More assertive vegetables that should be avoided in stocks include broccoli, cauliflower, cabbage, Brussels sprouts, and turnips. Asparagus should be used sparingly and only for soups featuring asparagus. Starchy potatoes will cloud the stock.

Meat Stock

Makes 8 cups

The heartiest, most assertive of all meat stocks, whether beef, veal, or lamb, are crafted not from meat or bones alone but from meaty bones like shank cuts. Look for the cuts that have a balanced ratio of bone to meat. You can make an even fuller-flavored stock by roasting the bones (meat removed) before adding them to the stock. Simply arrange them on a baking sheet and roast in a 400°F oven until the bones begin to brown. Blood on the bones can make a stock cloudy, so soak them in cold water for 30 minutes before roasting or using raw.

6 pounds shanks (beef, veal, or lamb), meat separated from the bones and reserved, fat trimmed and discarded, bones roasted if desired (see the side note)
1½ tablespoons extra virgin olive oil
1 large onion, coarsely chopped
1 carrot, coarsely chopped
1 rib celery, coarsely chopped
1 clove garlic, peeled and crushed
½ cup red wine (optional)
6 sprigs parsley
2 sprigs fresh thyme
1 fresh bay leaf
1 teaspoon black peppercorns, crushed
Salt, to taste

Heat the oil in a large stockpot over medium-high heat. Add the onion, carrot, and celery. Cook and stir until the vegetables are soft, fragrant, and beginning to brown slightly. Add the garlic and cook for an additional minute. Add the red wine and cook for a few additional minutes until the liquid has evaporated. Add the herbs and peppercorns. Add the bones and reserved meat, weighing down the other ingredients. (If the bones have been roasted, scrape any particles and juices from the pan into the stockpot.)

Cover with cold water to just above the bones. Bring to a boil, skimming any impurities that rise to the top. Reduce the heat to a simmer. Cook for 2 to 2½ hours, without stirring, until the meat is tender and the stock has achieved a rich, beefy flavor.

Strain the stock through a fine-mesh sieve lined with cheesecloth. Press gently on the solids to extract as much liquid as possible. Reserve the meat, shredding into small pieces for soups. Taste the stock and season with salt.

Cool the stock to room temperature. Cover and place in the refrigerator for up to 48 hours. The fat from the stock will rise and congeal at the surface. Remove carefully with a spoon and discard. Use the stock within 5 days, storing it in the refrigerator; or freeze for up to 6 months, packing and freezing the reserved meat separately.

• •

freezing stock

Chilled finished stocks can be frozen in a number of increments. Freeze one- or two-tablespoon-size portions in ice cube trays. When solid, transfer to freezer bags. Store larger quantities in freezer containers with tight-fitting lids, leaving an inch of headspace for expansion. An efficient way to store 4 to 8 cups of stock is in gallon-size freezer bags with sturdy zip-lock seals. After adding the stock, press out as much air as possible before sealing. Test the seal to make sure the bag is completely closed and no liquid is leaking out. Label the contents and place these bags flat on a sturdy baking sheet in the freezer until frozen solid. Remove and stack flat in the freezer.

in season ... *potatoes*

In the hierarchy of fresh fruits and vegetables, there is none more common, humble, or basic than a potato. Although it may be the "plain Jane" of ingredients, it's rare to find someone who doesn't appreciate or love a good spud mashed, baked, roasted, grilled, steamed, boiled, or fried.

Although a potato grows underground, it's technically not a root but a tuber, the part of the plant that swells as it stores food for the plant that grows overhead. While there are thousands of potato varieties, they basically break down into a few main groups by common characteristics. To simplify it even further, potatoes can be divided into two easy categories: baking potatoes and boiling potatoes.

Choosing the Best. Potatoes that are high in starch are better for mashing, frying, and baking. You can usually tell these baking varieties by the skin, which should be coarse and cork-like. Boiling potatoes or waxy potatoes have thin, smooth peels and a waxy flesh. They hold their shape when boiled or can be parboiled and roasted to a finish. Any potato should feel firm and heavy for its size and be free of blemishes and soft spots.

How to Store Fresh. Whether freshly dug or purchased, potatoes should never be washed before being stored. If stored at room temperature, potatoes will keep a week or two, but if you store them in a spot that is cool, dry, and dark, you'll add more time to their storage life. Never store potatoes in the refrigerator because they will darken when cooked.

To Prepare for Cooking. Whether to peel potatoes is a matter of preference and depends on the final goal of the recipe. On thin-skinned varieties, the peel cooks up soft and tender. Potatoes with a coarse peel have a rustic texture and chew. Peeled or cut potatoes exposed to air darken quickly at room temperature. To prevent this, place them in cold water until needed. Potatoes exposed to light often turn green or sprout—just remove these harmless spots with a knife.

Pick or Buy Now, Enjoy Later. For the home cook, freezing raw potatoes is rarely successful and canning is not a storage option. If you have a dark, dry cellar or an attached garage where the temperature holds between 45°F and 50°F, you can store potatoes throughout cold weather. Place them unwashed in a few layers, separating each layer with newspaper. On occasion, one will begin to rot, which you'll smell before you see the decay. Be sure to remove those.

If you're successful at long-term storage, potatoes can be a part of your menus throughout the winter, used in the same ways as when they are freshly harvested.

Chicken Thighs with Roasted Red Potato Crust

Makes 6 to 8 servings

Fresh red-skinned potatoes hold together when cooking, so they are the perfect option for the crust that crowns this dish. Underneath its golden finish wait meaty and richly flavored chicken thighs bathed in a garlicky balsamic sauce. Thick slices of crusty bread are recommended to catch every last drop.

8 chicken thighs, bone in, skin on, and trimmed of excess skin
Salt and pepper, to taste
4 tablespoons extra virgin olive oil, divided use
4 cloves garlic, smashed, plus 3 cloves, slivered
1/3 cup balsamic vinegar
1/2 cup chicken broth
1 1/2 tablespoons chopped fresh rosemary
3 to 4 large red potatoes, sliced 1/4 inch thick

Season the chicken thighs with salt and pepper. Heat 2 tablespoons of the oil in a heavy, 10-inch ovenproof pan over medium-high heat. Brown the chicken pieces on both sides, about 6 minutes per side. Remove the chicken from the pan and drain on a paper towel–lined plate. (The skin may be removed at this point, if desired.)

Drain all but 1 tablespoon of the excess oil and fat from the pan. Return the pan to the heat and add the smashed garlic and the vinegar, scraping the bottom to loosen any browned bits. Add the broth and the rosemary and let boil until the liquid is reduced by half. Return the chicken to the pan, cover, and lower the heat. Simmer for 10 minutes.

Preheat the oven to 400°F.

In a large bowl, toss the potato slices with the garlic slivers, remaining oil, and salt and pepper to taste until the slices are coated. Layer the potato slices over the top of the chicken, forming a crust all the way to the edges. Bake uncovered for 40 to 50 minutes or until the potato crust is golden brown.

To serve, spoon some of the pan juices over the chicken and potatoes with each serving.

what are new potatoes?

New potatoes often show up at markets in the spring or summer, tiny tots also known as creamers or fingerlings. Basically they are immature, freshly harvested versions of potatoes that left to grow will be much larger by the fall harvest. New potatoes are prized for their tender texture, and all that's necessary to enjoy their natural buttery flavor is to simply boil or roast them, toss with butter, and serve with a sprinkling of good salt and freshly ground black pepper. Mature red potatoes and new potatoes can be used interchangeably in recipes that call for either.

potato primer

A spud is a spud is a spud is not true. Each has particular nuances that make it a better candidate for one recipe than another. Select yellow, white, or red potatoes for boiling, steaming, roasting, or gratins. These potatoes have a firmer texture and won't fall apart when cut. Yellow and red potatoes can also be mashed, but they won't be as fluffy as russets.

New Potatoes, Fingerlings, or Creamers: Young, tender, naturally buttery, low in starch and best for baking, roasting, steaming, and boiling.

Russet: Very high in starch and best choice for mashed and baked potatoes.

Red: Low in starch and best in recipes where the potato needs to hold its shape. Good for boiling, steaming, and roasting and for scalloped and au gratin (covered with breadcrumbs or cheese) preparations. Does not make a fluffy mashed potato.

White: Another low-starch potato and a good choice for potato salads.

Yellow: Buttery-colored, all-purpose potatoes with medium starch that can be mashed or baked whole, steamed, boiled, or roasted, and are good choices for soups and chowders.

Blue-, Purple-, or Red-Fleshed Varieties: Medium in starch and tend to lose their vibrant color when boiled, steamed, and generally overcooked. Recipes that call for baking and roasting are better choices.

Roasted New Potatoes with Molasses

Makes 4 servings

Sweet, smoky bacon and thick, rich molasses deliver big flavors in this recipe. Bacon fat is certainly an indulgence, not for everyday use, and if you prefer, olive oil can be substituted for the bacon fat.

1 pound small red new potatoes, washed and unpeeled
2 or 3 strips of bacon
½ teaspoon salt
½ teaspoon freshly ground black pepper
1 to 2 tablespoons dark molasses
2 tablespoons chopped fresh parsley

Preheat the oven to 400°F.

Place the potatoes in a large pot and cover with water. Bring to a boil and cook for 10 to 15 minutes until almost tender. Drain.

Fry the bacon in an ovenproof skillet over medium heat until crisp. Drain on paper towels. Remove all but 2 tablespoons of fat from the skillet. Add the potatoes and sauté for 10 minutes or until lightly browned, turning frequently. Season with the salt and pepper.

Transfer to the oven and bake for 30 minutes or until browned, turning once. Remove from the oven and drizzle with the molasses and sprinkle with parsley. Serve immediately.

Laura's Potato Pancakes

Makes about 14 potato pancakes

Crispy on the outside, tender and buttery on the inside, this recipe will rival and replace any potato pancake recipe you are less than happy with. Be sure to use a high-starch potato such as a russet or a good all-purpose Yukon Gold, both easy to find at farmers markets.

Making your own crème fraîche is easy and delicious. For complete directions, see page 50.

9 large russet potatoes, washed and peeled
2 carrots, grated
2 medium onions, grated
¾ cup matzo meal or cracker crumbs
2 teaspoons salt
Freshly ground black pepper, to taste
Dash of freshly grated nutmeg
6 large eggs, lightly beaten
Vegetable oil for frying
Applesauce, to accompany
Sour cream or crème fraîche, to accompany
Chopped chives, for garnish

Place the peeled potatoes in a large bowl of cold water to slow discoloration. Coarsely grate, using a box grater. Drain well in a colander, squeezing to eliminate excess liquid.

In a large bowl, combine the potatoes with the grated carrots and onions, matzo meal, salt, pepper, and nutmeg. Add the eggs and mix well.

Pour enough oil in a large heavy frying pan to reach ¼ inch up the side. Heat over medium heat. When a shred of potato dropped into the oil sizzles and browns quickly, the oil is ready. Place about ¼ cup of the mixture into the hot oil and flatten slightly with a spatula. Fry until golden brown on the edges, then turn to the other side and fry until golden brown and crispy. Drain on paper towels. Serve immediately or keep warm in a 200°F oven, arranged in a single layer on a paper towel–lined baking sheet.

Serve with homemade applesauce and sour cream or crème fraîche and garnish with chopped chives, if desired.

the truth about sweet potatoes

Sweet potatoes and yams are two different vegetables: the first is a root vegetable, the second a tuber, and neither is related to the potato. True yams are neither sweet nor locally grown but prefer tropical growing climates. The candied yams with the soft texture and pumpkin-like flavor that have always been a part of Thanksgiving menus are actually a tender orange-fleshed sweet potato, one of a few varieties commonly available. You'll also find sweet potatoes with a very firm, pale yellow flesh, well suited for recipes where they need to hold their shape, like the Oven Fries, on page 149. Sweet potatoes often appear at farmers markets. They do not store well, so buy what you will use within 2 weeks.

Savory Potato and Cheese Pie

Makes 6 to 8 servings

The fall harvest of potatoes in this recipe absorbs the cream for an incredibly buttery finish. Serve this for lunch with a simple green salad or cup of light soup or in smaller portions at dinner to accompany roasted chicken.

Ingredients like these deserve a wonderful crust. Whether you're new to the art of making piecrusts or a skilled baker looking for a new recipe, try your hand at One Perfect Piecrust on page 128.

1 prebaked 9-inch piecrust shell
1 pound or 2 large russet or yellow-fleshed potatoes, peeled and cut into 1-inch cubes
2 cups heavy cream
1½ teaspoons salt
1½ teaspoons Dijon mustard
1 cup (4 ounces) Swiss cheese, grated
1 tablespoon chopped fresh parsley
1 tablespoon chopped fresh chives

Preheat the oven to 350°F.

In a small saucepan, combine the potatoes, cream, and salt. Place over medium heat and bring to a simmer, stirring frequently to prevent scorching. When the potatoes are fork tender, strain in a colander set over a bowl, reserving the cream. Brush the bottom of the pie shell with the mustard and sprinkle the cheese evenly over the bottom. Top with the potatoes and half of the reserved cream (use the remainder for a soup, if desired). Sprinkle with the herbs. Bake for 20 minutes or until golden brown in spots. Cool for 15 minutes before serving.

Oven Fries

Makes 4 servings

You can use russet potatoes or firm-fleshed sweet potatoes in this recipe that turns out crispy fries with a tender middle. And what goes better with fries than ketchup? Homemade ketchup! Learn to make your own Fresh Tomato Ketchup on page 124.

To spice up the fries a bit, season with paprika, garlic, onion powder, or the seasoning of your choice before baking.

2 to 3 large russet potatoes or sweet potatoes, peeled and cut into
    ½-inch-thick planks
1 teaspoon salt
½ teaspoon sugar
2 tablespoons extra virgin olive oil or vegetable oil
Coarse salt and freshly ground black pepper

Preheat the oven to 450°F.

Fill a large bowl with cold water. Add the salt and sugar, stirring to dissolve. Add the potatoes and let soak for 15 minutes. Drain and pat dry. Wipe the bowl dry.

Return the potatoes to the bowl. Drizzle with olive oil and toss until coated. Arrange the potatoes in a single layer on a large baking sheet. Sprinkle with salt and pepper. Bake for 45 minutes or until crispy and brown. Serve immediately.

Roasted Sweet Potato Mash with Cider and Ginger

Makes 6 servings

When the holidays roll around, it's time to indulge in great flavor, and that's what this recipe delivers. The natural sweetness of the concentrated cider and the kick of fresh ginger make this one side dish destined to become a holiday tradition.

3 large sweet potatoes
4 cups apple cider
2 to 3 tablespoons freshly grated ginger root, more or less to taste
2 tablespoons unsalted butter
Salt and freshly ground black pepper, to taste

Preheat the oven to 400°F.

Using a fork, pierce a few holes in the sweet potatoes. Bake for about 1 hour until soft. Let cool enough to handle easily. Scoop the potato from the skins into a large bowl and mash.

While the sweet potatoes are baking, bring the cider to a boil in a large heavy saucepan over high heat. Reduce the heat to medium low and simmer until the cider is reduced to about 1 cup. Stir in the ginger and butter.

Gradually stir the cider mixture into the sweet potatoes until the desired consistency is reached. Taste and season with salt and freshly ground black pepper to taste. Serve immediately.

Perfectly Mashed Potatoes

Makes 6 servings

Most cooks have beaten potatoes into a thick, gluey paste at least once. Follow this recipe to the letter and you'll be guaranteed better results next time. Here are a few additional tips to remember. First, choose the right potatoes, those higher in starch like russets or yellow-fleshed potatoes. This recipe uses a handheld electric beater to add "fluff" and volume without as much effort. Regardless of your mashing tool of choice—a wire mash, ricer, or mixer—know when to quit. Sample your work often for taste and texture.

2 pounds potatoes, peeled and cut into 1-inch cubes
1 tablespoon salt
¾ cup heavy cream or milk
2 tablespoons unsalted butter, softened
Salt and freshly ground black pepper, to taste
Freshly ground nutmeg, to taste (optional)

Put the prepared potatoes into a large pot. Add water to cover by an inch and add the salt. Bring to a boil, then lower heat to maintain a steady simmer. Reduce the heat and simmer until the potatoes pierce easily with a fork and fall apart, about 20 minutes. Meanwhile, gently warm the cream in a small saucepan or the microwave.

Drain the potatoes in a colander and return to the pot. Dry the potatoes over medium heat, shaking and stirring until some of the water has evaporated and the potatoes look "floury." Using a handheld electric mixer set to low speed, mix until most of the lumps have disappeared, only about 1 minute. Using a sturdy mixing spoon, mix in the butter. Stir in the warm cream until the desired consistency is reached. Season to taste with salt and pepper and a grating of fresh nutmeg, if desired.

Variations

Chive Mashed Potatoes: Omit the butter. Add ½ cup softened cream cheese with ¼ cup freshly chopped chives.

Feta Mashed Potatoes: Blend ¾ cup crumbled feta into the heavy cream or milk until smooth. Stir into the potatoes.

Pesto Mashed Potatoes: Omit the butter and add ⅓ cup prepared pesto.

Garlic Mashed Potatoes: Increase the amount of butter to 3 tablespoons. Melt butter in a small skillet. Add 4 to 6 crushed garlic cloves and sauté until lightly browned, about 1 minute. Stir into the potatoes.

New Potato Salad with Dill

Makes 8 servings

Make this the first potato salad of the picnic season when new potatoes and fresh dill arrive. Later in the fall, when larger red-skinned potatoes make their appearance, substitute dried dill weed for fresh, about ¼ cup.

4 pounds new potatoes
1 medium red onion, diced, or 1 cup thinly sliced scallions
1 cup mayonnaise
1 cup yogurt
2 tablespoons extra virgin olive oil
2 tablespoons lemon juice
1 tablespoon Dijon mustard
½ cup fresh dill, minced
1½ teaspoons salt
1½ teaspoons freshly ground black pepper
Sprigs of fresh dill, to garnish

Place the potatoes in a large pot and cover with water. Bring to a boil. Cook for about 15 minutes (more or less depending on size of the potatoes), until a fork easily pierces the potatoes yet they still hold their shape. Drain and allow to cool slightly. Slice the potatoes in half or quarters, depending on the size. Transfer to a large bowl. Add the red onion.

In a blender, combine the mayonnaise, yogurt, olive oil, lemon juice, mustard, minced dill, salt, and pepper and process until completely blended. Pour over the potatoes. Mix well. Chill at least 4 hours or overnight. Garnish with sprigs of dill and serve.

mushrooms

When you hear the word "mushroom," what's the image that pops into your head? Probably the ubiquitous white button mushroom. If so, you may not be spending enough time at your local farmers market. Other than the forest floor, farmers markets are the next best place to find fresh varieties of mushrooms with different flavors and textures, many of which will forever shatter your idea of what a mushroom tastes like.

It may come as a surprise, perhaps a shock, that there are hundreds of species of edible mushrooms, the majority of which are harvested from the wild—when the conditions allow in any given season. A fraction of those varieties can be cultivated, a labor-intensive process demanding that the grower create the perfect balance of humidity, air quality, and growing medium.

Different varieties of mushrooms have particular features to look for, but in general smell is a good indicator of what's in store. Fresh mushrooms should smell earthy, clean, and pleasant. Look for plump, meaty mushrooms that feel slightly spongy. The caps should be dry, not slimy, and show no signs of withering, spotty bruising, or pits. Avoid caps that are shriveled or broken. The caps on criminis should be closed where they meet the stem. On exotic varieties like oyster mushrooms, the gills under the cap are open and should be light in color, not black. If they need cleaning, gently rinse and pat dry.

Most varieties of mushroom can be eaten raw, thinly sliced and scattered over salads, used whole as crudités, or tossed into soups, stocks, and sauces. When you want to call out the rich earthy flavors and textures, choose a sauté.

mushroom primer

Here are some of the most popular cultivated and wild mushroom species you'll come across at farmers markets. Always be on the lookout for unusual varieties that may come and go with every visit.

Shiitakes are a popular variety of mushroom, highly fragrant with a powerful, distinct flavor, almost steak-like. Remove the tough stems and save to flavor soups and stocks.

Chanterelles are trumpet-shaped mushrooms ranging in color from yellow to bright orange. They have a chewy texture, a slightly nutty flavor, and don't like to be overcooked. Add to dishes at the end of cooking.

Criminis are shaped like the familiar button mushroom but firmer, darker brown, and fuller flavored.

Portabellos are mature versions of criminis. Dark brown and meaty in texture, they lack moisture although they hold up to the heat of the grill. Remove the woody stems and use to flavor stocks. Use the cap whole or slice for sautéing.

Lobster mushrooms, also called Lion's Mane mushrooms, are sweet, rich, and distinctively flavored. Good for sautéing, they are best standing alone because their flavor can get lost among other mushroom varieties.

Oyster Mushrooms are both cultivated and harvested from the wild. Fan shaped and in a range of colors (pink, golden, gray, and brown), they are robust and peppery eaten raw and mellowed by cooking—a good, all-purpose mushroom with great texture.

Mushrooms Sautéed in Wine

Experience the tremendously rich blend of earthy flavors in this simple sauté that you can use to top a burger or a fine steak.

Makes 4 servings

3 tablespoons unsalted butter
1 pound mushrooms, a single variety or a combination
1/3 cup dry red wine
2 tablespoons chopped fresh parsley
1 tablespoon balsamic vinegar or lemon juice
Salt and freshly ground black pepper, to taste

Melt the butter in a heavy skillet over medium high heat. Add the mushrooms and sauté until soft and lightly browned. Add the wine and continue to cook, stirring often, for 5 minutes. Sprinkle with vinegar and parsley and toss to combine. Season with salt and pepper. Serve immediately.

in season ... *peppers*

Bell peppers and chile peppers are members of the same family and, as families go, they exhibit a wide range of temperaments—from sweet and mild to hot and fiery. Knowing the differences ensures that your finished dish will have the flavor and degree of heat you want.

Early in the season, bell-shaped peppers arrive as green as grass, fully developed although immature, with a slightly bitter flavor. Left to ripen on the plant, they return in a few weeks showing their true colors—dark reds, deep purples and browns, creamy or vibrant yellows, and brilliant oranges—and full of sweet flavor.

Chile peppers are smaller and more tapered than bell peppers and are usually harvested fully ripe in a range of warm colors. They add heat and spice to a dish through capsaicin, a heat-producing compound, found in their membranes.

Choosing the Best.
Choose firm, shiny peppers and chiles with deep, even coloring and no signs of soft spots or wrinkled skin. A fully developed bell pepper is plump and blocky and features three or four lobes on the base.

When choosing chile peppers, remember that size, not color, is a fairly reliable clue to the heat within. As the varieties get smaller in size, the heat they deliver gets bigger, but it's still helpful to know specific varieties and their particular flavor nuances.

How to Store Fresh.
Keep fresh, unwashed peppers and chiles in the crisper drawer of the refrigerator. Those that have fully ripened will keep for about 5 days, while immature green peppers will keep a few days longer.

To Prepare for Cooking.
To cut up a whole pepper, slice off about a half inch from the top and bottom. Then split the pepper from top to bottom with one cut and open to lay flat. Remove the bitter seeds and white, spongy membranes with your fingers or a knife and discard. Then slice the pepper into the desired thickness, broad enough to scoop dips or in match-like slivers to scatter in salads. To create a dice, cut horizontally across the slices.

Working with chiles requires a cautious approach. Heat-producing capsaicin found in the membranes can be transferred from your hands to whatever you touch, producing an unpleasant burning sensation. Wearing disposable kitchen gloves when working with chiles and cleaning anything that comes in contact with them is good advice. One of the easiest ways to slice a chile pepper is to cut the top off, then slice in half from stem end down, exposing the membranes and seeds. Removing any portion of these will control how much heat that particular chile will deliver. Then chop or slice as desired.

Pick or Buy Now, Enjoy Later.
An abundance of red or yellow bell peppers can be roasted, peeled, and frozen. Fresh diced bell peppers can be frozen for about 3 months; they will lose their firm texture, but can be used in cooked recipes.

Chile peppers can be dried at room temperature, in a dehydrator, or in a low oven, then stemmed and ground for seasoning or frozen whole in small portions and used to flavor or season cooked dishes and soups.

Learn to make Roasted Red Peppers (page 158), a versatile ingredient whether pureed into dips and soups or cut into strips and scattered across a pizza crust.

Preserve the seasonal flavor of chile peppers with Hot Pepper Jelly on page 157.

Greek Stuffed Peppers

Makes 6 servings

Bell peppers make the greatest little containers for meat and vegetable mixtures, imparting flavor to dishes. Choose peppers with flat bottoms that with a little trimming can stand upright in the baking dish. This recipe can easily be tweaked to the classic version of bell peppers by substituting ground beef for the lamb and omitting the dill and mint.

6 green or red bell peppers, washed
3 tablespoons extra virgin olive oil
1 medium onion, diced
2 cloves garlic, minced
¼ cup finely chopped fresh parsley
¼ cup finely chopped fresh dill
1 teaspoon finely chopped fresh mint
3 cups tomato sauce, divided use
1 pound lean ground lamb
¾ cup rice, cooked
Salt and freshly ground black pepper, to taste
6 tablespoons crumbled feta cheese

Preheat the oven to 375°F.

Cut the tops off the peppers and hollow out the interior to remove the ribs and seeds. Set aside.

Heat the oil in a large skillet over medium-high heat. Add the onions and sauté for 6 minutes or until soft. Add the garlic and sauté for an additional minute. Add the parsley, dill, mint, and 1 cup of the tomato sauce. Simmer until the mixture has thickened. Cool slightly.

Mix the lamb and the cooked rice in a large bowl. Add the tomato mixture and mix all the ingredients with a wooden spoon. Season with salt and pepper, to taste. (Fry or microwave a spoonful of the mixture to taste for seasoning.)

Stuff the peppers with the mixture. Place them in a deep casserole dish. Add the remaining tomato sauce along with a little water to thin, if desired. Cover and bake for 1 hour or until the meat is cooked and the peppers are tender. Remove from the oven and top each pepper with 1 tablespoon feta. Let sit for 10 minutes before serving.

Corn and Bell Pepper Relish

Makes 5 half-pint jars

This relish keeps for up to 6 weeks in the refrigerator and doesn't call for processing in a hot water bath. It's a wonderful, seasonal gift from the locavore's kitchen. Make it often, share it freely.

2 cups cider vinegar
1½ cups sugar
½ teaspoon freshly ground black pepper
1 green bell pepper, diced
1 red bell pepper, diced
1 cup yellow or orange bell pepper, diced
3 cups cooked corn kernels
1 tablespoon freshly chopped basil

Combine the vinegar, sugar, and pepper in a large saucepan. Bring to a boil. Reduce heat and simmer 10 minutes. Add the bell peppers and simmer for 3 minutes. Stir in the corn and basil. Cool to room temperature. Spoon into sterilized jars, making sure to cover with the liquid. Cover and refrigerate for up to 6 weeks.

Pasta with Roasted Red Pepper Cream Sauce

Makes 4 servings

Roasting bell peppers makes the flesh so very tender and sweet and the perfect texture for pureeing into a smooth sauce. The cooked pasta gets folded into the sauce; a little of the cooking water added to the mix helps the noodles absorb the sauce so the flavor travels throughout. Enjoy with a slice of crusty bread and some fresh salad greens.

Learn to roast red peppers on page 158.

1 tablespoon extra virgin olive oil
1 medium onion, diced
½ to 1 teaspoon dried red pepper flakes
4 cloves garlic, minced
4 roasted red peppers, roughly chopped
½ cup fresh parsley or fresh basil, coarsely chopped
¼ cup heavy cream, room temperature
½ cup Parmesan cheese, grated
Salt and freshly ground black pepper, to taste
1 pound spaghetti, cooked according to package directions; keep warm and reserve 1 cup of the cooking water

Heat the oil in a large saucepan. Add the onion and sauté over medium heat for 6 minutes or until soft. Add the garlic and red pepper flakes and sauté for an additional minute. Add the roasted red peppers and cook for about 5 minutes. Add the herbs and cream and remove from heat. Cool for several minutes before pureeing in the pan with an immersion blender or transferring to a stand blender to puree.

Return to the saucepan and rewarm gently. Stir in the cheese and salt and pepper to taste. Combine the cooked pasta with the sauce in the saucepan, adding some of the reserved water if the mixture appears dry. Serve immediately.

- -

know your peppers and chiles

A beautiful display of colorful peppers and chiles at the farmers market tempts the most adventurous or curious cook to dive right in and try them all. Curiosity and a sense of culinary adventure is good—but when it comes to these vegetables, it's good to know what's in store. Although the smaller varieties look harmless, they can pack a hot punch that for the meek and unsuspecting can be an unpleasant experience. Here is a general guideline of some of the most common varieties and their flavor profiles. Remember that milder chiles have broad shoulders and blunt tips, while hotter chiles have narrow shoulders and pointed tips. When in doubt, talk to the farmer or grower, who can tell you exactly what's in store.

Bell Peppers and Pimentos: The mildest and sweetest varieties of peppers, they are the only ones that do not include capsaicin, the compound that produces heat in other peppers and chiles. Use these mild peppers raw in relish trays and salads; in a wide range of cooking methods, including stir-frying and roasting; or for stuffing.

Banana Peppers: Don't confuse these with yellow Hungarian wax peppers. Although they are similar in appearance, wax peppers have a strong bite. The bright "banana"-colored pepper is sweet and good on relish trays, in sandwiches and salads, and fried in a buttermilk batter.

Anaheim Peppers: These large, tapered, shiny, bright green peppers range in flavor from mild and sweet to moderately hot. Dice them and use for soups, casseroles, and Mexican dishes.

Cayenne Peppers: About as big as your pinky finger, these peppers show up at farmers markets green in the summer and red in the fall. Used in sauces, pickled recipes, and salsas, they are also good for drying and storing whole or grinding into a powder.

Poblano Peppers: Nicknamed the "bell pepper of Mexican cuisine," these mild, thick-walled, heart-shaped peppers are great for stuffing or adding to chilies, where they impart a deep, rich flavor.

Jalapeño Peppers: Grassy and fruity, jalapeños offer a good amount of heat, showing up green in the late summer and turning to red if left to completely ripen.

Serrano Chile: Medium to hot small (2-inch-long) waxy chiles that change to red and orange as they mature. The smaller they are, the more kick they have.

Thai Chiles: Small in size, mighty in the punch they pack. Ranging in color from red to green when fully mature. Use sparingly.

Habañeros: Hot, hot, hot—but underneath the heat is a fruity, apple-like flavor. Remove the seeds and membranes to tame the heat.

Red Pepper and Pear Soup

Makes 8 servings

Some of the season's naturally sweet vegetables "pear" up with ripe red peppers in this soup that looks and feels like a cream soup on the tongue yet doesn't contain a drop of cream. If you develop a taste for this soup in the winter, substitute about 6 roasted red peppers from the freezer.

....

This soup can also be served chilled. Allow to cool to room temperature before storing in the refrigerator for at least 6 hours or overnight.

2 tablespoons extra virgin olive oil
8 red, orange, or yellow bell peppers or a combination, seeded and coarsely chopped
2 carrots, peeled and cut into thin slices
1 medium onion, chopped
2 cloves garlic, minced
4 cups rich chicken or vegetable stock, plus extra, if needed
1 ripe pear, peeled and chopped
1 teaspoon salt
¼ teaspoon cayenne pepper
Crème fraîche, for garnish (optional)
Chopped parsley, for garnish

Heat the olive oil in a heavy pot over medium-high heat. Add the peppers, carrots, onion, and garlic and sauté for 2 minutes, stirring constantly. Reduce the heat to low, cover, and cook for 20 minutes, stirring frequently, until the peppers are soft and tender but not browned.

Add the chicken stock and pear. Increase the heat and bring to a boil, then reduce the heat so the soup remains at a simmer. Cover and cook for 20 minutes. Let cool.

Working in batches, puree the soup in a blender until smooth. Return to the pot and season to taste with salt and cayenne pepper. Thin the soup, if desired, with additional chicken stock. Serve hot with a dollop of crème fraîche, if desired, and a sprinkling of chopped parsley.

Buttermilk-Battered Banana Peppers

Makes 8 appetizer servings

Sweet banana peppers bathed in rich buttermilk and coated in crunchy cornmeal and salty cracker crumbs make it worth standing around the frying pan to make sure you get your share. Be careful to use the sweet banana peppers and not Hungarian wax peppers, similar in appearance but worlds apart in the heat they deliver and even hotter when fried.

8 banana peppers, washed, patted dry
1 cup buttermilk
1 cup finely ground cornmeal
1 cup crushed saltine crackers
Vegetable oil, for frying

Pour the vegetable oil into a deep frying pan to a depth of about ¾ inch. Heat over medium-high heat.

Slice the peppers in half lengthwise and remove the seeds and membrane. Pour the buttermilk into a wide, shallow bowl. In another wide, shallow bowl, mix together the cornmeal and crushed crackers. Dip the prepared peppers into the buttermilk, then coat in the cornmeal mixture.

When the oil is hot, add the peppers in batches and fry until golden brown, about 3 minutes. Drain on paper towels. Serve warm.

Jalapeño Poppers

Makes 4 servings

Plump, juicy jalapeños have a fresh, grassy flavor and a little heat that's tamed by the addition of cream cheese. Wrap in a strip of smoky bacon, cook over an open flame, and enjoy watching your friends devour the entire batch.

12 medium fresh red or green jalapeño peppers
4 ounces cream cheese, softened
1 teaspoon ground cumin (optional)
6 strips thick-sliced bacon, cut in half
Toothpicks
Cooking spray to coat

Preheat the oven to 400°F or heat a grill to medium-hot.

Cut the peppers in half lengthwise, leaving the stem intact. Remove the seeds and membranes. Mix the cream cheese with the cumin, if using. Stuff each half with about 1 teaspoon of cream cheese. Put the halves back together, wrap with a strip of bacon, and secure with a toothpick.

Place the peppers on a baking sheet that has been treated with cooking spray. Bake for about 20 minutes, turning once, or until the bacon is crispy. Or cook on the grill until the bacon is crispy. Remove from the heat, let cool slightly, and serve.

Poblano Chicken

Makes 4 servings

This southwest-style sauce adds great flavor to chicken. Poblanos are usually picked immature when their color is a dark forest green. On occasion you'll find them in their mature state, reddish brown and much sweeter. The first imparts an earthy quality to the sauce; the latter, a sweeter, richer flavor. Both work equally well in this recipe.

3 or 4 poblano chiles, seeded and chopped
½ cup heavy cream or whole milk
4 tablespoons unsalted butter, divided use, plus extra for buttering
1 tablespoon all-purpose flour
Salt, to taste
4 boneless, skinless chicken breasts
1 cup shredded Gouda cheese

Place the chiles and cream in a blender and puree until smooth.

In a medium saucepan, melt 2 tablespoons of the butter over medium heat. Whisk in the flour. Cook until golden brown, whisking constantly. Reduce the heat to low and whisk in the cream mixture. Continue whisking until the mixture thickens and begins to bubble. Remove from the heat and season with salt. (This sauce can be made a day in advance and refrigerated.)

Melt the remaining butter in a medium skillet. Sauté the chicken breasts for 4 minutes on each side. Transfer to a buttered baking dish. Pour the poblano cream sauce over the top and top with the grated cheese. Bake uncovered for 20 minutes or until the cheese is golden and bubbly. Let cool for 10 minutes and serve.

Sweet Bell Pepper and Tomato Crostini

Makes 6 appetizer servings

It's nature's gift to you that peppers and tomatoes both ripen to perfection at the same time. Combine two of the garden's best flavors in this quick preparation, perfect for appetizers or with a dinner salad. If there's any extra left over, store in the refrigerator for up to 2 days and enjoy warmed on a baked potato or as a condiment for sandwiches.

6 tablespoons extra virgin olive oil, divided use
1 medium onion, diced
2 yellow, orange, or red bell peppers, seeded and diced
2 ripe Roma tomatoes, seeded and chopped, juices reserved
¼ cup water
1 tablespoon chopped parsley
Salt and freshly ground black pepper, to taste
6 ½-inch slices rustic-style bread, toasted or grilled
Freshly grated Parmesan cheese, to garnish

Heat 3 tablespoons olive oil in a large skillet over medium heat. Add the onions and sauté for 6 minutes or until soft and transparent. Add peppers and sauté 7 to 10 minutes more or until the peppers are soft. Add the tomatoes and water. Bring to a boil, then reduce the heat and simmer for 15 minutes until the peppers are soft and most of the water has evaporated. Remove from the heat and let cool slightly.

Transfer the mixture to a blender and puree. Return to the skillet. Add the parsley and season with salt and pepper to taste. Cook until the mixture thickens and is spreadable, about 10 minutes. Spoon over the toasted bread, garnish with a grating of cheese, and serve immediately.

Hot Pepper Jelly

Makes 7 half-pint jars

When you need a little extra warmth in the winter, reach for a jar of this Hot Pepper Jelly. As long as your recipe measures 2¾ cups of peppers—really fresh, seasonal peppers— you can play with the combination, adding more sweet pepper varieties over hot or maybe even tossing in a habañero or two—for real chile heads. Pour a jar over softened cream cheese and serve with salty crackers for a simple yet delicious appetizer or use it to make the Pesto-Stuffed Pork Tenderloin with Hot Pepper Jelly on page 210.

3 red bell peppers, seeded and chopped
1 green bell pepper, seeded and chopped
2 Hungarian hot wax peppers, seeded and chopped
4 jalapeños, seeded and chopped
1 cup cider vinegar
1.75-ounce package powdered pectin
5 cups sugar
½ tablespoon crushed dried red pepper, more or less as desired

Combine the peppers, jalapeños, vinegar, and pectin in a large, heavy pot. Stir to combine. Stirring constantly, bring the mixture to a full rolling boil (one that won't stop when stirred) over high heat. Stir in the sugar and red pepper flakes and return to a full rolling boil, stirring constantly. Boil for one minute. Remove from the heat and skim off any foam that has developed.

Ladle the jelly into sterilized half-pint jars to within ¼ inch of the rim (headspace). Seal and process for 5 minutes.

New to making jams, jellies, and preserves? For a step-by-step guide to the basics, see "Jams, Jellies, and Preserves" on page 237.

Making Your Own: Roasted Red Peppers

A kitchen without sweet red peppers is not as sweet. When the end of summer rolls around, the green peppers of summer turn red—same shape, different color, and an entirely different flavor. The grassy bell peppers we sautéed for side dishes or for topping burgers have developed a sweet flavor that we can't get enough of in soups, salads, appetizers, sauces, and more. When they are roasted—blackened and caramelized under high heat—well, the sweet is on! Perfect this technique for roasting seasonal red, yellow, or orange peppers. Roast a lot—then freeze them in small batches. Thaw and use them to puree into dips or add to sauces, as a base or extra flavoring for soup, on pizzas, in sandwiches, and more—lots more!

Roasted Red Peppers

Save small sections of the trimmed tops and bottoms to chop and add to salads or freeze and add to soup stocks later.

Use roasted red peppers in the winter on the Chicken and Roasted Red Pepper Pizza on page 203.

- Choose red peppers that have firm, glossy skin, no wrinkles and certainly no soft spots. Rinse and pat it dry.

- Using a sharp knife, slice a portion off both ends, discarding the green stem and the bottom.

- Make one cut through the wall of the pepper and open the pepper up on your cutting surface so it lies flat. Using your knife or fingers, remove the membranes and the seeds from the interior of the pepper and discard.

- Place the cleaned peppers, skin side up, in a single layer on a broiler pan. Flatten them with the palm of your hand so they lie as flat as possible. (Alternatively, place the peppers skin side down on a hot grill and flatten with a spatula.)

- Broil or grill the peppers until the skins are just charred and blackened.

- Transfer the peppers to a paper or plastic bag and seal. Set aside for 20 minutes. During this time the pepper will continue to cook and the skin will soften and loosen from the flesh.

- Remove from the bag and slip or, using the dull edge of a knife, gently scrape away the charred skin. (Don't worry about removing every blackened fleck.)

- Let cool completely before packing in small portions, about 2 to 3 peppers, in freezer bags. Squeeze as much air from the bag as possible before storing in the freezer for about 6 months. Thaw before using.

Making Your Own: Dried Chile Peppers

There's more than one way to preserve the abundance of flavorful chiles the garden or the local harvest will hand you. Sun-drying is an option if you live somewhere where you're assured the sun beats down and the temperature will hover at 100°F to 140°F for a few days straight. Lacking a commercial dehydrator, you can turn to oven drying, an effective but not very energy-efficient method that also tends to fade the color of brightly hued chilies. Or you can simply take advantage of the air around you. Smaller, thinner-walled chilies like cayenne, habañero, jalapeño, and serrano are good choices for drying, shedding their moisture within weeks yet still retaining their heat.

From your garden or at the farmers market, chiles typically arrive in abundance, greater than your current need. Choose or harvest chiles that are fully ripe and have developed their color; they should be firm to the touch and smooth skinned, free of blemishes. Completely dried chilies can be stored up to a year, there to warm you up in recipes throughout the winter ahead.

Dried Chile Peppers

As an alternative to hanging, the chilies can be spread in a single layer on wire racks. It's just as effective as hanging, but will take up more room.

- Wash and dry fully ripe chiles.
- Thread a needle with about a yard of heavy-duty thread or thin fishing line. At one end, tie a small clean wooden stick. This will keep the chiles from slipping off the thread.
- Wearing protective gloves, thread the chiles by running the needle through the center of each pepper horizontally (wall to wall, not stem to tip), stacking them one on top of another in a rotating manner.
- When you have about 6 inches of string left, wrap the string around the last pepper and thread it under the loop you've just created to keep the peppers in place.
- Hang the strand in a warm, well-ventilated place and let nature do the work. Depending on the temperature and air circulation, drying the chilies can take as little as 2 weeks or as long as 5 weeks.
- When the peppers feel firm and smooth, dry to brittle, they are ready to use or store. Leave them threaded and hang in the kitchen (although they will become dusty), or remove them from the thread and store them in a jar with a tight-fitting lid in a cool, dark place. Perfectly dried chilies can be stored up to a year or ground into a powder for your spice cupboard.

grinding dried chiles into powder

Once the chiles are dried and brittle they can be ground into a powder and used in pinches or better for any recipe. To add a wonderful roasted quality to the dried chiles, lightly toast them in a hot skillet until fragrant, taking care not to burn them. Remove from the skillet and let cool completely before grinding.

To grind dried chiles into powder, remove the stems and break the pods into small pieces. Place in a spice grinder, blender, or food processor and process to a powder. Let the ground powder settle for a few minutes before opening the lid. Take care not to inhale the fine powder. If desired, sieve the powder through a fine-mesh kitchen sieve to remove unground flakes or large seeds. Store in tightly sealed jars in a cool, dark pantry.

rehydrating dried chiles

The need to rehydrate whole dried chiles depends on the recipe you're using. If you want to flavor a soup or stew, just toss the dried chiles straight into the pot and let the liquid do the work for you. When the recipe calls for chopped or sliced chiles, it's best to revive them to a soft, useful texture. Place the chiles in a bowl, cover with boiling water, and let sit for 30 minutes to an hour or until softened. (You may have to repeat this process a second time for larger, thicker-walled chiles.) Drain and slice or chop as desired. Wear protective gloves when handling the chiles and be aware that soaking chiles may give off some strong aromas. Sniff with caution!

Local Flavor

fish & aquaculture

The local fishing hole used to be a good way to kill time and catch supper all in one glorious afternoon. Fresh fish pulled from a pond or stream and brought home on the end of a string meant that dinner was not far off—just as soon as someone stepped up to clean the catch.

Over the past 30 years, our taste for fish has exceeded what nature can provide. The world's supplies of fresh and saltwater fish and shellfish have dwindled while the prices have soared. Natural fisheries—from small ponds and rivers to expansive lakes and oceans—have became sorely depleted, overfished and taxed to the point where the fish population is slow, sometimes unable, to recover. When the situation is compounded by pollution, contaminants, and troubling consumer advisories, the pleasure of snagging a fresh catch from local water is, in some ways, not what it used to be.

To keep fish on the table, aquaculture, also called aquafarming or fish farming, has emerged as a sustainable answer, a renewable food source and one of the fastest-growing sectors of agriculture throughout the country. Defined as the cultivation of fresh and saltwater fish in a controlled environment, aquaculture operations can range in size from a hobby farm pond to feed a family to small dedicated facilities where production, measured in thousands of pounds, feeds local communities to large commercial operations where the harvest is measured in millions of tons to feed populations around the world. More than half the fish we consume as a nation are farm raised.

Many varieties of fish are conducive to aquaculture practices and farm raising, including popular species such as yellow perch, rainbow trout, channel catfish, tilapia, hybrid striped bass—even shrimp. The process of raising fish for food has much in common with the way that farmers raise their crops and livestock, involving some of the same skills and activities as familiar agricultural practices. Think of it as underwater farming where instead of getting their hands dirty, farmers get their hands wet.

It begins with eggs hatched in incubator trays. The hatchlings develop into fry and then grow to "fingerlings," fish as big as a small finger. Like plants and animals, they need proper tending, feeding, and monitoring of water and growing conditions to thrive to adulthood or reach desired market weight, when they are harvested as food.

Aquaculture can be carried out in a natural environment like open water in large net enclosures that allow access to natural flows of water or in a man-made environment such as levee ponds, tanks, or water-recycling enclosures indoors where feed and nutrients are carefully controlled and fish are harvested year round.

Aquaculture is not a new idea. It has been developed over thousands of years in Asia. Today it is receiving increased attention and plays an even bigger role in putting fish on the table in our own communities where some small family farms have integrated aquaculture as a sidebar to existing practices. The practice has certainly skewed the definition of "locally raised fish," those we once pulled from local waters. Yet like farming, aquaculture is meeting the demands of a growing population by feeding our desire for healthy, nutritious seafood.

Baked Fish in Parchment Paper

Makes 1 serving

Fish baked in parchment paper is the perfect technique for oven baking thinner filets of fish, the kinds you'll find from aquaculture operations, without drying it out. The paper steams the food, trapping the juices released during baking to baste the contents.

You can modify this recipe by using your favorite seasonal herbs, seasonings, and thinly cut vegetables. This recipe serves only one, but you'll see that it would be easy to scale this to serve as many as you would like.

One small fish filet (perch, trout, or catfish), about 6 ounces
2 small red potatoes
12 fresh snow peas
¼ cup julienne carrots
Salt and freshly ground black pepper
1 teaspoon minced ginger root
1 clove garlic
Squeeze of fresh lemon or orange
Slice of lemon or orange
1 tablespoon butter or a drizzle of olive oil

Preheat the oven to 400°F.

Bring a small pot of water to a boil. Blanch the potatoes for 7 to 10 minutes, until a fork can be easily inserted. Remove potatoes from the water and set aside, reserving the water. Add the peas and carrots and blanch for 30 seconds. Remove and set aside to cool. Cut the potatoes into ¼-inch slices.

Cut a piece of parchment paper into a square, about 4 times the size of the filet. Arrange the filet on the paper, just to the right of center. Place the vegetables on top of the fish and season with salt and pepper. Sprinkle the ginger root, garlic, and lemon juice over the fish. Place the lemon slice and the butter on top. Bring the edges of the parchment together and fold down loosely over the fish, crimping to seal. Place on a sturdy baking sheet. Bake for 12 to 15 minutes (slightly longer for a thicker filet) or until the fish flakes easily when tested with a fork.

Place packet on a warmed dinner plate and serve immediately, opening slowly to allow the steam to escape.

Broiled Filet Rollups

Makes 4 to 6 servings

Rolling up thin filets into tidy bundles is an interesting way to present this dish, but there's a bigger reason at play. This method helps ensure that the filets emerge tender and moist, even when exposed to the high heat of the broiler. The bubbly, cheesy topping glazes the mild filets for an extra special presentation.

8 thin, skinless fish filets, 4 to 5 ounces each (such as tilapia)
Salt and freshly ground black pepper
⅓ cup mayonnaise
½ cup freshly grated Parmesan cheese
Grated zest from 1 large lemon
1 tablespoon freshly squeezed lemon juice
½ teaspoon Worcestershire sauce
1 small clove garlic, minced
2 tablespoons coarsely chopped Italian parsley

Position the oven rack 4 inches from the broiler element. Preheat the broiler. Spray a broiler pan with nonstick cooking spray. Set aside.

Lightly season the filets with salt and pepper. Beginning at the narrow end, roll up each filet and arrange seam side down on the broiler pan.

Broil until the tops are lightly browned, 7 to 8 minutes (more if the filets are bigger, less if smaller).

Meanwhile, whisk the mayonnaise, Parmesan, zest, juice, Worcestershire, and garlic in a small bowl. Season with pepper to taste.

Remove the pan from the broiler and spread a heaping tablespoon of the mayonnaise mixture evenly over the top of each filet, using a knife to smooth. Return to the broiler until the mayonnaise mixture is golden brown and bubbling, about 2 minutes. Transfer the filets to a serving platter or dinner plates, garnish with the parsley, and serve immediately.

in season ... *root vegetables*

At first blush, you might wonder what could be so wonderful about something that looks so rough and is often dressed with a fine dusting of soil. With a simple drizzle of oil, a sprinkle of salt and pepper, and some oven time, your answer arrives in the incomparable natural sweetness and earthy characteristics of root vegetables—beets, carrots, parsnips, and turnips. Technically, these are the taproots supplying the energy for the leafy green tops we see aboveground.

Proper steaming of these cool-season vegetables delivers vibrant colors and a genuine, fresh taste, while braising mellows the color and flavors. Roasting, on the other hand, deepens and intensifies colors and sweetness. This cooking method has undoubtedly converted former foes of root vegetables into the greatest of friends and fans.

Choosing the Best. There's a lot of information attached to the leafy greens of root vegetables—if the greens are still attached to the roots. The frilly fronds on carrots and parsnips should be fresh and green looking, with no signs of yellowing. Avoid roots that are dry, shriveled, cracked, limp, or sprouting hair-like rootlets, signs of overgrowth and old age. The deeper the color of the carrot, the fresher. Parsnips should be creamy white, not tan.

When it comes to beets and turnips, the stems should be only a few inches long and the edible leaves on top fresh, green, and small, not much bigger than the root itself. The roots should be firm, smooth skinned, and heavy for their size. Pass on those that are spongy or marred by cuts and brown spots.

How to Store Fresh. The rules for storing carrots, beets, parsnips, and turnips are basically the same. Remove the leaves, leaving about an inch of stem, and store, unwashed, in a perforated plastic bag in the crisper of the refrigerator. They should keep for about two weeks in the crisper. Keep in mind that as they age, turnips develop a stronger, more bitter taste; carrots and parsnips fade in color and develop a woody texture; and beets become tougher. If the beet or turnip greens are in good condition, store them unwashed in a perforated plastic bag.

To Prepare for Cooking. Parsnips and carrots need just a simple washing and removal of the tough outer skin with a vegetable peeler before you move on with a recipe. Young turnips do not need to be peeled, although more mature ones do. Beets, young or mature, need to be peeled, and the simplest method is to steam or roast them whole. The skins will slip off easily. Beet and turnip greens in good condition are edible. Simply wash, dry, and sauté with oil and garlic until soft or slice into thin strips and add to soups.

Pick or Buy Now, Enjoy Later. Root vegetables lose their characteristic crunch or firm texture when frozen in sections or pieces. Carrots and parsnips can be cooked into a puree and frozen for soups or in smaller portions, about two tablespoons to ¼ cup. Beets and carrots can also be pickled, later adding bright color to relish trays or served on the side with roasted meats.

Preserve the seasonal flavor of root vegetables with Carrot and Lemon Marmalade
or Pickled Beets with Caraway on page 166.

Carrot and Jalapeño Soup

Makes 6 servings

Sweet, sweet carrots enjoy a gentle (or a not so subtle) blast of heat from jalapeños. Your choice: discard the seeds and membranes where the heat lies and you'll end up with a pleasantly grassy overtone. Leave them be and this is a soup that will warm you to the core. Although you can use heavy cream to thicken this soup, consider giving crème fraîche a try. This thick and tangy substitute is perfect for cream soups because it resists curdling when added to hot liquids. Learn to make your own crème fraîche on page 50—it's easy!

4 tablespoons unsalted butter
1 large onion, chopped
1 celery stalk, chopped
1 pound carrots, peeled and chopped
2 or 3 jalapeño peppers, minced
1 teaspoon fresh thyme
1 fresh bay leaf
4 cups rich chicken stock
1 cup crème fraîche or heavy cream
½ teaspoon kosher salt
3 tablespoons chopped fresh cilantro or parsley

Melt the butter in a large pot over medium heat. Add the onion, celery, carrots, and peppers. Sauté until soft and fragrant, about 8 minutes. Reduce the heat to low and continue to cook for an additional 10 minutes, stirring frequently. Add the thyme, bay leaf, and chicken stock and bring to a boil. Reduce the heat to low and cook partially covered until the carrots are tender, about 30 minutes.

Working in batches, puree the soup in a blender. Return to the pot. Stir in the crème fraîche and salt. Gently reheat without boiling. To serve, ladle the soup into warmed bowls and garnish with chopped cilantro.

Honey Caramelized Turnips

Makes 4 servings

People harbor an impression of turnips as woody spheres, tasteless and colorless. As more and more farmers begin bringing turnip varieties to market—red skinned, purple tipped, pearly white, and golden yellow—cooks are beginning to take notice and rekindle their love affair with this root. Choose young turnips, on the smaller side, with fresh leafy greens for the best and mildest flavor— caramelize them and they'll win over even the most hardened skeptic.

2 tablespoons unsalted butter, divided use
1 small onion, chopped
3 cups diced peeled turnips, about ½-inch dice
1 cup chicken or vegetable stock
1 to 2 tablespoons honey
Salt and freshly ground black pepper, to taste

Melt a tablespoon of butter in a heavy skillet over medium heat. Add the onion and sauté until soft and fragrant, about 6 minutes. Transfer the onions from the skillet to a small bowl and set aside.

Return the skillet to the heat and add the turnips and chicken stock. Bring to a boil, then reduce the heat to low. Cover and simmer until turnips are tender, about 12 to 15 minutes. Remove the cover and let cook a few additional minutes until the liquid has evaporated. Stir in the remaining tablespoon of butter and drizzle with the honey. Add the reserved onions. Gently cook and stir the turnips until the butter and honey cook into a brown, sticky coating on the turnips, about 5 minutes. Serve hot.

a rainbow of root vegetables

Shop farmers markets or seed catalogs and you're likely to come across an array of root vegetables in colors that shatter traditional expectations. Sure, you'll find orange carrots, but you're also likely to find them in creamy white, yellow, violet, and burgundy. The expected ruby beets also show up in shades of ivory, rose, and gold with a few striped varieties just for fun. Turnips too can have the familiar lilac crowns or be completely white. There's really nothing new about these varieties. They've been around for ages and are enjoying a revival, one that we can also enjoy for their sweetness, scent, and rich flavor. To preserve the intense color of these delicious oddities from field to plate, choose recipes that feature them raw, very lightly steamed, or roasted and cook them until just tender. Overcooking and boiling typically leech the color and result in a paler version of the original.

Parsnip Chips

If you've never had parsnips at all, you're in for a treat. Thin slices of this humble root vegetable "fry" up in the oven and emerge like crispy potato chips. The thinner the slice, the crisper and sweeter the chip. For a hint of garlic flavor, season lightly with garlic salt.

Makes 6 servings

½ pound parsnips, peeled and sliced very thin
Extra virgin olive oil
Coarse sea salt

Preheat the oven to 350°F.

Place the sliced parsnips in a bowl and add 2 to 3 tablespoons of oil. Toss gently until the slices are coated. Spread the parsnips on baking sheets in a single layer. Roast, checking and stirring every few minutes, until lightly browned and crisp, about 10 to 12 minutes.

Season generously with salt and serve hot or at room temperature.

Fresh Beet Borscht

Borscht is a lovely vegetable soup that can be as simple as this recipe or embellished with mushrooms, cabbage, potatoes, or tomatoes. But the star ingredient is sweet, juicy beets, which give borscht a wonderful earthy flavor. Puree it smooth or leave it with pieces of grated beets floating in the sweet, red broth—and serve with a piece of dark, dense bread or hearty rye.

Vegetable stock or chicken stock can be substituted for the beef stock.

Makes 4 servings

6 medium beets, roots and stems trimmed
1 medium onion, finely chopped
1 teaspoon salt
5 cups beef stock, divided use
1 clove garlic, minced
Salt and freshly ground black pepper, to taste
Yogurt or crème fraîche, to accompany
Fresh dill sprigs, to garnish (optional)

Peel the beets with a paring knife or vegetable peeler. Coarsely grate the beets into a large bowl. Set aside.

In a large pot over medium heat, cook the onion with the salt in ¼ cup of stock until the onions are soft, about 3 minutes. Add garlic and cook, stirring, until fragrant, about 30 seconds.

Add the remaining beef broth and the beets and bring to a boil. Reduce the heat, cover, and cook until the beets are very tender, about 20 minutes.

Working in batches, transfer the soup to a blender and puree until smooth. Return to the pot and gently reheat. Season with salt and pepper, to taste. (If serving the soup chilled, remove from the heat and let cool to room temperature before refrigerating at least 8 hours or up to 2 days.)

Serve hot, at room temperature, or cold with a dollop of yogurt or crème fraîche and a sprig of dill.

Honey and Balsamic Glazed Parsnips and Carrots

The nutty and sweet tastes of carrots and parsnips combine perfectly in this easy-to-make side dish, drizzled with local honey. An added splash of balsamic vinegar and some quality roasting time lift these humble root vegetables to a new height of flavor.

Makes 6 servings

4 tablespoons extra virgin olive oil
2 tablespoons honey
2 tablespoons balsamic vinegar, white balsamic preferred
1 pound parsnips, peeled and cut into 1-inch pieces
½ pound carrots, peeled and cut into 1-inch pieces
Salt and freshly ground black pepper, to taste
4 tablespoons freshly chopped thyme

Preheat the oven to 425°F. Combine the olive oil, honey, and balsamic vinegar in a small saucepan. Warm gently over low heat until honey has liquefied.

Place the prepared parsnips and carrots in a large bowl and drizzle with the glaze, tossing to coat. Spread on a lightly oiled baking sheet and sprinkle with salt and pepper.

Bake for 15 minutes. Sprinkle the thyme over the vegetables, stirring to combine. Return to the oven and bake an additional 10 to 15 minutes or until the vegetables are tender and caramelized. Serve warm.

Slow-Roasted Beets

If you've never been a fan of beets, please give beets a chance with this method that slow-roasts them into an amazing candy-like finish.

Makes 4 servings

1 pound small or medium beets, any variety, scrubbed clean
1½ tablespoons extra virgin olive oil
1 teaspoon salt
4 sprigs fresh rosemary

Preheat the oven to 400°F. Place a large piece of aluminum foil on a heavy baking sheet.

Trim the stems and roots from the beets. Cut the beets into halves if the beets are small or into wedges if they are larger. Put the beets in a large bowl and drizzle with the olive oil. Toss until the beets are coated. Arrange the beets down the center of the foil. Sprinkle with the salt and arrange the sprigs of rosemary among the beets. Bring the sides of the foil up and around the beets and fold together to seal. Seal the open ends of the foil. Roast the beets for 1 hour. Check to see if they are tender by inserting the tip of a knife into a beet. If it pierces the beets easily and the beets are dark and caramelized and a bit wrinkled, they are done. If not, reseal the foil and return to the oven for 15 minutes. Let cool slightly before slipping the skins from the beets. Serve warm or at room temperature.

Cream of Turnip Soup with Seasoned Croutons

As humble and rustic as turnips may be, they make a sophisticated main course or appetizer soup that has a rich, nutty flavor. Choose younger, fresh turnips for a mild soup and top with crunchy croutons for the perfect complement and contrast.

Makes 4 to 6 servings

2 pounds young turnips, peeled and thinly sliced
6 cups rich chicken stock
2 tablespoons unsalted butter
½ teaspoon salt
½ teaspoon sugar
¼ teaspoon white pepper
¼ to ½ cup whipping cream

Croutons:
1 cup freshly cubed bread, crusts removed
2 tablespoons extra virgin olive oil
1 clove garlic, chopped
½ teaspoon paprika
Salt, to taste

Combine the turnips, stock, butter, salt, sugar, and white pepper in a heavy pot. Bring to a boil. Reduce the heat, cover, and simmer for 30 minutes or until the turnips are tender. Working in batches, puree the mixture in a blender until smooth. Return to the pot and stir in the cream. Gently reheat. Ladle the soup into warmed bowls and top with seasoned croutons.

To make the croutons, preheat the oven to 375°F. Toss the cubed bread with the olive oil, garlic, paprika, and salt until coated. Spread in a single layer on a baking sheet and bake for 15 to 18 minutes, stirring twice, until the croutons are crispy and golden. Remove and let cool completely.

Croutons may be made 3 days in advance and stored in an airtight container.

Carrot and Lemon Marmalade

Makes 3 half-pint jars

1 pound carrots, peeled, trimmed, and shredded
3 fresh lemons, scrubbed clean
3 cups sugar
1 cup water
1 teaspoon ground cinnamon
¼ teaspoon ground cloves

Marmalade is a sweet jelly in which pieces of fruit and citrus rind are suspended. The lemon rind lends a delightful bitterness to the sweetness of the jelly, which in this recipe is delivered courtesy of carrots. You'll love the amazing amber color of the finished marmalade, which is wonderful on toast and muffins or as a side relish to grilled or roasted chicken.

Place the prepared carrots in a large saucepan. Trim the ends from the lemon and cut each lemon into 8 wedges, removing any seeds and tough membrane. Add the lemons, sugar, and water to the saucepan and stir the contents. Bring to a boil over medium-high heat, stirring constantly. Reduce the heat to low and simmer for 30 minutes, stirring occasionally, until slightly thickened. Remove from the heat and cool for 30 minutes.

Puree the mixture in a food processor (some chunks of lemon may remain, which is fine), stopping once or twice to scrape down the sides of the bowl. Return to the pan and stir in the cinnamon and cloves. Bring to a boil. Reduce heat and cook until thickened, stirring often, about 5 to 7 minutes.

Ladle the mixture into sterilized half-pint jars to within ¼ inch of the rim (headspace). Seal and process for 10 minutes.

New to making jams, jellies, and preserves? For a step-by-step guide to the basics, see "Jams, Jellies, and Preserves" on page 237.

Pickled Beets with Caraway

Makes 4 pints

2 pounds fresh beets, leaves trimmed
1 large red onion, diced
3 teaspoons caraway seeds
2 teaspoons mustard seeds
2 cups cider vinegar
1½ cups sugar
½ cup water
2 teaspoons pickling salt

The earthy, sweet taste of fresh beets teams up with distinctly pungent, sweet, and tangy caraway in this recipe that tastes as good months from now as it does today. You can enjoy these beets from your pantry long into the winter—or store them submerged in the brine in a large jar with a tight-fitting lid and refrigerate for up to three months.

For a sweeter taste, substitute 2 teaspoons of celery seed for the caraway seeds.

Place the beets in a large pot, cover with water, and bring to a boil over high heat. Reduce the heat, cover, and simmer for 35 to 40 minutes or until beets are tender. Drain and rinse with cold water. When the beets are cool enough to handle, slip the skins off and slice the beets into ¼-inch slices or into bite-sized pieces. Place the sliced beets along with the onion, caraway seeds, and mustard seeds in a large bowl.

Combine the vinegar, sugar, water, and pickling salt in a saucepan. Bring to a boil, stirring occasionally until the sugar is dissolved. Pour over the beet mixture and gently stir to combine.

Ladle the mixture into the jars to within ½ inch of the rim (headspace), making sure that the beets are covered with the brine. Seal and process for 30 minutes.

New to pickling? For a step-by-step guide to the basics, see "Pickled Vegetables, Relishes, and Salsas" on page 239.

Making Your Own: Horseradish

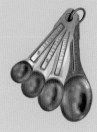

The journey to living and eating like a locavore is filled with pleasure . . . and maybe a little "pain," but all in the name of genuine flavor. That's true when it comes to horseradish, a ruddy, earthy root that doesn't get the same attention as the root vegetables we roast, puree, or steam into sweet submission. Yet take a fresh horseradish root, give it a workout on a box grater, and look out!

This one simple action unleashes the characteristic bite and strong aroma of this thick, fleshy root, in truth a member of the mustard family and kin to kale, radishes, and Brussels sprouts.

Freshly Grated Horseradish

Makes 2 cups or 2 half-pint jars

If you've never made your own horseradish before, you'll be amazed at not only how simple it is to make but also the clean and fresh taste, so unlike what you may have grabbed off a store shelf.

Horseradish is all about pungency, but grate it yourself and you have an opportunity to control it to some degree. Use really fresh roots—clean, firm, and free of cuts, splits, and blemishes. You can grate horseradish by hand using a box grater and firm, downward, crisscross motions, but a quicker and more efficient method is this one that uses a blender or food processor.

Do not process horseradish in a hot water bath. The oils that give horseradish its distinctive kick are heat sensitive.

¾ pound fresh horseradish root, scrubbed clean
½ cup plus additional chilled water, divided use
2 tablespoons crushed ice, more if necessary
1 teaspoon salt
¼ cup distilled vinegar

Trim the tough ends from the root and peel the thick skin with a paring knife or vegetable peeler. Cut the peeled root into small dice. Using a blender or food processor (fitted with a metal blade), fill halfway with the diced horseradish. (Depending on the size of the of the equipment, you may need to work in batches.)

Add 2 tablespoons each of chilled water and crushed ice. Blend or process until the mixture reaches the desired consistency, which can be anywhere between a fine and a coarse texture. Carefully remove the cover from the blender or food processor. (As horseradish is ground, it develops an extremely potent aroma that can be irritating.) The mixture will appear a bit dry. Add the salt.

Combine the ½ cup of water and the vinegar in a small measuring cup. Add enough of the water mixture to the ground horseradish to make it spreadable.

(The longer you process the root or let it rest without adding vinegar, the more heat it will develop. For a hotter finish, let the horseradish sit for up to 5 minutes before adding the vinegar.)

To preserve the horseradish, pack it into sterilized half-pint jars and refrigerate for up to a month or freeze for up to six months. Drain slightly before using. (After a month in the refrigerator, the flavor and pungency begin to wane, the horseradish begins to darken, and it will often develop an off flavor.)

heritage pork

Long before pork became known as "the other white meat," low in fat and in taste, farmers raised heritage breeds of pigs, hardy animals valued for their richly flavored meat, lean bacon, and lard, a superior cooking fat. Heritage breeds of pigs were bred over time to develop traits and characteristics that made them well adapted to the local landscape and environment, better suited to live off what nature and the land provided, and able to withstand disease and tolerate harsh climates. Their character was perfectly suited for sustainable and organic farming. These same qualities didn't translate well to the large, modern intensive-farming operations where pigs are confined indoors and growth hormones and antibiotics are used as a matter of course. The fat that carried the flavor was gone too, bred out in search of leaner meat and an animal that developed faster. As a result, heritage breeds were largely forgotten and pork lost its distinct taste.

The renewed focus on locally grown foods and the push to bring flavor back into our kitchens has thrust some of these endangered breeds back into the local limelight. Breeds like the Berkshire, a popular heritage breed, prized for juicy, flavorful pork that is red hued, heavily marbled, and suited for cooking for long times and at high temperatures. There's the "Bacon Hog," the handsome red Tamworth that develops an ample belly without developing a lot of fat. Seriously small in numbers, the Red Wattle is a good forager, is hardy, and grows rapidly; its meat is highly flavored, dark, and lean.

Good genetics, where the fat and marbling hasn't been bred away, is integral to juicy and flavor-rich heritage pork. But taste ultimately comes from the way the pigs are raised. Farmers who raise heritage breeds are typically good and responsible stewards of the land, paying close attention to the source of nutrition for their herds—lands that yield nutritious grasses and rich minerals from healthy soil; an abundance of fresh air, sunshine, and clean water. It will take about 7 months to raise these pigs to finish weight, almost twice as long as for those in larger commercial operations.

All this and the farmer's dedication and commitment to preserving diversity and choice in our foods pay off in pork that tastes like pork and not like anything else.

cooking heritage pork

Heritage pork has a higher fat content, more intramuscular fat, and better marbling, which makes it flavorful, moist, and a little more forgiving when you've left it on the grill or in the oven for just a little too long. For maximum tenderness, lean cuts like pork tenderloin and chops should be just slightly pink when served. Look for a finished temperature of 145°F; the pork will be slightly pink on the inside, still moist and juicy. For larger, tougher cuts, like pork shoulder, use a low oven temperature, a moist heat cooking method, like braising, and a long cooking time.

Cider Braised Pulled Pork

Makes 8 to 10 servings

The shoulder, butt, or Boston butt is a cut from the shoulder blade. Rich and fatty, it needs a low and slow cooking method to help break down the tough fibers. Patience pays off in this recipe. At the end, the meat simply falls off the bone and a fork will break it apart into thin shreds. Great for your next picnic or when you have to feed a crowd.

1 (5- to 6-pound) bone-in pork shoulder butt roast
½ tablespoon sweet or hot paprika
½ tablespoon coarse salt
Pinch of red pepper flakes
1½ cups apple cider
½ cup water
1 fresh bay leaf
8 to 10 crusty rolls, split and lightly toasted

Preheat the oven to 350°F.

Rub the meat all over with the paprika, salt, and pepper flakes. Place in a deep roasting pan. Add the apple cider, water, and bay leaf. Cover the pan tightly with foil and roast for 4 to 4½ hours or until the meat flakes and shreds effortlessly with a fork. Remove from the oven and let cool slightly. When cool enough to handle, shred the roast, discarding any fat. Cover and keep warm.

Pour the pan juices into a medium saucepan. Let rest for a bit and skim off the fat that rises to the surface. Bring to a boil and let boil for 1 minute. Remove from the heat and let cool slightly.

Pour the sauce over the shredded pork and toss to distribute. When ready to serve, use tongs or a slotted spoon to mound the pork on a crusty bun. Drizzle a little of the sauce over the top, if desired. Serve immediately.

Grilled Pork Chops with Oregano and Lemon Pepper Rub

Makes 4 servings

This grilling method is great for cuts of heritage pork where you want the smokiness of the grill to add flavor but want to make sure you don't overcook them. Using a disposable aluminum foil pan to cover the chops as they finish on the cooler side of the grill helps keeps the moisture in the chops. Try the same method for grilling chicken and lamb, too.

4 bone-in rib or loin chops, cut 1¼ inch to 1½ inch thick
Kosher salt
Grated zest of one fresh lemon
2 tablespoons coarsely crushed mixed peppercorns
3 tablespoons fresh or 1½ tablespoon dried oregano
2 tablespoons extra virgin olive oil
Disposable aluminum foil baking pan

Blot the surface of the chops dry with a paper towel. Season with salt.

Combine the zest, crushed peppercorns, and oregano in a small bowl. Stir in the oil to make a paste. Coat the chops with the paste. Set aside at room temperature for one hour.

Preheat the grill to medium-high with the cover closed. When the grill is hot, leave one burner on medium-high and turn the other burners to medium-low. Arrange the chops on the hotter part of the grill and grill for 2 minutes. Rotate the chops 180° and grill for an additional minute (this will give the presentation side nice crisscross grill marks). Turn the chops over and grill for an additional 3 minutes.

Move the chops to the cooler part of the grill, cover with the foil pan, and continue to cook for an additional 7 to 10 minutes with the grill cover down, until an instant-read thermometer inserted into the thickest part of the chop registers 140°F.

Transfer to a platter, cover with foil, and let rest for 5 minutes before serving. (The temperature will rise 5 to 10 degrees.)

in season ...
broccoli & cauliflower

Broccoli and cauliflower have a lot in common. As members of the cabbage family, their tastes include a cabbage-like undertone, but each has subtle and distinct differences. Cauliflower has a delicate, nutty flavor and is best suited for dishes that don't have a lot of strong flavors competing for attention. Broccoli packs a range of tastes and textures from the soft and flowery nature of the florets to the fibrous and crunchy character of the stems and stalks and is good at absorbing flavors like ginger, garlic, vinegars, and lemon.

More important is the cooking technique used, which should be quick to hang on to color and texture.

Choosing the Best. Broccoli bunches should feature compact clusters of florets with tightly closed buds. Broccoli with large, thick, pale stalks is overgrown, tough, and strong tasting, and any hint of yellowing or open, flowering florets is a sure sign of age.

A cauliflower head or curd, which is made up of multiple florets, should be creamy white and compact with bright green, firmly attached leaves. Sniff deeply. There should be no cabbage-like smell. Old cauliflower will show flecks of black mold on the florets; its leaves will be yellowed and curled, and it will have lost its firmness.

How to Store Fresh. While they look sturdy and durable, both broccoli and cauliflower deteriorate quickly, so buy or harvest them when you plan to use them. They will keep for a couple of days in the crisper drawer of the refrigerator. Store them unwashed and wrapped tightly in plastic.

To Prepare for Cooking. Broccoli provides a range of texture from soft and flowery florets to fibrous and crunchy stems and stalks. To prepare broccoli, remove the bottom two inches from the stalks and discard. Use a sharp knife to separate the stalks from the individual florets. Tender florets cook more quickly than the stalk. To create a balance, peel the stalk's tough outer layer and cut the stalks into pieces comparable in size to the florets or save and freeze them for other uses.

To prepare cauliflower, pull off and discard the green leaves, exposing the stem and core. Take a paring knife and remove the bottom core, cutting into it at an angle in a cone shape. The stalks on cauliflower are shorter and more tender than broccoli's, so as you separate florets from the head, they are likely to come with some stalks.

Pick or Buy Now, Enjoy Later. If properly blanched and frozen, broccoli will hold onto its color and flavor and a good amount of its texture. From the freezer, it will work well in dishes that require quick cooking techniques like the Broccoli Sauté with Garlic and Ginger on page 172 or cooked dishes as well as soups. Cauliflower, on the other hand, does not freeze well, turning rubbery and lifeless. Canning either vegetable is never recommended, although as part of a mix, pickling is sometimes an option.

Freeze this season's broccoli! To learn how, go to page 218.

Faux Mashed "Potatoes"

Makes 8 servings

This dish has everything mashed potatoes have, except for the starch and the calories. In every other way—texture, richness, and flavor—it's a dead ringer for spuds we love.

2 tablespoons unsalted butter
½ cup milk, more or less as needed
1 head cauliflower (about 1¾ to 2 pounds)
½ cup grated Parmesan cheese
¼ teaspoon cayenne pepper
Salt, to taste
Freshly grated nutmeg, to garnish

Heat the butter and milk in a small saucepan until very warm. Set aside.

Remove the florets and tender stalks from the cauliflower curd. Place in a large pot and add an inch of water. Cover and bring to a boil. Reduce the heat to low and steam for 15 to 20 minutes or until very soft. Drain.

In a food processor, process the cauliflower until mostly smooth, but with some of the pieces remaining for texture. Work in batches, if necessary.

Return the puree to the pot. Stir in half of the milk mixture, the cheese, and the cayenne and cook over medium heat, stirring often, for 5 to 10 minutes, until the mixture has the consistency of mashed potatoes, adding more milk if necessary. Season with salt to taste. Transfer to a warm serving dish and garnish with freshly grated nutmeg.

Cauliflower and Leek Bisque

Makes 4 to 6 servings

If you love cauliflower, you'll love this soup. If you're not sure how you feel about cauliflower, a bowl of this creamy soup might convert you. For the best puree, use a stand blender or an immersion "stick" blender. These kitchen tools do the best job of turning chunky vegetables into smooth, silky purees.

2 tablespoons unsalted butter
1 stalk celery, sliced
3 leeks, trimmed, rinsed, and sliced (white part only)
6 cups fresh cauliflower pieces (about ½ of a large head)
3 cups rich chicken stock
½ teaspoon salt, plus extra, if necessary
½ cup heavy cream (optional)
Cayenne pepper, to taste
2 tablespoons fresh chopped parsley

Melt the butter in a large saucepan over medium heat. Add the celery and the leeks and cook until very soft but not brown, about 10 minutes. Add the cauliflower pieces and the stock. Bring to a boil. Reduce to a simmer and cook for 20 to 25 minutes or until the cauliflower is very tender.

Working in batches, transfer the soup to a blender and puree. Return the soup to the saucepan, add the salt and gently reheat. Stir in the heavy cream and heat until hot, not boiling. Taste and season with cayenne pepper and additional salt, if necessary. Stir in the chopped parsley and serve immediately.

To make this a vegetarian dish, substitute highly flavored vegetable stock for the chicken stock.

Broccoli and Chickpea Salad with Feta Dressing

Makes 4 servings

Quick and easy, fresh and delicious, this crunchy salad is perfect for lunch or as a quick side for your dinner menu. Feta gives it a salty nature, so taste before adding salt.

½ cup crumbled feta cheese
⅓ cup plain yogurt
1 tablespoon freshly squeezed lemon juice
1 clove garlic, minced
Freshly ground pepper, to taste
4 cups chopped broccoli florets
1½ cups cooked chickpeas or 1 15-ounce can, drained
½ cup chopped red bell pepper
¼ cup chopped red onion
¼ cup golden raisins

In a medium bowl, whisk together the feta, yogurt, lemon juice, garlic, and pepper until combined.

Add the broccoli, chickpeas, bell pepper, onions, and raisins, tossing to coat. Let sit for 1 hour and serve at room temperature or refrigerate for 8 hours and serve chilled.

Broccoli Sauté with Garlic and Ginger

Makes 4 servings

This technique combines a quick sauté with a little steaming that turns broccoli a brilliant emerald green. Feel free to substitute cauliflower for the broccoli, just sauté and steam a little longer.

4 tablespoons extra virgin olive oil, divided use
1 head broccoli, florets removed and separated into bite-size pieces,
   stalks peeled and julienned
Salt and freshly ground black pepper, to taste
½ cup water
1 small red onion, diced
Pinch of red pepper flakes
2 cloves garlic, minced
1 tablespoon chopped fresh ginger

Heat 3 tablespoons of the oil in a large skillet over high heat. Add the broccoli florets and julienned stalks. Sprinkle with salt and pepper. Carefully add ½ cup water. Reduce the heat to medium-high and cook, stirring frequently, until the broccoli is tender, about 8 to 10 minutes. (If the pan begins to look dry, add a little more water to keep the broccoli from scorching.) Transfer the broccoli to a bowl and cover to keep warm.

Add the remaining tablespoon oil to the skillet over medium heat and add the onion and red pepper flakes. Cook until the onion is soft, about 6 minutes. Add the garlic and ginger and sauté until soft and fragrant, about 1 minute. Return the broccoli mixture to the skillet and cook, stirring, until all the ingredients are combined and the broccoli is heated through, about 2 minutes. Season to taste with salt and pepper. Serve warm.

Broccoli and Cauliflower Sformato

Makes 6 to 8 servings

A sformato is a soufflé-like creation but not quite as airy, so there's no need to fear a collapse in the oven. In this recipe, broccoli and cauliflower unite for one great seasonal side dish. You can also substitute the vegetable of the moment, such as asparagus in the spring or corn in the summer.

3 tablespoons salt
1 small head cauliflower, cut into bite-size florets
1 head broccoli, cut into bite-size florets
1 cup milk
3 tablespoons extra virgin olive oil
¼ cup all-purpose flour
¾ cup grated Parmesan cheese
Salt and freshly ground black pepper, to taste

You can substitute 1 cup of rich chicken stock for the cup of reserved cooking water.

Fill a large bowl with ice water. Set aside. Lightly butter a 9-inch square baking dish.

Fill a large stockpot with water and bring to a boil. Add 3 tablespoons salt. Add the cauliflower florets and cook for 10 minutes until tender. Using a handheld strainer, transfer the cauliflower to the ice water to halt the cooking.

Add the broccoli to the same pot and cook for 5 minutes until tender. Reserve 1 cup of the cooking water. Using a handheld strainer, transfer the broccoli to the ice water to halt the cooking. Drain the vegetables in a colander and set aside.

Preheat the oven to 375°F.

Heat the milk and reserved cooking water in a saucepan over low heat. In another saucepan, whisk the olive oil and flour together to make a roux. Cook over low heat for 5 minutes until lightly golden. Add the hot milk and whisk constantly until smooth and creamy. Remove from the heat, stir in the cheese, and season with salt and pepper.

Combine the sauce with the broccoli and cauliflower and transfer to the prepared baking dish. Bake 20 to 25 minutes, until bubbling. Cool for 5 minutes before serving.

Roasted Cauliflower

Makes 4 to 6 servings

Truly fresh cauliflower paired with the right cooking methods, like roasting or steaming until tender, has a mildly sweet taste that never comes across as strong. There's not much to get in the way of the truly mild and sweet flavor of fresh cauliflower in this recipe, but be sure to choose the freshest cauliflower you can find.

1 medium cauliflower, florets and tender stems separated,
    trimmed into bite-size pieces
¼ cup extra virgin olive oil
1 fresh lemon, juiced
1 tablespoon thinly sliced garlic
Salt and freshly ground black pepper, to taste

Preheat the oven to 500°F.

Place the cauliflower florets in a large bowl. Drizzle with olive oil and lemon juice. Add the garlic, salt, and pepper and toss until coated. Arrange on a shallow baking sheet and roast for 15 minutes, stirring occasionally, until just tender. Serve immediately.

cabbage & brussels sprouts

In the world of fresh vegetables, cabbage and Brussels sprouts may be among the most misunderstood and underrated. Childhood memories of strong-tasting, mushy, pale portions stood as the ultimate roadblocks to dessert.

Brussels sprouts look like tiny heads of cabbage and are closely related, but properly prepared sprouts have a milder taste and denser texture than cabbage. You'll find a few different varieties of cabbage, from compact, heavy heads to tender loose leaves, all of which can be served raw and crisp in salads where the taste comes through as mild, delicious, and easy to love. Cooked, not overcooked, cabbage is sweet and pleasant.

Choosing the Best. When choosing red or green cabbage, pick a crisp and fresh-looking head, tight and compact with no loose leaves. Leafy varieties like Savoy, Chinese cabbage (also called celery or Napa cabbage), and bok choy should have stems and ribs that are firm and crisp, not limp. The leaves on any type of cabbage should not appear wilted or have yellow or brown edges. Brussels sprouts should be bright green, firm, and compact with no sign of yellowing and no strong smell, a sure sign that they are old.

How to Store Fresh. Whole dense heads of cabbage will keep for a couple of weeks stored unwrapped in the coolest part of the refrigerator. Wrap unused portions in plastic and use within a week. Leafy varieties like Chinese cabbage and bok choy are more delicate and should be used within a few days.

Upon picking, Brussels sprouts begin to develop strong flavors, so they should be used fresh, the same day they are picked or purchased, or held no more than a day or two in the refrigerator, stored in a perforated plastic bag.

To Prepare for Cooking. Discard loose or limp outer leaves on head cabbage and rinse any signs of dirt. Cut into quarters, leaving the hard inner core intact to grip when slicing or shredding. When using individual cabbage leaves from either head or loose leaf cabbage, use a paring knife to remove the tough ribs to the point where they thin out.

On Brussels sprouts, remove just the outer leaves and cut a shallow 'x' in the bottom core with the tip of a knife so the fibrous stalk cooks evenly. Use them whole or cut in half or quartered.

Pick or Buy Now, Enjoy Later. Brussels sprouts can be blanched and frozen with fair results but canning is never recommended because the flavor intensifies in an unpleasant way and the bright green color wanes.

Fermenting cabbage into sauerkraut is simple and has only a few requirements for success. It's an easy, largely hands-off project that mostly requires a little daily monitoring. Learn to make your own sauerkraut on page 178.

Pickled Picnic Slaw

Make a quick trip to the farmers market or a stop at a roadside stand and you should find most of the vegetables that go into this colorful slaw with a slightly south of the border flavor. Use green, Savoy, or Chinese cabbage—each works perfectly in this recipe.

Makes 8 servings

4 cups finely shredded cabbage
½ red onion, thinly sliced
1 red bell pepper, seeded and julienned
2 to 3 jalapeño peppers, seeded and julienned
3 cloves garlic, minced
1 tablespoon chopped fresh oregano
⅓ cup chopped fresh cilantro
Salt and freshly ground black pepper, to taste

Dressing:
¼ cup cider vinegar
2 teaspoons honey
1 fresh lime, juiced, divided use
1 ½ teaspoons ground cumin
½ teaspoon salt
⅓ cup extra virgin olive oil

Combine the cabbage, red onion, red pepper, jalapeños, garlic, oregano, and cilantro in a large bowl. Season with salt and pepper and toss to distribute.

Stir together the vinegar, honey, lime juice, cumin, and salt in a small bowl. Whisk in the oil in a slow steady stream until blended. Pour over the slaw and toss to coat. Let sit at room temperature for 30 minutes or refrigerate for up to 4 hours, allowing to return to room temperature before tossing again and serving.

Warm Cabbage, Pepper, and Onion Sauté

Served as a salad or a side, this dish delivers a range of flavors from sweet to sour, smoky to spicy . . . and the short cooking time helps the cabbage retain more of its color and some of its firmness.

Makes 4 servings

2 slices bacon, cut into 1-inch pieces
½ red bell pepper, cut into 2-inch-long strips
½ green bell pepper, cut into 2-inch-long strips
½ yellow bell pepper, cut into 2-inch-long strips
1 medium onion, thinly sliced
½ head green cabbage or a small Savoy cabbage, cored and shredded

Dressing:
3 tablespoons cider vinegar
1 tablespoon vegetable oil
1 tablespoon water
1 ½ teaspoons brown sugar
1 ½ teaspoons Dijon mustard
½ teaspoon salt
½ teaspoon pepper

Cook the bacon in a large skillet until crisp. Drain off the excess oil. Return the pan to the stove. Add the bell peppers, onions, and cabbage. Toss gently over medium heat until slightly wilted, about 1 or 2 minutes.

In a small bowl, whisk together the vinegar, oil, water, brown sugar, mustard, salt, and pepper. Add to the vegetable mixture and stir gently. Toss over medium heat for about 3 minutes until the liquid has evaporated and the vegetables are tender with a little bite, not soft. Serve immediately.

Braised Bok Choy

In search of bok choy at the farmers markets? You might find it as "baby," young and tender and best when cooked whole. Mature or larger bok choy should be treated like chard, by separating the stalks from the leaves, chopping them into pieces, and giving them a head start in the pan before adding the chopped leaves.

Makes 4 servings

2 cups rich chicken stock
¼ cup unsalted butter
1 ½ pounds bok choy, tough stem ends trimmed

1 teaspoon sesame oil
Freshly ground black pepper, to taste

Combine the stock and butter in a deep heavy skillet. Bring to a simmer. Arrange the bok choy in a few even layers in the skillet, cover, and simmer until tender, about 5 minutes. Using tongs, transfer the bok choy to a serving dish and cover to keep warm.

Bring the broth mixture to a boil and let cook uncovered until greatly reduced to about ½ cup. Stir in the sesame oil and pepper. Pour the mixture over the bok choy and serve immediately.

Cabbage with Apples

Makes 8 servings

An autumn meal of roasted pork or sausages wouldn't seem complete without a side of warm braised red cabbage sweetened with locally grown apples and apple cider. This recipe can be prepared up to 2 days in advance and gently reheated before serving.

1 medium red cabbage (about 2 to 2½ pounds)
3 tablespoons unsalted butter
1 cup chopped onion
2 medium apples (such as Gala or Golden Delicious) peeled, cored, and chopped
½ cup red wine vinegar
2 tablespoons brown sugar
¼ teaspoon ground cinnamon
¼ teaspoon ground allspice
⅛ teaspoon ground cloves
Salt and freshly ground black pepper, to taste
1 cup apple cider or apple juice

Remove the outer leaves of the cabbage and the tough core. Quarter the cabbage and cut into shreds. You should have 9 to 10 cups.

Melt the butter in a large, heavy pan with a lid over medium heat. Add the onion and sauté until soft and translucent, about 6 minutes. Add the shredded cabbage in batches, adding more when the previous addition collapses and wilts. Stir in the chopped apples, vinegar, sugar, and spices. Season with salt and pepper to taste. Pour in the cider, cover, and cook until the cabbage is tender and the juices have thickened slightly, about one hour. Serve warm.

Cabbage and Mushroom Soup

Makes 8 to 10 servings

Economical ingredients add up to one delicious vegetarian soup. Great to make and serve in an afternoon, but better if you can let the soup sit in the refrigerator for 24 hours so the flavors can meld and mellow.

You can substitute 3 to 4 cups of drained sauerkraut for the fresh cabbage.

1½ pounds fresh mushrooms, trimmed, washed, and coarsely chopped
10 cups water or vegetable stock
2 carrots, peeled and chopped
2 ribs celery, chopped
1 small head green cabbage, thinly sliced
¼ cup chopped fresh parsley
1 teaspoon salt, more or less to taste
½ teaspoon pepper
3 tablespoons unsalted butter
1 medium onion, diced
1 to 1½ tablespoons paprika
1 cup orzo or any small egg noodles, cooked and drained

Place the mushrooms and water in a large stockpot. Bring to a boil. Reduce the heat to a gentle simmer and cook until the mushrooms are tender and the water takes on an earthy brown color, about 30 minutes. Add the carrots, celery, cabbage, and parsley. Let the liquid return to a simmer and continue to cook an additional 20 minutes until the vegetables are tender. Add the salt and pepper.

In the meantime, sauté the onion in butter over medium heat until soft and fragrant, about 5 minutes. When the onion is soft, stir in the paprika and cook until the mixture is highly fragrant, an additional minute or two. Add the onion mixture to the soup and mix well. Add the cooked noodles. Taste and adjust seasonings, if necessary. Serve hot.

The recipe calls for the noodles to be cooked before adding to the soup. Why not just toss them into the soup to cook? When dried noodles are cooked in a soup, they soak up the precious stock we expect to fill our soup bowls. Cooking noodles before adding helps the soup maintain a good balance between liquid and noodles.

Maple-Glazed Brussels Sprouts with Bacon

Makes 4 servings

If you've ever had to be coaxed to "eat your Brussels sprouts," it wasn't because of this recipe. These Brussels sprouts soak up the sweet smoky goodness of pure local maple syrup, and the crisp bits of bacon add a little welcome crunch.

1 pound Brussels sprouts, cored and trimmed
4 slices bacon, cut into ½-inch pieces
1 medium onion, thinly sliced

4 tablespoons pure maple syrup, divided use
½ teaspoon salt
Coarsely ground black pepper, to taste

Bring an inch of water to a boil in a medium skillet. Add the Brussels sprouts, reduce the heat to low, cover, and steam for 5 minutes, until they are crisp-tender. Drain and set aside. When cool enough to handle, slice the Brussels sprouts in half lengthwise.

In the same skillet, cook the bacon over medium heat until crisp. Transfer the bacon to a paper towel to drain the fat. Pour off all but 2 tablespoons of the bacon fat. Return the pan to medium heat and add the onion. Sauté until soft and tender, about 6 minutes. Add 3 tablespoons of the maple syrup and cook an additional minute. Add the Brussels sprouts and cook an additional 5 to 6 minutes, stirring occasionally, until the Brussels sprouts are lightly browned and glazed, and the liquid has evaporated. Stir in the remaining syrup and reserved bacon. Season with the salt and pepper. Cook 1 minute to heat through.

Warm Brussels Sprout, Shallot, and Nut Slaw

Makes 6 servings

Cool slaws are for summer, but come fall we like to warm things up. This simple slaw swaps out cabbage for Brussels sprouts and adds a salty, welcome crunch with the addition of nuts.

1 pound Brussels sprouts, cored and outer leaves removed
2 tablespoons extra virgin olive oil
6 shallots, thinly sliced (about ¾ cup)
Salt and freshly ground black pepper, to taste
¼ cup sherry vinegar or red wine vinegar
1 tablespoon light brown sugar
1 tablespoon grated orange zest
½ cup chopped salted cashews or peanuts

Thinly slice the Brussels sprouts in a food processor using a fitted slicing blade. Set aside.

Heat the oil in a large skillet. Add the Brussels sprouts and shallots and sauté until both are soft and tender, about 6 minutes. Season lightly with salt and pepper. Add the sherry vinegar and light brown sugar and sauté an additional 2 minutes or until liquid is evaporated. Add the orange zest and nuts, tossing to combine. Serve warm or at room temperature.

cabbage primer

Not all cabbage is green and round and while some can be interchanged in recipes, others prefer to reserve their distinct personality and flavor for their own glory. Here's an idea of some of the cabbage varieties you might find at farmers markets and roadside stands during the fall.

Savoy Cabbage: This looks like a rippled version of green cabbage with loosely layered leaves. It can be used just like green cabbage but does not have the keeping quality of its sturdier cousin. Delicious thinly sliced in salads, braised in butter, or in stir-fry.

Green Cabbage: Basic, solid, and stores well, long-cooking green cabbage brings out its natural sweetness; overcooking brings out its sulfur-like odor. Good cooked and in salads and slaws.

Red Cabbage: Similar to green in most respects except often smaller. Red cabbage is always cooked with some type of vinegar or a squeeze of lemon to prevent it from taking on a peculiar blue color. Good in salads and slaws, too.

Bok Choy: Bok choy has a mild but bright cabbage flavor. Its pale green stalks and leaves resemble Swiss chard. Often used in stir-fry, but braising brings out its sweet taste.

Chinese Cabbage: Also known as Napa or celery cabbage, it looks more like a head of Romaine. Crisp, light green leaves are mild tasting with a little hint of pepper. Good for salads and stir-fry.

Making Your Own: Sauerkraut

When life (or your neighbor) hands you cabbage, make sauerkraut. Lots of it! Turning mounds (or mountains) of shredded cabbage into salty, tangy sauerkraut is economical and easy to do in the locavore's kitchen, requiring little more than cabbage, salt, patience, and regular monitoring. A largely hands-off project, you can make it in giant batches or in smaller quantities, more often.

Cabbage turns into sauerkraut through *fermentation*, a natural transformation of the carbohydrates in certain foods into alcohol or acid through chemical changes caused by enzymes produced by naturally occurring bacteria. The same bacteria also prevent the growth of molds and yeast that would otherwise spoil your batch of sauerkraut. Fermentation is the process that turns grapes into wine and vinegar and milk products into yogurt (page 29), crème fraîche (page 50), and buttermilk. Properly fermented sauerkraut has a long shelf life and a distinctively tangy flavor, a result of the lactic acid that forms when bacteria ferment the sugars in the cabbage.

You can begin the process of making sauerkraut whenever fresh cabbage is available, although cabbage harvested in the fall is sweeter. Gather the following to get started:

- A ceramic-coated crock or plastic food grade container to hold the shredded cabbage. You can use anything from a container small enough to keep on your counter to a 2-foot-deep crock. How much finished sauerkraut you want will dictate the size of the container you should use. Five-gallon food grade plastic buckets are good for fermenting sauerkraut and will easily hold 15 pounds of shredded cabbage (that's 5 to 6 large, untrimmed heads), which will make about 7 quarts of finished sauerkraut. Check with local restaurants to see if they have any to give away or sell.

- A clean, finely woven lint-free cotton towel to cover the container as a barrier to dust and other foreign objects.

- Weights to compress the cabbage and keep it submerged in its juices. The best solution is to fill a large, sealable, heavy-duty plastic bag (or a double layer of bags) with water and place it directly on top of the cabbage. The water-filled bag disperses its weight over the surface, creating a seal to prevent exposure to air and the growth of film, yeast, or molds. You can also use a ceramic plate slightly smaller than the container opening and weigh it down with a heavy object such as water-filled mason jars or a heavy rock, scrubbed and wrapped in plastic.

location, location, location!

Before you proceed with the recipe, be sure that the container is located in an area of the house conducive to encouraging fermentation, such as a warm basement or an out-of-the-way corner in the kitchen where the temperature remains a consistent 65°F to 75°F with no dramatic fluctuations. At cooler temperatures, fermentation is slow, about 5 to 6 weeks, but yields crunchier sauerkraut with better flavor. At 75°F, the process takes place in about 4 weeks.

troubleshooting

Cabbage can spoil instead of fermenting if there is not enough salt or it is unevenly distributed, if the room temperature is too high or too low, or if it was improperly packed, leaving air pockets for mold growth.

You know your cabbage has spoiled instead of fermenting if

- It turns an undesirable color and has a strange odor, odd flavor, and soft texture
- It turns pink, a result of uneven salt distribution or too much salt, improper covering, or improper weighting during fermentation.
- It turns a shade of brown, which could be from unwashed or untrimmed cabbage, lack of juice covering the cabbage during fermentation, uneven salt distribution, or exposure to air.

Also, finished sauerkraut will spoil more quickly if you don't keep it cool (if it turns dark brown, it's spoiled), so keep it in a cool place, such as a refrigerator or root cellar, unless you plan to can it or eat it all within a few weeks.

Sauerkraut

Makes about 7 to 8 quarts or 15 pints

5 to 6 large, fresh heads of cabbage (about 15 pounds total)
9 tablespoons kosher salt or fine sea salt

Remove the outer leaves on the cabbage and trim away any damaged portions.
Cut into quarters and remove the core. Cut the cabbage into thin shreds, about the
thickness of a dime.

Working in 5-pound batches, thoroughly mix each batch with 3 tablespoons of salt. (Too
little salt allows the cabbage to spoil, too much prohibits proper fermentation.) Use your
hands to distribute the salt, crushing and breaking the strands to encourage the release
of water. You can also use a potato masher to crush the strands. Let sit until the cabbage
has wilted slightly and releases some water, about 5 minutes.

Transfer the salted cabbage and any liquid to the prepared crock or container (5-gallon
size). Using clean or gloved hands or the potato masher, press down firmly between
additions to tightly compact the cabbage until the juice comes to the surface. (If there is
not enough liquid, dissolve a teaspoon of salt to every one cup of water needed to cover
the cabbage.) Repeat the process with two more 5-pound batches of cabbage.

Weigh the cabbage down with the water-filled bag or other appropriate weight. Cover
the container with the cloth to keep out dust and other foreign objects. Set the crock or
bucket where it will not be disturbed and where the temperature will remain between
65°F and 75°F.

Fermentation begins immediately, but it will take a few days before you'll notice some
outward signs such as the formation of gas bubbles on the surface. Now it's time to
check the cabbage daily, removing any scum (a natural occurrence) that forms and
replacing the towel with a fresh one. As it ferments, the cabbage will reduce in volume.

Fermentation is usually complete in 4 to 6 weeks, and the cabbage is now sauerkraut.
How will you know? First, by appearance. Perfectly fermented cabbage ranges in color
from white to a light buttery yellow. Second, a taste will reveal a depth of flavor, a tang,
and a natural appeal to your taste buds. (If the flavor doesn't suit you, let the cabbage
continue to ferment so the flavor will continue to evolve.) Finally, by texture. The sauerkraut
should be somewhat firm to the bite, not crunchy but not mushy soft.

How you store your sauerkraut is now up to you. Either pack it into clean pint or quart
mason jars with tight-fitting lids and refrigerate for up to 3 months or preserve it longer
by canning.

For canning: Place the sauerkraut in a large stockpot with enough of the liquid to cover.
Heat over medium heat, stirring often to make sure none of the sauerkraut sticks to the
bottom of the pot. Heat until the mixture is hot and begins to bubble.

If you like caraway seed in
your sauerkraut, mix in one
tablespoon for every four
cups before canning.

Pack the sauerkraut into pint or quart jars with enough liquid to cover, to within ½ inch of
the rim (headspace). Seal and process 20 minutes for pints and 25 minutes for quarts.

"Canning" on page 227 provides a step-by-step guide to the basics.

local wine

Hold a glass of wine from a local winery to the light. Is it a luscious burgundy color with purple undertones or perhaps the color of golden straw? Give it a swirl in the glass, a couple of quick sniffs, then sip and savor the taste. Does it remind you of the juicy blackberries you ate straight from the vine this summer or does it hark back to the sweet, tender pears from the orchard down the road that you turned into a wonderfully chunky sauce last fall?

If you haven't decided on the perfect foods or cheese to pair with these wines, think a bit closer to home. The characters of local wines and of locally grown foods reflect the geography and climate where they are grown as well as regional winemaking and culinary traditions that have evolved over the years.

If you cook with the premise that "things that grow together, go together" then you can probably see that serving and using local wine in the locavore's kitchen makes perfectly delicious sense. As an ingredient, locally produced wines can be found and used all year round to add flavor to stocks, soups, stews, sauces, salad dressings, and desserts. But how do you know which wines to use? While there are some suggestions to point you in the direction of successful pairings both in the glass and at the stove, it's largely a matter of personal taste and what makes your taste buds happy.

There is one hard and fast rule about cooking with wine and that is never to cook with wine that you wouldn't drink. The same qualities that come through in the glass you're lifting will also come forward in the dish you bring to the table.

food + wine

When choosing a wine to use as an integral ingredient in your next recipe, consider the following guidelines. Always avoid any wines specifically labeled "cooking wine." They are usually flavorless, contain salt, and are anything but reflections of locally produced wines.

Full-Bodied Red Wines
Cabernet, Merlot, and Pinot Noir

Add to hearty dishes featuring beef, lamb, or duck, rich spaghetti sauces, or fruit sauces like Sweet Cherries in Wine on page 104 or the Drunken Leeks on page 139.

Light-Bodied White Wines
Chardonnay or Sauvignon Blanc

Use to flavor sauces for fish, poultry, veal, and cheese dishes or the Pumpkin Risotto on page 196.

Thick and Sweet Fortified Wines
Port and Sherry

Best used in recipes featuring fish, pork, poultry, veal, cream sauces, and salad dressings or as part of a marinade.

Sweet and Fruity Wines
Late Harvest Wines, Riesling, and Ice Wines

Use to flavor sweet desserts and dessert sauces or as a poaching liquid for Bay-Poached Pears on page 87.

Chocolate Red Wine Layer Cake

Makes 10 to 12 servings

Local red wine and chocolate are among the most perfect pairings at the dessert course and an especially clever way to add a truly local ingredient where you might least expect it. Snag a jar of raspberry preserves from the cupboard for another local component to this rich, chocolaty cake.

To get the best volume from the whipped cream, combine the cream and sugar in a mixing bowl. Place the bowl in the refrigerator for an hour before proceeding to whip.

1 ¾ cups all-purpose flour
½ cup unsweetened cocoa
1 ½ teaspoons baking soda
½ teaspoon salt
¾ cup unsalted butter, softened
1 ½ cups sugar
1 teaspoon pure vanilla extract

2 large eggs plus 1 egg yolk
1 cup local red wine (Cabernets and Merlots preferred)
2 cups heavy cream
2 to 3 tablespoons confectioners' sugar, more or less to taste
1 cup raspberry or strawberry preserves

Preheat the oven to 350°F. Butter and flour two 8-inch round cake pans. Set aside.

Whisk together the flour, cocoa, baking soda, and salt in a medium bowl. Set aside.

Using an electric mixer, beat the butter in a large bowl until fluffy, about 5 minutes. Add the sugar and continue beating until light and fluffy, about 2 minutes. Mix in the vanilla, eggs, and egg yolk until well combined. Add the dry ingredients and the wine, alternating and mixing well after each addition.

Divide the batter between the prepared pans and bake for 23 to 25 minutes or until a toothpick inserted in the center comes out clean.

Cool for 15 minutes before removing from the pans. Let cool completely on wire racks.

Using an electric mixer, whip the cream and the confectioners' sugar together until stiff peaks form.

Assemble the cake just before serving. Place one layer on a serving plate and spread the raspberry jam on top. Top with a layer of whipped cream. Place the second cake layer on top and spread with the remaining whipped cream. Garnish with a dusting of cocoa powder, if desired, and serve.

Sweet Wine and Lavender Cookies

Makes 12–14 cookies

To make the lavender sugar, combine 1 cup sugar and 3 tablespoons dried culinary lavender in a small container with a tight-fitting lid. Store in a dry spot for one week. Sift the sugar through a fine sieve to remove the flowers before using. Set aside one tablespoon of flowers. (Any leftover lavender sugar will keep in the cupboard for 3 months. Add to a vanilla cookie or cake recipe or stir into tea.)

Choose English lavender for recipes—it's sweet, with a delightful perfume.

1 cup plus 2 tablespoons all-purpose flour
⅓ cup lavender sugar, plus 1 tablespoon
Pinch of salt
4 tablespoons unsalted butter, cut into small dice and chilled

3 tablespoons sweet local wine (Riesling or ice wine)
½ tablespoon lavender leaves (sifted from the sugar)

Preheat the oven to 375°F.

In the bowl of a food processor, combine the flour, ⅓ cup lavender sugar, and salt until blended. Add the chilled butter and pulse until the mixture is coarse. Add the wine and the reserved lavender flowers and pulse until the mixture resembles wet sand. Let the mixture sit for 10 minutes and then pulse again a few times until it loosely comes together.

Press the dough evenly into a 4 x 14-inch tart pan or 7-inch round tart pan with removable bottoms. Sprinkle with the tablespoon of lavender sugar. Bake for 20 to 25 minutes or until the top is just lightly golden and looks dry. Let cool for a few minutes, then carefully remove from the tart pan and cut into small pieces or wedges. Let cool completely. Serve with fresh fruit and a sweet wine.

in season ... *fall greens*

Spring gives us soft, delicate, and tender greens, while summer delivers a salad bowl mix of greens with textures and taste ranging from crisp to buttery, bitter to sweet. In the fall, greens come on in hardy, full-flavored varieties including kale, collard, and mustard greens, and cool weather–loving greens like spinach make a return appearance.

Unlike their warm-weather counterparts, fall greens are rarely served raw in salads unless they are young and "wilted," with a warm dressing. One green can be substituted for another or mixed in most any recipe as long as you take into account those that have a bitter edge, like mustard greens, which require a quick blanching to tame that characteristic.

Choosing the Best. Fresh greens should have a deep green color, a firm, sturdy texture, and a little bounce to them. Any signs of softening, yellowing, or dried edges mean they are past their prime and have likely developed some undesirable flavors.

How to Store Fresh. Store fresh fall greens like you would any other green including salad greens—unwashed, wrapped in a layer or two of paper towels and refrigerated in a perforated plastic bag. Really fresh greens will keep up to a week if you change the towels once or twice.

To Prepare for Cooking. When you prepare greens for cooking, you'll likely be looking at a "heap" of greens. Keep in mind that they will cook down to a fraction, about a fourth or less, of their former raw selves. Wash greens thoroughly, especially those with ruffled edges that trap dirt and sand. Plunge them into a bowl or sink filled with water and blot or spin dry. The stems, unless they are small and tender, should be removed with a paring knife. Fall greens are usually chopped or cut into strips for recipes. To cut into strips, stack five to six like-sized leaves, roll up lengthwise, and slice perpendicularly.

Pick or Buy Now, Enjoy Later. Sturdier fall greens freeze well, and that will help keep green in your winter menus, going from the freezer to green up soups and stews. Greens that tend to have a bitter edge, like mustard greens, are best used in cream-based dishes.

Freeze this season's greens! To learn how, go to page 218.

Spicy Greens with Toasted Cumin

Makes 4 to 6 servings

Learning to love sturdy greens is not difficult if you're armed with the right cooking techniques. When it comes to mustard greens, the key is low and slow to soften the bitter edge. The texture will be tender and pleasant, not a soggy pile of mush, and the taste pleasantly sweet. After you've washed the greens, shake off the excess water but don't worry about drying them completely. A little water clinging to the leaves helps to steam and soften the greens while cooking.

2 tablespoons extra virgin olive oil
1 large onion, chopped
3 cloves garlic, chopped
¼ teaspoon dried red pepper flakes
1 ½ teaspoons cumin seed
1 large bunch mustard greens, washed, tough stems removed and discarded, leaves coarsely chopped
Cider vinegar
Coarse sea salt and freshly ground black pepper, to taste

Warm the oil in a large pot over medium heat. Sauté the onion until soft and fragrant, about 6 minutes. Add the garlic, pepper flakes, and cumin seed and sauté for an additional minute. Increase the heat and add the greens. Stir until wilted. Reduce the heat to low. Cover and steam for about 25 to 30 minutes, stirring occasionally and checking for tender, not mushy, greens. Add a splash of vinegar and stir to combine. Season with salt and pepper to taste and serve immediately.

Kale and Goat Cheese Appetizer

Makes 6 to 8 appetizer servings

Hardy fall greens are enhanced by the creamy texture and natural tang of goat cheese. You can also use about 1½ cups of of frozen kale to make this appetizer later in the year. Simply thaw and squeeze out most of the water before adding to the skillet and cooking lightly, just enough to warm.

2 tablespoons extra virgin olive oil
¼ cup chopped shallots
8 cups loosely packed kale, washed, drained, and roughly chopped
8 ounces goat cheese, softened
2 cloves garlic, minced
¼ teaspoon cayenne pepper
½ to ¾ cup mayonnaise or yogurt
½ cup freshly chopped parsley
Salt and pepper, to taste
¼ cup grated Parmesan cheese
¼ cup toasted, chopped nuts (walnuts, pecans, or pine nuts)
Toasted bread or crackers, to accompany

Preheat the oven to 350°F.

Heat the oil in a large skillet over medium heat. Add the shallots and cook until just translucent, about 5 minutes. Add the kale, cover, and cook until tender, about 5 to 10 minutes, tossing occasionally with tongs. When tender, remove from heat and transfer the mixture to a colander. Squeeze out excess moisture from greens.

In a large bowl, combine the goat cheese, garlic, and cayenne. Add just enough mayonnaise so the mixture is smooth and creamy. Add the cooked, squeezed kale, parsley, salt, and pepper. Transfer to an ovenproof dish or gratin pan and bake about 20 minutes or until bubbly. Sprinkle with the cheese and nuts and bake for an additional 5 minutes.

Serve with bread or crackers.

Wilted Collard Greens with Balsamic Vinegar

Rustic and humble collard greens cooked low and slow turn into a sweet side dish. This is the perfect recipe to use if you're trying greens for the first time. The ingredient list is simple, as is the cooking technique, and the genuine taste of collard greens shines.

Learn to make your own flavorful stocks on pages 143–45. They are versatile and valuable ingredients in a locavore's kitchen.

Makes 6 servings

2 pounds collard greens, stemmed and cleaned
1 teaspoon salt
1 tablespoon extra virgin olive oil
1 medium onion, chopped
1 clove garlic, minced
½ cup rich chicken stock or vegetable stock
1 tablespoon balsamic vinegar
Freshly ground black pepper, to taste

Fill a large pot with water and bring to a boil. Add the collard greens and the salt. Stir until wilted, about 1 minute. Drain and rinse immediately with cold water to stop the cooking. Squeeze the excess water from the greens. Coarsely chop and set aside.

Heat the oil in a large skillet over medium heat. Add the onion and sauté until soft and translucent, about 6 minutes. Add the garlic and sauté for an additional minute. Add the chopped greens and the stock and sauté, stirring occasionally, until the greens are tender and most of the stock has evaporated, about 5 minutes. Add the vinegar, stir well, and season with the pepper. Serve hot.

• •

fall greens primer

Greens are one of fall's best features, standing out among the reds, oranges, and golds of other fall vegetables. They're versatile and can often be exchanged for one another in a variety of recipes. Some varieties of greens show up in the spring and then make a return in the fall with leaves that are generally bigger and sturdier and more developed tastes. The key to enjoying any kind of green is to cook it just enough to soften and not so much that it turns into a soggy heap.

Kale: Kin to cabbage, these big, loose-leaf heads show up in green, purple, or cream colors. When fresh, young, and tender, they are an intense addition to salads and soups. Cooked to just tender, they can be mixed into mashed potatoes. Often available long into the fall and early winter, they are sweeter after exposed to a frost.

Collard Greens: Smooth leafed with a relatively mild flavor reminiscent of kale and cabbage. Use fresh; storing too long turns them bitter.

Mustard Greens: Leaves range from dark to light green. Among fall greens, this one delivers the sharpest flavor, zesty and peppery. Blanch to tame its bitter edge.

Spinach: This popular green is but a baby in the spring, tender and great for salads. The fall version is sturdier and better for recipes that call for braising, steaming, or mixing into soups.

Turnip Greens: The leafy tops from the sturdy, economical root vegetable that sometimes make an appearance at markets in the spring are young, tender, and mild in flavor; the fall versions are thick and sturdy. Mix with other greens to balance the sharp flavor or cut into thin strips and stir into Cream of Turnip Soup with Seasoned Croutons (page 165).

Sausage and Kale Sauté

Makes 4 servings

This is a hearty fall dish that calls on local and seasonal ingredients for its wonderful flavor. Eight cups of kale will look like a lot, but when this dish is finished, it will have cooked down to a little over 2 cups.

2 tablespoons extra virgin olive oil, divided use
1 pound bulk sausage, spicy or sweet variety
1 medium onion, diced
1 red bell pepper, diced
2 cloves garlic, minced
1 pound kale, chopped (about 8 cups)
1 tablespoon maple syrup
1 tablespoon water
Salt and freshly ground black pepper, to taste

Heat one tablespoon of olive oil in a large deep skillet. Add the sausage and cook for 10 minutes over medium-high heat, stirring frequently to break into small pieces, until thoroughly cooked. Remove with a slotted spoon to a paper towel–lined plate to drain. Scrape the excess fat from the pan.

Return the pan to the heat and add the remaining tablespoon of oil. Add the onion and red bell pepper to the pan. Sauté until soft, about 6 minutes. Add the garlic and sauté an additional minute. Add the kale and stir until wilted. Add the maple syrup, water, and reserved sausage. Cover and cook for 5 to 10 minutes or until the kale is tender and the dish is heated through. Season to taste with salt and pepper. Serve immediately.

Kale and Bacon Gratin

Makes 6 servings

Cream has a way of mellowing greens that have a pronounced or sharp taste. Here it coats the leaves with an infusion of garlic. The rich nature of this dish, which also features smoky bacon, complements the flavor of the kale without masking its true earthy flavor.

1 pound kale, stems removed and chopped, leaves coarsely chopped
1 tablespoon salt
3 tablespoons extra virgin olive oil, divided use
2 cloves garlic, minced
1 cup heavy cream
Grating of fresh nutmeg
Freshly ground black pepper, to taste
½ cup grated Parmesan cheese, divided use
6 strips bacon, cooked and crumbled
½ cup fresh breadcrumbs

Preheat the broiler.

Fill a large pot with water and bring to a boil. Stir in the kale and the salt. Boil for 5 to 6 minutes or until tender. Drain and cool slightly. Squeeze the excess water from the greens.

Heat 1 tablespoon of the oil in a large skillet over medium heat. Add the garlic and the cream and cook, stirring frequently, until reduced by a third. Season with the nutmeg and pepper. Add the cooked and drained greens to the cream and stir to coat evenly. Add half of the cheese and the cooked bacon. Transfer to a shallow casserole or gratin dish.

In a small bowl, toss the breadcrumbs with the remaining cheese and 2 tablespoons of extra virgin olive oil. Distribute evenly over the top of the kale mixture. Place under broiler (about 4 inches) to brown the topping, about 4 to 5 minutes. Serve immediately.

in season ...
green tomatoes

While they might be of the same "mother," red tomatoes and green tomatoes couldn't be more different. The first is soft, sweet, and compliant, obediently ripening throughout the summer months. The other is the "difficult" child—tart, firm, and stubbornly refusing to go beyond green when hot summer nights and days disappear. Seasoned cooks relish the always predictable fall crop of green tomatoes coveted for their unique flavor that hints of their ripe counterparts but is best know for its pleasantly sour tang.

Although they have been raised the same way, they can't be cooked the same way. Recipes developed specifically for green tomatoes will not have the same satisfying results if juicy ripe red tomatoes are substituted.

Choosing the Best. It's a rare but important tip to remember that this ingredient must be unripe, underripe, and firm. A hint of a red or yellow blush is fine. Do not use varieties of tomatoes that naturally stay green although the fruit softens and sweetens with maturity. Choose bigger tomatoes, the size of a tennis ball or bigger. Smaller ones will often have an acidic flavor.

How to Store Fresh. With a little coaxing and a few tricks you can get a green tomato to turn red—but then you would be depriving yourself of some delicious possibilities. Green tomatoes will begin to turn red at 65°F or more, so to keep them green, find a cool spot to store them for about one week, like the crisper drawer in the refrigerator. If the tomatoes are still on the vine, remove them as needed.

To Prepare for Cooking. Wash and remove the stem and tough center core, which extends about an inch below the top of the tomato. For fried green tomatoes, cut the fruit into thick slices.

If the tomatoes are cold, let them come to room temperature before adding to a recipe.

Pick or Buy Now, Enjoy Later. Green tomatoes are so acidic that canning is the best way to rescue every last one. Turn them into a salsa or relish or can ½-inch slices by packing them into pint jars. Add one teaspoon of salt, fill with boiling water, leaving ½-inch headspace, seal, and process for 15 minutes.

New to canning? For a step-by-step guide to the basics, see "Canning" on page 227.

Preserve the seasonal flavor of green tomatoes with Smoky Green Tomato Salsa on page 188.

New to pickling? For a step-by-step guide to the basics, see "Pickled Vegetables, Relishes, and Salsas" on page 239.

Fried Green Tomatoes
with Horseradish Mayonnaise

Makes 4 Servings

Fried green tomatoes should be crispy on the outside, soft and juicy on the inside. Using a cast iron skillet can get you these results. Take care not to crowd the pan with the tomatoes or they'll steam instead of quickly frying. The tangy horseradish mayonnaise is a great taste to top these delicious stragglers . . . and you can make your own mayonnaise on page 125 and horseradish on page 167 for the best flavor. And if you can't wait until fall for Fried Green Tomatoes, pluck a few from the vine in the spring!

½ cup mayonnaise
1 to 2 tablespoons grated horseradish
Salt and freshly ground black pepper to season
2 large green tomatoes
Flour, for dusting
1 egg, beaten with 1 tablespoon milk
½ cup dry unseasoned breadcrumbs
2 tablespoons cornmeal, medium grind preferred
Vegetable oil, for frying

Combine the mayonnaise and horseradish. Season to taste with salt and pepper. Cover and refrigerate until needed.

Slice the tomatoes into ½-inch-thick slices. Place the flour in a shallow bowl. Place the egg mixture in a shallow bowl. Combine the breadcrumbs and cornmeal with salt and pepper to taste and place in a shallow bowl.

Place a heavy skillet over medium-high heat and add ½ inch of oil. Allow to heat for 3 to 4 minutes or until a few breadcrumbs scattered over the top sizzle. Dust the tomatoes in the flour. Coat with the egg mixture. Dredge in the breadcrumb mixture. Fry in the hot oil until golden brown. Drain on paper towels.

Serve warm with horseradish mayonnaise.

• •

ripening green tomatoes

There are many techniques to encourage a green tomato to turn red. From layering in paper and storing in a dark place to pulling a plant out by the roots and hanging it from the cellar rafters, they all work to some degree. While the tomatoes will "ripen" to red, don't expect them to be as flavorful as the vine-ripened tomatoes enjoyed in the summer—yet, compared to store-bought tomatoes, your own home-ripened tomatoes will delight you.

However, if you can't get enough of the tart taste of green tomatoes, slice some for a sandwich layered with crisp bacon, basil leaves, and fresh mozzarella cheese between two slices of toasted bread.

Green Tomato Cake

Makes one 9 x 13-inch cake

It may seem an oxymoron to make a sweet cake out of tart green tomatoes, but this dense, moist cake is delicious proof. Enjoy it as the garden and farmers markets begin to wind down. Store a few tomatoes in the crisper drawer of the refrigerator and repeat this recipe when the first few snowflakes fly.

4 cups coarsely chopped green tomatoes
1 tablespoon salt
½ cup unsalted butter, at room temperature
2 cups sugar
2 eggs
2 cups all-purpose flour
1 teaspoon baking soda
1 teaspoon ground cinnamon
1 teaspoon ground nutmeg
¼ teaspoon salt
1 cup chopped walnuts or pecans
1 cup golden raisins (optional)
Confectioners' sugar, to dust (optional)

Place chopped tomatoes in colander and sprinkle with 1 tablespoon of salt. Let stand for 10 minutes. Rinse thoroughly with cold water and drain.

Preheat the oven to 350°F. Butter and flour a 9 x 13-inch baking pan.

Using a handheld electric mixer or a stand mixer, cream the butter and sugar together, about 5 minutes. Add eggs, one at a time, beating until blended after each addition.

Sift together the flour, baking soda, cinnamon, nutmeg, and salt. Add the dry ingredients to the creamed mixture. Add the nuts and raisins, if using. (The dough will be stiff.) Mix well. Add drained tomatoes and mix well. Pour into the prepared pan.

Bake for 40 to 45 minutes or until a toothpick inserted into the cake comes out clean.

Cool before dusting with confectioners' sugar (if desired) and slicing.

Smoky Green Tomato Salsa

Makes 4 half-pint jars

Charring the skin on green tomatoes adds a little smoke and a touch of caramelized sweetness to this spicy, tart salsa. Use as many chile peppers as you like to kick up or tone down the heat . . . then crack open a bag of salty tortilla chips and dig in.

New to pickling? For a step-by-step guide to the basics, see "Pickled Vegetables, Relishes, and Salsas" on page 239.

2½ pounds green tomatoes, cored and cut in half from stem end to blossom end
4 to 6 hot peppers, more or less to taste (jalapeño, serrano, habañero, or a mix, seeded and finely chopped)
1 large red onion, finely chopped
2 cloves garlic, minced
1 cup finely chopped fresh cilantro
½ cup lime juice or red wine vinegar
Salt and freshly ground black pepper, to taste
¼ cup water, if needed

Preheat the broiler. Line a baking sheet with foil and arrange the green tomatoes cut side down. Place under the broiler about 2 inches from the heat. Broil until charred and blackened, about 7 to 10 minutes. Remove from the heat. When cool enough to handle, slip the skins off. (A few blackened flecks left behind are fine.) Finely chop the tomatoes by hand or use a food processor.

Combine the tomatoes, peppers, onion, garlic, cilantro, and lime juice in a large nonreactive pot. Taste and season with salt and pepper. If the mixture appears somewhat dry, add the water. Bring to a boil over medium heat, stirring occasionally. Let boil for 5 minutes.

Ladle the hot salsa along with some of the liquid into half-pint jars to within ½ inch of the rim (headspace). Seal and process for 20 minutes.

in season ... *grapes*

Have you ever stood in the middle of a vineyard on a warm and sunny fall day and inhaled the scent of grapes ripening on the vine and wondered what could be better than this? Then you plucked one of the grapes, tasted, and had your answer. The sweet, perfectly "grape-y" taste of locally grown table grapes feels like a radical departure from a lifetime snacking on commercially produced varieties.

It's helpful to note that not all grapes are to be enjoyed in the same way. Wine grapes are thick-skinned, highly acidic, tart, and best reserved for the bottle. Sweet, thin-skinned table grapes are lower in acid and are best eaten out of hand, but they still have a place in the cook's kitchen.

Choosing the Best. Clusters should be heavy for their size and the grapes should look fresh, plump, and bright. The velvety powdery look you see on fresh grapes is "bloom," nature's protection against moisture loss and a good sign that the grapes are fresh and haven't been overhandled. Grapes that have firm, green stems are freshly harvested and the most flavorful. Once the stems have turned brown or black, the grapes have begun to age.

How to Store Fresh. Store unwashed grape clusters in a sealable plastic bag and refrigerate. Wet grapes will deteriorate faster, so blot surface moisture with a paper towel before storing. Wash them under cold running water when you're ready to use them.

To Prepare for Cooking. Wash the clusters under running water and drain in a colander. Remove the grapes from the stems, discarding any that are split or shriveled. Seedless varieties of table grapes are easy to prep for fresh eating or a recipe. Then there's the issue of dealing with varieties, highly flavorful varieties, containing seeds the size and texture of grains of uncooked rice. If you're up to the tedious task of removing them, simply split the grape in half and pick out the seeds. Otherwise, reserve these varieties for making grape jellies or juices where the grape is gently crushed and the seeds are strained out. Avoid crushing the seeds, which release a bitter taste.

Pick or Buy Now, Enjoy Later. Grapes are highly perishable, so enjoy them at their fresh best. Some varieties can be harvested, juiced, and used to make grape jellies and preserves. Homemade grape jelly and butter slathered on an English muffin or thick slice of homemade bread tastes extra special during the colder months.

For a frosty treat, separate the grapes from the stem and freeze. These "grape-sicles" hold their flavor for a few more weeks and are refreshing snack on a warm day.

Preserve the seasonal flavor of grapes with Grape Jelly on page 191.

Grilled Grapes

Makes 4 to 6 appetizer servings

A cluster of ripe grapes on the grill is not only a great conversation starter but also a great way to begin a fall meal. Fresh bunches entwined with sprigs of rosemary and dabbed with a little olive oil quickly caramelize without collapsing. Enjoy the warm, sweet taste in the company of a sharp or tangy cheese and some toasted breads.

1 bunch of hardy seedless red grapes, washed, dried, and left as a cluster
4 sprigs fresh rosemary
Extra virgin olive oil

Remove any shriveled or bruised grapes from the bunch. Tuck the sprigs of rosemary between the clusters of grapes. Lightly brush the surface of the grapes with olive oil.

Preheat the grill to medium-high or heat a grill pan over medium heat on the stove.

Place the grapes on the cooking surface and grill on all sides, 2 to 3 minutes per side, until the grapes are warm and show a few grill marks. Transfer from the grill onto a plate. Serve with toasted baguette slices, cheeses, and a glass of local wine.

Grape Focaccia

Makes 8 servings

Studded with sweet grapes and flecks of fresh rosemary, this wonderfully soft and tender focaccia makes it hard to decide whether it should be served as an appetizer, with dinner, or as a dessert. What's stopping you from trying all three?

1 tablespoon active dry yeast
1¼ cups warm water (90°F to 110°F)
3 cups all-purpose flour, plus extra
1 teaspoon salt
2 tablespoons chopped fresh rosemary
1 tablespoon extra virgin olive oil
1 cup seedless red or purple grapes, removed from the cluster, washed, dried
½ cup freshly grated Parmesan cheese
Coarse sea salt and freshly cracked black pepper

Stir the yeast into the warm water and let soften for 10 minutes.

Mix the flour, salt, and rosemary together in a large bowl. Make a well in the middle. Pour the oil into the well, followed by the yeast mixture. With a wooden spoon, mix the ingredients until they come together into a ball. Turn onto a floured surface and knead until the dough feels firm and elastic and looks smooth, about 10 minutes. Place in a lightly oiled bowl, turning to coat. Cover with plastic wrap or a damp towel and let rise in a warm place for 1 hour or until doubled in size.

Preheat the oven to 425°F.

Remove the dough from the bowl and place on a floured surface. Using your hands, stretch the dough into a 12-inch circle about ½ inch thick. Place on a baking sheet lined with parchment paper. Arrange the grapes over the surface of the bread and lightly press into the dough. Bake for 10 minutes. Sprinkle with Parmesan, salt, and pepper and bake for an additional 10 minutes or until golden brown. Let cool slightly before serving.

Grape Jelly
Makes 6 to 7 half-pint jars

3½ pounds Concord grapes or other highly flavorful variety
½ cup water
6 cups sugar
½ teaspoon unsalted butter (optional)
1 1.75-ounce package powdered pectin

As soon as you can smell the grapes on the vine when the sun beats down on them, it's time to make jelly. Grape jelly is one of the easiest to make, using pectin, a natural thickening agent made from apples and widely available in liquid and powder form. If you've made jams from recipes in this book during the spring and summer, you'll know that most did not call for added pectin, relying on their natural pectin and longer cooking times to thicken. Grapes, however, lack enough natural pectin to create a spreadable jelly, so commercial pectin is a must.

Remove the grapes from the cluster and discard the stems (if a few little stems remain, that's fine). Place the grapes in a large heavy pot and, using a wire potato masher, gently crush the grapes. Add the water. Bring to a boil. Reduce the heat, cover, and simmer for 10 minutes.

Line a colander with several layers of cheesecloth. Place the colander over a large clean pot or bowl that will collect the juice. Pour the cooked fruit into the cheesecloth. Gather the ends of the cheesecloth together and suspend the bundle, letting the juice drip into the bowl. (This may be done overnight.) Press gently to extract more juice. (Vigorous pressing will cloud the juice and the finished jelly.) You should have about 5 cups of juice. If you're just shy, add water to measure 5 cups.

Pour the juice into a large saucepan or Dutch oven. Stir in the pectin and ½ teaspoon butter to prevent the liquid from foaming, if desired. Bring the mixture to a full rolling boil (one that won't stop even when stirred) over high heat, stirring constantly. Stir in the sugar and return to a full rolling boil, stirring constantly. Boil for an additional minute, stirring constantly. Remove the pan from the heat and skim any foam that has developed.

Ladle the jelly into sterilized half-pint jars to within ¼ inch of the rim (headspace). Seal and process for 10 minutes.

New to making jams, jellies, and preserves? For a step-by-step guide to the basics, see "Jams, Jellies, and Preserves" on page 237.

concords

What would a peanut butter and jelly sandwich be without grape jelly? Certainly not the best it could be. Most grape jelly, whether commercially prepared or the half pints that home cooks put up, is made from Concord grapes, grown in great abundance on the east coast and regularly appearing at farmers markets and roadside stands at summer's end. These beautiful purple-black-skinned grapes are highly aromatic and have a sweet, juicy flesh and the classic grape flavor expected in jelly. Go ahead and experiment with different purple varieties, but few will top the Concord.

heritage breed turkey

To feed our yen for locally grown and raised foods, innovative farmers have responded in many ways such as growing specialty grains, crafting homestead and artisan cheeses, raising heirloom vegetables and fruits—foods that often have personal or historic connections to the land.

Some farmers have found their niche by raising and reviving interest in heritage breed turkeys, traditional "standard" breeds that graced Thanksgiving tables prior to the 1960s when Broad Breasted Whites began filling the freezer cases at grocery stores at a fast and furious pace. Cheap to feed, fast to grow, and unnaturally breast heavy were the special features of this new breed of bird, all at the expense of taste.

Heritage breeds have been quietly gaining a renewed popularity and respect, treasured for the flavor they return to the table along with a history that connects locavores to the way our families used to eat. There are more than a dozen heritage breeds raised for meat like the White Holland, a snowy white-feathered bird bred in Holland and very popular here before the 1960s; or the Bourbon Red, a fit and flavorful bird named for Bourbon County, Kentucky; or Standard Bronze, a beautiful, majestic bird with a coppery sheen, more than two centuries old, that has been the inspiration for children's drawings for centuries.

Heritage breeds are slow-growth birds, taking three times longer than broad-breasted varieties, about 30 weeks, to reach processing weight. These breeds thrive outdoors, scratching for bugs, enjoying a virtual salad bar of weeds and grasses, all while soaking up the sun. One breed is not necessarily better or tastier than another, although some are easier to raise, some grow larger, and each has its quirks. Farmers who raise these breeds attribute their superior taste and moist flesh to diverse diets, extended life spans, and greater care and respect for the animal, using no growth hormones or antibiotics and no preservatives or additives when processing.

Make one of these breeds part of your Thanksgiving table and the turkey, the traditional centerpiece of the meal, ceases to serve merely as the protein course and becomes another reason to give thanks.

estimated roasting times for turkey (unstuffed, brined, or unbrined) using the above method

Weight of Bird	Roasting Time
12 to 14 pounds	2¼ to 3 hours
15 to 17 pounds	3 to 3½ hours
18 to 20 pounds	3½ to 4 hours
21 to 22 pounds	4 to 4½ hours
23 to 24 pounds	4½ to 4¾ hours

Roasted Heritage Turkey

Makes 10 to 12 servings

Heritage breed turkeys won't yield the "mega" breasts of commercially raised birds nor do they have excessive amounts of fat. There's a better balance between dark and white meat so the trick is to roast it to perfection so both are done at the same time. This method gives the bird a blast of high heat followed by a longer cooking time at moderate heat. Don't skip the step of letting it rest before carving. That gives the natural juices time to redistribute back into the flesh where you want them, not in a pool on the cutting board.

1 turkey, 15 to 17 pounds
¼ cup extra virgin olive oil
¼ cup unsalted butter, softened
1 large onion, peeled and quartered
2 cloves garlic, peeled and crushed
1 fresh lemon, halved
1 apple, peeled, cored, and quartered
1 bunch fresh parsley
6 sprigs fresh thyme
Salt and freshly ground black pepper, to season

Preheat the oven to 450°F.

Pat the surface of the bird dry with paper towels. Mix the olive oil and butter together into a paste. Rub all over the surface of the turkey, under the breast skin, and into the cavity. Loosely stuff the cavity with onion, garlic, lemon, apple, parsley, and thyme. Place on a roasting rack in a roasting pan and roast for 30 minutes until the breast has browned slightly.

Drape a piece of oiled parchment paper over the breast. Reduce the oven temperature to 350°F and roast, basting frequently with the pan juices, until an instant-read thermometer inserted into the thickest portion of the thigh reaches 150°F. Total cooking time should be 3 to 3½ hours. Remove from the oven, cover loosely with foil and let rest for 30 minutes before carving.

Buttermilk Brine for Turkey

Brines one 15-pound turkey

Brining is a process that enhances flavor and increases the moisture content of lean meats using a salt, sugar, and liquid solution. Using cultured buttermilk is equally effective, adding subtle tang, and the milk cultures break down the proteins, tenderizing the meat for a tender and juicy bird.

1 15-pound turkey, rinsed and patted dry
1 cup kosher salt
1 gallon cold buttermilk
½ cup brown sugar
4 cloves garlic, crushed
2 tablespoons whole peppercorns, crushed

Rub the salt all over the outside and in the cavity of the bird. Place the bird in a large, heavy-duty plastic bag or a large, sturdy plastic container with a lid. Combine the buttermilk, brown sugar, garlic, and peppercorns. Add to the bag, squeeze out as much air as possible, and seal tightly. (The bird should be submerged or enveloped in the liquid. If needed, add cold water to increase the liquid level.) If using a bag, place it in a deep roasting pan or large container. Place in the refrigerator for 24 to 36 hours, turning occasionally.

When ready to roast, remove the turkey from the brine, rinse thoroughly and pat dry. Discard the brine. Let the bird sit at room temperature for one hour before roasting.

in season . . .
pumpkins & squash

When summer turns off the heat, pumpkins and squash begin to show up on roadside stands and markets in a multitude of colors, sizes, and shapes—huge, tiny, flat, short, tall, round, pear necked, smooth, ribbed . . . even warty. Colorful pumpkins have been used to add a fall motif to home decorating, but many of those same varieties are absolutely delicious and have long been overlooked in the kitchen.

The difference between pumpkins and winter squash is largely culinary rather than botanical, although in general one can be substituted for another in recipes, especially in pureed soups. Despite the name, winter squash is still a warm weather crop but unlike its summer counterpart, it keeps well into the winter.

Choosing the Best. By the time squash and pumpkin have reached monster proportions, the edible flesh becomes stringy, woody, and generally lacking moisture. Pie pumpkins or sugar pumpkins are better choices—small, weighing up to 4 pounds, and sweet, with dark orange flesh. Don't pass up on the oddly colored and unusual-shaped pumpkins, though. Many are heirloom varieties, thick and meaty, with sweet-tasting, intensely colored flesh.

Squash or pumpkin should feel heavy for their size, which means they have more tender, edible flesh, and the skin should appear fresh, glossy, and blemish free. It's best if the stem is intact and shows brown flecks or corking. These are also called "sugar spots"—good indicators of a mature, ripe squash or pumpkin.

How to Store. Pumpkins and squash like it cool, but because of their odd shapes and sizes, they might not be welcome in most fridges. If going from the farm or garden to the kitchen, a few days on the countertop won't hurt, but for longer storage, a cool (50°F to 60°F), dark, dry, ventilated place is best.

To Prepare for Cooking. Most pumpkin or squash have tough skin that poses a challenge to remove. If your recipe calls for peeling and cubing the squash or pumpkin, tackle the job in small pieces. It's best to use a large sturdy knife to cut round pumpkins into wedges, like cutting a slice of cake. If the squash is oddly shaped, try cutting it into large chunks. More manageable pieces make it easier to remove the skin with a paring knife and scrape away the seeds and stringy matter.

If the squash is to be steamed or roasted before pureeing for a soup or pumpkin puree, leave the skin intact. It's much easier to remove after the heat has softened the skin.

Pick or Buy Now, Enjoy Later. Pumpkin or squash that has been roasted, baked, or steamed in the shell can be scooped out, mashed into a pulp and frozen. Freeze it in the amounts needed for your favorite recipe and thaw in the refrigerator. In the months to come, the puree can be used to make Next-Day, No-Knead Squash Dinner Rolls on page 207 or Pumpkin Pancakes with Cider Syrup on page 208.

pumpkin and squash primer

There are subtle differences in flavor and texture between most varieties of pumpkin and squash. For the most part and taking into account the color differences in the flesh, varieties with the same qualities can be swapped for another in recipes. This primer will point you toward the flavor and best cooking techniques for each variety. Try them all to find your all-time favorite.

A word about pumpkins: while you'll only find a description for Pie Pumpkins, an easy-to-find variety, you will likely come across dozens of other large, oddly colored, and unusual-shaped pumpkins at roadside stands and farmers markets. Don't pass them up and certainly don't reserve them for fall decorating. Some of the varieties like Cinderella, Tan Cheese, Fairy Tale, and the blue-shelled Jarrahdale have fewer seeds, thick and meaty walls, and the richest and best taste you can find. These are good varieties to process into purees.

Acorn Squash: When you find this variety shaped, of course, like an oversized acorn missing its cap, choose those with a mostly green rind, which is thick and very firm and almost impossible to peel. Good for roasting or stuffing.

Ambercup Squash: A relative of the buttercup, this one looks like a little pumpkin. The bright orange flesh has a dry, sweet taste and can be used like or substituted for sweet potatoes.

Buttercup Squash: Squat and green and not to be confused with butternut squash, this is one of the most flavorful squash you'll find. The dark yellow-orange flesh lacks moisture, so use this one for soups and purees.

Butternut Squash: A good all-purpose squash with a smooth beige shell and a bell shape. Easy to peel, with a deep orange flesh and sweet, nutty flavor. A common substitute for pumpkin in recipes and vice versa.

Carnival Squash: The shell is splashed with cream, orange, and green. Inside, the yellow flesh can be used just like an acorn squash, baked or steamed and mixed with butter and herbs.

Delicata Squash: Oblong with a variegated shell, this tasty winter squash has a pale-colored pulp similar to sweet potatoes.

Hubbard: Large, lumpy, and grayish green, this squash is often sold cut into smaller pieces. Don't judge it by its cover. The intensely colored orange flesh is sweet, creamy, and moist—a good choice for pies.

Kabocha Squash: The thick, tough rind is worth getting through for the sweet flesh, which is somewhat drier and less fibrous than that of other winter squash. The taste will remind you of sweet potatoes.

Pie or Sugar Pumpkins: Typically around 4 pounds, these have a sweet taste, tender flesh, and smooth texture—a good choice for pies and baking. Their giant look-alikes are indeed edible but more challenging to work with and not as intensely flavored.

Spaghetti Squash: With the looks of a small golden watermelon, the larger ones with a golden yellow rind are the best choice. Once cooked, the insides pull out like long strands of noodles. The taste is mild and slightly nutty.

Sweet Dumpling Squash: Small, with cream-colored green-flecked skins, these are the perfect size for stuffing and baking as individual servings. The flesh is mild and sweet.

Fresh Pumpkin Puree

Yields about 1¾ cups or about 1 pound

Fresh pureed pumpkin has a lighter texture, brighter taste, and more vibrant color than canned pumpkin. You can use this same method to bake and puree most squash—just adjust the cooking time for the size of the squash. You can use this pumpkin puree in recipes that call for canned pumpkin. Be sure to drain it well before using or freezing.

When working with larger pumpkins, split the pumpkins in half, remove the seeds, brush with butter, and lay cut side down on a sturdy baking sheet. Bake until tender, an hour or more.

1 sugar pumpkin (about 4 pounds)
1½ tablespoons unsalted butter, melted

Preheat the oven to 400°F.

Slice off the stem end of the pumpkin 2½ inches from the top, reserving it. Scrape out the seeds and the membranes and brush the inside of the pumpkin with butter. Put the top back on the pumpkin. Put the pumpkin in a shallow baking pan and roast for 1 hour or until the pumpkin is soft to the touch.

Remove and let sit until cool enough to handle.

Discard any of the liquid accumulated in the pumpkin. Scoop out the pulp and, working in batches, process into a puree using a blender or food processor.

Line a large sieve or colander with large paper coffee filters and place over a large bowl. Cover the surface of the puree with plastic wrap. Place it in the refrigerator and let it drain overnight.

Pack in freezer containers in 1-pound increments and freeze for up to 6 to 9 months. Thaw in the refrigerator.

Pumpkin Risotto

Makes 6 servings

So many of the pumpkin recipes in our recipe collections call for pureeing the pumpkin to a silky texture. This recipe is all about experiencing the texture of fresh pumpkin that is so good at absorbing flavors during cooking and adding brilliant orange colors to dishes like risotto. Take note— there are no shortcuts for this dish, which requires stirring constantly for 20 minutes and serving immediately. One bite and you'll realize it's time well spent.

5 to 6 cups vegetable stock
¼ cup unsalted butter
1 tablespoon extra virgin olive oil
6 shallots, finely chopped
2 cloves garlic, chopped
1½ cups risotto
½ cup dry white wine
2 cups diced pumpkin or butternut squash, about 1-inch dice
½ cup chopped fresh flat-leaf parsley
1½ cups freshly grated Parmesan cheese, plus extra to accompany
Salt and freshly ground black pepper, to taste

Heat the stock in a saucepan until almost boiling. Reduce the heat to keep the stock at a bare simmer.

Heat the butter and olive oil in a large pan over medium heat. Add the shallots and cook for 2 minutes, until soft and translucent. Add the garlic and sauté for an additional 30 seconds.

Add the risotto and stir until the grains are coated, about one minute. Stir in the wine until it has been completely absorbed. Stir in the pumpkin and parsley. Begin adding the hot stock, a ladleful (about ½ cup) at a time, stirring until the liquid has been absorbed before adding the next ladleful. Continue to add stock at intervals until the rice is tender but firm (al dente) and the pumpkin is tender. This will take 18 to 20 minutes. Reserve one ladleful of stock.

Add the reserved stock, cheese, and salt and pepper to taste, mixing well. Remove from the heat, cover, and let rest two minutes before serving.

Spoon into warm bowls and serve with extra Parmesan cheese, if desired.

Spicy Pumpkin Ketchup

Makes about 1¼ cups

Why reserve ketchup for just tomatoes? Smooth and sweet, pumpkin is a great base for this recipe that puts an unusual spin on a classic favorite. Serve with Oven Fries (page 149) and you have a fitting salute to fall weather.

1 cup fresh pumpkin puree
1 small onion, minced
1 clove garlic, minced
½ cup water
¼ cup apple cider vinegar
2 tablespoons honey
½ teaspoon ground ginger
½ teaspoon ground allspice
½ teaspoon salt
¼ teaspoon ground mustard
¼ teaspoon ground cloves
¼ teaspoon black pepper

Combine all of the ingredients in a medium saucepan. Bring to a boil, stirring occasionally. Reduce the heat to low and simmer for 20 minutes, uncovered, until thick and the consistency of traditional ketchup. (If you find the mixture gets too thick before the cooking time is over, add more water in small increments.)

Let cool slightly, then process to a puree in a blender or food processor.

Refrigerate for a couple of hours and serve chilled as ketchup or hot as a sauce over a burger. The ketchup will keep for one week stored in the refrigerator in a covered container.

Acorn Squash with Garlic Oil and Sage

Makes 6 to 8 servings

Thick ruffled rings of acorn squash get a boost of flavor from garlic oil you make yourself. A simple, quick infusion does the trick. The fresh sage crisps in the oven and delivers bursts of flavor in every bite.

To make garlic oil: Crush a clove of garlic and put it in a small bowl with the olive oil. Let sit for 30 minutes to an hour before using.

2 acorn squash
2 tablespoons garlic-infused oil (see side note)
12 fresh sage leaves, more or less to taste, chopped
Salt and freshly ground black pepper, to taste

Preheat the oven to 400°F.

Using a large, heavy knife and working on a sturdy surface, slice the acorn squash widthwise into ½-inch-thick round slices. Remove the seeds and stringy membrane. You will have 6 to 8 slices. Arrange the slices in a single layer on a lightly oiled heavy baking sheet. Brush both sides with the garlic oil and sprinkle with the sage, salt, and pepper. Roast for 20 minutes or until the squash is tender. Remove with a spatula and serve warm.

Butternut Squash Soup
with Roasted Hazelnut Cream

Makes 6 servings

This rich and luscious soup highlights one of the best tastes of the season. Interestingly enough, it calls the seeds and strings into service where there's more flavor to be coaxed. You can also change up the flavor by substituting cider for some of the chicken stock.

1 cup heavy cream, divided use
¾ cup whole roasted hazelnuts, finely chopped
1 butternut squash (about 3 pounds total)
4 tablespoons unsalted butter
1 large shallot, chopped
6 cups water (vegetable stock or chicken stock may be substituted)
½ teaspoon salt
1 teaspoon dark brown sugar
Freshly grated nutmeg, to taste

Pour ½ cup of the cream into a saucepan and add the nuts. Warm over medium heat until hot, but not boiling. Remove from the heat and set aside.

Halve the unpeeled squash vertically and scoop out the seeds and strings and reserve. Cut the squash into about 8 large chunks.

Melt the butter in a large stockpot; add the shallot and sauté until soft and fragrant, about 4 minutes. Add the reserved strings and seeds from the squash and sauté for an additional 3 minutes. Add the water. Insert a steamer basket and add the chunks of squash. Cover tightly and bring the liquid to a boil. Reduce the heat to medium and steam the squash for 30 minutes until very soft.

Remove the squash from the steamer and set aside to cool. Strain the liquid into another container, discarding the solids (you should have approximately 3 cups of liquid). When the squash is cool enough to handle, remove the pulp and discard the skin.

Working in batches, puree the squash in a blender until smooth. Return to the stockpot. Stir in enough of the reserved liquid to achieve a creamy consistency. Return the pot to the stove and gently warm over medium heat. Add the salt, brown sugar, and nutmeg. Stir in the remaining ½ cup of cream. Heat until hot, but do not boil. Taste and adjust seasonings.

When ready to serve, whisk the hazelnut cream mixture until slightly thickened. Ladle the soup into bowls and top with some of the hazelnut cream and freshly grated nutmeg.

Spaghetti Squash with Feta and Pine Nuts

Makes 4 to 6 servings

When spaghetti squash is cooked, the pulp separates like glistening strands of golden pasta with a fresh buttery taste. This makes a great vegetarian main course or a satisfying side dish.

1 spaghetti squash, halved lengthwise and seeded
2 tablespoons unsalted butter, divided use
1 small onion, chopped
½ teaspoon red pepper flakes
¼ cup chopped flat-leaf parsley, plus extra for garnish
½ cup toasted pine nuts
1 cup crumbled feta cheese, divided use
Salt and freshly ground black pepper, to taste

Preheat the oven to 375°F.

Place the prepared squash, cut side down, on a heavy baking sheet. Bake for 40 to 45 minutes or until the shell is soft and yields to a gentle squeeze. Remove and let cool for 5 minutes. Using a fork, scrape the flesh from the shell into a large bowl.

While the squash cooks, melt the butter in a large skillet. Add the onion and sauté for 6 minutes or until soft. Add the red pepper flakes and sauté for an additional minute. Add the spaghetti squash and parsley and cook for 3 to 4 minutes, stirring occasionally, to heat and combine.

Transfer to a large bowl. Add the pine nuts and feta, tossing to combine. Season with salt and pepper and garnish with parsley. Serve immediately.

Pumpkin Fondue

Makes 8 to 10 appetizer servings

This recipe calls for a small pumpkin, and while you might be tempted to reach for a familiar pie pumpkin (small and sweet), try a Tan Cheese. It's beautiful and beige on the outside, brilliant orange and sweet on the inside. It looks almost like a serving dish!

3 to 4 cups whole wheat or whole grain bread chunks, lightly toasted
 or dried in the oven
1 4-pound pumpkin, preferably a Tan Cheese
1 cup half-and-half or heavy cream
½ cup rich chicken stock
½ teaspoon grated nutmeg, plus extra
1¼ cups grated Swiss or Gruyère cheese
1 tablespoon extra virgin olive oil

Preheat the oven to 400°F.

Cut the top off the pumpkin and remove the stringy pulp and seeds.

Combine the half-and-half, chicken stock, and grated nutmeg in a small bowl.

To assemble, place a layer of bread chunks inside the pumpkin. Add ⅓ of the cheese and ⅓ of the liquid. Repeat with two more layers, pressing and compacting the ingredients in the pumpkin shell. Place the top back on the pumpkin and brush the outside of the shell with the olive oil. (Can be prepared a few hours in advance and refrigerated.)

Place the pumpkin in a shallow baking dish or on a sturdy baking tray to catch any drips. Bake for about an hour, more or less time depending on the size and thickness of the pumpkin. If the pumpkin gets too charred for your liking, reduce the heat to 350°F.

The pumpkin fondue is done when the pulp on the inside is soft and buttery yet the shell is still intact.

Before serving, grate additional nutmeg over the fondue. Scoop out portions with a large spoon into small bowls, making sure to get some of the pulp.

Roasted Squash with Thyme and Honey

Makes 4 servings

Yes, this is a side dish, but it's so wonderfully sweet it will seem as if dessert arrived early. The honey adds a caramel-like finish, creating a golden glaze over the nuts and squash.

1 butternut squash, peeled, seeded, and cut into 1-inch cubes
¼ to ½ cup honey
4 tablespoons butter, melted
½ teaspoon dried thyme leaves
½ cup walnuts, coarsely chopped
Salt and freshly cracked black pepper

Preheat the oven to 400°F.

Combine the honey, butter, thyme, and nuts in a medium bowl and stir to combine. Add the cubed squash and toss until all the cubes are coated.

Arrange the squash in a shallow baking dish and season with salt and pepper to taste. Roast for 30 to 35 minutes or until tender. Serve immediately.

....

This recipe adapts beautifully for Buttercup or Ambercup squash. Cut the squash into thick slices, like cutting slices of cake. Remove the seeds and stringy matter and arrange the unpeeled slices on a lightly oiled baking sheet. Prepare the butter mixture without the nuts and brush on the squash. Roast until the flesh is tender. Remove with a spatula. Allow to cool slightly before slipping the skin off.

Sweet Pumpkin with Yogurt Sauce

This delicious vegetarian recipe is inspired by a traditional Afghan dish. The pumpkin cubes soak up the slightly spicy tomato sauce as they cook to a delightfully tender finish. A cooling, homemade yogurt sauce is the perfect crowning touch.

Learn to make your own yogurt on page 29. It's simple!

Makes 4 to 6 servings

¼ cup corn oil or canola oil
1 small pie pumpkin, peeled, seeded, and diced into 2-inch cubes
1 clove garlic, crushed
1 cup water
½ teaspoon salt
½ cup sugar
4 ounces tomato sauce
½ teaspoon ginger root, grated
1 teaspoon coriander seeds, crushed
¼ teaspoon freshly ground black pepper

Sauce:
¾ cup plain yogurt
1 clove garlic, crushed
¼ teaspoon salt

Crushed dried mint leaves
Cooked rice and pita bread slices, to accompany

Heat the oil in a large frying pan with a lid. Fry the pumpkin cubes on all sides until lightly browned.

In a small bowl, mix together the garlic, water, salt, sugar, tomato sauce, ginger root, coriander, and pepper. Add to the pumpkin mixture in the frying pan. Cover and cook 20 to 25 minutes over low heat until the pumpkin is tender and has absorbed most of the liquid.

In a small bowl, mix together the yogurt, garlic, and salt.

To serve, spread some of the yogurt mixture on a serving plate and arrange the pumpkin on top. Top with the remaining yogurt and sprinkle with dried mint. Serve with rice and pita bread.

Winter

Winter sends us back into the kitchen to cozy up with comfort foods . . . familiar, uncomplicated foods that we use as a special reward or that give us a sense of well-being.

If you've prepared your lovacore kitchen for the off-season by stocking your pantry and filling your freezer with locally grown and homegrown foods, then you've probably added another layer of definition to the term "comfort foods"—the comfort you find in knowing where they came from and that they were at their peak of flavor and quality when they were preserved.

There is also comfort in knowing that many of the distinctive flavors you preserved during the spring, summer, and fall are now waiting in the freezer or pantry to be enjoyed again in familiar or new recipes to bring to your table throughout the winter. Enjoy a few more recipes and be inspired to find other delicious ways to use these prized ingredients.

appetizers

Rosemary Meatballs with Tangy Red Raspberry Glaze

The sweet crimson glaze on these aromatic meatballs is sure to get your guests' attention during the holidays. Be sure to let them know which fabulous local flavors are straight from your locavore's kitchen: rosemary, raspberry preserves, mustard, or horseradish.

Makes about 32 meatballs

1 pound lean ground beef
1 clove garlic, minced
1 tablespoon fresh rosemary leaves, minced
1 tablespoon chopped fresh parsley
1 cup fresh breadcrumbs
1 egg, lightly beaten
½ tablespoon grated lemon zest
1 teaspoon salt
½ teaspoon freshly ground black pepper
1 cup red raspberry preserves
3 tablespoons Dijon mustard
1½ tablespoons horseradish

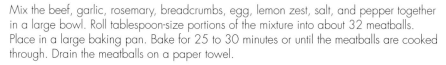

Preheat the oven to 350°F.

Mix the beef, garlic, rosemary, breadcrumbs, egg, lemon zest, salt, and pepper together in a large bowl. Roll tablespoon-size portions of the mixture into about 32 meatballs. Place in a large baking pan. Bake for 25 to 30 minutes or until the meatballs are cooked through. Drain the meatballs on a paper towel.

While the meatballs are baking, combine the preserves, mustard, and horseradish in a medium saucepan. Bring to a boil over medium heat and cook for 2 to 3 minutes, stirring occasionally. Remove from the heat and add the meatballs, tossing gently to coat in the glaze. Transfer to a serving dish and use toothpicks to serve.

Baked Brie with Orchard Chutney

This quick appetizer calls for Orchard Chutney from the pantry. Warmed in the oven, it recalls a morning in the orchard picking the ingredients as well as the afternoon well spent preserving them for moments like this.

Makes 6 appetizer servings

8-ounce wheel of Brie or other soft cheese
1 cup or ½ pint Orchard Chutney (page 136)
1 whole grain baguette, cut into ¼-inch slices and toasted

Preheat the oven to 350°F.

Place the Brie in a small glass pie plate or other ovenproof plate just large enough to hold the wheel of Brie. Spread the chutney over the top. Bake for 15 to 20 minutes or until the center of the Brie is soft. Serve with crusty slices of toasted bread.

Oven-Dried Tomato Spread

Makes about 1 cup

Intensely flavored oven-dried tomatoes makes this versatile spread one you won't soon forget. Thin it with a little milk, cream, or yogurt and use it as a dip with toasted pita chips or use as a spread for bagels or sandwiches.

½ cup oven-dried tomatoes (page 122)
¾ cup (6 ounces) cream cheese, softened
3 large cloves garlic or 1 large shallot
½ to 1 tablespoon extra virgin olive oil
2 tablespoons prepared pesto
Salt and pepper, to taste

Place the tomatoes, cream cheese, garlic, and ½ tablespoon of the oil in a blender or food processor. Process for about 1 minute until smooth. Add the pesto and process for an additional 10 seconds. If the mixture is not smooth and creamy, add additional olive oil in teaspoon portions. Taste and season with salt and pepper. Refrigerate for at least 2 and up to 24 hours to allow flavors to meld. Serve with crackers or toasted breads.

Variations
Add a roasted red bell pepper along with the tomatoes before processing or stir in finely chopped walnuts at the end.

Chicken and Roasted Red Pepper Pizza

Makes 6 to 8 servings

When the craving for this pizza hits, you're prepared with a stash of sweet, roasted red peppers in the freezer. The work is already done and your only job is to enjoy them.

Prepare the Whole Wheat Pizza Crust on page 115 and freeze half for later use. Shape the remaining portion of dough to form the crust; bake for 15 to 17 minutes at 425°F before topping.

1 recipe Whole Wheat Pizza Crust (page 115), see note
1 tablespoon extra virgin olive oil
1 medium onion, thinly sliced
1 clove garlic, minced
2 roasted red peppers, cut into strips
½ cup heavy cream
2 tablespoons tomato paste
¼ teaspoon crushed red pepper flakes
1 cup cooked slivered chicken
2 tablespoons chopped fresh parsley

Heat the oil in a large skillet over medium heat. Add the onion and sauté until soft and fragrant, about 6 minutes. Add the garlic and sauté an additional minute. Stir in the pepper strips, cream, tomato paste, and red pepper flakes. Cook until thickened and well blended, about 3 minutes. Add the chicken and heat through. Spoon the mixture over the prepared pizza crust. Garnish with chopped parsley. Serve warm.

Chicken Pesto Cheesecake

Frozen pesto is one of the handiest ingredients in the locavore's kitchen. Drop frozen chunks into soups like the Escarole Soup on page 60, thaw and spread on crostini, or blend it into this luncheon-style cheesecake. If you've frozen chives and chive blossoms, you get bonus points!

Makes 8 servings

1 pound cream cheese, softened
2 large eggs
2 tablespoons all-purpose flour, divided use
½ teaspoon salt
½ cup prepared Classic Basil Pesto (page 89)
1 cup chopped cooked chicken
8 ounces crème fraîche or sour cream
10 cups mixed salad greens
Chopped fresh chives, for garnish

Preheat the oven to 325°F.

Beat the cream cheese with an electric mixer on medium speed until smooth and fluffy, about 5 minutes. Add the eggs, one at a time, until just blended. Add 1 tablespoon flour, salt, and pesto, beating until blended. Stir in chopped chicken. Pour into a 9-inch springform pan. Bake for 25 minutes.

Stir together the remaining flour and crème fraîche. Spread over the cheesecake and bake an additional 15 minutes. Cool on a wire rack for 10 minutes. Run a knife around the edges of the cheesecake to release the sides. Remove the springform. Allow to cool for 1 hour before cutting into slices. Serve hot, cold, or at room temperature atop a bed of fresh salad greens. Garnish with chives and serve.

Spinach Balls

The spinach (or chard or fall greens) blanched and frozen last year is likely destined for at least one batch of these savory appetizers. Once the spinach is thawed, give it one final squeeze to remove any water before beginning with this recipe.

To make quick toasted breadcrumbs, toast 3 to 4 slices of bread, cool, and then process into coarse crumbs in the food processor.

Makes 30 balls

2½ cups thawed frozen spinach or chard, squeezed to remove
   as much excess water as possible
2 cups coarse whole wheat bread crumbs, toasted
1 cup grated Parmesan cheese
3 large eggs, lightly beaten
1 small onion, minced
2 cloves garlic, minced
½ cup unsalted butter, melted
½ teaspoon salt
½ teaspoon freshly ground black pepper

Preheat the oven to 350°F.

Mix all of the ingredients in a large bowl until combined. Roll tablespoon portions of the mixture into balls and arrange them on an ungreased baking pan, close but not touching.

Bake for 20 minutes until hot, lightly browned, and firm enough to pick up.

soups

Asparagus Soup with Blue Cheese

Makes 4 Servings

The fresh "green" taste of asparagus feels delightfully out of place on a cold winter day, and that's what makes the locavore's kitchen so special. It's where you can expect the unexpected. The blue cheese is a tangy complement.

4 tablespoons unsalted butter
1 large onion, diced
1 large leek, thinly sliced (white part only)
1 large potato, peeled and cubed
6 cups rich chicken stock or vegetable stock
1½ pounds asparagus, frozen, unthawed or fresh
4 ounces blue cheese, crumbled
Salt and freshly ground black pepper, to taste

Melt the butter in a large saucepan over medium heat. Add the onion and sauté for 2 minutes. Add the leek and continue to sauté for an additional 6 minutes or until soft. Add the potatoes and the broth. Bring to a boil. Reduce the heat to a simmer and cook until the potatoes are tender, about 10 minutes. Add the asparagus and cook until just tender, about 4 to 5 minutes.

Remove from the heat. Working in batches, puree the soup in a blender until smooth. Return to the saucepan and gently reheat. Season to taste with salt and pepper.

To serve, pour into warm bowls, top with blue cheese, and garnish with reserved asparagus tips.

Cream of Corn Soup with Rosemary

Makes 4 servings

A little advance planning is necessary when making this soup: start the day ahead to gently infuse the milk with the rosemary. This strong herb subtly scents and flavors the milk base, and the corn adds natural sweetness. Here's a good use for frozen kernels of corn from the summer harvest and for rosemary sprigs, too.

For a richer soup, substitute ½ cup heavy cream for ½ cup of the milk.

2 cups whole milk
3 sprigs fresh rosemary
1 tablespoon unsalted butter
3 tablespoons chopped shallots
3 cups fresh or frozen corn kernels
Salt and freshly ground black pepper
2 tablespoons prepared pesto (page 89)

The day before you plan to serve the soup, combine the milk and rosemary in a medium saucepan. Heat to a simmer. Cool to room temperature. Transfer milk and rosemary to a container with a lid and refrigerate overnight. The next day, strain the milk and discard the rosemary.

To make the soup, melt the butter in a medium saucepan. Add the shallots and sauté until soft and fragrant, about 3 minutes. Add the milk to the saucepan along with the corn kernels. Bring to a gentle boil over medium-low heat. Cook for 8 to 10 minutes or until the kernels are tender. Working in batches, carefully transfer the soup to a blender and blend until smooth. Return to the saucepan and gently reheat. Season to taste with salt and pepper.

To serve, ladle the soup into 4 warmed soup bowls and swirl ½ tablespoon of the prepared pesto into each bowl, if desired. Serve immediately.

Savory Lentil and Rhubarb Soup

The tart taste of rhubarb adds an unusual twist to this lentil soup. When winter rolls around, frozen rhubarb delivers the same delicious results and will remind you that spring is not far off.

Makes 6 servings

1 cup boiling water
1 cup lentils
2 tablespoons extra virgin olive oil
2 carrots, peeled and diced
2 stalks celery, diced
1 large onion, diced
2 cloves garlic, minced
1 cup diced rhubarb
1 tablespoon tomato paste
1 to 2 tablespoons honey
4 cups chicken stock or vegetable stock
¼ cup chopped fresh parsley, divided use
½ teaspoon salt
Freshly ground black pepper, to taste
6 tablespoons or more of plain yogurt or sour cream

Place the lentils in a small glass bowl and cover with boiling water. Set aside.

Heat a Dutch oven or stockpot over medium heat. Add the olive oil. Sauté the carrot, celery, and onion for 6 minutes, until vegetables are soft and aromatic. Add the garlic and sauté for an additional minute. Add the rhubarb and continue sautéing another minute. Add the tomato paste and honey and stir for another minute. Add the lentils and the liquid they were soaking in along with the chicken stock and half the parsley. Bring to a boil. Cover and reduce the heat. Simmer for 20 minutes or until the lentils are tender. Season with the salt and pepper to taste.

Serve with a dollop of yogurt or sour cream and a sprinkling of the remaining parsley.

Farmhouse Chowder

A pot of simmering chowder is great comfort food when it's cold outside and your insides need warming up. Having summer's sweet corn at hand is another comfort in the locavore's kitchen. If you've frozen some corn stock (see page 108 to learn how), you can use it in place of some or all of the chicken stock.

Makes 6 servings

3 slices thick-sliced bacon, chopped
1 small onion, chopped
½ red bell pepper, chopped
2 cloves garlic, chopped
2 cups cubed potatoes, about ½-inch cubes
4 cups chicken stock
2½ cups chopped cooked chicken (skin removed)
2 cups corn kernels, frozen or removed from the cob
1 tablespoon chopped fresh thyme
1 to 1½ cups heavy cream
2 tablespoons chopped fresh parsley
Salt and freshly ground black pepper

Cook the chopped bacon in a large Dutch oven over medium heat until crisp. Remove with a slotted spoon and drain on a paper towel. Set aside.

Drain off all but 2 tablespoons of the bacon fat. Return to the heat and add the onion and pepper, sautéing until soft and translucent, about 6 minutes. Add the garlic and sauté for an additional minute. Add the potatoes and chicken stock. Bring to a boil. Reduce the heat to medium and cook until the potatoes are soft and break apart easily with a fork, about 20 minutes. Reduce heat to medium-low and add the chicken, corn, and thyme. Return to a simmer and cook for 15 minutes. Slowly add the cream and heat through without boiling. Stir in the parsley and reserved bacon. Season to taste with salt and pepper. Let stand, or "cure," for an hour. Reheat gently, if necessary, and serve.

Next-Day, No-Knead Squash Dinner Rolls

It's worth waiting a day to taste these amazingly tender rolls. Be sure to drain the puree as it thaws to rid it of any excess liquid.

Makes 18 rolls

2 .25-ounce packages active dry yeast
¼ cup warm water (90°F to 110°F)
2 large eggs, beaten
1 cup squash or pumpkin puree, thawed if frozen
½ cup unsalted butter, at room temperature
½ cup sugar
1 tablespoon fresh minced thyme
2 teaspoons kosher salt
¼ teaspoon cayenne pepper
3½ cup all-purpose flour, plus extra if needed
3 tablespoons melted butter, for greasing the bowl and pans

Sprinkle the yeast over the warm water in a large mixing bowl and stir to dissolve. Stir in the eggs, pumpkin puree, butter, sugar, thyme, salt, and cayenne. Stir in the flour and beat with an electric beater until smooth, adding up to an additional ½ cup flour to make a soft dough (the dough should be tacky but manageable).

Brush another large bowl with butter and turn the dough into it, turning to coat the dough with butter on all sides. Cover with a kitchen towel and let rise in a warm spot for 1½ hours or until double in size. Punch the dough down, cover with plastic wrap, and refrigerate overnight.

Preheat the oven to 375°F. Grease two 8-inch round cake pans with the remaining butter.

Punch the dough down again and divide into 18 pieces. Shape each piece into a ball and arrange in the pans, leaving some space between each. Cover with a kitchen towel and let rise in a warm spot for 30 minutes or until double in size.

Bake for 25 to 30 minutes or until the rolls are browned. Serve hot or warm.

Yogurt Bread

Makes 2 loaves

Once you've learned to make your own yogurt on page 29, you'll be hooked on the fresh taste and texture. It will probably become a staple in your kitchen all year round and the perfect on-hand ingredient for this soft, silky bread. This recipe is one with which even those new to bread making will enjoy delicious success.

1 .25-ounce package active dry yeast
2 teaspoons sugar
¼ cup warm water (105°F to 115°F)
1 cup (8 ounces) plain yogurt, at room temperature
½ cup unsalted butter, melted and cooled
½ teaspoon baking soda
½ teaspoon baking powder
½ teaspoon salt
3 to 3½ cups all-purpose flour
1 egg, beaten with 1 tablespoon water
¼ cup sesame seeds (optional)

Dissolve the yeast and sugar in the warm water. Let sit for 5 minutes, and then blend with the yogurt, butter, baking soda, baking powder, and salt. Stir in the flour until a soft dough forms. Turn out onto a lightly floured surface and knead for about 5 minutes, until soft and smooth. Cover and let rest for 10 minutes.

Divide the dough into two equal portions. Shape into round or oblong loaves and place on lightly greased baking sheets. Cover loosely with plastic wrap or a slightly damp lint-free cotton towel and let rise for about 30 minutes, until about doubled in size.

Preheat the oven to 350°F.

Lightly brush each loaf with the egg wash. Sprinkle with sesame seeds, if desired. Bake for 35 to 40 minutes, until golden brown. Remove to a baking rack and allow the breads to cool before slicing.

Pumpkin Pancakes with Cider Syrup

Makes about 16 pancakes

Add a little twist to your Sunday breakfast routine with these nicely spiced pancakes and a drizzle of naturally sweet cider syrup, a perfect pairing of local, seasonal flavors. The pumpkin puree comes from the freezer, and the syrup? You did make some during apple cider season, didn't you? If not, there's always the next season . . . or maple syrup!

....

Apple Cider Syrup is a sweet treat over pancakes or waffles. Learn to make your own on page 137.

2 cups all-purpose flour
2 teaspoons baking soda
1 teaspoon ground allspice
1 teaspoon ground cinnamon
½ teaspoon ground ginger
½ teaspoon salt
1½ cups milk, plus extra to thin
1 cup pumpkin puree
1 egg
2 tablespoons vegetable oil, plus extra for the griddle
2 tablespoons apple cider vinegar
Apple cider syrup (page 137), to accompany

Combine the flour, soda, spices, and salt in a large bowl. In a separate bowl, combine the milk, pumpkin, egg, oil, and vinegar. Add the pumpkin mixture to the dry ingredients stirring until just combined. Add more milk, if needed, to thin the batter.

Heat a griddle over medium-high heat. Brush with oil. Working in batches, pour batter by ¼ cupfuls onto the griddle. Cook until bubbles form on the surface of the pancakes and the edges appear set. Flip and cook an additional minute. Keep the finished pancakes in a warm oven until finished. Serve with the cider syrup.

"Bring on the Jam" Muffins

Makes 12 muffins

If your pantry is lined with jars of jams and jellies lovingly created from fruits and berries, they are deserving of only the best muffins. These emerge from the oven with a rustic crown and a bread-like texture, tender yet sturdy enough to spread with any sweet preserve. Enjoy warm with softened butter.

1 cup water, room temperature
2 tablespoons sugar
1 .25-ounce package active dry yeast
4 cups all-purpose flour
3 teaspoons baking powder
1½ teaspoons salt
1 stick unsalted butter, cut into small pieces and chilled
1½ cups crème fraîche or sour cream
2 tablespoons unsalted butter, melted

Butter one standard 12-cup muffin tin. Combine the water, sugar, and yeast in a small bowl. Let stand until foamy, about 10 minutes.

Place the flour, baking powder, salt, and butter in a large mixing bowl. Mix until the mixture is coarse and crumbly and some of the butter chunks still remain the size of small peas. Add the yeast mixture and mix until blended. Add the crème fraîche and mix until all the ingredients are moistened. (The batter will be sticky and appear slightly chunky.)

Spoon the mixture into the prepared muffin tin. Let stand at room temperature for one hour.

Preheat the oven to 400°F.

Bake for 10 minutes, brush with the melted butter, and bake an additional 10 minutes or more until golden and a toothpick inserted in the center of a muffin comes out clean. Serve warm with jam from the cupboard and butter.

Pesto-Stuffed Pork Tenderloin with Hot Pepper Jelly Glaze

Makes 6 servings

Instead of heading to the grocery store for some of the key ingredients, simply gather as many as you can from your cupboard and freezer: pepper jelly, pesto, and locally raised pork. Not only is it delicious, there's plenty of satisfaction knowing you didn't have to rush off to a grocery store for the ingredients.

4 tablespoons hot pepper jelly (page 157)
6 tablespoons pesto (page 89), divided use
1 tablespoon balsamic vinegar
3 tablespoons crumbled feta cheese
2 cloves garlic
1 teaspoon freshly ground black pepper
1 teaspoon fresh thyme
2 tablespoons extra virgin olive oil
2 1-pound pork tenderloins, trimmed of fat and silver skin

To prepare the glaze, melt the hot pepper jelly in a small saucepan. Add 3 tablespoons of the pesto and the balsamic vinegar. Gently simmer for a few minutes, remove from heat, and set aside.

To prepare the filling, combine the remaining pesto and feta cheese in a small bowl.

To prepare the rub, mash together the garlic, pepper, and thyme (a mortar and pestle does the job best). Mix in the olive oil.

To prepare the tenderloins, slice a deep pocket down the length of each tenderloin but not all the way through and 1 inch from the ends. Stuff the pesto filling into the pockets. Close the pockets by tying the tenderloins with butcher twine.

Rub the exterior of the tenderloin with the olive oil mixture. (Can be wrapped in plastic and refrigerated for up to 6 hours.)

Preheat the oven to 450°F.

Place a large ovenproof skillet over medium-high heat. When the skillet is hot, brown the tenderloins on all sides, about 3 minutes per side.

Brush the tenderloin generously with the hot pepper jelly glaze. Transfer the skillet to the oven and roast for 12 to 15 minutes or until the internal temperature reads 140°F when tested with an instant-read thermometer.

Let the meat sit for 10 minutes before cutting into ½-inch-thick slices.

Plum-Glazed Chicken

Makes 4 to 6 servings

Jazz up Plum Jam from the cupboard with a few additional ingredients for this simple, sweet, and spicy glaze for chicken or pork. Serve with a side of Perfectly Mashed Potatoes (page 150) and think back (or ahead) to summer. Make a mental note to make more Plum Jam (page 105). It's that good.

1 whole chicken, cut into pieces
Extra virgin olive oil, for brushing
Salt and freshly ground black pepper, to taste
1 cup plum jam
1 teaspoon freshly ground black pepper
2 teaspoons freshly grated ginger root
1½ teaspoons prepared horseradish

Preheat the oven to 350°F. Brush a heavy baking sheet with the olive oil. Arrange the chicken skin side up on the tray and sprinkle with salt and pepper. Bake for 20 minutes.

Meanwhile, combine the jam, pepper, ginger root, and horseradish. Brush the chicken with the glaze and return to the oven. Bake for an additional 15 to 20 minutes or until an instant-read thermometer inserted into a thigh piece reads 160°F. Brush again lightly with the plum glaze. Let rest for 10 minutes before serving.

Local Chili

Makes 8 servings

Chili is one of winter's most satisfying dishes. When it's filled with ingredients that have local connections, including the beef, tomatoes, stock or beer, and cornmeal, it's all the more satisfying. Serve it with the Sweet Corn and Poppyseed Cornbread on page 110, which can be made with frozen corn kernels.

2 tablespoons extra virgin olive oil
1 large onion, diced
4 cloves garlic, minced
5 tablespoons chili powder,
   divided use
2 pounds ground beef
1 cup beef stock or locally brewed beer
1 quart whole tomatoes,
   undrained and chopped
1 teaspoon ground cumin
1 teaspoon dried oregano
1 teaspoon garlic powder
¼ teaspoon ground cayenne pepper, more or less to taste
Salt, to taste
1 15-ounce can beans, either kidney beans or black beans, drained and rinsed
2 tablespoons medium or finely ground cornmeal
1 tablespoon honey

Heat the oil in a large Dutch oven over medium heat. Add the onion and sauté for 6 minutes until tender. Add the garlic and sauté an additional minute. Sprinkle 3 tablespoons of the chili powder over the onion mixture and cook, stirring constantly, for an additional minute. Transfer the onion mixture to a separate bowl and set aside.

Wipe the interior of the Dutch oven with a paper towel. Increase the heat slightly and brown the ground beef. Drain off the excess fat, if necessary. Return the onion mixture to the pot and stir to combine with the beef. Add the stock or beer, tomatoes and their juices, cumin, oregano, garlic powder, cayenne pepper, and the remainder of the chili powder. Season with salt. Stir well. When the mixture comes to a boil, reduce the heat to low and simmer for 20 minutes.

Add the beans, cornmeal, and honey and cook for an additional 10 minutes. Taste and adjust seasonings, if necessary.

desserts

Rosemary and Walnut Shortbreads

Makes 16 shortbreads

Shortbreads rely on a few good ingredients for great flavor and texture. Toasty walnuts, fresh butter, and fragrant, tender rosemary leaves make this cookie a delicious accompaniment to iced tea in the summer. And since you've planned ahead by freezing some rosemary, your friends and family will enjoy this as a great holiday cookie.

¼ cup walnuts, coarsely chopped
½ cup unsalted butter, cut into pieces
½ cup confectioners' sugar
2 tablespoons chopped fresh rosemary
1 cup all-purpose flour

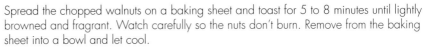

Preheat the oven to 350°F.

Spread the chopped walnuts on a baking sheet and toast for 5 to 8 minutes until lightly browned and fragrant. Watch carefully so the nuts don't burn. Remove from the baking sheet into a bowl and let cool.

In a medium saucepan, melt the butter over medium heat. Stir in the confectioners' sugar, the rosemary, and the nuts. Stir in the flour to make a stiff batter.

Distribute the dough in an ungreased 8-inch square baking pan, patting into place. Bake until the bars are golden brown, firm, and appear dry on the surface, about 20 minutes. Cool for about 2 minutes and then cut the shortbread into squares. Let cool completely before removing from the pan. Store tightly covered for up to 5 days or freeze for one month.

Simple Raspberry Mousse

Makes 4 servings

This creamy mousse is a great way to use frozen berries—whether raspberries, strawberries, or blackberries— especially when the season for fresh is just too far away. Enjoy it now . . . make it again in the summer.

1 cup fresh or frozen raspberries, thawed
2 egg yolks
2 tablespoons sugar
1 cup heavy cream, chilled
2 teaspoons grated lime zest

Puree the berries in a blender or food processor. Strain through a fine mesh sieve to remove the seeds. Discard.

In the top of a double boiler off the heat, whisk the berry puree with the egg yolks and sugar until blended. Place over gently simmering water and cook, whisking constantly for 10 minutes or until the mixture begins to thicken. Transfer to a medium bowl, cover, and refrigerate for 1 hour. The mixture will firm up as it chills.

In a large mixing bowl, whip the cream until stiff peaks form. Gently fold a third of the whipped cream into the raspberry mixture. Then fold the raspberry mixture into the remaining whipped cream.

Serve in chilled dessert glasses with a sprinkle of lime zest on the top.

Sour Cherry Slump

A slump is a simple, dumpling-like pudding, much like a cobbler, but prepared on the stovetop. The topping is steamed instead of baked. Frozen fruits find a good home all year round in recipes like slumps and cobblers. The cherries you froze this summer are already packed in sugar, so take that into account as you begin this recipe.

Makes 8 servings

Topping:
1 cup all-purpose flour
2 tablespoons sugar
1 teaspoon baking powder
¼ teaspoon baking soda
¼ teaspoon salt
2 tablespoons unsalted butter, melted
¼ cup sour cream, plus extra if needed

Filling:
4 cups sour cherries, drained
½ cup firmly packed brown sugar
3 tablespoons sugar
3 tablespoons water
1 tablespoon fresh lemon juice
Grated zest of 1 fresh lemon
Coarse sugar, for sprinkling
Freshly sweetened whipped cream, to accompany

In a large bowl, combine the flour, sugar, baking powder, baking soda, and salt. Add the melted butter and stir until combined. Stir in half of the sour cream, adding additional tablespoons as you stir until the dough feels wet. Set aside.

In a heavy 10-inch skillet (cast iron is best), combine the cherries, sugars, water, lemon juice, and zest. Cover loosely with a piece of aluminum foil and bring to a boil over medium heat. Remove from the heat and drop heaping tablespoons of the batter over the cherries, covering as much of the filling as possible. Sprinkle the top with coarse sugar. Cover the skillet tightly and return to the stove over low heat. Cook for 15 minutes without removing the lid. After 15 minutes, check to see if the topping is baked and dry to the touch, and a pale color (it will not brown). Serve directly from the pan, drizzling pan juices over the top and accompanying with whipped cream.

Pumpkin Custard with Peppered Brittle

Spicy, crunchy brittle and a slight drizzle of pure maple syrup are the perfect touches for this creamy custard. Grab some pumpkin puree from the freezer and get mixing. Be sure to drain the puree as it thaws for the densest custard possible.

Makes 6 servings

2 eggs, lightly beaten
1 cup pumpkin puree (thawed and drained, if frozen)
¾ cup half-and-half or heavy whipping cream
¼ cup packed brown sugar
½ teaspoon pumpkin pie spice (recipe below)
¼ teaspoon salt
1 cup coarsely chopped walnuts or pecans
3 tablespoons sugar
2 tablespoons light corn syrup
¼ teaspoon cayenne pepper
¼ cup pure maple syrup

Preheat the oven to 350°F.

Combine the eggs, pumpkin, cream, brown sugar, pumpkin pie spice, and salt in a medium bowl. Beat with a wire whisk until smooth.

Arrange 6 4-ounce ramekins in a shallow baking pan. Divide the pumpkin mixture between the ramekins. Place the pan on the oven rack and carefully add boiling water until it reaches halfway up the sides of the ramekins. Bake for 35 to 40 minutes or until a knife inserted in the center comes out clean. (The custards will still be wiggly but will firm as they chill.)

Remove from the water and cool on a wire rack. Chill in the refrigerator for at least 2 but up to 8 hours. Serve with a drizzle of maple syrup and a sprinkling of peppered nuts.

To make Peppered Brittle: Preheat the oven to 325°F. Combine the nuts, sugar, corn syrup, and cayenne pepper in a small bowl. Line a small baking sheet with foil. Butter the top of the foil. Spread the nut mixture on the foil and bake for 15 minutes, stirring twice. Allow to cool before breaking into small clusters. Sprinkle on top of the custards before serving.

Pumpkin Pie Spice: ½ teaspoon cinnamon + ¼ teaspoon ground ginger + ⅛ teaspoon ground allspice or ground cloves + ⅛ teaspoon ground nutmeg = 1 teaspoon pumpkin pie spice.

Preserving the Harvest

in the Locavore's Kitchen

Pretend for just a moment that it's the middle of January—unless, of course, it is. Outside, any hint of green is buried under a blanket of snow. Farmers markets are closed for the season and vegetable gardens, productive right up until the first hard frost, are also at rest. But step inside the locavore's kitchen and you'll find freshly baked bread waiting to be slathered with strawberry jam canned last spring. Blueberries picked and frozen last summer fill the sugary-crowned muffins coming out of the oven. The batter for pumpkin pancakes waiting to dot the hot griddle includes puree from heirloom pumpkins, and the syrup to drizzle over them is made from the apple cider crafted by an orchard down the road.

Moments, or meals, like these arrive with intention, some planning, and a dedication to capturing fresh homegrown flavors by preserving the harvest through canning or freezing. It takes effort—as much or as little as you want to put into it. Be assured, though, that your efforts will be rewarded with great taste.

No matter where you are right now in the local harvest season, it's a good time to think about preserving the flavors you love now so you can enjoy them later, too—when a taste of something so totally out of season feels perhaps a bit out of place, but oh, so welcome.

Just the Basics

This introduction to preserving takes a close look at a few basic techniques that will help you make the best choices using the simplest methods to preserve a variety of fresh, seasonal foods. "Canning" will take you through the basic steps of canning selected fruits and vegetables for more than 25 recipes found throughout the book. In "Freezing," you'll learn which fruits and vegetables freeze well and how to prepare them for a long life in the freezer.

Most important, this introduction to preserving will serve as inspiration and encouragement to get you into the kitchen following a morning of berry picking, or when bushels of fresh, fuzzy peaches brighten up farmstands, or when sweet corn arrives piled high in the back of a pickup truck at your favorite farmers market. Enjoy your fill of fresh, seasonal food while you can and then, with a little advanced planning and some time set aside for a morning in the kitchen, you can carry all of those great flavors into the winter and beyond.

Keys to Success When Preserving the Harvest

Choose only the best fruits or vegetables

Make sure that whatever fruit or vegetable you choose to can or freeze is deserving of your efforts. There is no magic feature in any preserving technique that will improve the taste or texture of underripe or overripe fruits or vegetables. As the saying goes, "it is what it is," and that's exactly what it will be when you pluck it from the freezer or pantry months from now. If it's not in peak condition, ask yourself if it is worth your time. If you don't appreciate the flavor now, you certainly won't later.

It's best to work with any fruit or vegetable as soon after picking or buying as possible. If you're not sure what to look for, "Choosing the Best" in each specific fruit or vegetable section in this book will be of help. Following these tips will ensure that the fruits or vegetables you get from a farmers market, roadside stand, or a CSA (defined on page xvi) are the best your money can buy and suitable for preserving.

Cleaning fruits and vegetables

Fresh homegrown and locally grown fruits and vegetables often arrive in the kitchen accompanied by a little dust or grit. It's not for lack of care. It's just better to wait to clean these foods until immediately before preparing them for recipes or preserving.

Sturdy vegetables like asparagus, pickling cucumbers, zucchini, and corn can be cleaned under running water, using a soft vegetable brush, if necessary, to dislodge any dirt.

Delicate berries and smooth-skinned vegetables like rhubarb, peas, green beans, and tomatoes fare better if you place them in a colander and submerge it in a sink or container filled with cool water. You can also place them directly in the water, gently swish to clean, then transfer with a strainer to a colander. Both methods are good for leaving any grit behind.

Spinach, chard, and fall greens trap a lot of dirt in the creases of the leaves, so you might need to give them more than one gentle washing in a sink or large water-filled container, changing the water once or twice until no more grit appears.

After washing vegetables headed for blanching, simply shake off the excess water in the sink. For foods like berries and fruit slices that will be frozen using the dry pack method (page 221), drain them in a colander, then spread them on a clean linen towel or several layers of paper towels. Using another towel, gently blot the excess moisture.

Choose an Appropriate Preserving Method

Become familiar with the best way to preserve individual fruits and vegetables before they arrive fresh and full of flavor in your kitchen. Each fruit and vegetable section in this book features a "Pick or Buy Now, Enjoy Later" section that includes suggestions on how to preserve the harvest now to use later in recipes. Some foods, like rhubarb and blueberries, can head straight for the freezer while others, like green beans and broccoli, must be blanched before being frozen. Beets are best pickled in an acidic vinegar solution. Turn peaches into jam or slice and freeze. Tomatoes can be frozen, or canned, or turned into a sauce and canned, or even oven-dried. Herbs can be dried or frozen. And then there are other foods, like tender salad greens and melons, that are only to be enjoyed fresh and really cannot be preserved beyond their fresh life.

Some fruits and vegetables take a different route to preserving. For example, you could simply freeze chopped red bell peppers, but because they keep for only 3 months in the freezer and lose texture when frozen, their use after freezing is limited to cooked dishes. Turn them instead into Roasted Red Peppers on page 158 and the taste, texture, and storage time improve; they can be used on sandwiches and pizzas and in dips as well as in cooked dishes. Roasting a fresh pumpkin for Fresh Pumpkin Puree (page 196) is not only easier than steaming it but also produces a more flavorful result, and roasted pumpkin freezes perfectly. And while some sources recommend freezing shredded cabbage, it will lose texture as it thaws—so consider a "Making Your Own" project to turn fresh cabbage into Sauerkraut (page 178), which can then be canned or refrigerated for an extended time.

The information on the following pages will help you decide which preserving projects or methods you might want to take on, depending on your tastes, energy, and time, as well as on the harvest. Can or freeze a little or a lot. If you preserve food properly, in any measure, you'll always be satisfied.

Freezing

Freezing Fresh Vegetables

Blanching and Shocking Vegetables for Freezing

Blanching is an essential step in preparing vegetables for freezing. A simple process, it's a quick, timed plunge into a pot of boiling water and then a reciprocating plunge into ice water to "shock" or halt the cooking. Blanching destroys the enzymes that cause vegetables to deteriorate quickly and helps vegetables maintain their vibrant color, fresh flavor, pleasing texture, and nutritional content. The technique of blanching also loosens the skins on fruits like tomatoes and peaches so that they slip away easily, making preparation for a recipe or canning that much simpler. Not all vegetables can or should be frozen—radishes and onions are examples of vegetables that do not freeze well—but all vegetables headed for the freezer, including asparagus, green beans, and corn, require blanching.

Here's what you'll need:

- A large stockpot, 8- to 10-quart size, with a properly fitting lid

- A blanching basket, pasta insert, or steamer basket sized for the stockpot

- A large container of iced water waiting to the side

- A supply of ice to replenish, as needed

- A large colander

- Clean, lint-free cotton towels

Preparing Vegetables for Blanching

Before you take the plunge and begin blanching the harvest, it's important that you know how to prepare the vegetables so they blanch quickly and evenly. Use the information provided in "Preparation and Blanching Times for Selected Vegetables" on page 220 as a guide to working with the specific produce found in this book.

Deciding Which Type of Blanching Method You Want to Use

- *Blanching in Boiling Water.* Easier than steaming, blanching in boiling water may leech some of the precious color from fresh vegetables and may weaken the flavor. Follow blanching times very closely. Fill the stockpot with about 4 quarts of water and bring to a rolling boil. Working in one-pound increments, arrange the prepared vegetables in the blanching basket and submerge in the boiling water. Begin timing once the basket is submerged. (See the chart of blanching times for specific vegetables.) With larger vegetables like asparagus, corn, or broccoli, you can use tongs or a handheld strainer to remove them after blanching.

- *Blanching with Steam.* This method yields the best results in terms of taste, color, and nutrition retention. You'll need a specially designed steamer pot or a steamer basket that fits into your stockpot and keeps the food just above the boiling water. Bring about 3 inches of water to a rolling boil in the stockpot. Working in one-pound increments, arrange the prepared vegetables in an even layer in the steamer basket, insert into the pot, and begin timing once the lid is in place. (See the chart of blanching times for recommended vegetables.) Replenish the water as needed and return to a boil before steam-blanching the next batch.

Immediately Following Blanching

Regardless of which blanching method you use, all blanched vegetables must be "shocked" by plunging them into an ice-water bath immediately following their blanching time. This halts the cooking process and helps maintain color, texture, and firmness. The vegetables should remain in the ice-water bath for twice the amount of time they were blanched. For example, blanch shelled peas for 3 minutes and keep them in the ice-water bath for 6 minutes.

Draining and Drying Blanched Vegetables

After the vegetables have sat in the ice-water bath, transfer them to a large colander using tongs or a strainer, leaving the ice behind. Let them drain for a few minutes, then transfer them to a clean lint-free cotton towel or several layers of paper towels to absorb additional moisture. Blot the surface of the cooled vegetables with another towel. Removing as much excess water as you can prevents excess ice crystals from forming during freezing—and the less ice accumulates, the better the vegetables will be preserved.

When working with leafy greens like spinach, chard, and kale, allow them to drain in the colander for a little longer, and then gently squeeze to remove as much water as possible before packaging for the freezer.

FREEZING

Preparation and Blanching Times for Selected Vegetables

The vegetables listed in the table "Preparation and Blanching Times for Selected Vegetables" are by far the best candidates for blanching and freezing. They hold their color, texture, and flavor better than most and perform well in recipes after freezer storage. If properly prepared and packaged, these vegetables will keep for 12 months at 0°F. If you don't see directions here for freezing your favorite seasonal vegetable, refer to the section "Pick or Buy Now, Enjoy Later" for that vegetable for more information and other preserving options. Remember that the vegetables should be shocked in the ice-water bath for twice the amount of time they were blanched.

Preparation and Blanching Times for Selected Vegetables

Vegetable	Preparation	Steam Blanch	Boiling Water Blanch
Asparagus	Medium stalks, remove and discard woody stems, leave whole or cut into 2-inch pieces	5 minutes	3 minutes
Beans, snap	Snip stem end, leave whole or cut into 2-inch lengths	5 minutes	3 minutes
Broccoli*	Trim to uniform sizes, about 1½ inches across	5 minutes	3 minutes
Brussels sprouts, medium*	Trim, remove outer leaves	6 minutes	4 minutes
Chard	Leaves only, cut into thick strips	3 to 4 minutes	3 minutes
Corn, sweet, whole ears, medium size, 1½ inches in diameter	Remove husks and silks	13 minutes	9 minutes
Corn, sweet, cut from cob	Remove husks and silks, trim ends	6 minutes	4 minutes
Fall greens (collards, kale, and mustard greens)	Remove any thick ribs and tough stems	3 minutes, add 2 minutes for collards	2 minutes, add 1 minute for collards
Peas (shelled)	Remove from pods	3 to 5 minutes	1½ to 2½ minutes
Peas (sugar or snap), small	Remove stems, blossom ends, and any string, leave whole or cut into smaller lengths	4 minutes	2 minutes
Spinach	Whole leaves, tough stems trimmed	3 minutes	2 minutes
Summer squash or Zucchini	Do not peel; cut into ½-inch slices	5 minutes	3 minutes

*Soak fresh-picked bunches of broccoli or Brussels sprouts in salted water for 30 minutes to purge of small insects.

[Adapted with permission from the Ohio State University Extension Fact Sheet: Family and Consumer Sciences HYG 5333-09, Freezing Vegetables.]

Freezing Fresh Fruits

After the fruit is cleaned, you'll want to prepare it for the way you plan on serving it. For example, while blueberries and raspberries are used whole in recipes, peaches can be halved, sliced, or coarsely chopped. Strawberries, especially small berries, are either left whole or halved, sometimes crushed to release the natural juices. Once you have decided on the preparation, your next step is to decide how to pack it for the freezer.

Three Methods for Packing and Freezing Fresh Fruits

Here are three commonly used treatments and packing methods for freezing fruits. Each has specific advantages for specific types of fruits. Read through these carefully and refer to the table "Preparation and Packing Methods for Selected Fruits" on page 222 before moving on.

Wet Pack Using Sugar

Some fruits hold their color, shape, and firmness better if packed in sugar syrup. Use these fruits later for desserts like cobblers, crisps, and pies. Because they are packed in syrup, taste before adding any additional sugar to the intended recipe. The strength of syrup used is largely a matter of preference, but a medium-weight syrup is a good all-purpose choice.

Sugar Syrups for Freezing and Canning Fruits

Type of Syrup	Sugar	Water	Yield
Light	1 cup	4 cups	4¾ cups
Medium	1¾ cups	4 cups	5 cups
Heavy	2¾ cups	4 cups	5⅓ cups

[Adapted with permission from the Ohio State University Extension Fact Sheet: Family and Consumer Sciences HGY-5349-19.]

To prepare sugar syrup, combine the sugar and water in a saucepan and warm over medium heat, stirring frequently, until the sugar is completely dissolved. If the syrup is to be used for canning peaches or other stone fruits, let it come to a boil, then reduce the heat to low and cover. Keep the syrup hot until needed. If the syrup is to be used for freezing fruit, transfer to a plastic container and chill completely in the refrigerator (it can be made a day or two ahead).

Note: Some canning manuals and guides publish conversions for substituting honey or corn syrup for a portion of the sugar. While this is a safe practice, both honey and corn syrup have an impact on the flavor and cost. Honey ranges in flavor from mild to robust. For medium syrup, gently heat 2 cups of mild honey with 3 cups of water and cool before using. Corn syrups often have added salt and vanilla. Intrigued but not sure? Experiment with one jar and taste for yourself.

Sugar Pack

This method works best with fruit that has been halved or sliced, such as strawberries, cherries, and peaches. Simply sprinkle the recommended amount of sugar on the prepared fruit and mix gently with a large spoon or clean hands. Let the fruit sit until juice has been drawn out and the sugar is dissolved.

Dry Pack or Unsweetened Pack

This is the easiest way to freeze fruit slices and berries without adding sugar. It allows for more versatile use later, and you won't have to make adjustments in recipes that call for sugar. The absence of sugar means juices are not drawn out, so this is a good method to use if you want berries to remain separate and loose. Making sure there is no excess moisture on the berries or fruit slices, scatter them in a single layer on a rimmed baking sheet. Place in the freezer and when frozen solid, in about 3 to 4 hours, pop them off the tray and store in freezer containers or heavy-duty freezer bags.

To Prevent Fruit from Browning

Fruits like peaches, apricots, and nectarines have a tendency to darken and lose flavor when exposed to air. They will do the same when stored in the freezer. An easy way to prevent this is to treat them with ascorbic acid (vitamin C), a readily available water-soluble powder packaged as Fruit-Fresh. It can be added to sugar syrups or sprinkled over fruit just before dry or sugar packing. Unsweetened fruit slices, like peaches, can also be soaked for a short time in cold water treated with ascorbic acid, drained, arranged in a single layer on a baking sheet, and frozen. Pop them off the tray once frozen and transfer to freezer bags. For the best results, follow the manufacturer's directions that come with the product.

Freezing Fruits

The fruits listed in the table "Preparation and Packing Methods for Selected Fruits" are by far the best candidates for freezing using any of the three methods described. They hold their color, texture, and flavor better than most and perform well in recipes after freezer storage. If properly prepared and packaged, these fruits will keep for 8 to 12 months at 0°F. If you don't see directions for freezing your favorite seasonal fruit, refer to that fruit's "Pick or Buy Now, Enjoy Later" section for more information and other preserving options.

Preparation and Packing Methods for Selected Fruits

Fruit	Preparation	Treat w/ Ascorbic	Wet Pack: Type of Sugar Syrup	Sugar Pack: Sugar per 4 Cups Fruit	Dry Pack, No Sugar
Apricots	Peel, pit; halve or slice	Yes	Medium	½ cup	Not recommended
Blackberries	Leave whole	No	Medium or Heavy	¾ cup	Yes
Blueberries	Leave whole	No	Medium or Heavy	⅔ cup	Yes
Cherries, sour	Pit	No	Medium	¾ cup	Yes
Cherries, sweet	Pit	No	Medium	Not recommended	Yes
Nectarines	Peel, pit; halve or slice	Yes	Medium	Not recommended	Yes*
Peaches	Peel, pit; halve or slice	Yes	Medium	⅔ cup	Yes*
Plums	Peel, pit; halve or slice	Yes	Medium	Not recommended	Not recommended
Raspberries	Leave whole	No	Medium	¾ cup	Yes
Rhubarb**	Remove leaves, cut stalks into 1-inch lengths	No	Medium	Not recommended	Yes
Strawberries	Remove caps, leave whole or slice	No	Heavy	¾ cup	Yes
Tomatoes	Core, peel, slice or chop	No	Not necessary	Not necessary	Not necessary

*Only if treated with ascorbic acid before freezing.

**If using brightly colored stalks, blanch prepared rhubarb for 1 minute in boiling water and cool in ice-water bath for another minute. This will help retain the color.

[Adapted with permission from the Ohio State University Extension Fact Sheet: Family and Consumer Sciences HYG 5349-09]

Guidelines for Freezing Fruits

Use rigid freezer containers or heavy-duty freezer bags that hold 2 to 4 cups of fruit. When packing fruits in sugar syrup or juice, add enough of the liquid so that the fruit is submerged. Leave ½ inch of headspace, seal, label, and freeze. Fruit prepared using the dry pack method can be stored loosely in heavy-duty freezer bags, squeezing out as much air as possible.

Thawing and Serving Frozen Fruits

Freezing may slow or halt the growth of bacteria, but it does not destroy them. Thawing slowly in the refrigerator is the best way to prevent bacteria growth, while thawing on a countertop in hot weather could encourage their growth.

If you are using frozen fruits in a fruit salad or as part of another cold or chilled dish, add them partially thawed for the best flavor and texture. For the best flavor and performance in baking, use fruits still frozen or just slightly thawed as substitutes for fresh fruit, measure for measure, in many recipes, including pies, breads, and desserts. Toss frozen fruits right from the freezer into the blender for smoothies and milkshakes or use them to top yogurt, oatmeal, or cereal.

Packaging Fruits or Vegetables for the Freezer

Most of the work in getting foods freezer ready is in proper preparation, but an equally important step is in packaging for long life in the freezer. Freezing temporarily stops spoilage and the growth of organisms and is the best way to preserve color, texture, flavor, and nutritional content in foods.

Begin by making sure that your freezer is in optimal working condition, that it has tight door seals, maintains a constant temperature of 0°F, and doesn't build up excessive frost or ice crystals. With that in order, the two elements that work most against frozen foods are air and moisture.

When air gets into the package as a result of a weak seal or improper packaging, it evaporates the moisture in frozen foods, causing freezer burn—dull, grayish streaks that are harmless but leave foods dry and tough.

Excessive moisture in foods and freezing foods too slowly both result in the formation of large ice crystals. Properly frozen foods will have some small ice crystals, but it's the large, excessive buildup that compromises taste and texture when food is thawed and cooked.

Here are some important guidelines for packaging all foods heading for the freezer, whether meats and poultry, fruits, vegetables, prepared foods, or breads and other baked goods.

- Package frozen fruits and vegetables in airtight containers, including plastic freezer-safe storage containers with tight-fitting lids or heavy-duty plastic storage bags that seal securely and completely.

- Squeeze or press as much air as possible out of freezer bags before putting them in the freezer.

- Be diligent about blotting vegetables and fruit after blanching to remove excess water. This will help prevent the formation of ice crystals in the freezer.

- If you can, chill foods in the refrigerator before packaging them for the freezer. They will freeze more quickly and form fewer ice crystals.

- Arrange foods as flat as possible in freezer bags, in single layers, to speed up freezing (and defrosting) and to use less space in the freezer. Flat packages can be stacked once frozen.

- Label and date everything, using freezer labels or a permanent marker. Include not only the name of the contents but when it was packaged and the weight or quantity.

Types of Packaging for the Freezer

You dress to protect yourself from the cold and frostbite. Use the same kind of thinking when you package your foods for freezer storage. There are many choices on the shelves that will protect foods from loss of color, texture, nutrients, and flavor. Here's a list of the most commonly found.

- Heavy-Duty Foil. Choose heavy-duty varieties made specifically for freezer storage. Foil has a few advantages over other freezer wraps in that it molds to the shape of the foods, eliminating air pockets, and won't tear or puncture easily. Use it to wrap foods like meats, breads, and other baked goods. Storing foil-wrapped food in freezer bags adds an extra measure of protection.

- Heavy-Duty Freezer Bags. Specifically designed for freezing food, these come in a variety of sizes, including pint (2 cups), quart (4 cups), and gallon (16 cups), with zippered closings. Make sure that they hold liquid well by filling with water and testing for leaks or gaps. If they hold water, they will also keep out air. Do not substitute thinner storage bags, which can split in the freezer, exposing or scattering the contents.

- Freezer-Grade Plastic Containers. Ideal for storing liquids, sauces, or cooked foods, they are also better choices for preserving more delicate foods that could be crushed in a crowded freezer, like raspberries.

- Plastic Freezer Wrap. This heavy-duty plastic wrap it usually lightly textured and designed to cling to foods, avoid air pockets, and let you easily see the contents.

temperature of freezer

A busy day preserving the harvest in the locavore's kitchen can be taxing on the freezer as well as its contents. If you've prepared large quantities of the local seasonal harvest for freezing or find yourself with a half dozen whole chickens you plan on freezing for use throughout the next few months, reduce the temperature of the freezer to its lowest point (about -10°F) 24 hours in advance before adding anything new to the freezer. In the next day or two, reset the temperature back to 0°F or the normal position. This little trick keeps the foods you've already stored in good condition while the new additions freeze solid.

freezing whole tomatoes

In recipes that call for removing the skins from tomatoes, blanching and shocking in an ice-water bath is a necessary step. However, if you want to freeze whole tomatoes to toss into stews, soups, or stocks, skip the blanching step. Simply core the tomatoes and place them whole on a heavy-duty baking sheet and freeze. When they are frozen solid, store them in heavy-duty freezer bags. Remove the tomatoes as you need them and let them sit at room temperature for a bit. As they thaw, the skins will slip right off, as easily as if they were blanched. Whole tomatoes will keep for 3 to 4 months in the freezer.

vacuum sealers

Vacuum sealers are an effective way to prolong the life and freshness of foods. These small electric countertop appliances remove the air from specially designed storage bags that hold food, heat-sealing the bag closed. They are great at prolonging the life of foods in the freezer but they do require an investment. Basic models start at about $150; deluxe models feature more vacuum power and a host of accessories, as well as a higher price tag. There's also the cost of the freezer bags, which usually come in rolls so you can cut the bags to the size you need. If you plan on making this investment, get the best model your budget can handle.

Here's an important tip about vacuum-sealing foods. Delicate fruits like berries, breads and other baked goods, and vegetables that have been softened somewhat by blanching can be crushed and ruined as the air is vacuumed out and the bags compress. One way to prevent crushing is to place these items in the freezer before packaging. As soon as they are frozen solid, pack them in the bag and then vacuum-seal. You'll avoid the problem of crushed food this way.

Removing the Skin on Whole Tomatoes, Peaches, and Other Stone Fruits

When a recipe calls for removing the skin on smooth-skinned fruits, there's always the option of peeling it away with a vegetable peeler, a paring knife, or a peeler with tiny serrated teeth designed specifically for these fruits. If you're peeling only a few fruits, this method will do, but if you're blessed with a basket, bushel, or bounty of fruit, it will be quicker to blanch them in boiling water and shock them in an ice bath. (See "Blanching and Shocking Vegetables for Freezing" on page {000} for full details.)

Simply use a paring knife to cut a small x in the bottom or blossom end of ripe fruit. Have water boiling in a stockpot. Working in batches so as to not overcrowd the stockpot, place some of the fruits, loose or using a blanching basket to dip them, into the boiling water for 30 to 60 seconds. The riper the fruit, the less time you'll need.

Transfer immediately to the ice bath to halt any cooking. Let the fruit sit for a minute, drain, and slip off the skins, then proceed with the recipe.

Freezing Meats and Poultry

Locavores seek out the best meat and poultry their money can buy, whether organic, pasture-raised, free-range, heritage breeds, or grain- or grass-fed. Locavores understand the dedication and work involved, and attach value to meat and poultry raised responsibly, without the aid of growth hormones or antibiotics, and with respect for the land and animal. If you've gone to any length to learn how to prepare and cook these meats for the best results, it only makes sense to be sure you know how to package and store them correctly.

Many meat and poultry producers will sell their products already vacuum-sealed and labeled for the freezer, a plus for the buyer. If they are not already frozen when you buy them, chill them in the refrigerator at 40°F for 24 hours. This small detour ensures that when they are placed in the freezer, they'll freeze more quickly and form fewer damaging ice crystals.

To prepare fresh, unpackaged meat and poultry for freezer storage, trim excess fat. Be sure to remove the giblets and any other parts from the cavities of whole chickens. If you must rinse the meats, do so after defrosting and before cooking, blotting excess moisture with a paper towel.

Use only quality heavy-duty plastic freezer wrap, aluminum foil, or freezer paper. For long-term storage (more than 3 months), the recommended method is to double-wrap, first in a layer of plastic freezer wrap, molding it around the meat or poultry to press out any air pockets, followed by another layer of foil or freezer paper or a heavy-duty plastic freezer bag. Heavy-duty freezer bags are good for ground meats and boneless cuts, as well as for smaller cuts like chops and steaks. For quicker freezing and defrosting, arrange meats in a single layer and avoid overcrowding the bags before sealing. Be sure to squeeze or press as much air as possible out of the bag before sealing. Always remember to label with the contents and date, and the weight, if desired. Properly packaged and stored, meats will last up to 9 months and poultry up to 12 months.

Thawing Meats and Poultry

Always thaw meats and poultry in the refrigerator on a tray to catch any moisture. Large turkeys, up to 24 pounds, can take 3 to 4 days, while a 4-pound chicken or large cuts of beef or pork will take from 24 to 48 hours. Smaller cut-up pieces such as chicken legs and breasts or ground meats will thaw in 12 to 24 hours.

Freezing Dairy Products and Eggs

When the season for farmers markets winds down, that favorite cheese or butter or the fresh eggs you bought on a weekly basis can still be enjoyed throughout the winter with some planning, proper packaging, and freezer space. Follow these guidelines and always ask the producer, cheesemaker, or farmer—those who know best—about whether it's possible or advisable to freeze their products.

Butter. Delicious, locally produced butter from the farmers market usually comes in a large roll, not neatly wrapped sticks. Divide the butter into small portions and wrap each tightly in plastic freezer wrap or store in small heavy-duty freezer bags. Frozen butter often becomes a little grainy and crumbly in texture once thawed. It won't make a difference in your cooking, but for a spread, stirring helps smooth the texture. Butter will keep up to 9 months in the freezer.

Cheeses. Another advantage of shopping locally or at a farmers market is that you often know the person who crafts the cheeses you love. Ask them about the freezing qualities of different varieties. Cheeses heading for the freezer should be tightly wrapped in plastic freezer wrap, never aluminum foil. Soft cheeses like goat cheese can be stored for about 2 months. If the cheese comes in vacuum-sealed packaging, the shelf life can be even longer. Semisoft varieties like Muenster and Havarti can be frozen for up to 3 months but will become crumbly when defrosted—okay for cooking purposes, not as great for a cheese board. Hard, aged cheeses like Cheddar should just be wrapped and refrigerated so they will continue to age and develop flavor. Soft cheeses like Brie should never be frozen, and the same goes for ricotta and cottage cheese.

Eggs. If the idea of being without fresh eggs for baking as you head into the winter months is worrisome, then get cracking. Eggs can be frozen in a variety of ways and still perform well in baking. Gently thaw in the refrigerator overnight.

Whole Eggs. Using a fork, combine the yolks and white with a pinch of salt. Pour into small containers, allowing for headspace, seal, and freeze for up to 9 months. Allow one or two eggs per container. Use for baking and scrambling.

Egg Yolks. Separate the eggs, reserving the whites, and stir the yolks together with a pinch of salt. Twelve egg yolks will yield 1 cup, so divide and package as desired. Use in sauces, mayonnaise, and custards.

Egg Whites. Separate the eggs and combine the egg whites in a container, allowing for headspace. (Make sure that no egg yolk gets into the white or it will affect the performance of the eggs when whipping.) Seal, label, and freeze. Use for meringues, cakes, and glazing for baked goods.

Canning

What are you going to get out of preserving food by canning? Certainly a lot of wonderful local and seasonal flavors sealed in a jar and waiting patiently in the pantry for when your taste buds demand the genuine flavors of homegrown or locally grown foods. It's a wonderful way to make the tastes of the seasons live on through jams and jellies, pickles, relishes, salsas, sauces, and more.

The information in this section will leave you with but a taste of the possibilities canning offers, using basic, easy, and safe techniques for canning high-acid fruits and vegetables, pickling, and making jams and jellies. It should not be regarded as a complete and comprehensive guide to all canning methods. *You will not find instructions for pressure canning, an entirely different technique and the only safe, acceptable technique for canning low-acid vegetables.* What you will find on the following pages is encouragement, motivation, and complete and detailed instructions to give you the basic working knowledge of canning necessary to prepare any (or all) of the recipes found in *The Locavore's Kitchen*.

Canning Guidelines

Safe canning techniques and good kitchen hygiene cannot be stressed enough and can make the difference between wholesome, delicious canned goods and food that can become contaminated, posing a health threat.

Here is a checklist of what you need to know and do before and during any canning project.

☐ Make sure that all equipment used in canning is perfectly clean. This includes the canner, cutting boards, knives, bowls, and towels . . . and especially your hands. Wash them often as you work.

☐ Use only fresh, quality fruits and vegetables. Those that show signs of spoilage and bruising may contain bacteria that will contaminate an entire recipe. Fruit sold as seconds can be used as long as bruises and damaged areas are removed.

☐ Clean all fruits and vegetables properly. See "Cleaning fruits and vegetables" on page 216 or refer to the instructions in each particular fruit and vegetable section. Do not soak any fruit or vegetable in water prior to canning.

☐ Use standard canning jars and lids. Readily available and easy to find, especially as the harvest begins, these come in a variety of sizes—quarts, pints, and half pints—as well as regular and widemouthed styles. Do not reuse commercial food jars, such as the ones that contained salad dressing, mayonnaise, or pickles. They may not seal properly and could break during heating.

☐ Check that canning jars are in good condition, whether new from the box or ones that are reused yearly. Discard any jars that have cracks or chips.

☐ Thoroughly wash all canning jars, whether new from the box or ones that are reused yearly. Wash them first with hot, soapy water and rinse thoroughly to remove all soap.

☐ Keep jars hot until ready to fill. This can be done by leaving them in the water bath canner as it heats, by filling them with very hot tap water, or by running them through a clean and empty dishwasher on the rinse cycle. Jars used in jam and jelly making should be sterilized for 10 minutes in boiling water before filling.

☐ Check canning lids and bands. Canning ring bands can be reused from season to season as long as they are in good condition with no dents, cracks, or rust. **Lids may only be used once.** If you attempt to reuse them, they may not seal properly.

A Word about Pressure Canning

Unless they are packed in vinegar brine, vegetables lack the natural acidity to make them good choices for canning with the boiling water bath method used for all the canning recipes found in this book. There are only two other ways to preserve vegetables. The first is to blanch and freeze them, which, if done properly, is an excellent way to preserve their color, texture, taste, and nutrition (see "Freezing Vegetables" on page 218). The only other safe way to preserve vegetables is by pressure canning.

A pressure canner is a metal kettle with a cover that clamps to make it steam tight and gauges to measure and regulate pressure. The principle of pressure canning is to expose low-acid foods (vegetables, meats, some fruits, and some prepared foods like soups) to high temperatures of 240°F and above, to sterilize the contents and destroy the microorganisms that cause botulism. Water bath canners can reach only 212°F, the boiling point of water, not hot enough to kill the bacteria in low-acid foods, but safe and recommended for high-acid fruits and vegetables and all the canning recipes found in this book.

If you're interested in exploring pressure canning, be prepared to make an investment. There are a handful of manufacturers who offer different models and sizes of pressure canners that cost upwards of $80. Don't confuse pressure canners with pressure cookers, which are not recommended for canning purposes. The canning publications and websites listed below should guide you in the right direction when it comes to pressure canning.

canning publications and websites

These books and websites are among the best sources for comprehensive information about canning, including pressure canning.

Ball Complete Book of Home Preserving, edited by Judi Kingry and Lauren Devine (2006)

Ball Blue Book of Preserving (2006)

Ball Canning Company online resource http://www.freshpreserving.com

Complete Guide to Home Canning, Bulletin No. 539, United States Department of Agriculture (2009 revision), available online, along with other publications, at the National Center for Home Food Preservation website, http://www.uga.edu/nchfp/

Canning and Preserving for Dummies (2nd edition), by Amelia Jeanroy and Karen Ward (2009)

cooperative extension services

There's something special and heartwarming about discovering a family recipe from long ago. When it comes to those that require canning, however, even some techniques used just a generation ago are no longer considered safe. To get more information on whether or not a recipe, family heirloom or not, is safe for canning or to find information on ways to safely adapt it to today's canning techniques, contact your local Cooperative Extension Service. Through the United States Department of Agriculture, every state hosts this valuable research-based resource, often through land grant universities, providing information on agriculture and food, home and family, the environment, and more. To find one in your area, go to the USDA's National Institute of Food and Agriculture website at http://www.nifa.usda.gov/extension.

What You Need to Get Started

Most of what you'll need to take on a canning project is probably already in your kitchen. If you don't already have a water bath canner, consider the size of your range and the burner it will occupy before making the investment, typically under $30. Once you have assembled all of this equipment, you're ready to begin canning.

- Water bath canner with lid
    21.5-quart size (holds 7 quart, pint, or half-pint jars)
    or 33-quart size (holds 9 of each)

- A wire jar rack (usually included when buying a water bath canner)

- Canning jars with ring bands and lids
    sold by cases of 12 in quart, pint, and half-pint sizes

- Large saucepan to hold ring bands and lids

- Teakettle with additional boiling water, if necessary

- Jar lifter or sturdy tongs, preferably with rubber grips
    necessary for lifting jars from boiling water

- Widemouthed canning funnel
    not essential, but very helpful in filling jars with liquids

- Kitchen timer

- Clean kitchen towels
    lint-free cotton towels preferred

- Flexible rubber spatula
    used to eliminate air pockets in filled jars

Canning Methods: Boiling Water, Raw Pack, and Hot Pack

About Boiling Water Bath Canning

To preserve any of the recipes found in this book by canning, you will be using a water bath canner. Filled jars are submerged in a boiling water bath. The heat destroys the molds, yeast, and bacteria that cause foods to spoil. High temperatures drive the air out of the jar, creating a vacuum that forms an airtight seal, preventing contamination of the food during storage. This is a safe and easy way to preserve high-acid foods—whole or sliced fruits, jams and jellies, relishes, chutney, and pickled foods.

The presence of acid, natural or added, in foods prevents bacteria from forming or flourishing. You'll notice that in all the recipes, there's a measure of vinegar or lemon juice added to boost the acidity for some foods to an optimal level. Don't skip or alter these measurements in any recipe.

Raw Pack Method or Hot Pack Method

There are two safe and acceptable methods used for the recipes found in this book for packing foods into canning jars.

The first is the *raw pack method.* Raw prepared fruits like tomatoes or peaches are packed tightly in jars, and hot syrup, juice, or water is added to cover. The jars are then sealed and processed. Raw pack fruit is more likely to float yet is perfectly safe to eat. This method is also used for pickling vegetables using vinegar brine. The process for Canned Whole Tomatoes on page 235 uses the raw pack method.

The other is the *hot pack method.* This is where prepared foods such as sauces, salsas, or pickles are heated before being packed in the jars. Additional hot liquid or juices released during cooking are also included. This method keeps fruits from floating to the top, so it's the preferred method to make Canned Peach Slices on page 236.

Basic Canning Techniques: A Step-by-Step Picture Guide

This picture guide will walk you through the basics of water bath canning. The same principles will apply when canning other recipes in this book. Look for important tips and information about specific preparations in "Jams, Jellies, and Preserves" on page 237 and "Pickles, Relishes, and Salsas" on page 239.

Place a rack in the bottom of the water bath canner and fill it with enough water to reach 1 to 2 inches above the rims of the jars you will be using when they're placed on the rack. It's also a good idea to have a kettle of boiling water on the side in case the water level drops and needs replenishing.

Fill a separate pan with water and heat over a low flame; do not boil. Add the bands and lids. The hot water gently softens the rubber on the underside of the lids, which helps create a good seal later.

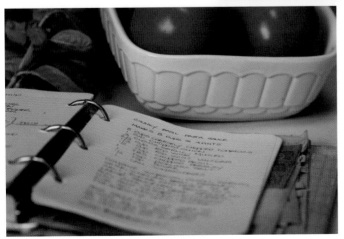

Be sure to follow recipes closely and to completion before filling jars. Pay close attention to the amount of headspace and the processing time called for in a recipe.

Fill the jars as the recipe directs, leaving the required amount of headspace, which allows for expansion of the food during processing. A canning funnel is helpful during this step to keep rims and threads on jars clean.

Run a flexible rubber spatula around the interior of filled jars to remove air pockets. Foods that are packed whole or have a chunky texture can trap pockets of air, and that could affect the seal. (This step is not necessary when the contents are liquid, like jelly.)

Wipe the contact surfaces (rims and threads of jars) with a clean lint-free cotton cloth or paper towel dipped in hot water. This ensures a good seal.

Remove the lids as needed from the hot water and place, rubber side down, on the rims of the jars. Add the bands, screw on snugly and securely, but do not over-tighten. Once the jars are filled and sealed, they should go directly into the canner.

Using a jar lifter or tongs, stand the jars on the rack in the canner. Always make sure the jars are on a rack, not sitting directly on the bottom of the canner, which could cause them to crack. Make sure the water covers the tops of the jars by at least 1 inch. Add additional boiling water, if necessary. Place the lid on the canner.

When water returns to a boil, begin timing for processing as directed in the recipe. (If the water falls below boiling during processing, stop the timing, wait for the water to return to a boil, and resume timing.)

Using the tongs, remove the jars from the canner and allow them to cool, undisturbed, at room temperature for 12 to 24 hours. Do not adjust, tighten, or remove ring bands during this time.

Once the jars have cooled, it's time to move them to a dark, cool storage place. Remove the ring bands and wipe the jars with a damp cloth. Label the jars with the contents and processing dates.

· ·

pop!

That's the sound you should listen for as the jars cool from the hot water bath. Within 5 to 15 minutes, the heat inside the jar will force out the air, creating a vacuum. When this happens, you'll hear a distinct "pop" or "ping," your sign that the jar has formed a good seal. Not sure? Hold the jar up and look across the lid. The surface should be concave, curved down in the center. If it's flat or bulging, or springs up when touched, the lid did not seal. Jars that did not form a seal should be refrigerated and used in the next few weeks.

Troubleshooting and Common Problems

The best part of a canning project is at the end. You can sit back and admire your work and know that some great flavor is in store for you in the months ahead. If you've closely followed the recipes and directions for canning, your efforts should pay off in delicious and safe foods. Here are some of the common problems you might experience, especially if this is your first attempt at canning. *Don't be discouraged—practice makes perfect. Keep canning!*

- If the lid did not form a seal after processing, do not reprocess. Instead, store the jar in the refrigerator and enjoy the contents within the next few weeks.

- If upon taking a jar from the pantry you find that the seal is broken or bulging, the jar is leaking or spurts upon opening, or the food has developed an off-odor, discard the contents. There are various reasons why the seal has failed and the food has spoiled. Here are some of the most common causes and ways to avoid these problems in the future:

  - Processing times were not followed.

  - Canning lids were not new or were not properly softened in hot water.

  - Ring bands were applied too tight or ring bands were adjusted following processing.

  - Not enough or too much headspace was left in the jar.

  - Recipe was not followed or ingredients were not properly measured.

No matter what else you decide to preserve for your pantry, tomatoes are a perennial favorite of canning enthusiasts. Canning novices, make this your first project. It will give you practical hands-on experience, knowledge, and confidence to take on any canning project. Best of all, in the middle of winter, a jar of canned tomatoes can be turned into sauces, added to stews and chili, made into or added to soups—used in any recipe searching for the garden-fresh taste of tomatoes.

Any variety of tomato can be used as long as you understand the result. Flavorful, meatier tomatoes like plum and Roma varieties are usually just the right size to be preserved whole without chopping or slicing; simply peel and core. When they are added to recipes later on, they will cook up into thicker sauces.

Beefsteak tomatoes and larger cherry tomatoes can be preserved, but because they are juicy to begin with, they will release even more water along the way and may not be as flavorful as other meatier varieties.

For this project, the raw pack method described on page 230 is used to help the tomatoes hold their shape. You'll notice that salt is listed as optional. It is used as a flavor enhancer, not a preservative.

Canned Whole Tomatoes

Makes 7 quart jars or 14 pint jars

20 pounds fresh meaty tomatoes of similar size, peeled and cored, bruises and soft
    or damaged areas removed, halved or quartered if very large
4 cups tomato juice or water, or a combination (approximate)
½ cup freshly squeezed lemon juice (approximate)
¼ cup kosher salt (approximate and optional)

For instructions on how to remove the skin on whole tomatoes, see "Removing the Skin on Whole Tomatoes, Peaches, and Other Stone Fruits" on page 225.

Bring the tomato juice or water to a boil in a medium saucepan. Reduce the heat to maintain the liquid at a simmer.

Pack the prepared tomatoes in hot jars to within ½ inch of the rim. Press the tomatoes down as you pack to fill the spaces and release some of the juice.
Add 1 tablespoon of lemon juice and 1 teaspoon of salt (optional) to quart jars, ½ tablespoon of lemon juice and ½ teaspoon of salt (optional) to pint jars.
Add enough hot juice or water to cover the contents to within ½ inch of the rim (headspace). Run a rubber spatula around the edges to release air pockets. Add more hot liquid, if necessary. Seal and process 40 minutes for pints or 45 minutes for quarts.

One of the most beautiful seasonal sights in the locavore's kitchen is freshly canned peach slices, bright, colorful, and promising the true taste of peaches long after the last are picked from the orchard down the road. Once the local peach season ends, the true taste of fresh peaches goes with it. You might find peaches at the local grocery off-season, but chances are very good the taste will not accompany them.

You'll want to choose the best-quality peaches, perfectly ripe, yielding to gentle pressure, free of bruises and blemishes, and giving off the aroma of a peach, sweet and highly perfumed. For perfect peach slices, use freestone varieties, whose fruit comes away cleanly from the pit. Cling peaches, which "cling" to the pit, can also be used but won't slice as neatly. Better to use these for jams and recipes where peaches do not need to hold their shape.

For this project, using the hot pack method described on page 230 is preferred to keep peach slices from floating to the top of the jar. Peaches must be packed in sugar syrup to enhance flavor, stabilize color, and hold the shape of the fruit.

Canned Peach Slices

Makes 4 quart jars or 8 pint jars

11 pounds fresh peaches, peeled, pitted, and sliced (soft or damaged areas removed)
¼ cup ascorbic acid or lemon juice, to prevent browning
1 recipe medium sugar syrup, page 221

For instructions on how to remove the skin on whole peaches, see "Removing the Skin on Whole Tomatoes, Peaches, and Other Stone Fruits" on page 225.

Place the prepared peach slices in a large bowl and toss with the ascorbic acid or lemon juice to coat the slices, preventing them from browning.

Bring the sugar syrup to a boil in a large stockpot. Reduce the heat just enough to keep the syrup at a gentle simmer. Add the peach slices to the syrup, stirring gently. Let them heat for 5 minutes.

Remove the peaches from the syrup with a slotted spoon and pack into hot jars to within 1 inch of the rim, pressing down gently to fill the spaces. Add enough hot syrup to cover the contents to within ½ inch of the rim (headspace). Run a rubber spatula around the edges to release air pockets. Add more hot syrup, if necessary. Seal and process 20 minutes for pints or 45 minutes for quarts.

other hot pack method recipes

Look for these recipes that also use the hot pack method of canning:

Chunky All-Purpose Tomato Sauce, page 121

Fresh Tomato Ketchup, page 124

Maple Applesauce, page 135

Pear Sauce, page 136

Jams, Jellies, and Preserves

When fruit is abundant, it's time to think about making jams, jellies, or preserves—you won't believe how much wonderful seasonal flavor you can fit into a little jar. But what is the difference between them?

Jams feature pieces of crushed fruit like strawberries, raspberries, or blueberries, often with the seeds left in berry jams. Jam will have more texture, will not spread as smoothly as jelly, and is usually made with added commercial pectin.

Jellies are made from only the juice of the fruit, which is crushed, strained, and then boiled with sugar and commercial pectin, a natural thickening agent derived from apples added to make the mixture gel, or set up. Grapes are best made into jelly because they contain too many hard seeds and tough skins to create a decent jam.

Preserves really don't differ much from jams. It's a term used long ago that means the fruit was cooked longer with extra sugar instead of added pectin and "preserved" by canning. You'll find the majority of recipes for spreads in this book are made without added pectin.

Marmalade is a cooked fruit preserve that features some kind of citrus in the mix.

All of these should be prepared according to the recipe directions and canned using the basic canning principles. For the best results in making jams, jellies, preserves, and marmalade, follow these rules:

- Always use fresh, fully ripe seasonal fruits. It's best if they are used within 24 hours of picking.

- Do not soak fruits in water.

- Unsweetened frozen fruit and juices may be substituted for fresh in recipes.

- Slightly underripe fruits contain a natural amount of pectin. If desired, substitute a small measure of these for fresh in recipes that do not use commercial pectin.

- Always measure ingredients carefully and never double recipes for jellies, jams, or preserves, especially those that use pectin.

- With pectin-free recipes, remember that when you've achieved the desired consistency after cooking the jam, the mixture will firm up even more when cooling.

- Jars for jams and jellies should be sterilized for 10 minutes in a boiling water bath before filling. (This is not required for foods that will be processed for 10 minutes or more.)

- Fill the jars completely, leaving ¼ inch of headspace.

- Follow processing times closely. Never underprocess and take care not to overprocess, which will overcook the contents. Most jellies and jam only require 10 minutes of processing.

- After processing, let the jars sit undisturbed for at least 24 hours before storing.

About Pectin

Pectin is a necessary component for quickly setting up or gelling jellies and jams. Whether to add pectin is a matter of personal preference. Most of the recipes in this book for jams and preserves are pectin free, relying on added sugar and natural pectin in the fruit to create a soft set. *Recipes that call for added pectin are formulated specifically for its use. Do not omit pectin from recipes that call for it.* For information on how to make jams and preserves using commercial pectin in both powdered and liquid forms, refer to the manufacturer's detailed instructions that come with the product.

Performing a Gel Test

Recipes for pectin-free jams and preserves require a gel test to determine if the mixture has set up properly and is ready to be added to the jars for processing. Here are two ways to perform a gel test:

Freezer Test: Chill a few small plates in the freezer. When ready to test for gel formation, place a tablespoon of the hot fruit mixture on a plate and return it to the freezer. Wait 3 minutes. (During this time, the pot should be off the heat to avoid overcooking). To test if the mixture is properly cooked, tilt the plate. If the mixture moves slowly, it will form a gel. If the mixture runs off the plate, return the pot to the heat and cook for another 2 minutes and repeat until the freezer test shows a gel has formed.

Spoon Test: Place a few metal spoons in the refrigerator. As the mixture nears the end of the cooking time, test for gel formation by dipping a spoon into the mixture and lifting it out so the mixture runs off the edge of the spoon. At first, the consistency will be light and syrupy. As it nears the gel stage, the mixture will get thicker and run off the spoon in big drops. When the mixture sheets off the spoon and two drops run together as one, a gel has formed and the mixture is ready to can.

• •

For delicious jams, jellies, and preserves, look for these recipes throughout the book.

recipes for jams, jellies, and preserves

Pickled Vegetables, Relishes, and Salsas

Simply put, pickling is a method of preserving foods in a vinegar solution, often seasoned with herbs and spices. It's a safe and effective way to preserve cucumbers, radishes, green beans, and other low-acid vegetables so that they keep their crunch and flavor.

Recipes for pickled vegetables use either the *Raw Pack Method* or the *Hot Pack Method* followed by processing in a boiling water bath. They should be prepared according to the recipe directions and canned following the basic canning principles. For the best results in making pickles, relishes, and salsas, follow these rules:

- Use nonreactive bowls, pots, and utensils when preparing pickled recipes. Glass, stainless steel, and ceramic bowls are acceptable; aluminum, copper, and cast iron pans and utensils react with the acids in vinegar and will affect the flavor, color, and quality of the finished product.

- Never reduce or increase the amounts of vinegar, lemon juice, other acids, or salt listed in pickling recipes.

- Pickling salt is formulated especially for canning, especially pure and fine grained so it dissolves easily. Kosher salt is a suitable substitute but might cause harmless clouding of the brine.

- The most economical vinegar to use is distilled white vinegar. Rice wine or white wine vinegars can be substituted for a milder flavor. Cider and red wine vinegars may darken the solution, so do not substitute them for white vinegar unless specified in the recipe.

- Pack the jars tightly with the prepared vegetables, always making sure vegetables like asparagus, pickles, and beans are trimmed to fit vertically in the jar. Vinegar brine should be added to cover the contents, leaving ½ inch of headspace.

- Follow processing times closely. Never underprocess and take care not to overprocess, which will overcook the contents, robbing them of their color and crisp texture.

- Store for a minimum of one month before opening to allow the flavors to meld.

For delicious pickles, relishes, and salsas, look for these recipes throughout the book.

recipes for pickled vegetables, relishes, and salsas

Resources

Sources and Inspiration

There's much to be learned about fresh, local, seasonal, and homegrown foods when you have the ear of a farmer, grower, producer, or skilled gardener, but for those times when you need inspiration, motivation, or confirmation, the following sources, both printed and electronic, are useful references.

Books

Ball Blue Book of Preserving. Muncie, IN: Jarden Home Brands, 2006.

Chesman, Andrea. *Serving Up the Harvest.* North Adams, MA: Storey, 2007.

Costenbader, Carol W. *The Big Book of Preserving the Harvest.* North Adams, MA: Storey, 2002.

Davis-Hollander, Lawrence. *The Tomato Festival Cookbook.* North Adams, MA: Storey, 2004.

Duea, Angela Williams. *The Complete Guide to Food Preservation.* Ocala, FL: Atlantic, 2011.

Herbst, Sharon Tyler, and Ron Herbst. *The Deluxe Food Lover's Companion.* Hauppauge, NY: Barron's Educational Series, 2009.

Jeanroy, Amelia, and Karen Ward. *Canning and Preserving for Dummies.* Hoboken, NJ: Wiley, 2009.

Jones, Bridget. *The Farmers' Market Guide to Vegetables.* Naperville, IL: Sourcebooks, 2001. Kafka, Barbara. *Vegetable Love.* New York: Artisan, 2005.

Kingry, Judi, and Lauren Devine, eds. *Ball Complete Book of Home Preserving.* Toronto, Ontario: Robert Rose, 2006.

Landau, Lois M., and Laura G. Myers. *Too Many Tomatoes, Squash, Beans and Other Good Things.* Thorndike, ME: G. K. Hall, 1997.

Lind, Mary Beth, and Cathleen Hockman-Wert. *Simply in Season.* Scottsdale, PA: Herald, 2005.

Morash, Marian. *The Victory Garden Cookbook.* New York: Alfred A. Knopf, 2010.

Parsons, Russ. *How to Pick a Peach.* New York: Houghton Mifflin, 2007.

Schneider, Elizabeth. *Vegetables from Amaranth to Zucchini.* New York: Morrow, 2001.

Snow, Keith. *The Harvest Eating Cookbook.* Philadelphia: Running, 2009.

Topp, Ellie, and Margaret Howard. *The Complete Book of Small-Batch Preserving.* Buffalo, NY: Firefly Books, 2007.

Towne, Marion K. *A Midwest Gardener's Cookbook.* Bloomington: Indiana University Press, 1996.

Websites

Ball Canning Company

http://www.freshpreserving.com

Michigan State University Extension

http://www.msue.msu.edu/

Ohio State University Extension Service

http://extension.osu.edu/

University of Illinois Extension Service

http://urbanext.illinois.edu/veggies

Finding Locally Grown Food,
No Matter Where You Live

Where does your food come from? Whether you're a dedicated locavore who knows all the best sources for locally grown fruits and vegetables, meats and poultry, dairy and more or you're new to living the life of a locavore, it's important to create a network of resources that will point you to farms, farmers markets, CSAs, and artisan or homestead producers in or close to your community. Here are a few reliable and popular websites to help in your search, no matter where you live.

Farm Bureaus

Also remember that most states have large farming organizations such as farm bureaus that provide information to consumers on how to find products, farms, and farmers markets in their state. To find the link to the farm bureau in your state, start with the American Farm Bureau website.

http://www.fb.org

Finding a Winter Farmers Market

http://www.farmaid.org

Food Routes

http://www.foodroutes.org

Local Dirt

http://www.localdirt.com

Local Harvest

http://www.localharvest.org

National Sustainable Agriculture Information Service

http://attra.ncat.org/attra-pub/local_food/search.php

Real Time Farms

http://www.realtimefarms.com/markets

Rodale Institute Farm Locator

http://www.rodaleinstitute.org/farm_locator

Slow Food USA

http://www.slowfoodusa.org

University Extension Services

Through the United States Department of Agriculture, every state hosts research-based resources through land grant universities. Use them to find information on local agriculture, food, home and family, the environment, and more. To find one in your area, go to the USDA's National Institute of Food and Agriculture website and click on your state.

http://www.nifa.usda.gov/extension

USDA Farmers Market Listing

http://apps.ams.usda.gov/FarmersMarkets

Recipe Credits

Chard Pancakes, page 36
Adapted from a recipe by Karen Conant, Ridge Bridge Farm, Avon, Ohio

Linguine with Chard and Bacon, page 36
Adapted from a recipe by Peace Angel Garlic Farm, Morrow, OH

Greens with Goat Cheese Croutons and Honey Thyme Vinaigrette, page 59
Adapted from a recipe by Parker Bosley, Cleveland, Ohio

Escarole Soup, page 60
Adapted from a recipe by Diane Firestone, Vermilion, Ohio

Cornmeal Cookies, page 114
Adapted from a recipe by Heather Haviland, Lucky's Café, Tremont, Ohio

Heirloom Pasta Sauce with Maple Syrup, page 118
Recipe courtesy of Lisa Sippel, Sippel Family Farms, Mt. Gilead, Ohio

Heirloom Tomato Bisque, page 120
Adapted from a recipe by Karen Conant, Ridge Bridge Farm, Avon, Ohio

Margaret's Salsa, page 121
Recipe courtesy of Margaret Bellis, Vermilion, Ohio

Laura's Potato Pancakes, page 148
Recipe courtesy of Laura Taxel, Cleveland Heights, Ohio

Index

INDEX